Profiting from Emerging Market Stocks

MITCHELL POSNER

President of Kirkwood Financial, Inc.

NEW YORK INSTITUTE OF FINANCE

NEW YORK • TORONTO • SYDNEY • TOKYO • SINGAPORE

Library of Congress Cataloging-in-Publication Data
Posner, Mitchell J.
  Profiting from emerging market stocks / Mitchell Posner.
    p. cm.
  Includes index.
  ISBN 0-7352-0023-8
    1. Investments, Foreign—Developing countries. 2. Stocks—
-Developing countries. I. Title.
  HG5993.P68 1998
  332.67'3'091724—dc21   97-32819
                                                          CIP

This publication is designed to provide accurate and authoritative information in regard to the subject matter covered. It is sold with the understanding that the publisher is not engaged in rendering legal, accounting, or other professional service. If legal advice or other expert assistance is required, the services of a competent professional person should be sought.

From a Declaration of Principles Jointly Adapted by a Committee of the American Bar Association and a Committee of Publishers and Associations

Printed in the United States of America

10 9 8 7 6 5 4 3 2 1

ISBN 0-7352-0023-8

ATTENTION: CORPORATIONS AND SCHOOLS

NYIF books are available at quantity discounts with bulk purchase for educational, business, or sales promotional use. For information, please write to: Prentice Hall Special Sales, 240 Frisch Court, Paramus, NJ 07652. Please supply: title of book, ISBN, quantity, how the book will be used, date needed.

NEW YORK INSTITUTE OF FINANCE
An imprint of Prentice Hall Press
Paramus, NJ 07652
A Simon & Schuster Company

On the World Wide Web at http://www.phdirect.com

Prentice Hall International (UK) Limited, *London*
Prentice Hall of Australia Pty. Limited, *Sydney*
Prentice Hall Canada, Inc., *Toronto*
Prentice Hall Hispanoamericana, S.A., *Mexico*
Prentice Hall of India Private Limited, *New Delhi*
Prentice Hall of Japan, Inc., *Tokyo*
Simon & Schuster Asia Pte. Ltd., *Singapore*
Editora Prentice Hall do Brasil, Ltda., *Rio de Janeiro*

Contents

3

Where the Action Is in Emerging Markets
35

4

Emerging Stock Markets
69

5

ADRs and GDRs: Emerging Market Stocks in the USA
85

6

Privatizations: The Blue Chips of Emerging Market Stocks
101

7

Bonds: Investing in Emerging Market Debt
121

8

Currencies: The Hidden Emerging Market Investment
137

9

Emerging Market Indexes
155

10

Emerging Market Mutual Funds
175

11

Constructing an Emerging Market Portfolio
189

Introduction

The term "emerging markets" is probably not new to you. Your interest in this book is probably due in part to casual contact with the subject in the business press, personal finance magazines, or television news features. But in a market filled with buzzwords this one announces the most promising invested opportunity through the next several decades.

Emerging markets are more easily defined by those that aren't—the United States, Canada, Western Europe, and Japan—than by those that are. The entire world is emerging except for a handful of economies that are already very rich, productive, and advanced.

Journalists love this field because it makes for good copy. Stories of exotic places and "overnight millionaires" have fascinated readers over the years.

Financial services firms love emerging markets because they generate another product line for investors. "You've made lots of money on Wall Street, so why not risk some of it in exotic markets?" Or, "Keeping all your dollars in the U.S. stock market is risky, so why not diversify into world markets, which often move independently of the S&P?" "Are you bored and looking for adventure? Why not buy into a Russian company, or an Indian or an Egyptian firm?"

Unlike some of the gimmicks cooked up by Wall Street, emerging market investing has—more often than not—been worthy of the hype. For example, consider the year-end performance data for 1996. It was a great year for the Dow, but look at which markets did best:

Country	Return Local stock index, $US dollars
Russia	68.9%
Turkey	49.9%
Greece	41.5%
Brazil	28.5%
Mexico	19.2%

The top five stock markets were emerging markets, an impressive showing. But the greatest benefits of this exciting sector will emerge over the long term. Emerging market stocks are not a fad.

In 1997, the year of the Asian currency crisis, emerging stock markets were among the leading gainers. Mexico, Venezuela, Brazil, Russia, and Hungary all outperformed the United States.

I believe that the case for emerging markets is compelling, no matter what your predisposition toward investing. As an *offensive* strategy, emerging-market companies offer greater growth and profit potential over the next ten years than all but the best performers in the United States and Europe. As a *defensive* strategy, sound emerging-market investing provides an excellent way to diversify a portfolio and reduce the risk.

This book examines the logic behind emerging-market investing in great detail. Its goal is to provide you with techniques and insights gleaned from the community of financial professionals who are dedicated to this asset class. I believe that the facts support the view that emerging market securities are now mainstream investments and arguably deserve a place in any well-diversified portfolio. Emerging-market investing at its best is a reasonable way to profit from the world's rapid and steady development, which for years had trailed a small number of leading economies. It is essentially the same as the road taken for over a century by those insightful men and women who invested in a young and growing America.

Indeed, investors today have it better and easier than our predecessors. Those who invested in early America had little to protect them from schemes and swindles and much less data to go on than does today's emerging market player. No matter that some say emerging markets are best left to experts or that these stocks and bonds are not for the faint of heart, for this argument is fading rapidly. Many world stock markets, once illiquid, poorly regulated places with "men's-club" rules, have matured into regulated, computerized exchanges linked to financial markets around the globe.

Unlike the situation in U.S. markets, individual investors in emerging markets have a fair chance of outperforming the pros. There are three basic reasons for this. First, demand for emerging market professionals has outstripped supply: Many of the so-called "pros" have very little or no experience in this area. Second, emerging market data are "democratic": Most of the information available to professionals is available to individual investors as well. Third, emerging markets are less efficient: It is still possible to (legally) gain an edge by learning something about a stock that the other guy does not know.

Naturally, any book on emerging markets must discuss the countries in question. The differences lie in what *else* is included. I have made a conscious effort to cover all the topics I believe are important to the sophisticated investor, while avoiding technical material of interest only to the professional portfolio manager.

The book is divided into four sections. Chapters 1 and 2 give the reader some background on the development and rise of emerging market investing and place it in a global perspective. I believe that a basic overview of the history of emerging market investment and the development of emerging stock markets will heighten the readers' perception of what is happening there today. Chapter 3 includes capsule summaries of the most promising markets for investment.

Chapters 4 through 8 survey the most important emerging market investment vehicles, from privatization issues to mutual funds and emerging market bonds and derivatives.

Chapters 9 through 12 are devoted to the tools of the trade. How does an emerging market investor go about selecting stocks and building a portfolio? This section devotes a chapter to a discussion of portfolio analysis in emerging markets and one to stock picking and investment styles.

Chapter 13 is a comprehensive view of country risk and all its components—including political, economic, financial, and social—and a guide to compiling and using country risk reports.

I have included four appendixes: a list of ADRs (American Depositary Receipts), an atlas of world stock markets, an annotated list of notable Web sites, and Nasdaq emerging market listings.

A final note: "Timely" investment books are rapidly becoming a thing of the past. The markets are moving too fast and so is the information that feeds them. Most books require months of preparation and pre-publication, so the author runs the risk of offering dated material to the reader. You need not rely on stale data and outdated analyses and forecasts when you can get the latest via the Internet, a global brokerage, or other information service. For this reason, I have chosen to focus on investment principles, techniques, and insights that I believe will serve the emerging markets investor over the next few years rather than over the next few months. I offer no short-term recommendations and few suggestions specific to a given market or stock at a given time.

My personal interest in emerging markets developed serendipitously. As a consultant, I have been involved in share offerings for companies doing business in Latin America, Russia, China, Africa, Tajikistan, and Azerbaijan, among others. I find emerging market investing to be exciting, challenging, and yes, romantic. When was the last time you could say that about a stock you purchased? So read on, and begin your tour of emerging markets. It offers a lot more promise than Las Vegas or even Wall Street. And it's a lot more fun.

A Note on the Data Used in This Book

The data and statistics cited in this book are intended to illustrate and clarify key points and concepts. They are not intended to make investment decisions, which require more timely data than a book prepared months in advance can provide. While I have cited data sources where appropriate, I would like to collectively thank the various research organizations, government agencies, banks, and brokerage firms that assisted by making their data available.

Acknowledgments

Writing a book that deals with so many countries and complexities was a difficult task. It was made easier through the patience and guidance of my editor, Ellen Coleman, and the rest of the team at Prentice Hall, including Barry Richardson, Jackie Roulette, and Barbara Palumbo.

In addition, I'd like to thank George Gregor, Gerrit B. Parker, Jr., Alan Cohen, Charles Lieb, James Nelson, Jeff Evans, Jorge Pierrestegui, Steve Posner, Newton Bleffe, and, finally, my wife Renée and my children Sara and Josh, who endured the nights and weekends I spent on this project.

MITCHELL POSNER

CHAPTER 1

Why Bother Investing in Emerging Markets?

"Getting in on the ground floor" of a good investment is an attractive notion. But sophisticated investors know that such opportunities aren't served on silver platters. You must seek them everywhere, whether around the corner or on the other side of the globe.

Indeed, the global search for a good deal has been going on for centuries. "Emerging markets"—economies in transition from agrarian or controlled economies to industrialized free markets—have long been part of the investment scene. The Foreign and Colonial Investment Trust, for example, was established in 1868 and is still investing in developing markets today. During the 1890s, a typical edition of the *Financial Times* was filled with tantalizing tales about high-flying railway companies in Argentina and about the Panama Canal Company and Turkish stocks. Indeed, some romantics may long for those "good old days," when the world seemed to teem with new situations in exotic foreign lands.

Consider the following investment "opportunities":

Country A recently endured a long and ugly civil war, the assassination of its president, a financial panic, and a disruptive influx of poor immigrants.

Country B was formed from the ruins of a vanquished army forced from its mainland to a small island.

Country C stands divided and completely cut off from its northern half after a bloody and destructive civil war.

Country D suffered a humiliating defeat and heavy bombing that severely damaged its infrastructure.

Doesn't sound like a very promising investment portfolio, does it? But country A defines the United States in the 1880s and Country B, Taiwan after the defeat of the Nationalist Army. Country C is Korea, and D, Japan. All were once considered emerging markets.

Similar opportunities might seem elusive in today's investment environment, but they are not. The good old days are still with us. The second half of the twentieth century has seen more wealth created than during any other era, and much of it is finally falling into the hands of those in less-developed nations. Imagine what kind of fortunes were made by those with the insight—and the guts—to invest in a defeated nation rebuilding from the devastation of World War II. At the end of the 1960s, Japan—now the richest nation in Asia—had a per capita gross domestic product (GDP) of less than $400. South Korea and Taiwan were on par with some sub-Saharan nations. Today, Taiwan's per-capita GDP is over $10,000 and Korea's exceeds $7,500.

THE BULL MARKET IN GLOBAL INVESTING

You haven't missed the boat. In fact, this may be the best time ever for global investments. A unique combination of economic forces—ignited by the collapse of communism—has created a new bull market for the twenty-first century. The political reaction to the end of the cold war turned out to be far less important than were the economic effects.

In the late 1980s, Berlin was two cities, the Soviet Union a single country, Latin American nations were defaulting on loans, Chinese private enterprise barely existed, and almost 70 percent of the planet lived under communist or socialist systems. The United States, Soviet Union, and Maoist China were showering their client states with trade credits, foreign aid, loans, subsidized goods, and weaponry.

The end of the Cold War put an end to such patronage on both sides. No longer could countries get foreign aid simply by following either a capitalist or a Marxist line and hosting military bases. With less to fear and economic troubles of their own, the superpowers turned a deaf ear to large-scale aid requests. The dependent economies had to create their own wealth instead of freeloading off wealthy nations. According to the World Bank, official government loans to developing countries fell from $27.1 billion in 1990 to just $9.5 billion six years later. The *type* of loan has also changed. Much of the current loan funds are earmarked for repayment of past debt or for short-term humanitarian aid.

Without the ability to play the former cold warriors against each other, countries could no longer afford to remain "global deadbeats," defaulting on loans, erecting tax and currency barriers, and nationalizing foreign-owned businesses. Developing nations responded the only way they could, by joining the global marketplace.

Many emerging nations hit the ground running. They reformed their economies, privatized state-owned enterprises, turned to the International Monetary Fund for help in restructuring debt, and never looked back.

Now, for the first time in recorded history, nearly every country on the globe has a market-oriented economy, is competing for capital, and is buying and selling products and services. As such, the world free market has gained about three billion new customers, and thousands of listed companies opened for investment in the past decade.

Taken together, the emerging-nations' consumer market is by far the world's largest. Developing markets combine to make up 70 percent of the world's land area and 85 percent of the population, but account for only 20 percent of the world's total GDP. When adjusted for purchasing power, however, emerging markets include six of the world's largest economies and account for a little more than half of the world's output.

By the year 2010—in what's been called "the Pacific Century"—700 million Asians in China, India, and Indonesia will have an average income roughly equivalent to that of Spain today. That's a population group as

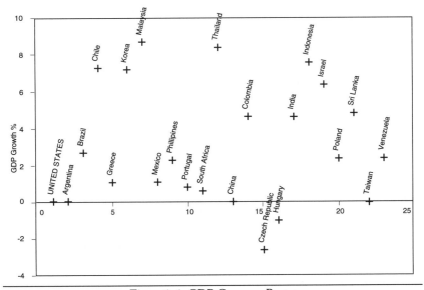

Figure 1–1. GDP Growth Rates
Source: IMF, OECD, J. P. Morgan, UBS, The Wall Street Journal, The World Bank, Euromoney, IFC Emerging Markets Database.

large as the United States, Japan, and Europe combined, with buying power on par with that of a western European nation.

Well-managed multinational firms have already responded to this phenomenal growth spurt. Companies such as Gillette, Procter & Gamble, Coke, and Pepsi are finding faster sales growth in markets where items such as liquid soap, cartridge razors, and diet sodas are relatively new.

Stock and bond markets are sprouting across the globe, and the international investment community is buying and selling securities on emerging market exchanges. As of this writing, equity investment dollars are flowing into emerging stock markets at a near record pace.

Ironically, you may already be a player in emerging markets without realizing it. According to Kleiman International, in 1995, U.S. pension funds invested about $150 billion in emerging markets, about 7.5 percent of total emerging market capitalization.[1] So, if you are in a pension or perhaps a mutual fund with an international mandate, you may well be invested in emerging markets. In fact, some pension funds are actually increasing their emerging market allocations in light of the Asian financial crisis. Today, the bargains are bigger than ever.

WHAT'S IN A NAME?

The World Bank has set a definition of a "developing nation" as one with a per capita GNP of less than U.S. $7,910. Emerging markets are developing nations that are "investable." No universal definition of emerging markets exists. Even if experts could agree on which nations are "emerging" and which are not, the list would be dated in a matter of months.

The International Finance Corporation (IFC) classifies more than 150 economies as "emerging." The IFC uses the term broadly, as the rough equivalent of "nonindustrialized," and classifies nearly every country in the world as emerging. Most are "emerging" in one form or another, but the differences are significant. IFC's Emerging Markets range from those with per capita GNPs of $300+ to those with $8,000+.

This list includes many marginal economies, which are probably too small or too dependent on larger economies to be of interest to investors, such as Guadeloupe, Réunion, and Tonga.

The IFC is dedicated to assisting these nations and therefore uses criteria that offer the widest latitude. The investment community, on the other hand, bears no such responsibility and is principally concerned with the state of a nation's capital markets. If the stock and bond markets work smoothly and freely, they will attract investors, no matter how poor the population or how bad the roads.

Another characteristic of emerging markets is growth. In its *Emerging Market Factbook*, the IFC acknowledges that "emerging" implies a country that "has begun a process of change, growing in size and sophistication in contrast to markets that are small and give little appearance of change."[2]

FOUR WAYS TO RECOGNIZE
AN EMERGING MARKET

1. By its Gross National Product (GNP). GNP is the defining measure for emerging markets in both the public and private sector. Emerging markets have GNPs considerably lower than those of the developed nations. The average emerging market as defined by MSCI's (Morgan Stanley Capital International) latest definition has a per capita GNP of around $3,100, as compared with $20,535 for the 21 developed markets in the MSCI indexes. The IFC considers any economy with a per capita GNP of less than $8,626 to be emerging.

The GNP is a popular measure of a nation's financial standing, computed by multiplying the number of goods and services produced by their respective market value. Gross Domestic Product (GDP) measures strictly domestic output, excluding income produced outside the country.

The GNP benchmark has many shortcomings because it measures just output. For one thing, it does not reflect the differing costs of living around the world. It doesn't reflect *purchasing power,* the amount of goods and services that the average citizen can purchase, as compared to that in other countries. (See Chapter 8.)

Another drawback to per capita GNP is that it does not reflect differences *within* a nation. In the United States and Brazil, the gap between rich and poor is much wider than in Europe. The former communist nations, such as Poland, also have narrow gaps.

2. By its free market limitations. While some emerging markets are considered free-market economies, few, if any, are the equal of developed markets when it comes to regulations regarding foreign investment, financial disclosure, free capital flows and sophisticated, mature stock markets, and restrictions on repatriation, dividends, and capital gains. Most emerging markets have some limitations on foreign investment in local stock markets, and many have restrictions on currency movements and repatriation of capital assets.

3. By its risks. In general, emerging markets carry greater "country risk" than do developed markets. Risks of political turmoil, hyperinflation, and social unrest, while not unknown in developed markets, are much higher in emerging markets.

4. By its growth rate. Given the attendant risks, financial professionals are willing to consider an emerging market only if it offers the potential of high returns. While there is no hard-and-fast rule, a high growth rate is *de rigueur* for a country to be interesting. A real GDP growth rate of 4% or more over a multi-year period is a reasonable expectation, if we discount the no-growth period caused by the Asian meltdown.

As with all investment rules of thumb, allowances must be made for special situations. Some of the most attractive emerging markets have had recessions, resulting in severely contracting economies. Mexico is a perfect example. It contracted more than 8 percent after the peso devaluation in 1995, and has grown in excess of 5% per annum since then, astounding the experts and making it one of the most attractive emerging markets. Nevertheless, it is one of the most attractive emerging markets.

The Asian crisis will trigger a period of negligible—or even negative economic growth. But over the long view, these fast-track nations will return to growth rates befitting an emerging market nation.

FRONTIER MARKETS

Frontier markets, a.k.a. "pioneer" or "embryo" markets, is Wall Street parlance for the really new, sometimes obscure, and often underdeveloped investment arenas around the world.

With so much money flowing into emerging markets, aggressive investors in search of bargains are forced to blaze new trails. This "embryo" stage can be short-lived. Privatization programs, new and improved stock markets, and economic reform programs are transforming even the most backward economies. Communications, financial, and other technologies needed for economic development have been growing rapidly, so it is no surprise that embryo markets are maturing much faster than their predecessors did in the seventies and eighties and early nineties.

Today's embryo-stage investors are venturing into Kazakhstan, Swaziland, and even Iran. Two Morgan Stanley strategists began recommending investments in Cambodia in the spring of '94, even though the country has no stock market and most of its business and professional caste was eliminated by the Khmer Rouge in the seventies.

The goal of such investing is a very big score, perhaps a 1,000 percent return or more. In order to realize such gains, you have to be positioned in the market before the arrival of conventional emerging market investors, who are hardly latecomers themselves. Embryo-market investors are pioneers, often making direct investments that provide no liquidity and require a long-term commitment. They might purchase an equity interest in a local company, buy real estate, or buy shares on an exchange that is barely functioning.

When an embryo market evolves in the right direction, the payoff can be huge. Peru, once considered too unstable and dangerous because of the Shining Path guerrillas, is now booming, with certain companies worth over five times more than when terrorists roamed free. In 1991, when the Shining Path seemed on the verge of toppling the government, the price of Peru's principal telecom company, Compañía Peruana de Teléfonos (CPT), collapsed. Its market cap dropped to U.S. $150 million. Shortly thereafter, the group's leader was captured, weakening the terrorists, and investors began to return. CPT's market cap (now Telefonica del Peru) is currently more than $3 billion, nearly 20 times the market cap at the low.

Embryo investors don't always guess right. Anticipated reforms and political stability may not materialize, the country may not develop at the expected pace, and the investment vehicle itself may not pan out. For example, once promising Mongolia has squandered its foreign aid package and privatization proceeds. Inflation and interest rates are up, production is down.

Unfortunately, there are few embryo markets left. Today, most countries have some professional-investor-participation interest. Still, there are places where "the water is hot, but hasn't yet begun to boil." Consider small Latin markets such as Paraguay, former Communist regimes such as Romania, formerly closed nations such as Myanmar (Bulgaria), and virtually all of Africa.

Embryo investors typically leave their politics at home. Many of these nations, while emerging economically, are still very repressive. Human rights are severely restricted, and dissent isn't tolerated. The business community—in some cases a brand new social class—may consist of former generals, communist officials, or spies.

Sometimes, an emerging market "backslides." A political or economic reversal throws the country into a tailspin. Several years ago, a few of the former Soviet republics looked as if they were about to emerge; today, they are lagging behind in the embryo stage.

Obviously, the frontier market strategy is not for the faint of heart. "In the old days, even bad companies would go up a lot, because a cascade of money would eventually come into these thinly capitalized markets," says Jim Rogers, a pioneer in emerging market investing. "I'd just buy the ten largest stocks and wait. . . . But that game is coming to an end." Today, you have to be part scout, part daredevil, and go into countries that are considered "uninvestable" by most. You won't find reliable financial reporting, the markets won't be liquid, and the regimes could turn on you at any time. Since it is possible, although not likely, you could lose most or all of your investment for reasons having little to do with the viability of the company you invest in, most individuals shy away.

Embryo markets to watch include Laos, Cambodia, Vietnam, Myanmar, North Korea, Mongolia, Croatia, Bulgaria, Slovenia, Jordan, Egypt, Latvia, Oman, Lebanon, Saudi Arabia, Qatar, Kuwait, Morocco, Tunisia, Cuba, Swaziland, Papua New Guinea, Ghana, Bangladesh, and Paraguay.

THE CASE FOR EMERGING MARKETS

As the argument in favor of investing in emerging markets grows stronger, here are 12 sound reasons to include emerging markets securities in your portfolio.

1. Emerging markets often outperform U.S. markets. Emerging markets investing has paid off. According to Micropal, Inc., $100 invested on December 31, 1994 in the International Finance Corporation's Global

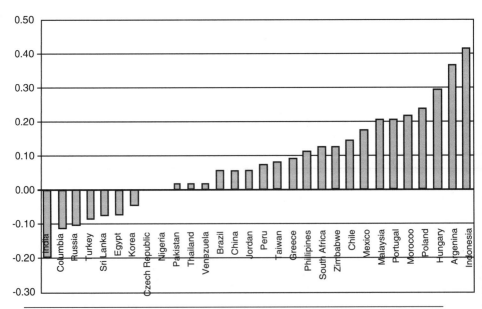

Figure 1–2. Emerging Market Indices vs. the S&P 500.
Source: The World Bank.

Index (IFC Global) would have grown to $528.07 as of June 22, 1995. The same $100 invested on the same date in the Morgan Stanley Capital International's World Index would have returned $461.91.

No market rise continues unabated, and the early nineties saw significant reversals in certain emerging markets, erasing some of the prior gains. They have resumed their climb, however, and the outlook is positive well into the next century.

In 1997, the Mexican (up 54.21%) and Brazilian (up 28.94%) stock markets easily outpaced the Dow.

By contrast, the Dow and the Standard & Poors (S&P) were both up less than 10 percent!

2. Emerging market stocks can reduce portfolio risk. Correlations of emerging markets with developed markets have been low, suggesting that emerging market movements aren't related to the direction of developed markets. Sometimes an emerging market correlation is negative, meaning it moves in an opposing direction. Domestic and regional factors exert more influence on Latin American and Asian stocks than do world events and economic trends in developed nations. Even the '87 crash and the Persian Gulf War had relatively little effect on emerging market stock prices.

Because emerging markets go their own way, they are an excellent way to reduce portfolio risk by reducing volatility and enhancing returns. A study by A. Divecha, J. Drach, and D. Stefek of the years 1986–1989 showed that a portfolio with a 20 percent allocation of emerging market stocks could have achieved annual returns 2.1 percent higher than portfolios with only industrialized-market stocks, with .81 percent less risk.[3]

3. Emerging markets are growing at a faster rate than are developed markets. The World Bank projects average annual GDP growth in emerging markets at 4.9 percent, almost twice as fast as for developing nations. Chile's per-capita GDP grew an impressive 10 percent per year from the mid-80's to the mid-90's. Countries such as China might grow nearly as fast. Over ten years, the entire East Asia region will resume its rapid expansion and grow more than 7 percent annually. Latin America and the Middle East could grow by 4 percent as well.

More important, it is the *right* kind of growth. In addition to the typically low-tech exports and raw materials shipped to more advanced countries, emerging market growth also includes state-of-the-art manufacturing driven by domestic and regional consumption.

4. Many experts believe that emerging markets will offer the best returns over the next ten years. Historical evidence points to a positive correlation between economic growth and stock market returns. Buoyed by strong growth rates and solid fundamentals, emerging market portfolios should perform well over a five- to ten-year holding period.

5. Many emerging market companies compare favorably with U.S. counterparts. From Argentine oil companies such as YPF to Malaysian resort operators such as Genting Berhad, many emerging market companies are competitive and profitable. Hungarian pharmaceutical company Chinoin has posted gains of 20 percent return on equity for the past several years while mounting a successful R&D program. Chosun Brewery of Korea has an astonishing 46 percent market share and earnings per share prior to the Asia crisis of 1997, was growing at about 25 percent per annum. (Watch out, Anheuser-Busch.)

Several analysts expect Chilean businesses to see profits grow by 15 percent or more per year over the next five years, Peruvian businesses by 18 percent, and Brazilian businesses by a whopping 25 percent per year.

6. The U.S. market will be challenged to keep pace. As growth slows, U.S. companies will be under pressure to increase profit margins to maintain earnings growth. Margins are at a 15-year high, and productivity gains have been impressive. Unless the United States and other nations can continue to achieve such gains, the U.S. stock market will slow down. With the market capitalization as of this writing equal to about 115 percent of the nation's GDP—a level last reached in 1968—the U.S. markets may be approaching the limits of overvaluation

7. While emerging markets have been "hot" for nearly a decade, they are still at an early stage. There is still time for you to participate. International investing—especially in emerging markets—is a relatively new field. As these markets grow, they will tend to reward those who have gained some experience.

The statistics dramatize the upside potential in emerging markets. Emerging markets account for about 85 percent of the world's population, but only 20 percent of world GNP. Emerging markets produce approximately 45 percent of the world's goods and services, but account for only 13 percent of the world's stock market capitalization. That means there are hundreds, perhaps thousands, of productive companies with little or no investor participation.

According to analyst Michael Howell, by the year 2010 emerging markets could account for 45 percent of total capitalization, and China,

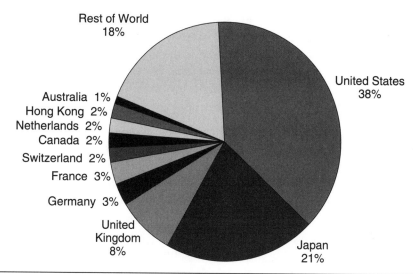

Figure 1–3. WORLD EQUITY MARKET CAPITALIZATION, 1996.
SOURCE: DATA SOURCE: THE WORLD BANK, IFC, THE WORLD BANK. AS OF AUGUST 1996.

Brazil, India, and Russia could rank with the United States, Japan, and the U.K. as the world's biggest stock markets.[4]

8. Institutions are increasing their participation. According to a recent survey, 25 percent of more than 65 corporate- and public-pension funds intended to increase their emerging market allocations. There is plenty of room to grow, since the pension funds surveyed had an average of just 3.8 percent of assets allocated to emerging markets.

9. Reforms have held in recent years. In the past, developing nations have altered trade and fiscal policies almost as often as they have changed regimes. Governments have been quick to reverse reforms at the first sign of crisis.

The nineties have been different. Most emerging market nations have stuck with reform. In Latin America, Mexico struggles with inflation, Argentina is plagued with high unemployment, and Brazil wrestles with debt, but open-market reforms remain in place. After a devastating peso devaluation crisis, Mexico opted for a painful austerity program rather than abandon reform, and it is bouncing back. Argentina gained financial respect by standing firm on its currency's one-for-one link to the dollar, even though the policy contributed to a serious recession. Brazil wavered at first, instituting tariffs and other anti-free market controls, but then abandoned them. Even the crises in Bosnia and the Middle East haven't altered plans for economic liberalization in their respective regions.

Ironically, the crisis in Asia is accelerating the pace of economic liberalization as Asian nations move away from Japanese-style state capitalism toward the American-style free-market model.

Governments are toeing the line on reform because it works. Indonesia, once hostile to most foreign investors, has seen annual investment multiply since it began a policy of deregulation in 1987.

10. Emerging market small caps are untapped. Most institutions have invested in emerging market equities by buying shares in the largest emerging market companies. Many good companies have been overlooked simply because they are too small to attract the attention of institutional investors. Consequently, few analysts specialize in small emerging market companies. Without investor interest, these small stocks are often underpriced, creating buying opportunities for aggressive investors.

In the next few years, smaller companies will enter the markets. As the emerging markets grow and become more liquid, these small stocks will become more popular. Big-picture, macroeconomic stock picking will give way to the micro-bet.

11. Emerging market stocks are becoming easier to buy and sell. All over the world, from Cambodia to Zambia, markets are opening to investors. Stock exchanges are tightening securities regulations to protect the public and make markets more investor friendly. For example, Brazil recently abolished its 1/2 percent stamp tax on stock purchases, acknowledging that it was a disincentive to investment.

12. Information is more readily available. Government and private publications and on-line databases provide a wealth of information. Travel is easier and more affordable, and emerging markets, with international airports and modern roads, are more accessible.

Many emerging stock markets have their own Web sites on the Internet and "publish" news releases, financial data, and other information on their listed companies. Investment banks such as Morgan Stanley and ING Barings are currently supplying valuable data to nonclients.

FIVE MISCONCEPTIONS ABOUT EMERGING MARKET STOCKS

1. Investing overseas is risky. Quite the contrary: Global investing—*when part of an overall strategy*—is a conservative tactic. Research has shown that diversifying investments among world markets is actually *less risky* than a diversified all-U.S. portfolio. World markets do not move in step; some markets are "linked," tending to move in the same direction, while others go their own way. While some emerging markets have, from time to time, been linked to established markets, there are enough independent factors that will keep them diverging.

2. Emerging market stocks are overpriced. "Hot money"—large, short-term capital inflows from around the world, can drive emerging market stocks to unrealistically high prices, prompting many stories of outrageous valuations. This fear is overblown. True, foreign and especially emerging market stocks have had quite a run in recent years, but recent corrections have brought values back in line. Every year brings new listings and new "investable" stock markets. In many cases, emerging stocks trade at lower valuations than U.S. stocks.

As of this writing, the Morgan Stanley Capital International Eastern European index is selling for around 13 times (trailing) earnings. But Poland's economy is growing at around 5 percent per year. The Czech Republic's stock market goes for just 12 times earnings, and its economy is growing at over 4 percent. Russian oil giant Lukoil, which now has the world's largest proven oil reserves, was, as of this writing, trading at only 12 times earnings.

3. There are too few listings. The numbers are rising fast. India, for example, has thousands of listed companies (although many are multiple listings), second only to the United States. According to the IFC, 36 emerging markets have total listings that lag those of the 26 established markets by less than one-third.

4. The regulations are insurmountable. Around the world, with a few exceptions, markets are becoming easier—and safer—to trade.

While some restrictions make trading difficult or impossible in certain emerging markets, the trend is clearly toward reform. Since the global securities markets are the primary conduits of capital in the world today, every emerging economy must eventually render its local exchanges "investor friendly." Any loss of confidence could cause the flow of capital to slow. Most nations will not run that risk.

5. You have to be a pro to profit. In fact, you might even do *better* than the pros. Emerging market investing may be the last great opportunity of the decade for the private investor.

Individual investors may even have an edge over the pros. While the professional fund managers have formidable resources with which to find opportunities, they are hampered by mutual fund inflows and redemptions, rules, and by-laws. They trade large blocks of stock, which makes it difficult to enter and exit markets. And they rarely have time to ferret out those little-known companies.

TWENTY-FIVE TRENDS THAT WILL CHANGE THE WAY YOU INVEST

The pace of growth has been accelerating since the dawn of civilization. But the first half of the twenty-first century will be known as the time when most of the world gains the status of advanced nations.

1. Market forces are accelerating development, generating above-average growth and rising demand. Industrial companies seek the lowest-cost producers, regardless of national borders; this creates rapid growth in lesser-developed nations, such as China, India, and the Philippines. Production rises and exports soar. In turn, the resulting inflow of capital creates an expanding middle class, higher living standards, and increased consumer demand. As countries develop, citizens demand more goods and services, improved infrastructure, and a better standard of living. From Mexico to Egypt, consumer demand is rising.

2. Privatization—the sale of state-owned assets to the private sector—is growing around the world. This process provides needed capital to local government, attracts outside investment, and makes the economy more competitive.

Privatizations will continue for years to come, adding to the supply of new listings. The number of international carriers with any private ownership has more than tripled since 1996, as dozens of nations sell stock in their national telecommunications companies.

Electric power utilities in more than a dozen countries have come to market through privatization; international power companies raised some $4 billion in 1995 on the capital markets.

3. Advances in telecommunications make it easier to conduct business, move capital, advertise, and market products. Satellite television brings the outside world to local citizens, spurring demand for consumer goods and a higher quality of life. In addition, it exposes local government to the scrutiny of the local and world community.

4. Emerging markets' development will fuel the world's economy, not just their own. In the eighties and early nineties, low inflation, lower bond yields, and a rise in valuations lifted stock markets. In the next decade, however, huge capital demand for modernizing emerging market infrastructures, plus the high volume of world trade, will drive the markets.

5. High-tech industries will develop and prosper. As factories are built and technology is transferred, producers in Asia, Latin America, and Eastern Europe are making televisions, computers, microchips, telecommunications equipment, autos, and pharmaceuticals and are selling them in their own regions. Thus, they are becoming less dependent on advanced nations. Consequently, they are less vulnerable to changes in the industrialized nations and can solidify their ability to move independently. The emergence of more economies that move independently of the developed nations should engender stock markets with low or negative correlations to our own.

6. Emerging markets will sell more goods and services to each other. Emerging markets were once considered suppliers of low-tech items such as garments and hand-assembled goods for export to the developed nations. Now that these markets are maturing, they will supply goods and services once purchased only from Japan and the West. In years to come, local and regional consumer spending, infrastructure projects, and regional trade will fuel much of the growth, while furthering their economic independence from the West.

7. Funds will continue to flow toward developing stock markets. Cross-border equity flows into emerging markets rose steadily in the late eighties and early nineties. There was a brief pause in the wake of the Mexican peso crisis in December 1994. But, despite predictions of gloom and doom and an immediate pullback in its wake, emerging market portfolio equity flows recovered quickly, to a record $45.7 billion in 1996. The decline in capital flows in wake of the Asian crisis will be longer and steeper, but capital flows will undoubtedly increase again.

8. We are entering a period of relative price stability. Central bankers and fiscal policymakers around the world have proven more adept at coping with inflation and shortening recessions. While there will always be exceptions to the rule, nations around the world have been doing a better job of managing their economies to prevent wide swings, whether inflationary or deflationary. Ironically, many emerging markets, often considered less stable, have done a better job than some advanced nations have in managing their economies in the wake of negative influences, IMF bailouts notwithstanding.

9. Fund managers are increasingly turning to emerging markets to balance portfolio risk. For years, portfolio managers have used international stocks as a means to optimize their portfolios. There are signs, however, that foreign stocks represent too broad an asset class. The industrialized countries are coordinating their monetary policies. The European Union will harmonize most of Western Europe. The result could be an increasingly positive correlation in developed stock markets, thus reducing their "diversification" value. In fact, there are signs that the major world economies are beginning to move in the same direction.

According to a recent five-year study by Morningstar, the U.S. markets are highly correlated with Canada, Australia, Germany, Hong Kong, and the Netherlands. The only industrialized market to show meaningful negative correlation is Japan.

In contrast, emerging markets are less dependent on the United States, Japan, and Europe as trading partners and markets for their goods. Consumption is increasing in their own markets, as is infrastructure spending and trade among neighbors. As a result, portfolio managers treat emerging markets as a separate and distinct asset class, with risks and rewards that differ from other foreign stocks. The correlation between the U.S. and emerging markets from 1994 to 1997 was less than 0.25.

10. As emerging markets mature, investors will be more discriminating, taking a more in-depth look at companies and searching for bargains, possibly among small firms. With longer operating histories and better disclosure, investors will have more data and money managers will be more willing to "buy the company, not the country."

11. Smart companies will go where the growth is, expanding into emerging markets. Even with the innovations and productivity gains of U.S. industry, domestic companies will be hard-pressed to increase earnings as American economic growth starts slowing down. Many companies will expand abroad to keep pace and will disconnect their fate from the conditions of the U.S. market. They will increasingly manufacture, market, and sell goods and services anywhere in the world, especially in emerging markets.

In order to achieve higher share prices, American companies will have to go global. For many companies, emerging markets are where the action is. Aggressive expansion is already underway, with Procter & Gamble moving into China, Wal-Mart into Argentina, and so forth. As the U.S. corporate machine throws its weight into emerging markets, many local companies will benefit.

While such moves, if well-executed, will help bolster U.S. competitiveness and lift the local stock markets, they will stimulate emerging markets and consequently increase share prices on local exchanges.

12. There is a growing fear of being "left behind." The globalization of finance is unstoppable. As world markets open up, as trade and internal capital flow increase, no nation will be able to resist the pressure to join the world financial community. Today, politics takes a back seat to business. Isolation from the international business community means certain suffering for the population. Nations must establish or reform their stock markets, stand behind their sovereign debt, and open their borders to foreign investment. Every government—from neo-fascist to communist—is learning the rules of global business and is playing by them.

Developing nations have watched in amazement as one of the most isolationist and xenophobic regimes in history—the People's Republic of China—has opened to capitalism, and they are following suit. Even holdouts such as Cuba, Myanmar (Burma), and North Korea will join the fold. Eventually, Iraq, Iran, and other "pariah" nations will accommodate some form of open-market capitalism.

13. Many emerging market currencies will disengage from the dollar. Economic communities may link their currencies, follow the lead of the European Union and create a single one, or tie their currencies to a regional slant like the yen.

14. Central banks will cooperate. Central bankers often see speculators as obstacles to sound fiscal management. In the future, they are likely to cooperate in an attempt to discourage such moves as currency gambles made by hedge funds.

There will be a move to create a "global" central bank, perhaps by transforming the role of the International Monetary Fund or the Bank of International Settlements.

15. The Internet will create a free market of information and will facilitate transactions. Hype notwithstanding, the Internet is ideally suited to global finance. While the Internet may or may not become a great entertainment or shopping medium, it will certainly transform emerging markets. Companies will use it to disseminate information. Underwriters will canvass potential investors. Most important, essential investment data will be available worldwide in real time. It's even possible that some form of trading markets will eventually spring up on line.

16. The world is running out of emerging markets. Many of the world's emerging markets are on the verge of becoming established.

Several emerging markets, growing at rates of 8 percent or more, could become Newly Industrialized Countries (NICs) by the end of the century.

17. The pace of development is accelerating. What took ten years to accomplish in Mexico might take just two in Pakistan. Indeed, the entire process of development takes less time than it did decades ago. Even the boom that occurred after World War II, which transformed Japan and rebuilt Germany, seems like slow motion today.

The speed of technology transfer is accelerating. High technology, computer-assisted manufacturing, and improvements in fiscal management have shortened the amount of time it takes to develop industry, improve productivity, increase production, and manage the economy. Personnel are trained, buildings and roads are designed and built, and plants are commissioned faster and better than ever before. For this reason, the infrastructures of emerging markets will develop at a faster rate than they did in the developed countries.

18. U.S. businesses will form global partnerships. From the *maquiladora* plants in Mexico to manufacturing in China and oil prospecting in Kazakhstan, the United States looks abroad for everything from natural resources to low-cost skilled labor. As the U.S. labor market polarizes—Microsoft or McDonald's, with little in between—U.S. companies will seek overseas partners.

19. The emerging nations will spend massively on infrastructure. While the mature economies rebuild, the emerging nations build. Emerging nations are spending billions on highways, telecommunications, supermarkets, power plants, and so forth. Trade opportunities increase, as the need for capital equipment, machinery, power-transmission equipment, transportation equipment, and high-technology rises rapidly.

Asian countries, not including Japan, Hong Kong, Australia, or New Zealand, will spend about $232 billion on telecommunications infrastructure by the year 2000. Latin America will spend $90 billion, Africa and the Middle East $60 billion, and Russia about $363 billion.[5]

20. Basic industries will regain momentum. The telephone companies, retailers, banks, and manufacturers of emerging nations are often decades behind U.S. companies. Emerging market "telco's" will grow faster by installing telephone lines and service where limited—or no—service exists. Cement companies are among the most popular emerging market stocks from Brazil to Thailand, due to ongoing construction booms.

21. American culture and the English language are spreading. Like it or not, English is the real *Esperanto*, dominating business transactions, entertainment, and telecommunications. Those who speak English have access to the largest information base available in any language. According to the University of Washington, as of 1989, approximately 443 million people speak English, exceeded only by Hindi and Chinese dialects.

America is the market leader in "lifestyle" products. America will prosper by marketing its lifestyle and culture to other nations who are only now creating a middle class.

22. The securities market has gained in popularity over the loan window. As markets mature, the favored source of capital switches from banks to the securities markets. Mature markets mean greater comfort with risk, hence a tilt toward equity. This shift increases market capitalization and liquidity. In time, healthy, growing businesses will again turn to banks to finance expansion, but this time as creditworthy, competitive companies.

23. U.S. stock markets are actively seeking to list more foreign stocks. The New York Stock Exchange (NYSE), National Association of Securities Dealers Automated Quotation System (NASDAQ), American Stock Exchange (AMEX), and other exchanges are lobbying the SEC to change certain regulations and financial reporting requirements to make it easier for foreign companies to list on principal U.S. exchanges. In addition, the growth of American Depositary Receipts, or ADRs, and Global Depositary Receipts, or GDRs (see Chapter 5), will make it much easier to trade foreign stocks on U.S. exchanges.

24. The world commodity markets are in transition as demand increases for raw materials to feed consumption and fuel growth. African companies are likely to benefit because they have vast resources and are among the lowest-cost producers. Russia, the nations of the former Soviet Union, and Latin America should also benefit. Commodity exchanges are linking across borders, further increasing liquidity and efficient pricing.

25. A revolution in telecommunications is driving deregulation and reform around the world. In 1993, overseas calling totaled 47 billion minutes, up from 23 billion only five years earlier. Countries with regulated, national telecom systems have little choice but to deregulate as customers demand less expensive, state-of-the-art services. Companies can't be competitive if customers receive outmoded service and pay 15 percent to 50 percent more than do counterparts in other nations. As nations liberalize telecom laws and privatize their telephone systems, they attract outside investment capital and joint ventures with international giants. The improving efficiency and rapid growth not only improve communications, but spawn many smaller telecommunications companies. This trend deserves much of the credit for the recent surge in emerging markets, and it shows no sign of abating.

The best way to approach the world of emerging markets is to gain an overview of the universe of potential markets, the subject of Chapter 2.

ENDNOTES

1. Survey by Kleiman International in "Survey: Pension Funds to Boost Emerging Markets Holdings," *Dow Jones News.* New York, March 25, 1996.

2. IFC, *Emerging Stock Markets Factbook 1995*, 2.

3. Divecha, A., J. Drach, and D. Stefek, "Emerging Markets: A Quantitative Perspective," *The Journal of Portfolio Management,* Fall 1992.

4. "Emerging Market Indicators," *The Economist.* London, October 21, 1995, 112.

5. Moody's Investors Service Estimate, in John T. Mulqueen, "Developing World Lures Investors," *Telecom Infrastructure.* Published on the Internet.

CHAPTER 2

The Flow of Wealth

WHAT IS THE WORLD'S WEALTH MADE OF?

Most of the world's wealth is concentrated in three regions: the United States and Canada; Western Europe; and the Far East, in a string of nations from Japan to New Zealand. With few exceptions, the rest of the world lives in relative poverty.

Asia's economies are growing fast, but the continent is still home to most of the world's poverty. China and India have the largest number of poor people. Bangladesh, Cambodia, Vietnam, and Myanmar (Burma) are also impoverished.

The Middle East has several indigent countries: Iran, Egypt, and Iraq, have more than 185 million poor people combined. Iran and Iraq have significant oil revenues, but the IFC still ranks them as lower middle income. The oil-rich Gulf states and Israel enjoy relatively high standards of living.

The sub-Saharan region of Africa is one of the poorest regions in the world. Only South Africa and Gabon—a tiny, oil-rich nation—are in the upper middle income ranking. Ethiopia, Chad, Western Somalia, and Eritrea rank among the poorest nations in the world. The ten poorest nations in terms of per capita GDP are all in Africa.

Latin American countries straddle the middle, with some ranked upper middle income and others in the lower middle income group. The Americas do have their share of poor people, notably in Central

America and the Caribbean, in nations such as Haiti, Nicaragua, and Cuba and Brazil.

North America is a rich region, with the poorest nation—Mexico— a relatively prosperous emerging market in terms of GDP, with a higher per capita GDP than that of Hungary.

All of Western Europe is near the top of the per capita GNP table. Eastern Europe is comparatively poor. Greece, Malta, Portugal, and Turkey lag behind Europe.

Not all emerging market nations are poor in GNP terms. Israel ranks seventeenth in the world; the upper middle of the pack, ranking from 21 to 30, includes Greece, South Korea, the Czech Republic, Iran, Hungary, Brazil, South Africa, and some of the CIS republics.

HOW MUCH MONEY IS AVAILABLE AROUND THE WORLD FOR INVESTMENT?

In 1990, the financial wealth of the world amounted to $44.4 trillion, with most of it held outside the United States. Real estate and bonds are both worth more than the world's stock markets, but real estate is often illiquid and obviously cannot be moved.

Very few members of the human race gain an opportunity to invest. Roughly 70 percent of the world's population is currently sitting on the sidelines, making no investments, directly or indirectly, through the world financial system (except perhaps through the taxes they pay to governments). Russia, China, India, and the rest of Southeast Asia have literally billions of people with little or no capital available for investment.

So while financial services firms have been flocking to these markets, there hasn't been much money to manage, except among the elite. However, times are changing, as new sources of capital enter the investment pool. For example, the Chinese and Indian middle classes—growing at a rate of 15–20 percent per year—are becoming potential investors, joined by others from other developing nations. Pension funds, which once disappeared in the black hole of emerging market government mismanagement and corruption, are entering the global capital markets, adding perhaps trillions of dollars to the investment pool.

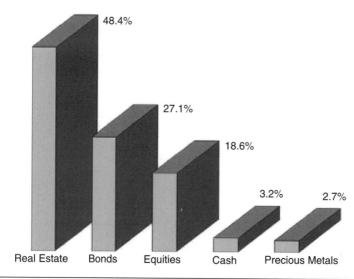

Figure 2–1. FINANCIAL WEALTH OF THE WORLD.

THE WEALTH OF WORLD STOCK MARKETS. Market capitalization—the total value of all the shares traded on a stock exchange—is even more concentrated than the world's wealth. Most of the world's total stock market capitalization is still concentrated in just three places: the United States, Japan, and Western Europe.

The total trading value of the world's public shares, while much more liquid than most of the remaining forms of global wealth, is not fully available to the investment community. Much of it—private family-share holdings, government-share ownership, stock restricted from foreign ownership, and cross ownership between companies—is less readily bought and sold.

While equities comprise only about 20 percent of world financial assets, their importance is far greater. The world stock markets are good indications of the consensus regarding the value of a nation's corporate sector. Stock prices reflect movements in the economy, the political situation, fiscal policy, capital flows, and just about everything that's important to a nation's economic performance.

SAVINGS. We know that approximately $20.6 trillion of world savings is currently held in institutional portfolios including mutual and pension funds and life insurance programs.

Wealthy individuals and families hold another $12 trillion, a good portion of which is probably invested or accessible for investment.

OTHER FINANCIAL ASSETS. Economists estimate that government and corporate war chests hold a combined surplus of around $4 trillion. Another $3 trillion sits in personal savings accounts and time deposits in banks around the world.

UNACCOUNTED FOR OR "HIDDEN" MONEY. Citizens around the world have about $1.5 trillion "in the cookie jar," and another $132 billion in gold sits in jewelry boxes, coin collections, and safe-deposit boxes. No one knows how much gold and silver is under the mattress in India. It has been smuggled in for decades, and the population values it highly. As world economic reforms take hold, some of this money may surface as capital available for investment.

The tally comes to a little over forty-four trillion, with at least half—and probably more—considered "investable" wealth. In short, most of the investment capital is accounted for. Each day, Wall Street and its international counterparts pitch deals at this money. This is why the direction and rate of flow of capital is so important. **World economies are competing for the same investment dollars, and emerging economies are gaining ground.**

TYPES OF CAPITAL FLOW

Cross-border investors are pouring capital into emerging markets in several forms and channels.

DEBT. Global borrowing, in the form of capital raised on international financial markets, hit a record $1,258 billion in 1995, up 32 percent from 1994. OECD countries accounted for 90 percent of total financing. International bank credit is rising sharply, as are commitments for project finance.

Globalization has reduced the role of traditional banking. Once a principal source of cross-border funds for debt and equity investment, they are no longer the major players. Banks got badly burned in the seventies and eighties, especially in Latin America, and things have not been the same since. In 1970, bank loans accounted for some 49.5 percent of cross-border capital flows from the private sector of the industrialized nations. According to Barings Securities, that share had dwindled to about 9 percent by the 1990's.

Don't count the banks out yet. While their *share* of capital outflows has declined, international loans outstanding are a respectable $4 trillion, more than three times that of a decade earlier. And emerging market bonds acount for only 5 percent of the total global bond market.

During the first quarter of 1997, Russian companies borrowed more than U.S. $3 billion from Western banks, and Russian sovereign guarantees were not required.

EQUITY. Equity is the principal vehicle for cross-border finance in emerging markets, and accounts for a large portion of cross-border investment. According to Barings Global Strategy Unit, direct and portfolio equity flows to emerging markets now account for almost 50 percent of the world total, up from a mere 12 percent in the late eighties. Half of this equity flow will come from local regions, as opposed to from America, Japan, or Europe.

Investment dollars, which went almost exclusively into country or regional mutual funds, now include the direct purchase of new issues and shares on local stock exchanges or via ADRs and GDRs.

NEW EQUITIES AND DERIVATIVES. The number of new international equities in emerging markets has been growing, as have new derivatives, including options and futures based on emerging market bonds, commodities, and stocks.

FOREIGN DIRECT INVESTMENT (FDI) has grown even faster. The amount of world wealth flowing from one nation to another is increasing. FDI has grown 27 percent, or about seven times faster than the output of the investor nations. Underscoring America's place in the world economy is the fact that it ranks first among recipients (22 percent of the world's FDI) *and* first among investors (accounting for 25 percent of world FDI).

FDI to developing countries has been increasing and now accounts for about 40 percent of the world total.

OFFICIAL FLOWS. Aid from multilateral and bilateral agencies is an important source of capital for emerging markets. This aid takes the form of loans, loan guarantees, investments, and outright grants. For example, donors have pledged $2.3 billion to Vietnam and $500 million to Bosnia for reconstruction.

The least-developed nations of the world still have limited access to the private capital markets. One reason is that their economies are often based purely on exports of commodities, which are subject to fluctuation.

A 10 percent drop in the price of a key export crop might leave a nation unable to service its debt. Should this occur, the country must choose either to use what little foreign reserves it has to make debt payments or simply to stop paying.

With so little room to maneuver, these countries have become dependent on official international flows. Organizations such as the Paris Club and the International Monetary Fund (IMF) have programs to rescue poor nations from debt crises.

DEBT RELIEF. Both commercial and official creditors provide assistance in the form of debt relief. If the arrangement involves forgiveness of debt—a form of income—it could be considered a capital inflow. Recently, Russia reached an agreement to reschedule billions of dollars in principal and interest arrears.

FLIGHT CAPITAL refers to capital owned by local citizens and institutions that has been held offshore due to heavy tax burdens, political instability, and so forth. When countries make their wealthy citizens more comfortable, this capital is more likely to return from its foreign home in Switzerland, the Grand Caymans, or the like.

Flight capital is both a cause and an effect of a change in capital flows; when the market recognizes that wealthy citizens are willing to repatriate capital, it is often willing to follow their lead. Conversely, local citizens sometimes follow the lead of the market, taking money out of the country as global investors retreat, then bringing it home when they return.

TRADE AND TECHNOLOGY TRANSFERS. Every year, the percentage of transactions involving international flows increases, taking the form of goods, services, capital, and technology transfers.

Goods and services move around the world more readily than does capital. In 1994, international trade was approximately U.S. $4 trillion. Since 1950, world merchandise exports have grown an average of 6 percent per year, as compared with a 4.5 percent average annual growth in world output. In the past 30 years, trade in services has grown faster than has trade in goods.

Technology has been flowing, as technical expertise, patents, R&D, and facilities are dispersing around the globe. It is no longer a one-way street, with all the world's technology flowing out of the United States and Japan. While U.S. exports of advanced technology products have been rising at twice the rate of merchandise exports, imports of advanced technology products have been rising three times as fast as merchandise imports. No single country can take the lead in every high-tech sector, because global markets can support only a few production sites. For example, although the U.S. no longer manufactures televisions, it is the market leader in more sophisticated computer and telecommunications equipment. United States computer makers dominate the world, but none of the laptop computer displays in widespread use are made stateside.

Necessity remains the mother of invention. Israeli scientists were motivated to develop high-tech solutions to water desalinization and advanced encryption and communication technologies because of the country's lack of water and political isolation. The result was the spawning of several companies that market their high-tech products worldwide.

THE FLOW OF CAPITAL TO EMERGING MARKETS

The flow of capital to and from emerging market countries changes rapidly, and these changes can have an impact on your investments. In the 1977–1982 period, capital inflows were $30 billion; between 1983 and 1989 they fell to only $9 billion, but skyrocketed to nearly $92 billion in the 1990–1993 period. A year-by-year look reveals even more volatility: In 1981 net inflow was over $51 billion; in 1989 it was minus $14 billion.

In the mid-eighties there was relatively little capital flowing to the emerging market nations. Things picked up in the early nineties, with equity largely superseding debt as the principal form of investment.

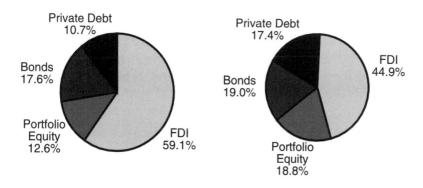

Figure 2–2. COMPOSITION OF PRIVATE FLOWS, 1991 AND 1996. THE PORTFOLIO EQUITY SHARE GREW BY OVER 6%.
SOURCE: THE WORLD BANK.

Passive investors now favor short-term, liquid investments in stocks and bonds over the more long-term lendings of the seventies and eighties. Theoretically, then, capital flows are even more volatile today, since positions are more easily reversed.

The Asian currency crisis triggered a net private capital outflow of over $12 billion in 1997 from Thailand, Malaysia, Indonesia, South Korea and the Philippines. The outflows were primarily from Southeast Asia. Net inflows to emerging markets were actually up slightly and if Asia was excluded, they were up 50 percent over the prior year.

In 1996, capital flows to emerging markets were an astounding $285 billion, a 20 percent jump from the previous year, and a record sum. Portfolio investments accounted for over $45 billion. Government loans and assistance to poor countries decreased by 23 percent during the same year, as developed nations continued to withdraw from the foreign aid business. In 1996, private money accounted for more than 80 percent of net long-term flows to emerging markets, according to the World Bank. This wasn't always the case. As recently as 1991, half the money flowing into emerging markets came from governments and international financial institutions.

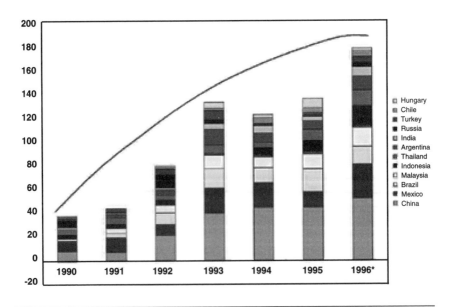

Figure 2–3. Net private capital flows to emerging markets by country. Source: The World Bank.

Not surprisingly, the beneficiaries are a small elite group of emerging markets. In 1996, three-quarters of the funds were invested in just twelve countries, with China and Mexico together receiving one-third. Fifty percent of emerging market "investable" stocks are found in Brazil, South Africa, and Malaysia.

Recent beneficiaries of large net inflows include China and India, as wealthy Asian residents and institutions in Hong Kong and Taiwan invest there. In Latin America, Mexico, Chile, and Argentina have large net inflows. Turkey and Israel have received substantial private investment in the Middle East. Saudi Arabia and the Gulf States are usually the recipients of huge net inflows, but much of it is oil revenue cash surpluses held by its citizens outside the country.

If China and India are excluded, the world's poorest countries combined received less than 3 percent of investment capital. Without sufficient capital for development, they are in danger of falling even farther behind.

African nations continue to attract very little in the way of private capital, with Nigeria, Morocco, Egypt, and Tunisia being the largest recipients. Recently, of every $20 invested, only one-third went to sub-Saharan Africa. The continent still receives much of its inflow in the form of development aid which amounts to around $13 billion annually.

Size and economic potential are not the only determinants of foreign inflows. The emerging markets likely to receive the largest share of portfolio investment are those with the largest and most open capital markets. That is why Asian nations, in spite of spectacular growth, aren't as attractive to emerging market securities investors. Many of their markets are restricted and inaccessible.

THE NET RESULT

Money flows in two directions at the same time. No nation is just a recipient or just an investor. Therefore, capital flows are measured in terms of "gross" and "net" inflows. Billions may get pumped into a nation, but at the end of the day, how much investment capital stays?

Recent figures show a sevenfold increase in gross portfolio investment capital to the developing nations, but net inflow has only doubled. So, as investors were pouring money into emerging markets, investors in emerging markets were sending much of it out. It seems that developing nations, especially those in Asia, have created sufficient wealth to become a source of capital for their less-developed neighbors and a source of capital for business in the United States and Europe.

WHAT CAN WE LEARN FROM LOOKING AT CAPITAL FLOWS?

Do large inflows of capital to an emerging market suggest that it is a good place to invest? Not necessarily. You must examine the nature of the inflows. What is the *reason* for capital inflows? Increased capital inflows may be due to policy changes alone, rather than an improvement in economic performance. For example, a rise in short-term interest rates will attract capital.

What is the *response* to capital inflows? Is the money being invested? Used to pay off debt? Is it reaching the real economy, where it is increasing savings? Or is it being spent on imported consumer goods?

How are the inflows managed? When an emerging market is the recipient of such largesse, the government must take steps to ensure that the inflows are used wisely, for long-term investment and to stimulate production. If mismanaged, capital inflows can result in inflation, an appreciating currency, and a vulnerable economy.

Consider two regions that have attracted large capital inflows, Asia and Latin America. In several Asian economies, until the recent crisis, the ratio of private investment to GDP actually rose in response to increasing capital inflows, because productivity rose even more than investment. GDP has grown at a faster rate than private foreign investment. Those same countries saw reductions in their deficits and annual growth rates as high as 7 percent, a further indication of prudent use of capital.

Now let's consider Latin America. The ratio of private investment to GDP has remained constant, indicating that the increased capital flows are not translating into increased productivity. So where is the money going? It appears to be financing private consumption. Indeed, the ratio of private consumption to GDP has risen. Domestic savings have decreased. While this is a cause for concern in the long term, in the near term it is often bullish for the local stock market.

The flow of money has a direct impact on global liquidity, which in turn moves emerging financial markets.

WHAT CAUSES CAPITAL FLOWS TO CHANGE DIRECTION?

Any factor that alters the attractiveness of a country as an investment target causes capital flow to change direction:

- Poor economic and fiscal policies
- Economic and fiscal reform
- Changes in rules regarding foreign ownership
- Increases, decreases, or restructuring of foreign debt
- Changes in real interest rates and
- Repatriation of flight capital

THE IMPORTANCE OF LIQUIDITY

Global money flows have a profound effect on asset values, especially emerging market securities. If the rate of flow of investment capital into an emerging market increases, stock prices will rise, even if the profits are falling or nonexistent and fundamentals remain unchanged. "Investor power (liquidity and savings flows)," says Barings Global Strategy Unit, "is fast replacing earnings power (profits); as the driver of stock markets . . . money matters most."[1] A few fund managers' decision to increase participation in an emerging stock market can send the bulls charging.

In each economy, the central bank—or outside foreign investors—creates money. The financial sector is the distributor, and the real economy is the end-user. As money flows from the central bank to the real economy, asset prices increase.

One theory holds that as an economy becomes more liquid, bond prices rise first, followed by stocks, then real estate and commodities. More money is available to purchase these assets.

LIQUIDITY AND STOCK MARKET FORECASTING

Some firms, such as Barings, poll fund managers to track foreign capital flows in and out of emerging markets. Liquidity analysts are concerned about two factors only: how tight or loose the money is in each emerging stock market and the amount of cross-border capital flow. By analyzing the data and using them to predict future flows of capital, they can generate buy and sell signals for the stock and bond markets. The goal is to anticipate increasing or decreasing liquidity and enter and exit the market ahead of the crowd.

Emerging market analysts monitor capital flows in "investing" countries as well. An increase in liquidity in the United States, Japan, the U.K., or Europe will often coincide with a rise in emerging stock markets as the "excess" capital seeks a home. A lowering of interest rates will often send investors in search of higher returns, which can lead to an increase in emerging market stocks or bonds.

POTENTIAL PROBLEMS WITH CAPITAL FLOW

The system is far from perfect, and since emerging markets are so dependent on capital flows, a sudden reversal could trigger a fall in the local stock market as occurred in Malaysia in 1992. The following list shows some ways in which problems could develop.

1. Deficit spending and poor fiscal policy in "investor" nations. Suppose vote-hungry politicians accuse emerging market nations of draining the United States of its capital, making it more difficult for domestic businesses to receive funding? With a net $50 billion leaving the developed countries each year, it is only a matter of time before some politicians in call for capital controls. Germany appears to be a likely candidate, as its corporations turn in record profits on their overseas operations, but the domestic economy suffers from record unemployment.

2. The wrong kind of capital inflows. "Hot money"—too much capital flowing into a country—could cause inflation and turmoil. Some governments might attempt to discourage the short-term cash going into securities in the hope of forcing investors to park their money in less liquid direct investments.

3. Poor use of capital inflows. Incoming capital is used to finance government spending and trade imbalances, rather than going into long-term investment, reducing the deficits, and reforming taxes.

4. Changing conditions in investor nations. Studies suggest that a reduction—or reversal—of funds into an emerging market nation is due in part to changing conditions in the *investing* nation. A poor economic environment in the developed "investor" nations—lower growth, higher inflation, and higher interest rates in the industrialized nations—might result in a reduced flow of capital to emerging markets. Such factors account for some 30–50 percent of the variation in capital flows to developing countries.

5. A rise of nationalism. Political forces, resentful of the changes taking place, could stir up fears of "economic colonialism," in which the rich Western nations try to enslave the Third World, this time with dollars instead of bullets. If such a conspiracy theory were to catch on, a nation might halt direct investment altogether and might even nationalize foreign investments, as some did in decades past.

6. A weakening of resolve by the government. The local government is responsible for smoothing the transition to a market economy, and ensuring that the newly created wealth is well distributed and that the population eventually will benefit from the sacrifices they may have to endure. For example, the high unemployment rate and recession that Argentines have endured must bear fruit for the majority of the population, or social unrest is likely.

7. Too much capital. The flow of funds has many implications for the recipient country, not all of them good. Capital flows aren't always put to good use. Sometimes, too much capital triggers increased consumption, as happened in Mexico and Argentina, where it sparked a spending spree on imported goods. An increased flow of funds can be potentially inflationary, and by accentuating the gap between rich and poor, can stir political and social unrest. As the money supply increases, interest rates fall, further fueling domestic demand and spurring inflation.

Large capital flows increase the potential for a rapid appreciation of the exchange rate, which could trigger a reduction in exports (because it would make local goods more expensive on world markets) and a resulting reduction in the current account.

In the wake of the December 1994 peso crisis, capital was diverted from Mexico and other countries to more promising emerging markets. Countries such as Malaysia, Poland, Thailand, the Czech Republic, and even Brazil were forced to manage increasing capital inflows. The inflows were more than the economy could absorb, which increased foreign exchange reserves and threatened to destabilize the economy.

Governments combat this problem with a tight monetary policy, which reduces demand. A more radical approach is to soak up the extra cash by "sterilizing" it. To sterilize capital inflows, the government absorbs the excess by issuing bonds, or forcing banks to do the same, and by increasing the reserve requirements for banks, forcing them to take money out of circulation.

Sterilization is not a long-term solution. It is expensive, because of the interest rate the government pays on the bonds it issues. And it taxes the private banking system by forcing it to do the same.

MONEY FLOWS IN THE FUTURE

Local and Regional Flows Will Become More Important. In 1995, half of the estimated equity flows came from local regions, not from Britain, Japan, or Europe. Emerging market regions such as Asia and South America are getting richer and are developing financial sectors of their own.

Emerging Market Foreign Exchange Reserves Are Increasing. As money flows from developed nations to China and other emerging markets, their hard currency reserves will increase, and their currencies are likely to appreciate.

Someday, the World's Capital Will Coalesce into a Large Pool that will be utilized much more efficiently than it is today. The best projects and companies will get financed under the most attractive terms. More risky—or less promising—ones will pay more. Deals done based on cronyism or political expediency will be outdated. Well, maybe. It may seem theoretically possible for such changes to come about, but it is unlikely that the human factor—contacts, opinions, greed, trust and mistrust, favoritism—will ever totally disappear from the investment scene.

ENDNOTES

1. ING Barings Global Strategy, "Main Argument," *Cross Border Equity Flows: The Financial Silk Road* (1995). Published on the Internet.

Where the Action Is in Emerging Markets

During the cold war, the globe had three worlds: the free and developed "First World," the Communist "Second World," and the "Third World," which comprised much of the developing world. A more contemporary model divides the world into *market democracies; transitional states*—former dictatorships, communist regimes, and closed economies that are beginning to make progress; and the *troubled states*, which by some measures are falling behind the rest of the world, due to extremism, isolationism, religious fanaticism, some other "ism," or just chaos.

The market democracies include a fair number of emerging markets in Asia and South America and some in Eastern Europe. Transitional states include nations such as Romania in Eastern Europe, Pakistan, and many others in Africa and Asia. Troubled states are few and far between, but North Korea, Iran, and Iraq seem to be logical members. As this is not a book about politics or the new world order, we will confine ourselves to a discussion of each nation as a potential investment market. Politics and social unrest matter only to the extent that they affect investment risk and reward. As one might expect, the level of investment risk is lowest in market democracies and highest in troubled states.

This chapter is not intended as an "investment guide," because investment climates are always changing. It provides some useful background insights that will prove valuable as you read the later chapters and formulate an approach to emerging market investing.

	Best			*Worst*		
1984	Brazil	Korea	Mexico	Greece	Argentina	Chile
	53%	20%	6%	-15%	-18%	-24%
1985	Brazil	Argentina	Chile	Colombia	Malaysia	Venezuela
	94%	75%	49%	-11%	-14%	-27%
1986	Philippines	Columbia	Chile	Malaysia	Brazil	Argentina
	383%	155%	150%	12%	-25%	-27%
1987	Turkey	Portugal	Greece	Malaysia	Mexico	Brazil
	262%	224%	152%	1%	-5%	-63%
1988	Brazil	Korea	Mexico	Portugal	Greece	Turkey
	126%	113%	108%	-28%	-38%	-61%
1989	Turkey	Argentina	Thailand	Colombia	Korea	Venezuela
	503%	176%	101%	12%	7%	-33%
1990	Venezuela	Greece	Chile	Taiwan	Philippines	Brazil
	602%	104%	40%	-51%	-54%	-66%
1991	Argentina	Colombia	Mexico	Greece	Turkey	Indonesia
	307%	191%	107%	-19%	-42%	-42%
1992	Thailand	Colombia	Malaysia	Greece	Venezuela	Turkey
	40%	39%	28%	-19%	-42%	-42%
1993	Poland	Turkey	Philippines	Venezuela	Nigeria	Jamaica
	970%	214%	132%	-11%	-18%	-57%
1994	Brazil	Peru	Chile	Poland	Turkey	China
	65%	48.10%	42%	-43%	-43%	-49%
1995	Jordan	South Africa	Peru	Pakistan	India	Sri Lanka
	23%	15%	11%	-34%	-35%	-40%
1996	Russia	Hungary	Venezuela	South Africa	Korea	Thailand
	143%	133%	101%	-17%	-33%	-36%

Table 3–1. Best and Worst Performing Emerging Markets, 1984-1996. *Source:* BCA Publications, Ltd., Montreal, The BCA Emerging Markets Analyst, January 1998.

ASIA

The securities markets of Asia are arguably the most important emerging markets in the world. Most Asian economies will grow faster than the developed world for 10 or perhaps 20 years. At their current rate of growth, they will overtake Japan sometime around the year 2010. A short time after that, their stock markets will surpass Japan's in market capitalization. Greater China's (China, Hong Kong, and Taiwan combined) GNP is already larger than Japan's in terms of purchasing power.

The economic region defined by members of the Association of Southeast Asian Nations (ASEAN) and its observers constitutes another economic powerhouse. This includes the rapidly expanding economies of Indonesia, Malaysia, Singapore, and Thailand, and up-and-comers such as the Philippines. It also includes Brunei, Myanmar (formerly Burma), Vietnam (with 72 million literate citizens and an economy opening to foreign investment), Cambodia, and Papua New Guinea. Thailand, Indonesia, and Malaysia are attracting direct investment and stock market participation and are among the world's most dynamic economies.

In spite of the region's spectacular gains over the last ten years, there is plenty of room for continued development. Most of Asia still lags the world's leading economies in income and output. At current growth rates, it will take Thailand more than 10 years to grow to within 60 percent of the leading global income levels; it will take China 75 years. While growth rates will vary from year to year, the Asian economic miracle is still in its early stages. Only a major political or social upheaval can impede continued growth.

East Asia

CHINA is the ultimate emerging market and an investment paradox. Every nation seems to buy more from China that it sells to China, with the U.S. posting a $35 billion trade deficit, Japan $14 billion, and Europe, $13 billion. China's exports are no longer limited to textiles, toys, and other low-tech items, made by workers who average about $100 per month. It is now producing TVs, computer chips, cellular telephones, engines, and automobiles, reaching a projected annual value of $100 billion within four years. Measured on a purchasing power parity basis (PPP), China's 1994 GDP was a little less than $3 trillion, making it the second largest economy in the world.

In spite of economic growth, however, China is of another era politically. The government continues to crack down on dissent. The role of the military is rising. The regime seems determined to maintain control over the social order. While many figured that open markets would eventually trigger a movement toward an open society, the Communist party remains firmly in control.

China's path to radical economic change began in the late 1970s. In 1981, the Chinese government began issuing bonds to individuals. As

China prospered, the savings rate increased, but there weren't any liquid investment vehicles. You could buy government bonds, but couldn't sell them; the bonds weren't transferable.

In 1984, the government prompted companies to issue corporate paper, mainly to employees. But what good were corporate bonuses paid in bonds or stocks if there was no place to trade them? A year later, Beijing made securities transferable and created a secondary market; banks and other financial institutions set up securities firms. In December 1990, STAQ, a bond trading system, was implemented nationwide. Shanghai officials were given a mandate to restore the city to its former glory as a world money center and the financial capital of China and open the Shanghai Stock Exchange.

Between 1904 and 1949, the Shanghai Stock Exchange was one of the largest in Asia. A major financial center filled with wheeler-dealers, swindlers, and tycoons, the old Shanghai exchange reminds us that Chinese capitalism is not new, it is just coming back from a 50-year break. Nevertheless, the current Shanghai Stock Exchange is not a grand reopening of the old exchange. The name is the same, and that's about it.

Other regional population centers in China have applied for permission to open exchanges; some will undoubtedly win approval, but the central government seems intent on regarding Shanghai as the "national" exchange. A regional exchange—the Shenzen Securities Exchange—was formed in 1991. That same year, foreigners were permitted to buy shares. Stocks are quoted and settled in Hong Kong or U.S. dollars. Currently, Shanghai and Shenzen are the only two exchanges tracked by the IMF. The two exchanges combine for more than 320 listings.

Foreign ownership of stocks is limited to classes of shares issued expressly for that purpose, and the market is very fragile as investors wonder how committed Beijing is to maintaining the integrity of the markets. As with many legal issues in China, the government seems either unwilling or unable to enforce regulations regarded as sacrosanct by the international community. Rumors of price-fixing and insider trading abound. Still, there are many investors willing to bet that the maturation of the Chinese stock markets is just a matter of time. Beijing buoys hopes—and often, the market—when it periodically announces a series of reforms designed to improve the situation.

Fortunately, there are many ways to add China to a portfolio. Several Chinese companies are listed on the Hong Kong Exchange; there are also ADRs (see Chapter 5). But the best route is probably through companies that do a significant portion of their business in China or as joint-venture partners. There are many such companies trading around the world, especially in Hong Kong.

Investors who look only at the bottom line might see opportunities in this huge export machine and local consumer market. Many of the best companies have yet to be privatized, however, and there are signs that the current regime won't be selling them in the near future. Rather than opting for large privatizations, the government intends to streamline its nearly 80,000 state-owned enterprises (SOEs) by selling off the less-desirable parts and holding onto the most promising operations. In other cases, smaller SOEs will be sold to larger ones. The government is also instructing banks to offer SOEs the most favorable loans.

The result will be a more efficient galaxy of about 1,000 large SOEs, all controlled by Beijing. More efficient, but hardly more open. Investors won't be able to buy into these SOEs, but they can purchase shares of companies that have joint ventures with them. Other investment opportunities lie with China's many joint-venture partners or affiliates in the United States, Japan, Korea, ASEAN, and even China itself.

From an economic perspective, China's recent growth is only the tip of the iceberg. It has a per capita annual income of $450, 700 million peasants, and unemployment running at around 7 percent, which means about 54 million people are out of work.

China seems to be moving toward a convertible currency. It is cutting tariffs and adopting regulations to protect foreign investors. While hardened veterans of a Marxist revolution once controlled the nation, the reins are now being taken up by a younger generation, many of whom were educated elsewhere, that may choose a more open route.

SOUTH KOREA. South Korea, Taiwan, Singapore, and Hong Kong are in a class by themselves, known as "newly industrialized countries" (NICs), which are not authentic emerging markets. With past annual growth rate of 8 percent to 10 percent and profits growing by as much as 30 percent, one shouldn't quibble over such technicalities. South Korea has been able to take advantage of the strong Japanese yen by competing directly with Japanese goods for a share of the export market. South Korea competes with the Japanese in cars, electronics, steel, chemicals and other products.

The recent crisis in Asia is not likely to affect South Korea's continued growth in the long term. Unemployment is an incredibly low 2 percent, exports are booming, and foreign investment is strong. The big news, however, is South Korea's admittance to the Organization for Economic

Cooperation and Development (OECD), the principal trade organization of the industrialized nations. (The only other emerging market members at this writing are Mexico and the Czech Republic.) A condition of OECD membership is the lifting of certain restrictions and deregulation of the economy.

The Korea Stock Exchange was founded in 1956 and remained a backwater market until the middle eighties; from 1985 to 1989, equities rose 514 percent in local currency. In 1996, it accounted for more than 11 percent of the market cap of the IFC Emerging Markets Global Index and is larger than the Swiss stock market. The South Korean economy is still dominated by large, family-held conglomerates. As such, only a small portion, perhaps 25 percent of the more than 700 listings, are "investable." Some of the listed companies are household names around the world, such as Daewoo and Samsung. Others of interest include Korea Mobile Telecom and Samsung Fire & Marine Insurance, and Pohang Steel.

Unfortunately, South Korea restricts total foreign ownership to no more than 18 percent of a company, which often makes investments problematic. Observers currently expect the South Korean government to increase the limit to 20 or 25 percent.

INDONESIA is a vigorous economy, fueled by increasing foreign investment, rising domestic consumption, and growth in exports. A combination of income tax cuts and a rise in the minimum wage have helped make Indonesians more prosperous. The recent banking and currency crisis will halve Indonesia's growth until reforms are implemented. Potential problem areas are high inflation and high foreign debt.

Indonesia is an important oil and gas producer, and this sector is an important source of exports. However, non-oil exports have been growing steadily. The government has opened the country to outside investment, triggering an influx of imports of capital goods designed to bolster manufacturing. This has increased imports and hurts the trade balance, but in the long run, it's a positive step. It should smooth Indonesia's transition to an economy less dependent on oil and gas by expanding the industrial base. Increasing internal demand for oil seems to be offsetting any potential gains from higher oil prices. The government wisely has ruled out using a devaluation of the rupiah as a way to deal with the trade balance. (See Chapter 8 for more on currency devaluations). In the past year, Indonesia has addressed the needs of foreign investors by reforming laws regulating the formation of new companies, securities regulation and tariffs.

Indonesia's stock market activity originated with the Dutch early this century, but the markets were closed with the onset of World War II. The market reopened in 1952, but when Dutch companies were nationalized in 1958, the market closed again. The Jakarta Exchange began in earnest in 1989 following a series of deregulation and reform measures. Listing requirements were simplified, and foreigners were allowed to purchase shares in certain companies. Trading is now automated.

While it continues to have growing pains, Jakarta is a key exchange for Asian emerging market investors. Among the larger listed companies are PT Unilever Indonesia, which owns the right to all Unilever products and trademarks in Indonesia; Astra International, a 70-affiliate holding company that, among other things, assembles and distributes autos, including Toyota and BMW; and Indocement Tunggal, one of the largest cement producers in the world. In 1995, they were joined by telecommunications giant PT Telecom. There are more than 230 listings, but most are illiquid.

MALAYSIA is on a fast track, growing 7.4 percent in 1997 and embarking on a "Vision 2020" program designed to maintain growth of at least 7 percent over the next 30 years with the goal of becoming a developed nation by the year 2020. There is a tremendous amount of activity in exports, imports, and consumer and infrastructure spending. But the pro-growth policy has its downside—a mounting trade deficit, increased public spending and an overheated economy. The government has acted aggressively to tighten money to control inflation and keep price hikes from eliminating its advantage as a low-wage nation. The currency appears to be rebounding from the currency crisis that drove the ringgit down by nearly 50 percent.

The Malaysian stock market—the Kuala Lumpur Stock Exchange—is well developed and very liquid. Share trading has been part of Malaysian society since the nineteenth century and has been open to foreigners.

Until 1965, Singapore was part of Malaysia, and the Singapore Exchange was preeminent, continuing to list Malaysian companies. In 1973, the Kuala Lumpur Exchange was formed, and it severed ties to the Singapore Exchange in 1990. There are more than 520 companies listed, offering some of the best investment opportunities in Asia. Listings include newly privatized Petronas Gas, Telekom Malaysia, and Genting, a holding company active in real estate, resorts, and transportation. The Malaysian stock market rose 4 percent in 1995 and an impressive 24 percent in 1996.

In 1995, the Kuala Lumpur Options & Financial Futures Exchange became the third futures exchange in Southeast Asia.

PHILIPPINES, a nation of 7,100 islands, has endured Japanese invasions, dictatorships and coups during this century. While it has many problems, the Philippines is not without prospects.

The economy has received several shocks in recent years. The inflation rate has been running slightly over the government's 7 percent target, partially the result of an increase in food prices, especially rice. The government has begun to tighten monetary policy to meet inflation and money supply targets set by the IMF. The good news is that foreign investment continues to flow, boosting production and exports, especially of computer chips and microcircuits. Clearly, capital inflows are building industrial production. As in other emerging markets, foreign investment also means increases in imports of capital goods, which is expanding the trade deficit.

The Manila Stock Exchange is one of the oldest in Asia, founded in 1927 and later merged with another to form the Philippines Stock Exchange. It lists more than 200 companies, but less than a dozen make up more than half of the total market capitalization and most foreigners have been sticking with the larger companies.

Important stocks include Ayala Property Ventures, Benguet Corporation (a leading gold producer), Philippine National Bank, Philippine Long Distance, and San Miguel (a food producer and brewery). Recently, the government announced plans to set aside at least 10 percent of all future IPOs for small investors.

In the future, the government must take firm action to control inflation and the trade balance and to keep foreign capital flowing in. It must also deal with Islamic groups in the south, which could result in renewed violence if talks on self-rule break down. Coup attempts and power outages are also problems that tend to crop up in the Philippines. Keep in mind that this country is strategically located, has close ties to the United States, and has a growing industrial sector and the need to spend big on telecommunications and electric power to put an end to those brownouts.

TAIWAN. One hundred miles off the Chinese mainland, about the size of Holland, Taiwan is a thorn in the side of Sino-U.S. relations. However, the country is a major export power with a very favorable trade balance. Foreign investment, particularly in high-tech, continues to flow in from OECD and ASEAN nations, and even China.

Although the economy is healthy, the stock market has had to cope with financial scandals, Chinese saber rattling, and a drop in private consumption. In recent years, it has suffered a liquidity squeeze, in part triggered by a loss of investor confidence.

A dramatic increase in exports to Hong Kong may indicate that Taiwanese goods are flowing into China through a more politically expedient route. This places Taiwan in an enviable position of having diverse trading partners in the ASEAN nations, mainland China, and the United States. Even with shifting political winds, Taiwan will always find a market for its goods. There are many good companies that enable investors to cash in on this export-driven economy.

The stock market traces its roots to land reform in 1953, when the government issued bonds to compensate wealthy landowners. In 1960, the government formed its SEC and two years later, the Taiwan Stock Exchange. There are more than 340 listings, including Evergreen Marine, the world's largest container fleet; Compeq a circuit board maker; and Microtek, a computer technology firm. As of this writing, Taiwan limits foreign stock ownership by individuals to 15 percent and stock ownership of a company by a foreign entity to 7.5 percent. This is a considerable improvement over more severe restrictions in the past. Since the start of gradual reforms on the Taipei Stock Exchange in the late eighties, the market has exploded. There is now one active brokerage account for every four Taiwanese.

THAILAND is growing at a rate of over 6 percent per year, but will certainly contract for two or three years in light of the recent currency crisis. Stocks are attractively priced. Exports are booming, from rubber, rice, and frozen shrimp to computers and computer parts. The Board of Investment (BOI) has acted to improve conditions for investors, and foreign investment is at near-record highs. Foreign investment continues and the stock market is growing. In spite of its exports, Thailand has a mounting trade deficit.

A large current account deficit, foreign debt, and an economic slowdown have sent the market reeling. Thailand's banks, which account for one-third of the Bangkok Stock Exchange, are dangerously overextended.

The Bangkok Stock Exchange was founded in the sixties and folded in the seventies. But the Stock Exchange of Thailand (SET), which began in 1975 with 16 listings, was a winner almost from the start. Listings and volume have grown along with the Thai economy—with corresponding booms and busts—then climbed steadily in the mid-eighties. It took the Iraqi invasion of Kuwait in 1990 to give the market the excuse it needed to correct. This ended a decade-long rise that saw only one losing year and a brief drop after the 1987 crash. The Kuwait invasion was not the reason for the sell-off, only the excuse. The market was overvalued and the economy was slowing. A military coup the following year didn't help.

In 1992, the Thai "SEC" was founded to regulate the market. Foreign ownership of listed companies is restricted to 49 percent, and financial reporting can sometimes be a problem. Today there are more than 415 corporations and more than 65 mutual funds on the exchange, and market turnover often exceeds that of Hong Kong, even though the market cap is much smaller. In 1995, the Ministry of Finance decided to allow SET listings for foreign-registered companies provided they have partial Thai ownership.

Excellent liquidity. Computerized trading. Good regulations (although the head of the SEC was removed in a scandal in 1996). And brokers that make money—or at least some of it—the old-fashioned way, on fees. Companies worthy of note include Siam Cement, with the second-largest market cap; Bangkok Bank, the largest; and Sino-Thai Engineering, one of the nation's largest construction companies.

VIETNAM is on the verge of a major transformation. It was admitted to ASEAN and normalized relations with the United States in 1995, the fiftieth anniversary of Vietnam's independence and the twentieth year of the unification of the North and South. It's *doi moi*, or economic renewal policy, has been very successful so far. The country has surpassed its economic targets and continues to grow at more than 8 percent per year, although the Asian currency crisis is expected to slow the economy somewhat. Exports are mainly commodities—oil, rice, coffee, coal—and some low-tech manufactured goods such as textiles and garments. Imports such as autos, steel, cement, and home appliances are flowing in.

The government remains Communist, and Communists love their five-year plans. The sixth, which began in 1996, has the goal of catching its neighbors in terms of economic development by the year 2000, pushing the growth rate to more than 10 percent. Inflation and trade imbalances could pose a problem, but as the country enters the world economic community, it should be able to finance its deficits with outside help. This will require a comprehensive legal framework and other reforms, which have yet to materialize. At the moment, the only way to participate in Vietnam's growth is through direct investment or through a closed-end fund that makes direct investments.

South Asia

INDIA is a giant, sprawling, multicultural democracy with one of the world's busiest stock markets. India and China combined contain more than 40 percent of the world's population; at present, India has many more investment opportunities. To sustain growth, India is dependent on foreign investment and has little choice but to reform the rules for direct and portfolio investment. But Indian politics is turbulent, and there will be lots of infighting first. Things could get worse before they get better.

Most experts believe that, unlike China, India is on an irreversible path to a market-driven economy. Once hostile to outside investment, recent reforms have encouraged foreign investment and bolstered the emerging middle class. Statistics are sketchy, but the current middle class may number 200 million or more, and they may be earning incomes on par with the West.

While growth will continue in the range of 7 percent, it will not achieve the near-10 percent level until economic reforms reach the agricultural sector. Ironically, agriculture is a source of national pride. Once barely able to feed their own people, agricultural products now contribute 70 percent of India's export income. Farmers are prospering, due in part to government investment and tax-free income. Unlike China, where agricultural workers are the nation's poorest, India's rural population accounts for 40 percent of the consumption of packaged goods, up from 28 percent ten years ago.

On the negative side, there is some fear that economic liberalization, which is widening the gap between rich and poor, will lead to political instability. Also, a recent rise in religious agitation is worrisome. The lack of a clear majority in the Indian government could slow reforms. Although exports are growing at a rate of 18 percent per year, imports are rising faster and the trade deficit is growing. With an export economy led by agricultural products, nature is an important player. Bad weather can have a significant impact on the economy.

Bombay is a city with the world's largest film industry and a stock market with thousands of listings and more intriguing subplots than the movies. The Bombay Stock Exchange is the oldest in Asia and the largest in India. In 1995, the number of listed companies jumped 22 percent to more than 5,300 companies. There are 21 other exchanges and nearly 7,000 listed companies.

The Indian stock markets are not highly correlated with those in the United States, leading some portfolio managers to conclude that ownership of Indian stocks is a hedge against the risk of a U.S. market sell-off. In spite of the large number of new listings, only three were "international" in scope in 1995.

Cows may be sacred, but the Indian stock market also has an ancient tradition of fleecing the lambs. Financial disclosure is a problem. Companies float new issues without informing existing shareholders. And trade settlement is often late: More than 20 percent fail to settle on time. Part of the problem is the increase in volume, which has overwhelmed the securities industry infrastructure. The government is addressing all these issues, as indeed it must if foreign participation is to rise, or even continue. In 1994, Indian stock brokers responded to certain reform measures in a curious way—they staged a boycott and slowed trading volume.

PAKISTAN. Discouraging economic and political news brought about a market collapse in 1995. However, a recent wave of economic reforms and privatizations has attracted attention. Virtually every area is open to private-sector investment, and IMF-sponsored programs are pushing reforms and economic stability.

Pakistan's primary export is cotton, which is vulnerable to weather and world prices, and the country runs a trade deficit as it seeks to purchase machinery, iron, and steel from the outside. Ethnic conflicts could pose a threat to political stability. In 1995, the State Bank of Pakistan devalued the rupee 7.5 percent against the dollar to aid exports, but this could increase inflation, which is already running at 11 percent.

Pakistan will be an important source of privatization deals in the years to come. Double-digit inflation and high deficits remain the trouble spots for the near future. Pakistan is well positioned geographically and culturally to be a major swing player between the Muslim republics of central Asia and the giants of southern and eastern Asia. It has several stock exchanges; the principal ones are in Karachi, which has more than 760 listings, and Lahore. Listed companies include subsidiaries of Unilever and Glaxo, Pakistan Tobacco, Rupali Polyester, and state-owned companies such as Karachi Electric and Pakistan State Oil.

SRI LANKA, an island nation off the tip of India, has a rapidly expanding economy and a real problem with a separatist movement among the Tamil ethnic minority. But the Colombo Stock Exchange, founded in 1986, is one of the best-managed emerging stock markets. It got off to a shaky start, with slow and inefficient operations. In 1990, the market and liquidity improved dramatically when the government lifted a tax on stock purchases by foreigners and took steps to combat insider trading and regulate takeovers and mergers. Foreign ownership is restricted to 40 percent of the shares outstanding, however. The market has more than 225 listed companies. It is likely to remain in the doldrums until the political situation stabilizes. But the exchange is modernizing, moving to an electronic, screen-based trading system.

OTHERS. The region also includes Nepal, Bhutan, Bangladesh, Afghanistan, and the Maldives, which are all very poor. Only Bangladesh has a stock market.

THE AMERICAS

Latin America has been roaring along. According to Morgan Stanley, the region posted the best emerging market gain over the 10-year period from 1986 to 1996, with average growth of 21.7 percent a year, besting the emerging Pacific Rim, at 15.6 percent. Chile's per capita GDP has grown an average 10 percent per year since 1986.

The nations of Argentina, Brazil, Paraguay, and Uruguay have formed a common market of sorts (Mercosur) and are increasingly trading among themselves. The Andean nations—Bolivia, Colombia, Ecuador, Peru, and Venezuela—are also growing, with notable progress in Peru.

ARGENTINA is one of Latin America's most important markets with a young and literate population of 33 million and the second-largest land area after Brazil. Long an economy based on "meat and wheat," industrial production is rising and the nation is finally exploiting its natural resources, such as oil, copper, and precious metals. It has been recovering slowly from a deep recession triggered by the Mexican peso crisis. The signs of recovery are evident, however, as inflation is low, and the economy continues to grow in excess of 5 percent per year. Foreign direct investment is rising again, and the government is determined to maintain the direct link between the Argentine peso and the U.S. dollar at virtual parity. Argentina does face many problems, however, and some are a direct result of the dollar-peso link. Unemployment remains a serious problem, and reform of the pension and welfare systems will be painful. So far, political infighting has not dampened Argentina's recovery.

Founded in 1854, the Argentine stock market, the Bolsa de Comercio de Buenos Aires, is the oldest in Latin America. At first it was just a "club" for wealthy aristocrats and merchants. Trading began in 1872 and grew as the country prospered. By the turn of the century, Argentina was one of the world's top seven economies, which explains the beautiful buildings and wide boulevards of Buenos Aires. Agriculture fueled growth, and the Argentines imported nearly everything else from the United States and Europe.

The double whammy of the Great Depression and World War II sent the agricultural sector into a nosedive, and hard times led ultimately to a military regime. For the next half century, Argentina was populist, isolationist, sometimes repressive, and politically unstable. Foreign companies fled or were tossed out.

It wasn't until sweeping economic reforms, beginning in 1989, took place that the Argentine stock market began to show real signs of life. A few adventurous country funds jumped in 1986 and 1987, but a 1989 reform package, followed by a privatization program begun in 1991, created demand for Argentine securities. Although there are 10 other exchanges, Buenos Aires is far and away the most active, with around 150 listings. Among the listed stocks, YPF is a recently privatized world-class oil company; Telefonica and Telecom are outgrowths of the privatization of the telephone company; Banco Frances and Banco Galicia are two leading banks.

BRAZIL is Latin America's largest nation—and the world's eighth largest economy—and the dominant player in Mercosur. Recent reforms by the government have curbed inflation and triggered rapid growth. However, national debt and real interest rates remain high. With a population exceeding 150 million, a large land mass, great natural resources, and an expanding manufacturing base, Brazil is an attractive market for foreign investment and is on virtually every emerging market expert's list.

The Brazilian stock market is like *carnaval*—sexy, with a whole lotta shakin' goin' on. Its swings reflect the roller-coaster ride that has characterized the economy in recent years. The government has announced eight economic adjustment plans since 1985.

The Bolsa de Valores, founded in Rio de Janeiro in 1877, was followed in 1895 by Bovespa in São Paulo, which is now the larger of the two exchanges. Early years were dominated by bond trading, but an economic boom in the seventies brought additional depth to the markets. In 1976, the Brazilian "SEC," called the Comissao de Valores Mobilarios (CVM), was formed, and in 1978, the government required insurance companies to invest part of their reserves in the stock market.

The eighties brought an end to the boom, and when the country plunged deeply into recession for the first half of the decade, the stock market followed. In 1985, over 20 years of military rule came to an end. The following year the government announced the Cruzado Plan, designed to rescue the nation from hyperinflation, and the market boomed again, for several months anyway, until it was clear that the Cruzado Plan was about as good as "Plan 9 from Outer Space." Stocks were so cheap by 1988 that the market began to recover on bargain-basement buying. In 1990, the Bovespa licensed the Computer Assisted Trading System (CATS) from the Toronto Stock Exchange.

Brazil has cash markets, forward markets, options, and commodities as well, and settlement is smooth. The latest economic reform effort—the Real Plan—has been working well, sharply reducing inflation and boosting the stock market. However, inflation is still a worry.

The recent success of the Brazilian economic plan underscores difficulty in maintaining smooth growth in emerging markets. Reforms drove up the value of the real; anti-inflationary measures drove up interest rates, further increasing the value of the real against other currencies. Now, Brazilian exports are more expensive, reducing demand for Brazilian goods around the world, and increasing the trade deficit. If the government responds by loosening credit, domestic spending could well increase, and demand for foreign *imports* could increase.

Most experts believe that Brazilian officials are finally capable of guiding the economy and expect steady growth to continue along with favorable economic conditions.

Only the Bovespa (65-75 percent of the volume) and Rio (25-30 percent) exchanges are sufficiently liquid to merit investment, but Brazil does have seven regional exchanges, which together account for 5 percent of the total volume. There are more than 1,000 listed companies, and the market is dominated by telecom, banks, energy, and mining. Current restrictions on foreign investment are not insurmountable.

CHILE, a benchmark for emerging market development, is on everyone's dance card. For a small country, Chile is remarkably diverse. Long and narrow—roughly 2,600 miles long but only 150 miles at its widest point, Chile has lots of copper and other metals in the north, rich soil and forests in the south, abundant fishing along its Pacific coast, and two-thirds of its people living in its temperate midsection.

The leading copper producer in the Western Hemisphere, Chile is also the third largest wine exporter to the United States (after France and Italy), a major exporter of "out-of-season" fruit to the the Northern Hemisphere, and an important seafood exporter. If that weren't enough, Chile's aggressive companies are fanning out across the rest of Latin America, buying assets and companies, and forming joint ventures. Indeed, many Chilean companies offer a nice play in Argentine, Brazilian, or Peruvian assets. Some experts say that Chilean management skills are a decade ahead of the rest of the continent.

Chile's economy continues to be the envy of the continent and is growing steadily. But even this "jewel of Latin America" has its problems. It has a heavy exposure to Asian weakness, since Asia accounts for 33 percent of its exports. Tensions between the government and the military contributed to a depreciation of the currency, which, combined with increasing domestic demand, resulted in increasing inflation and a trade deficit. Declining prices of principal exports such as copper and wood pulp have also taken their toll. Most experts agree that the Chilean economy will take these reversals in stride. Chile's GDP is expected to continue growing at 5–6 percent per year for the near future, while the government takes steps to bring inflation under control. Chile remains one the most stable and progressive economies in Latin America, and one of the most resilient.

Chile has a problem that many emerging markets wish they had— so much foreign capital flowing into the economy that the government has had to restrict it. Chile has restrictions on both foreign ownership and investment, restricting repatriation of capital, but allowing repatriation of profit. This helps keep out "hot money," or short-term flows seeking a quick hit.

The Bolsa de Comercio de Santiago grew steadily from its founding in 1873 through the 1930s. The country turned isolationist, and the market went downhill, reaching a low point under the Marxist Allende regime. In 1973, a coup brought General Pinochet to power, and his regime began a program of free-market reform, which included large-scale privatization of state-owned firms as well as the pension system. Chile's fundamentals improved, and in 1985, the stock market began to move. In 1989, the exchange went electronic.

The following decade was a textbook case in economic development—strong economic growth, high profits for local companies, well-managed privatizations, and growing institutional investment fueled by private pension funds. The outlook is for more of the same. Companies are reinvesting profits and expanding into new markets. Some of the biggest listed companies are in forestry, such as Copec and Cartones. Endesa is Chile's largest power company. Many companies are closely held by investment groups and are therefore illiquid.

COLOMBIA has been buffeted by scandal involving accusations that government officials accepted bribes from Colombian drug cartels. In addition, the government is at odds with the United States over its "war on drugs" policy. Despite the political uncertainty and some concern surrounding the economic effect of the assumed demise of the drug trade, prospects are favorable.

Colombia's drug problem is a paradox for would-be investors. A gutting of the drug cartels is generally considered positive for the stock market and the country's economic prospects. But like it or not, the drug trade pumps a great deal of liquid foreign exchange into the economy, and those "drug dollars" will vanish.

Tight monetary policy and a strong peso have contributed to a slowing of the economy, but Colombia's GDP is expected to grow modestly and exports are good. With an inflation rate exceeding 20 percent annually, restrictive monetary policy is likely to continue. However, the government is easing interest rates to stimulate the economy.

Colombia's three stock exchanges are the Bolsa de Bogotá, the Medellin Stock Exchange, and the recently formed Bolsa de Occidente in Cali. It's good to know that there are other ways to make money in Cali and Medellin besides cultivating poppies. Cali has all-electronic trading; the other exchanges are soon to follow. The three exchanges have more than 100 listings between them.

ECUADOR, emerging from a series of political crises, including a border war with Peru, appears poised for a round of economic reforms designed to stimulate growth. While manufacturing and agriculture have been growing, the mining and oil sectors have contracted. The stock exchange, the Bolsa de Valores de Quito, has about 145 listings; it was formed in 1992. The Guayaquil Stock Exchange has 40 listings.

MEXICO is the third largest country in Latin America and an important oil producer. Its stock market, the Bolsa Mexicana de Valores (BMV), has the second-largest market cap, after Brazil. It should come as no surprise that Mexico is one of the easiest emerging markets in which to invest. The stock market is heavily influenced, if not controlled by, Wall Street, and the leading source of investment is through ADRs traded in

New York. The big stocks are Telefonos de Mexico, or Telmex, which is highly correlated with the BMV index; Banco Nacional de Mexico, the largest bank; Cifra, the largest retailer; and Cementos Mexicanos, the fourth-largest cement producer in the world.

Mexico is in the midst of a recovery, with manufacturing and construction sectors fueling a boom in industrial output. The current account surplus shows only a slight deficit, as Mexican exports remain very competitive.

Currently, the big risks for investors in Mexico are related to political unrest. Recent political violence raises the specter of instability. At the same time, the purchasing power of the average Mexican has eroded over the years as the peso weakened, sowing the seeds of discontent.

Since the peso crisis of December 1994, Mexico has been kicked around, perhaps unfairly, as the Mexican stock market has had a long and impressive run. Mexico enjoyed 50 years of growth, which accelerated when oil prices rose in 1973–1974, averaging 6 percent. It finally hit an air pocket in August 1982, when combined effects of lower oil prices and high interest rates caused a serious debt crisis, and the government announced it could not meet its obligations. That December, the market plunged to a 30-year low.

The market recovered. In the period beginning December 1982 and ending October 1991, the Mexican market rose 8,900 percent in U.S.-dollar terms, even though GDP growth was -2 percent on average from 1981 to 1988. In 1990, the Brady Plan (see Chapter 7 on Emerging Market Bonds) restructured Mexico's debt and enabled the government to focus on reforms. President de la Madrid instituted reforms that helped Mexico move away from an oil-export economy, broadening the industrial base and opening the economy. Hyperinflation continued, however, and the market sold off 8 percent in concert with the 1987 crash. Again the market recovered.

"Tequila, anyone?"

Here begins the object lesson that is referred to in emerging market lore as the "Tequila Effect."

Buoyed by NAFTA-inspired optimism, Mexicans began a spending spree, while foreigners invested heavily, some $91 billion between 1990 and 1993. But two-thirds of that money was in portfolio investment—the money was "hot," easy-in and easy-out, rather than long-term capital investment.

With all that money flowing in search of high returns, the Mexican government succumbed to temptation, borrowing heavily to balance its budget, instead of curbing expenditures. In the meantime, Mexicans were spending instead of saving. The foreign inflows offset high local consumption rather than financing investments. The government and consumers were mortgaging Mexico's future.

With the current account deficit at 6.5 percent in 1993 and 7.7 percent in 1995, someone should have noticed. The World Bank and several noted economists did and sounded meek warnings: The peso was overvalued, making foreign goods cheaper and encouraging imports.

The Mexican government ruled out a devaluation, which would reduce imports by making them more costly. It feared the nation would lose hard-won credibility. Besides, devaluations tend to be inflationary. The government hoped to solve the problem *without* devaluing the currency, as Argentina later did. The Mexican government failed to come up with a remedy. Instead, it gambled that with exports growing and the "NAFTA effect" about to kick in, the current account would improve. In the meantime, it reasoned, don't do anything to discourage the flow of foreign capital.

The government lost the gamble when events conspired against it. (What's Spanish for "Murphy's Law"?) Early in 1994, there was an uprising in Chiapas, a state led by a charismatic leader. A few months later the ruling party's presidential candidate was assassinated. In September, the party's secretary-general suffered the same fate. A scandal erupted, with charges of cover-up and conspiracy leveled against the president's brother. At the end of the year, there was more violence in Chiapas. If that weren't enough to drive foreign capital from Mexico, the steady yearlong rise of U.S. interest rates made Mexican debt less attractive.

Each crisis was like a body blow to the midsection of the Mexican republic. Foreign reserves began the year at $25 billion; by year's end they were only $6 billion, and the government responded with operation head-in-the-sand. It delayed publication of the figures and began issuing short-term dollar-indexed bonds in a last-ditch bid to attract foreign capital. This visit to the global loan shark worked too well, as the government was able to get $29 billion worth of these bonds to market.

There was plenty of blame to go around. With IMF experts sheepishly apologizing for being "asleep at the wheel," President Salinas left the dirty work to the incoming President Zedillo, who behaved like a teenager on his first date.

The week of December 19, 1994, was much harder on the stomach than were the chiles. It began on Tuesday, when the finance minister—after assuring everyone the prior week that Mexico was committed to its exchange rate—announced he was raising the rate band by 13 percent, an invitation for the markets to devalue the peso. Instead of informing the market through the usual channels, he went on TV. Even worse, the news wasn't accompanied by a carefully considered rescue plan, designed to restore confidence and avoid default. So, what was the market to assume?

On Wednesday, foreign and domestic capital promptly fled the country, with local Mexican investors at the head of the line. The Mexican Central Bank tried to defend the peso and ran through an estimated $6 billion, like a poker player on a losing streak. By the end of the day the Bank had only $6 billion left. President Zedillo boldly affirmed Mexico's commitment to support the peso.

On Thursday, the government let the peso float, and it fell another 15 percent. The following Monday, after what must have been a working weekend, the President scheduled a news conference at which investors were to be told precisely what steps Mexico would take to address the crisis. At the last minute, the press conference was canceled, and the peso fell further.

On Tuesday, the peso fell to a level that was 36 percent less than the previous week, and fear of economic chaos spread through the market. An auction failed, attracting only $27.6 million in bids on a refinance of $774 million in bonds. Prices begin to rise, and labor leaders, sensing the inevitable, pushed for higher wages.

The crisis spread like a stubborn winter flu, with Brazil, Argentina, and the rest of Latin America getting sick. The bug hit the jetstream and floated across to Asia, where it destabilized local exchanges, prompting fears that this peso crisis would take all emerging markets down with it. Money managers—many of whom had too much money in Mexico—struggled against mounting losses and redemptions. Many were forced to cut back holdings in other countries.

President Clinton, sensing the cure couldn't possibly be worse than the disease, arranged a $50 billion rescue. Mexico is, after all, the third largest consumer of American exports. The political opposition protested, but many business leaders breathed a sigh of relief.

By March 1995, with the bailout loans in place and a credible economic rescue plan on the Mexican agenda, things began to turn around. By then the peso—and the stock market—had lost half their value. By some accounts, $5 billion had fled the country. Eventually, the peso stabilized, the stock market rebounded, the trade balance improved, and even the short-term dollar bonds were largely paid back. And the problem of holding back important financial data? The Mexican government now maintains a Web site to release these figures to the world. *Immediately.* (See Appendix C.)

Argentina and Brazil got badly bruised during the Mexican crisis, but came roaring back. Other emerging markets went relatively unscathed. Today, Mexico is still dealing with inflation and a weak peso. However, the depreciation has kept labor costs low and goods competitive. Long-term prospects are good. With 90 million people, a developing stock market, and a role as the United States' largest trading partner, Mexico is an emerging market that should be on everyone's "watch" list. Many consider the peso crisis a watershed event in emerging market investing. It showed emerging market governments the dangers of hot money, lack of fiscal discipline, and indecision. But it also demonstrated the resilence of emerging markets. In the long view, the peso crisis did not alter the prospects of emerging markets. Nor did it prevent countries such as Malaysia from stumbling into their own currency crises. Investors should take two lessons from the peso crisis. First, that blunders in emerging market fiscal policies are inevitable. Second, that they eventually recover.

PERU has been growing rapidly in the 1990s. While growth slowed somewhat in 1996 and 1997, the effects of the turnaround should kick in during 1998. Peru recently signed a Brady-style agreement that will make financing easier and marks the end of a 13-year period during which Peru was blacklisted by the world's leading banks. The privatization program raised more than $1 billion in 1995. Peru's government has increased the percentage of pension funds that may be invested in stocks from 20 percent to 35 percent.

The Bolsa de Valores de Lima has more than 240 listings and has been a favorite with investors the past several years. Liquidity has been increasing as well as market capitalization. In 1995, the Bolsa de Valores was up 22.1 percent, the best performer of all the Morgan Stanley Emerging Market Indices, due in part to investor optimism in privatization, which encourages small-investor participation. A number of companies trade simultaneously on the NYSE and the Bolsa de Valores.

VENEZUELA is one of the most volatile markets in the region, and still among the riskiest. Several years ago, the country responded to a crisis by returning President Rafael Caldera to power. He immediately reverted to populism, abandoned reforms, and instituted foreign exchange controls. The impact was severe, and it would have been even worse if not for the nation's oil wealth. Venezuela created its own banking crisis even before Mexico's infamous Tequila Effect. In 1994, the government seized 14 banks, which collectively held 54 percent of the country's deposits. President Caldera's bold reforms appear to have the economy moving again. However, the country is still vulnerable to discontent in the labor sector.

The 1995 Venezuelan stock market is a classic example of the impact of currency rates on returns. That year, the International Finance Corp.'s Investable Index (IFCI) for Venezuela rose 35 percent in local currency, but dropped 32.4 percent in dollar terms.

In 1996, Venezuela's fortunes reversed and its stock market was one of the world leaders, with its Merinvest Index up over 232 percent, and rose 20.7 percent in 1997 in dollar terms. The government's decision to devalue Venezuela's currency, the bolivar, under pressure from the IMF, contributed by making exports cheaper. The booming oil industry also helped.

Venezuelan political reforms are relatively new. Inflation is slowing and confidence in reforms is increasing. Approach this market with caution.

EUROPE AND CENTRAL ASIA

Eastern Europe has turned an important corner. The population, while generally euphoric over the collapse of the communist regimes, has also been quite tentative. "What if it doesn't last?" was the question on everyone's lips. The population was cautious and did not engage in the spending that comes with consumer confidence about the future. Today, after more than five years of capitalism, the local population is on the go, and the governments are maintaining momentum by continuing economic reforms. By the end of the century, Eastern Europe may account for nearly a quarter of the world's market capitalization.

This region, led by Poland, is emerging as one of Europe's low-cost producers of goods and services. It supplies both Russia and Western Europe.

BULGARIA is in the midst of a reform program, the aftermath of a financial crisis. The government has established a currency board, and is now receiving aid from the IMF. In 1996, Bulgaria began a large-scale privatization designed to increase foreign reserves and reduce the deficit, but the program still has a long way to go. Currently, foreign ownership is limited to 34 percent. A great deal hinges on the privatization program and on the quality of the companies that emerge. On balance, Bulgaria is becoming a market worthy of investor interest, but the economy and the banking system are too shaky in the short term. Nevertheless, there are indications that it will be a popular destination for frontier investors in 1998 and 1999.

CROATIA appears to be moving in the right direction. Its territorial borders are set, and internal conflict appears unlikely. The country should grow at a 5 percent rate, higher if it is able to attract large-scale foreign investment. Several industries were competitive before the regional conflict, such as tourism, shipbuilding, pharmaceuticals, and engineering. Tourism and other service sectors are driving the recovery, while industries remain depressed. As of this writing, a new securities law is due for implementation. Significant political risks remain, and the IMF and the U.S. may withold financial assistance to put pressure on Croatia to live up to the Dayton peace agreement.

THE CZECH REPUBLIC was recently admitted to the OECD, which conveys the status of an industrialized nation, but requires an almost irrevocable commitment to free-market capitalism. With a skilled labor force, a rich cultural tradition, and easy access to markets in Europe, Russia, central Asia, and the Middle East, the Czech Republic holds promise.

Foreign portfolio investment is already at a high level and is expected to increase in the coming years. A disciplined monetary policy has resulted in the lowest inflation rate in Eastern Europe, at 8.8 percent. Growth should continue at around 5 percent. In addition, the currency is moving toward full convertibility, which would make it the leading currency in Eastern Europe.

The Czech Republic also has one of the lowest unemployment rates on the continent, although this statistic is somewhat misleading. The privatization process took longer than expected. The resulting private companies have dragged their feet on restructuring, delaying the job reductions that usually accompany the privatization of a state enterprise. When these enterprises get around to cost cutting, unemployment is sure to rise.

In the near term, rising real wages will increase domestic demand and investment. But the government's tight money policies, implemented to fight inflation, and its growing domestic and trade deficits will probably keep the economy from growing even faster.

The Czech stock market has been plagued by trade settlement and custody problems, so buyer beware. On the plus side, this market is relatively liquid, and plans are underway to improve investment options for foreigners.

GREECE, a full member of the European Community (EC) and in the fold of Western Europe, is often omitted from emerging market lists. It is included in the IFC's "upper middle income" group of emerging markets, although Greece—with a per capita GNP of $7,390—is near the top end of the range.

The Greek economy is largely agricultural, with that sector using 70 percent of the land surface. A tight money policy and strong currency have recently contributed to a drop in inflation. However, growth has been slow, below the EU average at around 2+ percent, and the trade deficit is mounting. Labor negotiations could contribute to inflation.

The Athens Stock Exchange has become more important as a source of financing in recent years. In the past, the business sector relied on banks and family-style financing. Undoubtedly, the country's goal of admittance to the European Union (EU) by the year 2002 has helped, as the economy struggles to meet the demands and opportunities of membership in one of the world's most prestigious economic blocs.

In 1990, the Athens Stock Market was the second-best performer in the world. The market was automated. Listings increased, liquidity improved, and a regulatory framework was placed in service. Since the base year of 1990, the IFC index for Greece has increased over 700 percent. While the ten largest companies still dominate trading, the market is quite liquid, with more than 200 listings and a healthy turnover. The listed companies are a diverse mix of banks, bottlers, shipping, construction, and several high techs. Companies of note include Credit Bank; aluminum producer Aluminum de Grece; Delta Dairies; Intracom, S.A., a telecom company; and the Coca-Cola bottler, Hellenic Bottling. The Athens market was up over 39 percent in 1997.

HUNGARY was the first in Eastern Europe to move to a market economy, withdrawing from the Warsaw Pact in 1990 and beginning widespread economic reforms less than a year later. As with any emerging economy, Hungary has had its share of ups and downs, but has accomplished one of the fastest transitions in economic history. The country is relatively free of the ethnic tensions that plague its neighbors, and, in spite of the discontent engendered by capitalism, is very stable. There are many millionaires and a growing middle class. But there are growing numbers of poor as well.

The Budapest Stock Exchange has a proud tradition dating from its founding in 1864, except for a 35-year hiatus. Closed by the Communists in 1948, it was reopened in 1983. In 1990, the government created a Stock Exchange Commission to regulate the exchange and instituted a series of laws and regulations designed to protect investors. There are many active brokerage firms, a computerized trading system, and more than 40 listings. The privatization of Magyar Hitelbank (MHB) raised U.S. $89 million, part of a program that will bring in several billion and increase the number of listings on the Budapest Exchange. The BUX index was up 56.5% in 1997.

The outlook for Hungary is bright. The economy should continue to grow for years to come, although not at the pace of some of its neighbors. A recent austerity program and devaluation of the currency, designed to reduce the deficit, have not slowed growth. Inflation appears to be slowing and should soon fall below 20 percent. Devaluations mean higher prices on imports and stimulation of inflation, but the worst seems past. Surging exports have kept the economy moving. The currency is convertible for most—but not all—transactions. By all accounts, Hungary's admittance into the OECD is imminent. Currently, just a few companies, including hotel chain Denubius, dominate the stock market. Hungary has been invited to begin negotiations to join the EU and NATO.

POLAND, with 38 million people, is the largest country in Eastern Europe and is rapidly emerging as an economic power. The economy was among the first of the former Iron Curtain nations to expand, posting positive GDP growth in 1992. Inflation continues to be high, but has been dropping steadily. Growth is running at over 5 percent per year. The budget deficit is rising, but foreign exchange reserves are strong due to foreign equity investment, cross-border trade, and repatriated assets. A new currency law lifts restrictions on hard-currency bank accounts for private companies. With a population that is 98 percent Polish, there is no risk of ethnic strife.

The Warsaw Stock Exchange (WSE) began operating in 1991 after being closed for 50 years by Fascist and Communist regimes. It has boomed since reopening. According to the IFC, there were 65 listed companies at the end of 1995, including Bank Slaski, with the largest market cap; Elektrim, a trading company; and Zywiec, a construction company. The market also includes promising breweries, distilleries and garment manufacturers.

Curiously, privatization has been lagging, although it is now in progress with a program covering more than 400 state-run companies with a combined book value of over $2.5 billion. One hundred additional companies are under consideration, and the next phase will bring 500 to

600 new companies to market. As of this writing, Poland is considered one of the most attractive emerging markets for foreign investment.

PORTUGAL is another "semi-emerging" market, with a per capita GDP about $800 below the IFC cutoff. It's had a stock market since the Oporto Stock Exchange was founded in 1891. The Lisbon Stock Exchange, founded ten years later, went largely unregulated until the mid-1970s. The market was hit by the 1987 stock market crash and is one of the few in the world that hasn't fully rebounded. Liquidity has declined as well.

Privatizations are attracting foreign investors. The government sold portions of Portugal Telecom and an electric utility, and the shares were well-received.

Portugal needs investment to grow. Recently, its location on the European coast with relatively low-cost labor has been attracting attention. A new Volkswagen plant should increase the value of exports by as much as 10–15 percent. Fiscal management has improved recently, and inflation is under 4 percent. Economic growth rate is a respectable 3 percent, and the OECD forecasts higher rates in coming years.

Portugal does not receive much attention from mainstream European equity funds. Yet, as part of industrialized Europe, it is also neglected by many emerging market funds in search of higher risk-and-reward scenarios. The Lisbon Stock Exchange is worth a look. Liquidity has increased, but watch for distorted valuations.

ROMANIA is now instituting much-needed economic reforms. The growth trend is positive, on the heels of a decline brought about by an austerity program. Production and foreign investment are improving, although most global investors await an IMF program. The currency, the *leu*, has been devalued as part of an overall program to increase exports, but privatization of heavy industries is moving slowly. Romania is a laggard in Eastern Europe, but the government is expected to accelerate reforms and privatization.

The Bucharest Stock Market is beginning to show signs of life and generating interest among frontier investors.

RUSSIA AND THE FORMER SOVIET REPUBLICS. As this book goes to press, foreign investors are lining up to invest in Russian stocks. Fourteen Russian companies have floated ADR issues in the United States, and at least 15 more are waiting in the wings. Investors from around the world have pumped billions of dollars into Russian equities. The Moscow Stock Market enjoyed a spectacular rise in 1996, which carried through to 1997.

Market watchers attribute the rise in the Moscow Stock Market to a series of confidence-boosting events: the reelection of Boris Yeltsin, Russia's successful offering of U.S. $ 1 billion in Eurobonds, and a decision by the IFC to add Russia to its emerging market indexes, making it easier for portfolio managers to monitor and invest. A drop in local interest rates has lured many investors from the bond markets, and 20 percent of the trading volume has come from Russians. Another reason for the rise is the simple fact that the U.S. bull market has created a great deal of wealth that is looking for new opportunities.

Is the Russian market out of hand? Many insist that Russian stocks are still cheap, given the potential. The better-managed telecoms and banks are growing fast and posting large gains and some of the oil companies are priced lower than their counterparts in the U.S. and Europe. But there is still a shortage of experienced, capable management, so meeting aggressive growth targets may be easier said than done.

One prominent naysayer is Jim Rogers a pioneer in emerging markets investing and author of *Investment Biker*. "As far as I'm concerned," he writes in the May 1996 issue of *Worth*, "the former Soviet Union is still the world's great economic, political and social disaster in the making. It will be so for years, if not decades." Rogers believes that the 15 former Soviet republics will split further, into perhaps 50 or 100 smaller nations. Infrastructure is crumbling, and there is no political stability. "It's important to look not just for an emerging country but for emerging stability as well," said Rogers. Furthermore, Russia's external debt situation is nearly as bad as that of Indonesia and Malaysia before the decline of their currencies in late 1997.

A central problem for Russia is that people are unhappy with the status quo. In one poll, about 75 percent said they were "deeply dissatisfied." This has opened the political scene to reactionaries, populists, demagogues, and communists. It is a sad irony that this is happening just as Russia is beginning to make progress, reducing inflation from 20 percent per month to less than 3 percent. The government is making use of ruble "bands," which allow the currency to float freely within a certain range. If it trades above or below the band, the central bank intervenes. The intended effect is a stabilization of the currency and a reduction in speculation. As a result, the currency has been appreciating against the dollar. Continued reforms and liberalization and adherence to the IMF guidelines should keep the economy growing slightly over the next several years. The optimists believe that a solid economic policy will generate growth of 7–8 percent per year.

These milestones are very important on the emerging market scene, but mean little in the short run to a population ravaged by crime, falling real wages, and increasing unemployment. Production has been falling in many industries, and there are working capital shortages everywhere.

As Rogers points out, big obstacles remain at the political level. Rules of law are difficult to enforce, and the country's institutions and legal framework are weak. A notable example: The government has been unable to collect taxes due. This problem extends to Moscow's stock exchanges, banks, and other financial institutions.

Russia's stock exchanges are anarchic. The major exchanges are in Moscow and St. Petersburg, but there are many others. Unfortunately, while Russia may be a diamond in the rough, its stock markets are too treacherous for most investors. Regulations are still lax, and it can be difficult to determine the true worth of a company or even the actual shareholders. Perhaps the best news is the increasing number of ADRs and GDRs, which will require disclosures that meet international standards. Major companies include Lukoil, a major world oil company; smaller oil concerns such as Yukos; regional telecoms such as Perm Uralsvyazinform; the Siberian electric company Irkutskenergo; and well-known banks such as Inkombank and Menatep.

It would seem unfair to leave this section without an encouraging note. Russia had no stock exchanges and little private enterprise from 1917 to 1990. As *The Economist* points out, "Russia has more than 3,000 commercial banks, 800 insurance companies, 600 mutual funds and 200 commodity and stock exchanges. That they exist at all in a society where most forms of private economic activity were a crime four years ago is remarkable." Stock market liquidity has improved, and listings are becoming more diverse.

At least a few of the former Soviet republics should fare better. Odds are that one or several, rich in resources, will be able to achieve sufficient stability to succeed.

TURKEY has always been a strategically important country by virtue of its unique location straddling Europe, Asia, and Russia. With a population of over 60 million and an economic renaissance that has made the Istanbul stock market one of the world's busiest, Turkey continues in its traditional role as the crossroad of Europe and Asia. Turkey stands to benefit from the economic development of the Balkans, the southern former Soviet republics, Russia, even Iran and Iraq and the rest of the Middle East. Surrounded by such growth, the Turkish economy is bound to benefit. The economy has been growing at an average rate of 4.5 percent since 1990, with annual rates as high as 7 percent.

When it comes to volatility, the Istanbul Market is in a class by itself. In 1992, it was off by 49.2 percent, making it the worst-performing emerging market. In 1993, Istanbul gave new meaning to the term "rebound," as it climbed 207.7 percent on the year, only to roll over hard, down 52.6 percent, in 1994. In 1995, the Istanbul Stock Exchange Index (ISE) rose 46.8 percent, but the local curency (lira) fell more than 36 percent against the dollar. The IFCI index was down 13.4 percent on the year.

The Turkish political situation is perpetually uncertain, with a formidable Islamic fundamentalist movement and six political parties vying for power. Inflation and the deficit are high.

Stock market activity dates back to the Ottoman Empire, but the modern Istanbul Stock Market was founded in 1986, and there are now more than 200 listings. Notable companies include Ege Biracilik, a brewery; Migros, a supermarket chain; Koc Holding, a holding company; and Petrol Ofisi. A privatization program began in 1997 with a U.S. $10 billion target. Turkish Telecom, wireless telephone licenses, and state properties will be on the block.

THE MIDDLE EAST AND NORTH AFRICA

The Middle East may well be "the last undiscovered pool of credible emerging markets in the Old World," says Frank Gardner of London merchant bankers Robert Fleming. The IMF has supervised financial reforms in Jordan, Morocco, Egypt, and Tunisia, and investors such as Fleming and Salomon Brothers are entering the markets.

The Islamic world (which extends into Asia as well) is a big player on the world scene because of its sheer size. With 900 million people in 49 countries, Koranic law may have more influence on the investment climate than do government policies, especially since the Koran speaks to financial matters directly and with respect to how one treats one's neighbors.

The question remains, How will the Islamic nations incorporate Koranic law into the global financial system? While great differences exist among these nations, they will all have to come to terms with the fundamentalist segments of their populations.

The Koranic law forbids the charging of interest, so stock materials and the equity may well become the favored method of raising capital.

EGYPT could be one of the biggest beneficiaries of a Middle East peace. One of the more interesting positive developments is the prospect of regional economic integration, complete with a free trade zone and a regional development bank. In addition, Egypt is pressing for membership in the European Community's Euromed free trade zone. In 1996, the

IMF approved Egypt's reform program, which will relieve the country of some of its debt.

Egypt has a relatively large stock market, Bourse de Valeurs du Cairo, with more than 700 listings. The country has reduced its budget deficit from 20 percent of GDP in 1989 to 10 percent in 1995 and is growing at over 3.5 percent per year.

The government is expected to enact a series of economic reforms including several directed at foreign investment.

The Cairo Stock Market is poised for a boom. The IFC recently included it in its daily indexes, and this should attract investors. New IPOs have offered solid assets at favorable valuations. Privatizations will continue, and several Egypt large-country funds have been formed recently.

The future of Egypt's stock market is closely tied to the progress of economic reforms and privatization.

ISRAEL. Israel's Tel Aviv Stock Exchange, buoyed by a takeoff in high-tech issues, is soaring. The Israeli stock exchange includes several of the largest emerging market companies in the world, such as Israel Chemicals, Teva Pharmaceutical, Bank Hapoalim, and Bank Leumi. There are more than 400 listings.

Because Israel is neither truly emerging nor truly developed, it is fertile field for investment bankers. It has a financial infrastructure with a skilled brokerage community; company managers understand the rewards and risks of stock market participation. Since the country is so small, however, a Wall Street consensus that "Tel Aviv is hot" can cause a rapid increase in price, and the market can get overheated. In addition, many of Israel's young companies are in the volatile technology sector.

Technology spun off from Israel's defense industry as well as a highly skilled work force enhanced by well-trained and educated Russian immigrants have helped create some of the world's most advanced technology companies. As such, they may be subject to the same market forces that move U.S. technology stocks. In 1996, two offerings, NICE Systems, Ltd. (NICEY) and ESC Medical Systems (ESCMF) raised a combined $66.5 million.

Israel's prospects look good, provided there are no extraordinary shocks. Growth is slowing, but is still healthy. Inflation—a persistent problem—appears to be under control, back in single digits. Cooperation between the government and the Central Bank is improving. On the downside, domestic consumption and trade deficits are high.

JORDAN is a leader in stock market maturity, although the Amman Financial Market hasn't been very exciting. Established in 1976, it began trading in 1978. The government is planning privatizations of the airline, telephone company, and electric utilities, among others. New investment and tax laws aimed at encouraging foreign investment helped shock the Amman market out of its torpor; the AFM rose 10.5 percent in 1995 in local currency, and the IFCI rose 23.1 percent in dollars. The new investment law grants equal treatment to all investors and makes it easier for foreign investors to trade on the stock exchange.

A small country with few large companies, poor in natural resources, Jordan seeks to become the money center of the Middle East, kind of a financial demilitarized zone. It has a skilled workforce, many of whom are Palestinian, and the country has managed to avoid deep-seated blood feuds with most of its neighbors, no easy task.

In October 1995, Jordan signed a peace agreement with Israel. The agreement acknowledges the economic gap between the two countries, and while taking steps toward removing trade barriers, it gives Jordan special protections and advantages designed to make the situation more equitable. The stronger Israeli market has little chance of becoming the money center of the Middle East for obvious political reasons. Therefore, Jordan has as good a chance as any to assume that role. The AFM has about 100 listings.

Jordan has made tremendous progress since a debt crisis in the late eighties, when the Gulf states began reducing aid. From 1992 to 1994, GDP growth averaged an impressive 7–8 percent; inflation dropped from 16 percent in 1990 to under 4 percent in 1995. Unfortunately, the Jordanian economy cannot escape the effects of every Middle East Crisis.

LEBANON is preparing to reopen Beirut's bourse for the first time since civil war closed its doors in 1983. Should the peace initiative hold, Beirut is in the running as a receiving center for the capital inflows to the Middle East, but it needs rules against money laundering and insider trading. It has poor commercial and financial laws and a policy of weak enforcement. Lebanon is a hotbed of drug and terrorist money. To date, the nation's banks have benefited from banking secrecy laws, but the international community will require greater scrutiny of clients. If Beirut forms a regulatory commission for its securities markets, it could become the Wall Street of the Middle East. It has an advantage over Amman in that there is already lots of cash in town and enough banks to hold it.

SUB-SAHARAN AFRICA

In some ways the final frontier, Africa is abound with "embryo markets," emerging markets to be. Anchored by the established South African stock market and invigorated by the reforms there, the continent is beginning to show signs of life.

COTE D'IVOIRE is very small and lacks the resources to fully qualify as an emerging market. It is worthy of mention because it is one of the most impressive economies in sub-Saharan Africa. It is growing at a rate of 6+ percent. Inflation has come down to around 4 percent, and the developed countries are supporting the government's commitment to economic reform. A devaluation in 1993 has benefited the economy, and the government has a firm hand on tax collection, public sector wages, the deficit, and inflation.

Cote d'Ivoire has one of the most extensive privatization plans in Africa. Several offshore oil discoveries have been announced, but their viability is as of yet unclear. The country has a working stock market, the Abidjan Stock Exchange, with about 30 listings. It has a reputation for good economic management and relative political stability, making it a good choice for those interested in investing in Africa. A new Brady Plan and agreements with the London and Paris clubs and the IMF will help reduce and restructure some of the nation's obligations, but it will remain heavily in debt for years to come.

GHANA has made excellent progress since 1983, but has recently suffered setbacks due to inflation, a credit crisis, and uncertainty after the end of military rule in 1992. Inflation is high, but the IMF has agreed to a loan package and an assistance program aimed at boosting Ghana's GDP growth to 6 percent by the end of the decade. In 1996, Coca-Cola opened a bottling plant in Acra, a further indication of progress.

In 1994, Ashanti Goldfields Company Ltd. was floated on the London and Ghana Stock Exchanges, raising $454 million, and in February 1996, it became the first African company to list an ADR on the New York Stock Exchange. The company has 10,000 employees, has been strike-free since 1985, and had annual profits exceeding $100 million in 1995 and 1996. The Ghana Stock Exchange has undergone improvements, and the government appears commited to economic reform.

KENYA is growing at nearly 3-4 percent per year. The economy is dependent on tea, coffee, and tourism, which are extremely vulnerable to market forces. At the present time, restrictions on foreign exchange and investment make Kenya "uninvestable."

The third largest economy in sub-Saharan Africa, Kenya has had a stock market, the Nairobi Stock Exchange, since 1954. The largest stocks make up nearly three quarters of its market cap and consist mainly of banks, breweries, coffee and tea, and natural resources.

NIGERIA, an oil-rich nation, is currently in the grip of a repressive military regime. Worldwide condemnation has not yet resulted in sanctions, probably because of Nigeria's importance as an oil exporter. Although oil and agriculture have kept the economy growing, industry is in deep recession and the government is running a deficit. Talks with the IMF have been suspended indefinitely, but the government is hoping to open a dialogue. The Lagos Stock Exchange has a market cap that probably exceeds $1.9 billion, but is closed to foreign investment.

SOUTH AFRICA. The African National Congress (ANC) retains the support of the voting majority, and the nation is getting used to elections in which both blacks and whites have a vote. Inflation is falling gradually; the economy should continue to grow modestly.

Import barriers are falling as the economy opens to foreign investment, and the rand/dollar exchange rate is stabilizing. The downside is that local suppliers are forced to compete with foreign companies offering lower prices. Foreign reserves are very low, even by emerging market standards, covering only about one month's worth of imports, excluding gold reserves.

The Johannesburg Stock Exchange is by far Africa's largest stock market with about 650 listed companies and a market cap of over $230 billion. The exchange listings are dominated by diamond, gold and other mining concerns, and have attracted investment dollars from all over the world as a way to invest in precious metals and diamonds.

In some respects, South Africa isn't an emerging market at all. The previous political system developed the financial markets to a high level of sophistication, and there are some very well-run companies that have been around for more than a century. On the other hand, the victims of apartheid constitute the majority, and based on overall standards of living, income, and GDP, South Africa is every inch an emerging market. The country has more infrastructure than most emerging markets, and if it can muster the political will to shed its painful past, South Africa could become a world economic power and certainly the economic leader of the continent.

Curiously, South Africa attracts only a small share of emerging market investment capital. This may be the result of its own early success. South Africa has a more established investment history than, for example, the Latin American nations. More is expected of South Africa. A more tangible reason for this lack of interest is the confusing policy signals from the government.

The JSE is now actively wooing foreign investors, admitting foreign brokerage firms and banks, and allowing them to trade directly. It now allows market making, has abolished fixed commissions, and has initiated screen-based trading.

ZIMBABWE has been on a roller coaster in terms of growth. Its most serious problem is unemployment, which hovers at around 50 percent, followed closely behind by 20+ percent inflation. The country missed 1995 IMF targets and failed to reach a new agreement. Tighter fiscal management will undoubtedly be required, and it will be painful. Drought has hurt this agricultural economy by reducing exports and forcing the importation of food, but the situation has improved.

The Zimbabwe Stock Exchange (ZSE), located in Harare, lists 64 companies and is very illiquid. The market and liquidity have begun to pick up. Banks and mining stocks dominate trading.

Emerging Stock Markets

A common misconception is that stock markets are venerable institutions, quasi-governmental organizations that exist for the benefit of the nation. Stock markets are fundamentally capitalist businesses established to meet the needs of consumers. They are no different, in a sense, from the roadside produce stand.

The founding of a new stock exchange is always cause for some excitement in the financial community. But the majority of the world's nations already have stock markets, and most have been around for quite some time.

As with the telephone system or the railroad, the sign of a solid institution is not how long it's been around, but how well it functions. In addition, emerging stock markets largely reflect the health and openness of the local economy. If the late 1980s and 1990s have brought a rebirth of free-market economies and the triumph of capitalism over communism, it's no surprise that many stock markets have been reborn as well.

THE ORIGINS OF GLOBAL INVESTING

In the 50 years preceding World War I, Britain—and to a lesser degree, other countries of Western Europe—were the world's economic superstars. For most of this period, the British had a current account surplus in excess of 8 percent of its GDP. They were taking in a lot of cash. And they were saving it; by 1914, total annual income was $11 billion, and the British saved $1.8 billion of it.

Growth, on the other hand, wasn't so spectacular. From 1870 to 1913, Britain grew at an annual rate of 1.9 percent, France by 1.9 percent. Only Germany posted respectable expansion of 2.8 percent.

With large domestic savings and slow growth at home, Europeans looked across the oceans, where the United States was growing at 4.3 percent per year, Canada and Australia at 3.2 percent, and Argentina at a fierce 6.4 percent. The Europeans, especially the British and the Dutch, poured money into stocks in all industry sectors of these countries. They bought bonds that financed infrastructure projects such as railways and dams. This was the capital that financed the growth and development of North and South America and Australia, just as capital from the United States, Japan, and Europe is financing development today.

World War I brought this boom to an end. Russia went communist; Germany was vanquished; France and Britain were forced to liquidate certain overseas holdings. The United States became protectionist, raising tariffs and turning inward.

After a flurry of local activity inspired by the roaring twenties in the United States, most small stock markets around the world grew quiet. A lack of foreign capital and the worldwide depression of the thirties closed many, or turned them into private "clubs" for aristocrats.

After World War II, many of the developed nations tried to recapture the glory days before World War I, but the tides were against them. A large portion of Europe fell behind the Iron Curtain.

Newly liberated nations in Africa and Asia, created from former European colonies, were insecure political entities. They restricted economic and political freedom, often turning to totalitarianism. In South America, even such nations as Uruguay and Argentina, which had so benefited from free trade, turned away from the free market, and much of the continent followed suit.

Heavy taxation and exchange controls made it difficult for foreign money to invest in "Lesser Developed Countries," or LDCs. Overtaxed and overregulated locals turned their wealth into "flight capital," taking their cash out of their home countries and placing it in overseas banks or investments.

In spite of all this, there was still a lot of lending going on: official flows, in the form of loans and aid from developed nations and private bank loans. However, there was virtually no activity in LDC securities markets, and few stocks or bonds.

THE RISE OF EMERGING STOCK MARKETS

Ironically, it was during this time that many stock exchanges were formed. Newly formed nations, eager for prestige, established stock markets just as they formed national airlines and acquired arms. A local stock market was viewed as a sign of sophistication and prestige but was not taken seriously as a tool of economic development. In fact, many politicians in these countries preferred to trash stock markets as tools of oppression and dens of thieves.

By 1970, 32 developing countries had working securities markets. The Philippines and Argentina even had a form of regulatory commission; six others had some form of regulations.

In 1971, Robert McNamara assumed the presidency of the World Bank. Under his tenure, the World Bank became more involved in capital markets as a method of raising capital. LDCs were forced to take securities more seriously, dependent as they were on the World Bank's assistance.

Then came the triple whammy that changed everything.

1. Cheap Fuel No More

In 1979, OPEC raised oil prices dramatically, triggering a worldwide recession that put an end to three decades of post-war growth.

Lesser-developed countries endured not only the oil shock, but the adverse reaction of the developed nations as well. The developed nations were less willing—and less able—to shower them with aid.

By the early 1980s, many of the world's nations had begun the long road to economic reform. In Latin America, Chile and Mexico began the transition to market-based economies. Newly industrialized countries in Southeast Asia and the Pacific Rim joined developing European countries such as Spain and Portugal. The LDC's governments could no longer afford generous subsidies, protectionist policies, and government inefficiencies.

Ironically, the oil crisis produced a new savior. The OPEC nations now had a large surplus of cash, which they promptly put into banks. The banks then lent much of this money to the LDCs.

2. The Loan Window Closes

From 1981 to 1982, central bankers around the world tried to tighten the money supply and control inflation, due in part to the oil shock, by raising interest rates. Economies slowed and commodity prices collapsed. In August 1982, Mexico decided to default on its bank loans, and by the end of the year, it was very difficult for LDC governments to borrow money. The problem was especially severe in Latin America and caused great hardship there.

Making matters worse, the United States had become a competitor as the federal government began borrowing money to fund budget deficits. The United States was now the world's largest importer of capital, competing with less creditworthy nations for available funds.

A string of loan defaults and a credit squeeze led to the rebirth of the capital markets.

Assisted by the World Bank, the IMF, the United States, and Latin American countries began to explore alternate ways to raise capital. There were possibilities to explore, but first, these countries had to make significant changes in economic and fiscal policy.

3. The Wall Falls

The collapse of communism was a loud wake-up call for stock markets in Eastern Europe. Many of these nations had active stock markets before the advent of communism, but they lay dormant during the period of state-directed investment. Virtually every former communist nation was forced to reach out to the capitalist world for assistance.

The developed nations, with problems of their own, were not willing to lend a hand unless these nations moved toward self-sufficiency. So from the ashes of communism, state-run companies were privatized. In many cases, shares were issued and sold to the public and overseas investors. Newly minted entrepreneurs were forced to look for funds. With the attendant risks of political and economic instability, equity investors with a high risk orientation were more likely candidates than were banks. Stock exchanges in the Czech Republic, Hungary, Slovakia, and Poland were in business in near-record time, and closed-end funds, eager to get in early, were not far behind.

THE REBIRTH OF GLOBAL STOCK MARKETS

Stock markets, old and newly formed, seemed to come to life all at once. Spurred on by the globalization of markets around the world, local policymakers and central bankers, many trained in leading business schools, saw the advantages.

A working stock market is often a good way to lure money out from "under the mattress." It can increase the savings and investment rate, which is important for any emerging economy. It can serve as a more efficient, long-term source of financing for local companies, and it helps distribute wealth. In many Third World countries, the wealth has been concentrated in the hands of a few. A few wealthy families own large businesses, such as construction, supermarkets, mining, and so forth. When their companies go public, these families often see their net worth increase as valuations go up. They have a chance to liquidate part of their holdings. And, since the shareholder base is broadened, the benefits of ownership are spread among a larger number of citizens. This phenomenon has been called "shareholder democracy," and rightly so.

With reform came new emphasis on stock markets. In Korea, where common stocks were listed as a response to government pressure and incentives, the stock market became a viable source of new capital, as stocks began to trade in the range of 15 times earnings, up from 4-5 times earnings in the seventies.

In Chile, where a collapse of the banking system forced a government bailout of banks and businesses, officials acted to stimulate the equity markets. The government implemented tax reforms, established a local pension fund system, and created incentives to convert certain debt to equity. In 1982, Chile's equity market cap was approximately $1.2 billion. Ten years later, it was over $25 billion.

The Developed Nations Provide the Stimuli

The emerging market boom of today would not be possible without the financial innovations pioneered in the developed countries. In the years after World War II, most people kept their savings in banks, and businesses borrowed from them to finance growth. The growth of the securities industry and nonbank financial institutions has changed all that. Today, in the United States, mutual fund assets equal nearly 85 percent of total bank deposits, not including money held in pension funds and life insurance companies.

As cross-border stock deals increased in volume and number, the world's investment bankers scrambled to design all manner of financial instruments to accommodate them. The stock exchanges, the leading financial information services and the National Association of Securities

Dealers (NASD) all responded with increasing levels of sophistication. In short, it was the stock market boom, and the globalization of securities markets in the developed nations, that made the emerging markets boom possible.

BUILDING A CREDIBLE EXCHANGE

It takes more than a grand headquarters and a press release to establish a viable market. Suppose that you were the president of an emerging security exchange and you were charged with the task of building credibility. To do this, you must create a stock market that is known for its integrity, gives every investor a fair chance, and functions efficiently.

By *integrity*, we mean that you wish to safeguard the solvency of the key participants in the market in order to protect investors and maintain confidence. The payment and settlement system should be smooth and effective in order to minimize risks to counterparties and ensure that the players can effectively manage their exposure. You must reduce or eliminate the possibility of financial panic that might arise from fears over the market's ability to function. You must prevent stock market abuses, or at least seriously discourage them.

You also must create a *fair* market, one that provides small, less sophisticated investors with the same protections afforded larger ones. Every investor should be able to enter, get quotes and other market data, and exit with equal ease.

Finally, a good market is one that performs its intended functions *efficiently*. Companies should be able to raise capital on the stock market. Equity holders should be able to sell their stakes. The market should create the proper environment for investors to make money. The market should efficiently assist people in managing assets, and companies in financing growth and adding value.

In the beginning, many officials considered building credibility to be much ado about nothing, because there were so few players to police. First *establish* a stock market, they felt, and then worry about protecting those who come to the party. They have since learned that investor protection is a crucial first step in wooing financial institutions around the world.

For example, Lebanon reopened its stock exchange in October 1995 after a 12-year hiatus due to war and instability. Eager to rebuild their economy, the Lebanese were understandably in a hurry. The exchange had no stocks listed and no trading rules, however, and it won't become active until it adopts and enforces an investor protection program.

EIGHT STEPS TO VIABILITY

Those emerging stock markets that are serious about attracting investors from around the world take the following steps:

1. DEFINE THE FINANCIAL SYSTEM. What is the basic structure of the financial system? The roles of banks, brokerage firms, clearing and settlement firms, and regulatory bodies are clearly spelled out, as are the qualifications of firms allowed to engage in these practices.

2. ESTABLISH A SECURITIES COMMISSION. First and foremost, a stock market must win the confidence of investors by ensuring both (a) fair trading practices, and (b) full, accurate and timely disclosure and financial reporting by the listed companies. Ideally, this involves the establishment of a securities commission.

3. IMPROVE FINANCIAL REPORTING. As of this date, accounting principles and financial disclosure still differ widely around the world. The situation is changing, however, thanks to the power of the U.S. investment dollar. To put it bluntly, sooner or later, emerging stock market companies must please those who would invest capital. Standards will therefore become more uniform. Wall Street analysts have thus far been willing to issue recommendations with caveats about poor financial disclosure, but increasingly, they are expected to justify "buy" recommendations with the same scrutiny that they apply to domestic companies.

4. CREATE AN INVESTOR PROTECTION PROGRAM WITH INCENTIVES AND PENALTIES. For example, Chile requires that public issues of securities be rated by a licensed rating agency. So a company eager to access the capital markets will be forced to make the disclosures necessary to qualify for a rating.

Disincentives are perhaps even more important. What good are regulations unless there are stiff penalties for violating them? Any market that means business will have strict penalties for stock manipulation, front running, self-dealing, and insider trading, as well as for failures to file or disclose or for making false statements.

Many believe that the world is moving toward a single investment standard. With Americans the most aggressive in moving cash abroad, Wall Street will have a lot of influence over that standard. If such a standard is adopted, expect still another emerging market "boomlet," because it will alleviate some of the primary risk factors.

5. TIGHTEN THE LEGAL ENVIRONMENT to guarantee the enforcement of contracts. Say a company signs a deal to acquire another company, and it induces an investor to buy the stock. If one company changes its mind and breaks the deal, and there is no way to enforce the contract, the business environment is too shaky to merit investment. This may seem obvious to us, but in many Third World nations, contracts have not been held in the same high regard as they (supposedly) are in the developed world. Good banking laws and a workable justice system are equally important.

6. PROVIDE TAX RELIEF. Tax policies are a nightmare the world over. Tax laws are used in many different ways by many different countries, and their policies reflect the varying points of view. In the past, many Third World tax policies were designed to "soak" those from the developed nations who were seeking to do business locally. In other cases, the tax system favored borrowers over risk takers.

In order to encourage investment, governments must create favorable tax treatment for capital gains and dividends, and institutions and pension funds should receive incentives to invest in the stock market. Most important, foreign investors should not be subjected to prohibitive taxes.

7. ENCOURAGE STOCK OFFERINGS. As in any business, you can't attract buyers unless you have something to sell. Stock exchanges need listings. In many LDCs, the larger companies were hooked on bank debt, and officials could encourage them to forgo debt in favor of selling equity through tax incentives.

Another method for creating listings is the privatization of state-owned companies. There is nothing like the addition of utility companies, oil companies and telecommunications firms to increase the market capitalization of a fledgling stock market. One of the principal reasons for the rush to create viable stock markets among the formerly communist and still-communist nations is the need for a place to list state-owned companies when they are privatized (see Chapter 6).

8. TELL THE WORLD THAT YOU ARE OPEN FOR BUSINESS. You have to get the message out. Proudly send out copies of your securities regulations, showing potential investors the safety and security of your exchange. Invite analysts and money managers down to see your beautiful building and modern computer system.

Most of the stock exchanges discussed in this book have already taken these eight steps. Indeed, the number of stock exchange regulations enacted since the 1970s probably exceeds the total number devised before then, back to the invention of the stock market centuries ago.

They must have done something right. Funds invested by foreigners in emerging stock market equities grew from almost nothing in 1980 to $17 billion in 1990.[1] In 1994, about $39.5 billion was used to purchase emerging market stocks. That year, there were more than 17,000 listed companies on 74 emerging market exchanges, according to the IFC.

In September 1995, the Jakarta (Indonesia) Stock Exchange moved into a new 30,000 square-foot building. Exchanges in São Paulo (Brazil), Moscow, and Turkey are building new trading facilities. Romania, Latvia, and Estonia all opened stock exchanges in 1995. In China, seven different groups are planning new stock exchanges. (One group apparently told a noted U.S. expert that it wanted a market where the stocks go only up.) There are rumors that the North Koreans are planning one.

STOCK MARKET DEVELOPMENT AND EMERGING MARKET GROWTH

Do emerging market stock exchanges promote long-term growth? Or are they merely cosmetic image builders, or worse, local gambling dens? Ross Levine of the World Bank and Sara Zervos of the University of Rochester analyzed data from 41 countries for the period from 1976 to 1993 and concluded that measures of stock market and bank development are "robustly correlated" with the current and future growth rates of the local economy, capital accumulation and productivity. Their key findings follow.

GOOD MARKETS MAKE GOOD ECONOMIES. The development of well-functioning emerging stock markets appears to play a crucial role in promoting economic growth. A developing banking and financial services sector also contributes.

Levine and Zervos concluded that stock market and banking development spurs the accumulation of capital (possibly by attracting capital inflows) and improves both productivity (possibly because the stock market rewards improvements in productivity) and allocation of resources. Well-functioning stock markets, then, are seen to stimulate and promote growth by "fueling the engines."

THE BETTER THE STOCK PRICING, THE GREATER THE GROWTH. The authors also studied "mis-pricing," that is, the extent to which stocks of an emerging market are not efficiently priced when compared to several models based on standard deviations from expected returns compared to a benchmark. They concluded that in all 41 countries, the more efficiently priced a stock market was, the greater the economic growth.

POSITIVE MEASURES OF EMERGING STOCK MARKET DEVELOPMENT MAY BE USEFUL IN FORECASTING ECONOMIC GROWTH. Levine and Zervos found that measures of both stock market and banking development "independently *predict* long-run economic growth even when entered together in cross-country growth regressions."[2]

For investors, this appears to suggest a self-fulfilling prophecy. Earlier research shows that liberalized capital flows tend to improve stock market development. Levine and Zervos show that improved stock market development spurs economic growth. This implies that, over the long term, an investment in a stock market that is benefiting from capital inflows will function better and spur growth in the economy. It would appear, then, that time is on your side.

ARE THESE STOCK EXCHANGES
READY FOR PRIME TIME?

Now that these emerging stock markets have done all the proper things, you can comfortably invest your money, right? Not exactly. It will take many years for most stock markets to achieve the level of maturity of New York, Tokyo, or London, if they ever do. Even when trading stocks in the United States, it pays to study the playing field. The rules of the game at the NYSE differ from those at NASDAQ. In emerging markets, a thorough analysis of the local exchange is critical.

Although emerging markets are lumped together in the press—and, indeed, on Wall Street—under a common banner, keep in mind that each market is different. Not only are the fundamentals and the levels of sophistication different, but the markets are evolving at different speeds. Some are growing faster than others. Some are instituting reforms at a more rapid pace.

At one end of the scale are the "frontier" markets, such as Vietnam and Lebanon, that are so new that there are few data and no history.

Next come emerging markets that are in the early stage of development, such as the stock markets in Jordan, Nigeria, Colombia, Zimbabwe, and Kazakhstan.

Brazil and India lie farther up the scale because they are improving operations and investor protection. Finally, there are the emerging markets on the verge of being considered fully developed—Mexico, Thailand, Malaysia, and, especially, Korea and Taiwan.

Here are some practical issues to consider when considering buying stocks on a local exchange:

SIZE. Not all emerging stock markets are created equal. It is best to stick with the 33 emerging markets defined by the World Bank. To narrow the list further, consider that 20 of these markets accounted for more than 98 percent of total emerging market capitalization.

Argentina	India	Mexico	Taiwan
Brazil	Indonesia	Nigeria	Thailand
Chile	Jordan	Pakistan	Turkey
Columbia	Korea	Philippines	Venezuela
Greece	Malaysia	Portugal	Zimbabwe

Table 4–1. The 20 largest emerging stock markets.

Size is measured in two ways. Total market capitalization is simply the sum total value of all the shares listed on that exchange on any given day. The other measure is even simpler—the actual number of companies listed on the exchange. Put these two measures together and you can get a feel for whether or not the market is spread too thinly. A large market cap divided among too few companies isn't a healthy trading environment; neither is a small market cap in an exchange with many listings.

MARKET ACTIVITY. There are three basic measures of market activity.

- **Total value traded.** The total value traded *ratio* is the total value of shares traded divided by the GDP. A market may have a large capitalization, but there may be little trading.

- **Turnover.** The turnover ratio equals the total value of shares traded divided by the market capitalization. A large but inactive stock market will have a large market cap ratio but a small turnover ratio. A small but liquid market will have a small total value traded ratio but a high turnover ratio.

- **Market capitalization ratio.** The market capitalization *ratio* is equal to the value of listed shares divided by the GDP.

Emerging markets are characterized by low turnover and small traded value. In addition, expect the "top ten" effect: In almost every case, the top ten largest listed companies in an emerging market tend to dominate trading volume and market capitalization. This situation reflects a vicious cycle. Large financial institutions tend to favor stocks in the largest, supposedly safest companies, which in turn increases their dominance of the local stock exchanges.

Country	Number of Equity Issues	Total Raised ($ billion)
India	47	$3.0
China	36	$2.4
Mexico	36	$1.7
Indonesia	27	$1.5

Table 4-2. The Top Four Emerging Markets for Equity Issues, 1994. *Source:* IFR Securities Data, London. In addition, Argentina, Brazil, the Philippines, Korea, and Pakistan all raised more than $1 billion.

LIQUIDITY. The speed at which one can buy, sell, and convert stocks to cash is a serious problem in emerging markets. To this definition we should add cost, since you can get out of even the most illiquid stock if you are willing to take a very low price. While this may seem like a tough problem for the individual investor or money manager, it is a nightmare for institutions that like to take sizable positions and trade blocks of stock. Lack of liquidity is one of the principal reasons certain emerging market stock exchanges are excluded from the IFC's "investable list." Peter Marber of Wasserstein Perella likens this problem to "roach motels"—you can get in [to a stock], but you can't get out. In a recent *New York Times* article, he described a problem with a stock purchase he made on Slovenia's Ljubljana stock exchange, a tiny market with only 17 listings, according to the IFC. He was able to buy $1 million worth of stocks in less than a month, but it took him more than eight months to sell.

According to an article posted on ING Barings' Web site, emerging markets are roughly twice as sensitive as are mature markets to changes in liquidity.

VOLATILITY is a fact of life in many emerging markets. This is directly related to liquidity, as foreign portfolio investors move money in and out. In defense, emerging markets are encouraging local investment and the establishment of local mutual funds, which will commit to market participation over the long term.

Market	Current Rank	Previous Week	Four Weeks Ago	Twelve Weeks Ago
Indonesia	1	1	1	3
Thailand	2	2	4	1
Malaysia	3	3	2	15
Turkey	4	4	6	5
China	5	5	3	9
Brazil	6	6	7	4
Philippines	7	7	5	2
Hungary	8	13	11	16
Korea	9	8	17	13
Asia	10	9	8	23
Greece	11	12	15	14
Mexico	12	10	16	21
Latin America	13	11	21	17
Zimbabwe	14	14	10	11
Poland	15	17	12	7
Taiwan	16	16	20	22
EMEA	17	19	28	29
Czech Rep.	18	22	23	10
Argentina	19	15	26	20
Venezuela	20	20	22	8
Composite	21	18	24	25
India	22	25	13	18
Portugal	23	24	14	26
S. Africa	24	21	29	27
Colombia	25	26	18	28
Pakistan	26	23	9	6
Peru	27	27	25	19
Sri Lanka	28	28	19	12
Jordan	29	29	27	30
Chile	30	30	30	24
Israel	31	31	31	31
Slovakia	32	32	32	32
Russia	33	33	33	33
Morocco	34	34	34	34
Egypt	35	35	35	35

Table 4–3. BARRA Emerging Markets Volatility Index for the 13-week period ending November 14, 1997. The lower the number, the higher the volatility. BARRA Emerging Markets Volatility Index calculations are based upon the International Finance Corporation (IFC) investable total return indexes (in $U.S.). "Asia," "EMEA" (Europe/Mideast/Africa), and "Latin America" are regional IFC investable indexes.

BUSINESS ENVIRONMENT. How good is the accounting in the home market? Are the custodial and settlement arrangements reliable? How open are these markets to foreign investment? Are there any limitations on repatriation of dividends and/or capital gains? Are there withholding taxes?

THE KEY PLAYERS IN EMERGING STOCK MARKETS

AMERICANS. While Americans sometimes appear xenophobic to the rest of the world, speaking only English, suspicious of foreigners, and relative newcomers to the export scene, they love to make money. More than that, they love to take risks on stocks and bonds. In the five years between 1989 and 1994, Americans poured more than $330 billion into foreign stocks and bonds. According to the IMF, international investments account for 12 percent of the nation's $9 trillion in pension and mutual fund assets.

Probably the most important reason Americans have so much money abroad is Wall Street itself, which sells investments better than anyone in the world and is always in search of a new spin. Mutual fund sponsors and brokerage firms, from Morgan Stanley to Merrill Lynch, have committed their resources to educating—and selling—the public and financial professionals on foreign and even emerging markets.

Much of the American money is invested through financial capitals in Europe and Asia, and local institutions there are intimately involved.

MUTUAL FUNDS. Mutual funds have been players in emerging markets almost from the beginning, with the rise of "country funds." They are still important today, and there are country funds devoted to virtually every emerging market, from Chile to Vietnam. Some country funds are even formed in the *anticipation* of a viable stock market. Some let the money sit, but most content themselves with direct investment or real estate while they wait for the securities market to get cranking. When the market finally does open, money managers often buy the only stocks listed, the top ten, or a little bit of everything. Emerging market mutual funds deserve a chapter all their own (see Chapter 10).

PENSION FUNDS. InterSec Research Corp., a financial consultant, estimates that U.S. pension fund international assets will reach $725 billion by the year 2000. Greenwich Associates surveyed 1,620 U.S. pension funds in 1994 and found that more than 65 percent already invest abroad.

At that time, 17 percent were investing in emerging markets. Today that number is undoubtedly higher.

THE FUTURE OF EMERGING STOCK MARKETS

REGIONAL CENTERS WILL REPLACE INDIVIDUAL EXCHANGES. Ironically, the financial marketplace is evolving toward fewer exchanges, not more. National stock exchanges exist because there are national differences. As these fade, stock exchanges will be organized around time zones and accessibility. This is likely to mean the development of regional trading centers. Investors will benefit, because these regional exchanges will offer greater liquidity, pricing, and settlement procedures.

The growth of ADRs points the way. Rather than attempt to trade in local exchanges, investors around the world traded over $1.9 trillion in foreign shares, usually as ADRs and GDRs, on large international exchanges such as the New York Stock Exchange and SEAQ International in London.

London is a likely candidate for a European regional exchange. New York has a lock on North America, and may well be the center of choice for Latin American securities as well. In Asia, Hong Kong is the logical choice, but its future under Chinese rule is currently a wild card. Singapore and Shanghai are in the running, while Tokyo still seems a bit xenophobic in its outlook.

MORE PORTFOLIOS WILL INCLUDE EMERGING MARKET SECURITIES. Institutional investors in the industrialized countries are increasingly diversifying into emerging markets. As the pension funds and money managers join the mutual funds in adding emerging markets to their portfolios, share prices could be in for another meteoric run.

A Barings report concluded that from 1986 to 1994 each $1 billion in net inflows to emerging markets produced a 1 percent rise in stock prices. Some pension experts believe that cross-border investments by pension funds will rise to between $3 and $9 trillion by 1999. If only 30 percent were allocated to emerging markets, we could theoretically—and I emphasize *theoretically*—see an average rise of between 1,000 and 3,000 percent.

THE NUMBER OF EMERGING MARKET IPOS PROBABLY WILL OVER-TAKE THOSE IN INDUSTRIALIZED COUNTRIES. This is a debatable point, because it pits the rapidly growing emerging market economies against the rapidly innovating business environment in the United States, Japan, and Europe.

The boom in U.S. IPOs will continue, as technology and entrepreneurship spawn thousands of companies that are increasingly turning to the equity markets for capital. However, the emerging markets have a greater pent-up demand for investment capital and a large supply of potential IPOs in companies marked for privatization and successful private businesses.

Most experts agree that emerging market IPOs will pass Europe in the next few years.

Is it safe to invest in emerging market stock exchanges? The answer is a qualified yes. One can avoid the transaction risks, if not the market risks, however, by buying and selling ADRs and GDRs, the topic of the next chapter.

ENDNOTES

1. *The Economist*, November 16, 1991, p. 93.
2. Levine, Ross, and Sara Zervos, "Stock Markets and Banks: Revving the Engines of Growth." January 1995, p. 25. Private World Bank publication.

ADRs and GDRs: Emerging Market Stocks in the USA

The year 1927 is remembered for Babe Ruth's 60 home runs and Lindbergh's transatlantic flight. However, a nifty little manuever by J. P. Morgan may turn out to be the biggest thing to happen in a very big year.

Morgan created the American Depositary Receipt, or ADR, to allow Americans the chance to buy shares in London's famous Selfridge's department store. Until that time, there was no way to buy shares in a foreign company short of going to the local country, opening an account with a local broker, depositing your money, and making the trade. With so few investors willing to do this, there was virtually no information available on foreign companies and no way to get a price other than a telegram from your overseas broker. Worse, Great Britain and several other countries required foreign shareholders to present their share certificates to receive dividend checks. So collecting a payout meant one or several transatlantic voyages for the shares and/or the shareholder. Unless, of course, you were a friend of Lindbergh.

Morgan, a banker accustomed to holding other people's money, figured it would be just as easy to hold other people's share certificates in the U.K. The shares would be held in his "custody" in London. He could then present the shares as needed and collect the dividends, annual reports, and other shareholder entitlements on behalf of his clients. When a customer turned Selfridge's shares over to Morgan, he or she got a receipt. The receipt was called an American Depositary Receipt. Things have hardly changed since then.

If the ADR gave the bearer the legal and enforceable right to ownership of 1,000 shares of Selfridge's, why not trade the ADR, rather than the underlying shares? True, the shares were in custody in London. But they were under the protection of the esteemed J. P. Morgan Bank. Therefore, the ADR was worth approximately as much as the shares themselves. Suppose you wanted to buy Selfridge's and you met a fellow American who wanted to sell. Why waste time and money on a trip to England to retrieve the shares? Why take the time or the risk of waiting for the shares to make the round trip (home for the transfer and back to England to J. P.'s custody)? Just trade the ADR and that's it.

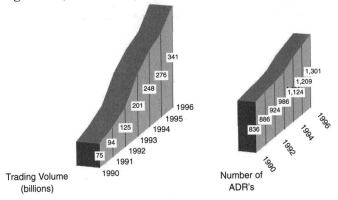

Figure 5–1. Growth of Listed ADRs and Trading Volume

HOW TO INVEST WHEN YOU DON'T KNOW MUCH ABOUT FOREIGN SECURITIES

Until recently, ADRs were not much of a business on Wall Street. In fact, until World War II, foreign stocks were dominated by a single broker, Carl Marks (no kidding) and Company. In the early fifties, Marks decided to distill his vast knowledge of overseas stocks into a single volume called *What I Know About Foreign Securities*. Before you rush out and buy the book, I should tell you that every one of the 300 pages was blank.

Of course, in the fifties there was no Sony or Lukoil to buy. There wasn't much action in ADRs until after the war, and things didn't really heat up until the 1980s, when investors began to realize that there were indeed profitable companies that weren't American.

ADRs are now serious business. Annual trading volume in exchange-listed ADRs has more than tripled since 1990.

U.S. investors can now trade shares in well over 1,100 foreign companies without leaving home, in essentially the same way they buy and sell domestic companies. To buy an ADR, you call your broker, and you pay standard commissions. Compare this with the hassle of buying foreign stocks—high commissions, settlement issues, minimum trade requirements, and so forth—and you can see why ADRs are so popular.

Some issues are referred to as "GDRs," or Global Depositary Receipts. GDR's differ from ADR's in that they do not trade in the United States. They are often listed in Luxembourg or London.

HOW ADRs WORK

A broker or a U.S. depositary bank purchases securities (that is, shares, preferred stock, or debt) of a foreign company in a foreign market. Through a local market custodian, the depositary accepts delivery of the shares and holds them for safekeeping while the depositary bank issues U.S.-dollar-denominated American Depositary Receipts for ownership of those shares. The ADR, then, is a negotiable certificate representing the company's publicly traded shares or debt. In a sense, ADRs are a type of derivative, because their value is derived from another instrument, in this case the price of the underlying stock. ADR prices reflect the price and dividend rate of the underlying shares and the U.S. dollar exchange rate against the local currency.

In order for an ADR to exist, there must be a depositary. If the foreign company selects an exclusive Depositary agent bank and pays it a fee to provide services to ADR holders, it is called a *sponsored* ADR.

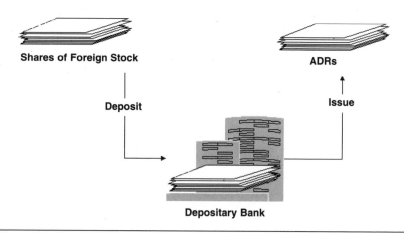

Shares of Foreign Stock

ADRs

Deposit

Issue

Depositary Bank

Figure 5–2. The ADR Process. Shares of stock in a foreign company are held by the depositary bank, which then issues ADRs, which are traded in the U.S.

ADRs trade like any other U.S. security, either over the counter or on an exchange, depending on the "Level" of SEC compliance. They can also trade on foreign exchanges. The underlying shares may be bought out of the existing float in the home market, or they may be part of an offering of new shares or an IPO.

One ADR doesn't necessarily represent one ordinary share of the underlying stock. The sponsor seeks to make the ADR a practical trading instrument. In some countries, such as Brazil, even a large company might have shares that trade for a few cents. The Telebras ADR, for example, represents 1000 shares of the underlying stock. In the case of a Brazilian company whose stock was trading at U.S. 12 cents, the sponsor might offer an ADR representing 1,000 shares, which would sell in the range of U.S. $126.

ADRs sometimes trade at a discount to the value of the underlying shares. As in any case where there are two or more liquid markets, traders are quick to arbitrage, which bring prices back in line, provided that the transaction cost of the "arb" allows for a profit.

When the number of ADRs in the United States rises to about 3–6 percent of the company's float, a trading market often emerges and investors buy and sell the ADRs between them. But until that time, the depositary bank *issues* them as needed to meet investor demand. Likewise, if an investor wishes to sell and there are no buyers in the United States, the depositary bank will sell the underlying shares in the home market, *cancelling* the ADR.

When a trading market exists, the purchase and sale of an ADR is an "intramarket" transaction; the ADR is transferred from the buyer to the seller. The trade settles just like any other, on the fifth business day after the trade date, with the depositary bank acting (if sponsored) as transfer agent and registrar. Almost all ADR trades (95 percent) in the United States are transacted this way, without the need for issuance or cancellation of an ADR. Continuous buying and selling of liquid ADRs tends to increase market efficiency, minimizing the price differential between local and U.S. markets.

SPONSORED ADRs

Sponsored ADRs come about when the foreign company seeking to issue an ADR selects a U.S. depositary bank to "sponsor" it. The bank holds the shares on deposit and serves as the transfer agent for the ADR. It performs a variety of other services on behalf of the company, which may include providing information to the SEC, communicating with holders of ADRs, distributing dividend payments, and so forth.

The sponsor charges a fee for each of its services, including creation and cancellation of an ADR, administration, custody of the shares, and dividend processing.

Publicly Traded ADRs

The SEC recognizes three levels of publicly traded ADRs.

LEVEL I. This is the simplest and cheapest method of creating a sponsored ADR. The depositary bank files for an exemption of the U.S. reporting requirements on behalf of the foreign company. The company files with the SEC for an information exemption, which requires only the current financial statement in English and all other information required by the regulatory body in the company's home market.

If accepted, all the foreign company need do is file a Form F-6 registration statement, which asks for little more than the name and address of the company and its depositary bank and the signatures of the officers and directors. About eight weeks later, ADR trading begins.

The company also signs a service agreement with the depositary bank and the receipt holders, the original purchasers.

The foreign company now has gained access to the U.S. publicly traded market, without adopting U.S. GAAP (generally accepted accounting principles) or altering its financial reporting in any way. It has simply furnished the SEC with the same information it provides to authorities and shareholders in its own country. Often, this means that it may not have to disclose such items as hidden reserves, cross-stock ownerships, executive pay, insider selling, lines of business, and the like. The issuer may not offer new shares in the U.S.

Financial reporting standards are different in other countries, and many of these companies would rather not conform to the disclosure and reporting requirements of the SEC. Occasionally they have something to hide, but this does not necessarily mean that they are bad investments.

Level I is the fastest-growing segment of the ADR business. While foreign companies are permitted to list ordinary shares in the United States, they must be listed on a national exchange and must meet SEC disclosure and exchange listing requirements. A Level I listing is, therefore, a lot simpler. However, a Level I ADR behaves like an over-the-counter stock and should be treated as such.

Most sponsored ADRs are Level I, and they include such multinationals as ANZ Bank, Rolls Royce, Shiseido Volkswagen, and Dresdner Bank.

LEVEL II is intended for foreign companies seeking to list their securities on a U.S. exchange. By definition, a Level II ADR program must be sponsored and has stricter reporting requirements than a Level I ADR. The foreign company must file a comprehensive annual report with the SEC, which is similar in content to those filed by U.S. firms. In addition, the filing must adhere to SEC guidelines regarding the calculation of earnings and cash flow. In essence, the SEC says to the foreign company, "Do the numbers as American companies do them." Thus, it is easier for investors to analyze Level II companies. In short, Level II ADRs walk and talk like U.S. stocks. Korea Electric Power and Pohang Iron & Steel are Level II ADRs.

While a company could simply list its shares directly on a U.S. exchange, it must meet certain obligations, such as providing shareholder services and a transfer and registration mechanism. If the company issues ADRs, the depositary bank serves as liaison with the home market operations and performs these services on behalf of the company. In most cases, an ADR program is cheaper and less complicated than a direct listing.

As of this writing, the SEC gives Level II issuers up to 180 days beyond their fiscal year-end to file a financial statement; it gives U.S. companies only 90 days. That means you may be in the dark about a company's annual performance for up to six months after the books were closed. So don't rely on the SEC for your information. It's a good idea to check with the sponsor or the company to find out when and in what form it will issue information on the company's performance. SEC requirements in this regard are meant to comply with host country rules. For example, if the overseas stock exchange requires a financial statement within 120 days, the SEC will expect the paperwork in the same period.

LEVEL III. This level permits the foreign company to issue new equity in the United States. ADRs of this type are created when the company decides to offer shares for sale in the United States, just as in an IPO or secondary offering. Companies issuing Level IIIs are subjected to the same reporting requirements as Level IIs, although in practice, compliance is stricter, as the SEC and the stock exchanges scrutinize their accounting and reporting methods. Level III's can also offer debt.

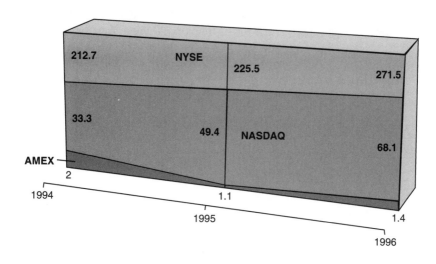

Figure 5–3. ADR Volume by Exchange. Source:

Private Placement ADRs

144A **Depositary Receipts** are sponsored ADRs purchased through a private placement. They allow a foreign company to raise capital through a placement of shares—in the form of ADRs—to large institutional investors and non-U.S. investors. The 144a label is a nonexclusive designation; companies can issue 144a ADRs alongside Level I ADRs.

These issues do not offer much liquidity.

UNSPONSORED ADRS

Unsponsored ADRs are created without the participation of the foreign company. This occurs when demand for a foreign company is sufficient that a depositary bank decides to create an ADR on its own. Without the participation of the company itself, don't expect the ADR to be very investor-friendly. You can buy the stock, period. Shareholder services are minimal, and the company may be ill-equipped to manage an ADR program. Never assume that the mere existence of an ADR automatically implies that the company is large or well known in its home market.

Suppose a foreign company attracts lots of attention, perhaps a small firm in Kazakhstan that wins a McDonald's franchise for Almaty. A bank, acting without the consent of the foreign company, may, through a custodian, buy shares on the local stock exchange, hold them, and issue an ADR. Since the company itself is not involved, there will be probably very little, if any shareholder services. In fact, the company is not even obligated to respond to ADR holders.

While they must meet all SEC "Level" qualifications for trading, unsponsored ADRs are rarely permitted beyond Level I.

Depositary banks charge fees on unsponsored ADRs, and they are usually borne by the broker, although in practice, the depositary often provides a rebate to the broker. The investors' commission structure usually takes the charges, but not the rebate, into account.

HOW COMPANIES BENEFIT FROM ADRs

- **Broader shareholder base.** Shares are available to investors in the United States and other markets, increasing—and diversifying—the market for the company's shares. This helps stabilize the price. Nestle's, through an unlisted ADR, has been able to boost its U.S. shareholder base to 15 percent since its ADR began trading in 1985.

- **Increased liquidity.** ADRs are regarded as U.S. securities, which often increases overall liquidity of the stock. Many ADR issues are more liquid than the underlying shares, with ADRs sometimes accounting for as much as 15-20 percent of a company's float. Nevertheless, most smaller ADR issues are illiquid relative to U.S. exchange traded shares.

- **Higher company profile.** Companies trading on a principal U.S. exchange receive press coverage and analysts' coverage. Therefore, the company's name, trading history, products and services, and financial structure receive wide exposure.

- **Improved financing mechanism.** The foreign company gains a U.S. shareholder base and, often, a stepping-stone to other types of U.S.-based financing, such as raising equity, borrowing, or acquiring U.S. companies. Foreign companies can raise capital on U.S. markets through the use of Level III ADRs.

- **Increased participation** of employees, customers, and suppliers around the world, who can now buy stock easily and safely. Employees have more confidence in stock-ownership programs and the company can more readily use stock plans to attract executives from overseas.

- **Avoidance of certain local regulations** that may restrict the transfer of shares out of the home country.

- **Reduce costs of listing shares in the United States.** In most cases, ADRs provide an easier and cheaper way to offer shares in the U.S. market.

HOW INVESTORS BENEFIT FROM ADRS

- **ADRs pay dividends and interest in U.S. dollars,** rather than in the currency of the host country.

- **ADRs establish a price** for the underlying shares in U.S. dollars on a U.S. exchange. ADR quotes are as easy to come by as are quotes for U.S. stocks. In addition to brokers and the financial papers, you can rely on all the major on-line services and the Internet as well.

- **ADRs follow U.S. standards.** Trading, clearing, and settlement of ADRs follow U.S. regulations and practice.

- **ADR holders have the same rights and privileges as ordinary share-holders.** They are not a separate class of security.

- **Shareholder communication is in English,** usually forwarded from the depositary bank.

- **Ease of purchase and sale.** In an active market, U.S. investors can buy and sell ADRs as they would any U.S. stock.

- **Lower commissions, fees, and requirements** than foreign stock purchases. There are no global custodian charges, which saves investors 30 to 60 basis points.

- **ADRs can represent debt securities, convertibles, preferred, and other types of securities.**

- **Often, ADRs are more liquid** than the underlying stock in the local markets.

- **Wider choice of investment vehicles.** Many mutual funds and pension funds are not permitted to trade on foreign exchanges, but they can buy ADRs.

Drawbacks to ADRs

- **Illiquidity.** Many ADR programs are still plagued by liquidity problems, usually among the unlisted, unsponsored, or very small or little-known companies. Liquidity is easy to check if a company is trading on a major exchange. It's more difficult—and the figures are less reliable—on the pink sheets.

- **Taxes.** Overseas governments often levy withholding taxes on ADR dividends. As of this writing, this tax amounts to 35 percent in India, which takes a deep bite out of the yield. Fortunately, you can request a credit against your U.S. tax bill. If you keep your ADRs in a tax-free account, however, you will have a more difficult time recovering the withholding, since such accounts are usually not eligible for the tax credit.

- **Abuses.** Unscrupulous brokers in foreign markets sometimes use ADRs to play the angles. For example, fast-moving foreign bankers and brokers can purchase a block of thinly traded stock on a foreign exchange, repackage it as an unsponsored ADR, and then sell it at

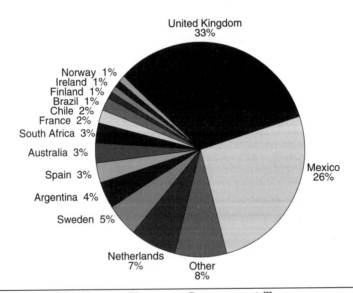

Figure 5–4. ADR TRADING VOLUME BY COUNTRY, 1996. TRADING IN EMERGING-MARKET ADRs HAS GROWN SUBSTANTIALLY. *SOURCE:* DEUTSCHE MORGAN GRANFELL, THE BANK OF NEW YORK.

the highest-quoted asking price. They make the "spread," but hide it in the pricing structure of the ADR. It's another good reason for checking the price and liquidity of the underlying stock before you buy the ADR.

TRENDS INVOLVING ADRs

ADRs are one of the most important investment vehicles for emerging market investors. They are altering the global investment scene, and the U.S. markets as well.

DEMAND HAS BEEN GROWING. Foreign companies want access to the world's largest equity markets. U.S. investors want to buy solid companies that aren't necessarily American.

In 1996, 50 percent of companies that established ADR programs were in emerging markets. Companies from India, Pakistan, South Africa, Ghana, Peru, Colombia, Russia, and Sri Lanka are among those that have been issuing ADRs.

EMERGING MARKET ADRs ARE BECOMING MORE LIQUID AND EFFICIENT. Citibank estimated the total value of Latin American Depositary Receipts traded in 1994 was $104 billion, which was equivalent to about 51 percent of the total trading volume for all the stocks in the home markets in Latin America. In 1993, three of the top ten most actively traded stocks in the United States were ADRs. In 1997, total U.S. exchange trading totaled 10.7 ADRs worth about $337 billion, representing a 63 percent increase over 1995.

THERE ARE MORE LEVEL III ISSUES, as the SEC helps the U.S. stock exchanges maintain their worldwide lead in listings. The SEC is streamlining the process, encouraging foreign companies and making it easier for them to raise money in the United States. This helps the exchanges that are competing against exchanges such as London for listings and helps Wall Street as well.

Level III ADRs are the current method of choice for large privatizations. If a foreign government is privatizing a state-owned company, it would probably like to sell some of the shares in the U.S. market and would do so by issuing Level III ADRs. For example, when the Argentine government privatized its large state-owned oil company, YPF, in 1993, it simultaneously issued ordinary shares to Argentine investors and Level III ADRs to U.S. investors.

COMPETITION IS HEATING UP AMONG DEPOSITARY BANKS seeking to sponsor ADRs. The business has been dominated by the Bank of New York, which has more than a 60 percent market share of public ADR programs, Citibank and Morgan Guaranty. Lately, other players such as Bankers Trust, Deutsche Morgan, and Morgan Stanley have entered the business.

LEVEL II ADRs ARE GROWING. Obviously, companies seeking the broad market exposure in the United States want the legitimacy provided by a listing, not to mention access to retail and institutional investors. Level-II ADR prices are readily available through print and electronic media. You can get a price without having to wait for a market maker to return your call.

THERE ARE FEWER UNSPONSORED ADRs. NASDAQ is discouraging new listings of unsponsored ADRs that do not provide more detailed information. Investors tend to shy away from them, and some consider them obsolete.

	Unsponsored	Level I	Level II	Level III	Rule 144A	GDR
Sponsor Required	No	Yes	Yes	Yes	No	N/A
U.S. Exchange Listing	No	No	Yes	Yes	No	No
Issue Equity in US Placement	No	No	No	No	Private Placement	Private
Comments	Liquidity can be a problem		Stricter reporting and compliance			Non-US listing

Table 5–1. Types of ADRs.

CREATING AN ADR PORTFOLIO

ADRs represent the safest—and possibly the best—way to play emerging market stocks. Don't be surprised if your ADR portfolio outperforms many of the mutual funds in the markets you trade. You will be buying some truly great foreign companies from the same broker that sells Microsoft right here at home.

As the number and quality of ADRs increase, so does the practicality of building an emerging markets portfolio entirely of ADRs. There are three principal issues to consider.

1. Do the ADRs make up a significant portion of the home market? In order for ADRs to be a reflection of the local market, they must serve as a proxy for a meaningful percentage of the market cap of the local exchange. As of this writing, if you were to buy the ten largest ADRs from Argentina, you would own 75 percent of the market weight of the IFCI Argentina Index. Thus, you would own stocks that, taken together, comprise the rough equivalent of 75 percent of the Buenos Aires Stock Market's (investable companies only) market cap. By contrast, the four Malaysian ADRs account for only 9.73 percent of the IFCI market weight for Malaysia.

2. Are the ADR issues diverse? All three Colombian ADRs are banking stocks. Two of Malaysia's four ADRs are in the hotel and leisure sector. Many ADRs are telecoms, and some investors erroneously conclude that these stocks are proxies for the entire local stock market. This is a serious mistake. To be a useful "country basket," the universe of available ADRs for a given country must represent a broad distribution of industrial sectors.

3. Are they liquid? What good is an ADR portfolio if the issues in it are rarely traded in the home markets?

For those who prefer to pick individual stocks, but lack the time, money, or resolve to trade on emerging market exchanges, ADRs are clearly the best alternative. According to analysts at the Bank Credit Analyst Research Group, markets offering the best coverage and liquidity through ADR baskets are in Latin America.

Country/ Stock	Ticker	Sector	Market Cap	IFCI Weight (%)	Ratio	Listing	Avg. Daily Volume (000)	Trading Frequency
ARGENTINA								
YPF	YPF	Oil Majors	$9.35 bn	21.13	1=1	NYSE	18,607	***
Perez Companc	CNPZY	Oil Majors	$5.18 bn	20.16	2=1	OTC	1,019	***
Telefonica de Argentina	TAR	Telecom	$7.22 bn	10.13	10=1	NYSE	18,483	***
Banco de Galicia y Buenos Aires	BGALY	Banks	$1.68 bn	6.07	4=1	OTC	6,350	***
Telecom Argentina	TEO	Telecom	$4.63 bn	5.43	10=1	NYSE	7,140	***
Banco Frances del Rio de la Plata	BFR	Banks	$1.48 bn	4.91	3=1	NYSE	3,580	***
Transportation de Gas del Sur	TGS	Oil & Gas		2.69	5=1	NYSE	667	***
Irsa Inversiones	IRSA	Investment		1.51	10=1	NYSE	4,848	***
Capex S.A	CPDS	Utilities		1.19	2=1	LDN		***
Buenos Aires Embotelladora (BAESA)	BAE	Food		0.44	2=1	NYSE	1,622	
				75.09			57,467	
BRAZIL								
Telecomunicacoes Brasileiras (TELEBRAS)	TBR	Telecom	$20.8 bn	21.58	1000=1	NYSE	128,403	***
Petroleo Brasilero (PETROBRAS)	PEBRY	Oil Majors	$9.26 bn	9.73	100=1	OTC	2,281	***

Table 5–2. ADR Country Baskets proposed by *The BCA Emerging Markets Analyst*, BCA Publications, Ltd., Montreal, May 1997. These baskets are, naturally, subject to change and revision.

Country/Stock	Ticker	Sector	Market Cap	IFCI Weight (%)	Ratio	Listing	Avg. Daily Volume (000)	Trading Frequency
ELECTROBRAS - "Common"	CAIFY	Utilities	$589 m	7.43	50=1	OTC	1,615	***
Companhia Vale do rio Doce (CVRD)	CVROY	Mining	$427 m	3.55	250=1	OTC	3,490	***
ELECTROBRAS - "Preferred"	CAIGY	Utilities	$714 m	3.38	50=1	OTC	2,633	***
Companhia Cervejaria Brahma "Preferred"	CCBJY	Beverages		3.32	20=1	OTC	647	**
Companhia Energetica de Minas (CEMIG)	CEMCY	Utilities	$1.46 bn	2.66	1000=1	OTC	3,842	***
CESP - Companhia Energetica de Saõ Paulo	CMPSY	Utilities/ Electricity		2.08	300=1	OTC	455	**
Companhia Siderurgica Nacional	CSNNY	Iron/Steel	$2.77 bn	1.43	1000=1	OTC	708	**
Aracruz Celulose	ARA	Paper & Forest Products	$764.8 m	1.04	5=1	NYSE	1,942	***
Multicanal Participacoes	MPARY	Other	$180 m		10=1	NASDAQ	4,664	***
Brasil Distribuidora Pao Acucar	GPASY	Utilities					227	**
				56.2			150,957	

Table 5-2. (cont.)

Country	No. of Stocks	Coverage of index (%)	Coverage with "Top Ten" ADRs	Daily Trading ($m)	Trading Frequency
Argentina	10	75.1	56.2	>57.5	***
Brazil	12	56.2+	52.7	151.0	***
Chile	18	57.2+		40.2	***
Colombia	2	16.2		0.8	***
Mexico	31	54.9+	46.6	136.3	***
Venezuela	4	34.4		17.8	***
Hungary	4	62.5		..	***
Israel	6	19.7		34.5	***
Portugal	1	1.3		2.8	***
Poland	2	27.8		..	***
South Africa	24	32.4	26.7	11.2	**
Turkey	2	2.4		..	***
China	4	12.9+		2.4	***
India	31	47.4	34.0	>7.8	***
Indonesia	3	29.7		>6.5	***
Malaysia	4	9.7+		0.3	**
Philippines	2	23.8		5.8	***
South Korea	13	42.4	41.3	>8.9	***
Taiwan	7	9.4		>1.8	***
Thailand	2	7.6		<0.01	*

Table 5–3. Size and liquidity of ADR/GDR Baskets. *Source:* BCA Publications Ltd., Montreal, *The BCA Emerging Markets Analyst,* May 1997.

Many of the newly listed ADR issues you are likely to see are the result of large privatizations, which are a primary source of emerging market investment opportunities and the subject of the next chapter.

Privatizations:
The Blue Chips of
Emerging Market Stocks

Like the term "football," privatization means something different to the rest of the world from what it means to us.

In the United States, politicians often talk of privatizing garbage collection, prisons, and even the mails. This refers to the granting of government contracts to a private company to perform services for the public good.

To the rest of the world, privatization usually means the conversion of state-owned assets into private companies. Governments around the world have sold—and are continuing to sell—water and power utilities, railways, airports, oil companies, airlines, and telephone companies.

In spite of our boasts about less government, this sort of wholesale disposal of state-owned assets is almost unheard of in the United States. One reason is the fact that the federal and state governments have less to sell, perhaps the postal system or federal prisons. Unlike the European and Latin countries, Uncle Sam never owned any airlines, oil companies, or telecoms. Another reason is that such sales make many people nervous.

Most emerging markets have little choice. After years of economic isolation, state socialism, and a variety of other "isms," they were left with economies that were ill-prepared to compete in the free market. Privatizations—the simple act of turning a government-run enterprise into a private or publicly traded company—has done more to jump-start emerging economies than any other single strategy.

Hailed by many of the ivory-tower economists, privatization is in many respects the closest thing there is to a magic bullet. Introduced by Britain in the early 1980s, privatization has caught on all over the world, on every continent.

The pace of privatizations is enough to make investment bankers drool. And they have been. After all, how often do you get a chance to create a blue chip stock overnight? Imagine taking a large state-owned company—a near monopoly with huge revenues and dominant market share—and converting it into a public company. The deals are huge.

Brazil's large iron ore producer, Companhia Vale do Rio Dolce (CVRD), recently went private with a valuation of $11.7 billion. CVRD is the third-largest mining company in the world and the largest producer and exporter of iron ore. CVRD owns 66 businesses and employs 17,000 people. Before the end of 1997, the Brazilian government is expected to shed its remaining shares, bringing the total proceeds from the privatization to nearly $5 billion.

Merrill Lynch managed the offering, earning around 1.9 percent commission on CVRD's sale price, definitely something to drool over. Even though fees are not high by corporate standards, investment banking firms continue to field costly privatization teams.

CHILE: MAKING PRIVATIZATION WORK

Consider Chile, one of Latin America's shining stars and one of the earliest emerging markets to jump on the privatization bandwagon. It began its program shortly after the coup that overthrew Salvador Allende in 1973. The military government wanted to reverse the socialist "reforms" of the Allende government, which not only increased the number of state enterprises from 68 to 596 in just three years, but allowed losses from these state-owned enterprises—or "SOEs"—to balloon to a quarter of the Chilean GDP.

First, the *generalissimos* began returning companies to the previous owners, a total of 325, with a net book value of approximately $1 billion, in 1974. From 1975 to 1979, they sold 207 more, generating about $1.2 billion in revenue for the state. By 1980, there were only 48 SOEs left, about 92 percent fewer than when they started in 1973.

In the early 1980s, an economic crisis hit Chile, contributing to the bankruptcy of many privatized companies, which were highly leveraged. The government managed to do a kind of "socialism but not really socialism" two-step that created a group of companies aptly named the "odd sector." The government rescued these companies, assuming control of the management and absorbing their debts. Technically, the government did not take back ownership, so they weren't "unprivatizing" them.

When the crisis blew over, the government turned these companies out into the world to go it alone, selling interests it had earned in the bailout. This went well and triggered a new wave of privatizations of the largest SOEs. Until this point, most of the privatizations were of companies that had been previously seized from the private sector. Now, Chile was ready to privatize state firms created from scratch or nationalized by law.

The Chilean government offered the international community an incentive. Investors could use foreign debt issues—then trading at a 40 percent discount—to pay for privatized shares. The exchange would be at face value. So a $1,000 note worth only $600 could be used to purchase $1,000 worth of shares in a privatized company.

Chile went on to become what is often called "an economic miracle" and serve as an example for the rest of Latin America and emerging markets around the world to aspire to emulate. However, privatization by itself should not get most, or even much, of the credit. Chile also undertook an aggressive program of full-scale economic reforms and changes in fiscal policy, which reduced the deficit, increased tax revenues, and boosted international confidence.

WHY GOVERNMENTS CHOOSE PRIVATIZATION

1. To raise money for the government. As emerging markets enter the world financial community, they need cash. Sell a state-owned business, and the money goes directly into the Treasury. The proceeds may be used to improve creditworthiness, reduce the national debt, and fund social programs.

2. To pay off debt. Sometimes, the proceeds of a privatization are used to pay off debt. In other words, debt is retired through a debt/equity swap in which lenders to the state enterprise are willing to exchange their notes for equity in a newly privatized company. Often, it is a little bit of both.

3. To stem losses and end subsidies. State-owned companies are notoriously inefficient because, at the end of the day, they are controlled by politicians. These companies have been used to grant political favors, such as jobs and contracts. They have been used to win or keep votes. The result is bloated, inefficient companies with too many workers, too many offices, and little or no profits. Such companies commonly lose money and must be subsidized by the government. In the late seventies, state enterprises in developing countries ran deficits that averaged 4 percent of the total GDP.

4. To get lean and mean. As private enterprises, they can worship the bottom line, which means becoming more efficient and competitive. Sure, it causes pain and suffering, but the government doesn't wield the ax, and the government no longer has to carry the company.

That isn't to say that citizens always acquiesce. They often greet announcements of large privatizations with fear and trembling. However, in many cases government leaders have done such an effective job of selling economic reform that the population appears willing to accept the pain of layoffs and other cost-cutting measures.

5. To raise capital. Would you invest in a money-losing state-run enterprise? That's like asking if you would buy shares in the Postal Service or the Social Security Administration. On the other hand, you might take a chance with Federal Express. This argument is not lost on the financial community, or on government leaders. Privatizing a company also gives it access to the global capital markets.

6. To give the local stock market something to list. Emerging market stock exchanges need large companies to attract attention and bring in investors. Local private companies, unfamiliar with the stock market, don't want to be the first on the box.

7. A privatization can attract attention to a small stock market. When Ghana floated its partial ownership of Ashanti Gold, it increased the local stock market capitalization fivefold. A blip appeared on the fund managers' radar screens, and suddenly, Ghana was at least worth a look.

8. To improve management. Although every country has skilled and dedicated public servants, the caliber of management talent and experience tends to be lower in the public sector than in the private. Experience shows that newly privatized or to-be-privatized—companies are more capable of attracting quality managers than are state-owned enterprises.

9. To cut the red tape. Government means bureaucracy, and bureaucracy means red tape, usually a negative for a striving business. Eliminate the government intervention and reduce red tape, or so the theory goes. On the government side, privatization frees up administrative resources for other projects.

10. To curry favor with the IMF and the World Bank. International finance agencies that hold the financial aid checkbooks are still very important to emerging nations. They will be dependent on loans, if not outright aid programs, for many years to come. Such agencies demand signs that the country is committed to economic reform.

11. To send a signal to the world. Perception plays an important role in investor confidence, whether it be Apple Computer or Albania. Privatizations signal the commitment to free-market reform and the capital market system.

GOOD FOR INVESTORS, BUT NOT NECESSARILY GOOD FOR CITIZENS

Privatizations provide investment opportunities for global investors, but they don't necessarily accomplish their intended purpose. A recent study by Armando Pinheiro and Ben Schneider of four Latin countries showed that revenues from privatizations didn't really provide much short-term help in bringing fiscal balance.

In some countries, such as Argentina, proceeds from privatizations are sufficient to close the budget deficit, and even generate a surplus. However, even in Argentina's case, the government took other measures, to help balance the budget, such as eliminating subsidies of private companies. In other countries, the reduction of the budget deficit was underway long before the privatizations hit the street.

There are other problems. In Argentina, the state labor force dropped from 295,000 in 1990 to 50,000 at the end of 1992. According to the World Bank, two-thirds of this decline was due to divestment of SOEs. It is hardly surprising, therefore, that the strongest resistance to privatizations usually comes from organized labor unions.

The government's plans to privatize the Yacyreta hydroelectric plant were criticized in an Argentine Energy Institute study. It concluded that the deal would create a government debt burden more than double the proceeds it would receive from the sale.

Privatization offerings don't always go well. Consider Indonesia's privatization of its domestic telephone company, PT Telkom. Investors apparently thought the price was too high. When demand failed to materialize, Indonesia was forced to halve the size of the offering to $1.59 billion and reduce the price of the shares. Indonesian President Suharto came close to scrapping the international portion of the issue.

This wasn't a case of Indonesia lacking expert guidance. The four global underwriters were Merrill Lynch, Goldman Sachs, SBC Warburg, and Lehman Brothers. There were four domestic underwriters as well. The underwriters pitched PT Telkom at 130 meetings in 30 cities on 4 continents.

In addition, PT Telkom had a compelling story to tell, having transformed itself from a bureaucratic government utility to a world-class telecommunications giant in six years. In the year before the offering, it eliminated two divisions, offered early retirement to 16 percent of its 43,000 employees, and signed pioneering regional-management agreements with private consortia.

No matter how promising a company—or its home market— appears, one cannot assume that demand for shares will be strong.

The official explanation for the poor initial response was softness in demand for emerging market new issues, due in part to fallout from the Mexican peso crisis. In addition, the sheer size of the offering gave potential buyers the jitters. The feeling was magnified when an Indonesian underwriter offered foreign buyers shares that had been reserved for Indonesians, adding to a suspicion that there was an over-supply of stock.

Perhaps the lower share price and smaller equity raise was a blessing. A little more than five weeks after the offering, PT Telkom was trading at more than 40 percent above the initial offering price.

Privatization by itself is not enough to turn around an economy. However, the message that privatization sends to citizens and to the world—a commitment to free markets and private enterprise—may be worth more than the revenue it generates. Hand in hand with a comprehensive reform program, privatization can be a genuine confidence builder. In the wake of Argentine privatizations and reforms, wealthy private citizens who hid money offshore began to bring it home, investing locally again and even paying their fair share of taxes.

WHAT TO WATCH FOR WHEN INVESTING IN PRIVATIZATIONS

A SHORT-TERM PRICE RISE. Emerging market privatizations often outperform the local stock market in the short run, for the following reasons:

1. Pent-up demand. In any given emerging market, there are a limited number of large-cap companies to invest in. The new company often becomes a "must-own" for portfolio managers. This is especially true of emerging market fund and portfolio managers, who tend to favor large, established companies.

2. Demand created by index funds. A large company will make up a significant portion of a developing nation's market capitalization, so it will be included in the various indexes. This makes it an essential component of funds that try to recreate that index by owning a basket of stocks.

3. Increased efficiency. Privatizations are often packaged with a corporate reorganization designed to transform the company from a bureaucratic state-owned enterprise to a "lean-and-mean" competitor.

4. Better management. Highly respected managers are often recruited.

5. Local buying. Native investors, unaccustomed to stock market investments, tend to go with names they know.

DEALS RUSHED TO MARKET. Is the company ready for prime time? Some companies are rushed to market before their restructuring into a competitive private company is complete. If the company is perceived as untested, buyers may not want to take a chance.

HYPE. There is no *inherent* reason that a privatized company is better than a conventional corporate issue. Behind every deal is a government that is trying to get top dollar on the sale of its assets and a highly competitive group of investment bankers who tend to over-promise.

COMPARISONS WITH OTHER DEALS. No two privatizations are alike. Each privatization seems to have its own history and dynamics, so you must adopt a case-by-case approach rather than trying to formulate a simplified model.

OVERVALUATION. As long as they remain hot commodities, newly privatized stock offerings are more likely to be overvalued than undervalued. When in doubt, assume the issue is overvalued. That doesn't necessarily mean that the stock isn't worth owning at the offering price, especially if you are a long-term investor.

ARROGANCE. Don't think you can fool the Street. When it comes to large privatizations, it is unlikely that you will know something the institutions do not.

HOT ISSUES. Remember, a privatization deal is essentially an IPO. If demand is there, you can expect the stock to trade at an immediate premium, just like a "hot" domestic IPO. Unless you can get an allocation, it may make more sense to step back and let the stock trade awhile, gradually integrating it into your portfolio. Occasionally, privatizations are secondary offerings, in which the government sells all or part of its remaining stake in a company that is already publicly traded.

When a deal is hot, it can be very hot. When YPF, Argentina's largest company, was privatized, it was at once the largest privatization ever, one of the largest IPOs, and the number-one company on the Buenos Aires exchange in terms of market cap. Offered at U.S. $19, it traded up to $23 on the first day of trading. The offering of more than U.S. $2.66 billion was oversubscribed and went into overallotment, bringing the deal to $3.04 billion. The company was originally hoping to raise $1 billion. The deal added $7 billion to the Buenos Aires Bolsa's total market cap, increasing it by some 35 percent. When the dust had settled, 160 million shares of YPF had been sold, up from the 110 million the underwriters had planned on originally.

LOCAL OPPOSITION. Don't underestimate the power of local opposition. Organized and effective resistance often comes from unionized labor, prompting governments to devise various ways of managing labor-related problems. The deal, the share price, and/or the company may be affected. In Malaysia, special guidelines state that all privatization plans must ensure that employees will not lose the benefits they held and that they will be absorbed into divested firms under terms "no less favorable" than those they enjoyed while working for the government. In Chile, special efforts were made to sell shares to labor and pension funds, and special quotas were often reserved for them at public auctions and offerings of shares.

Sometimes, resistance turns ugly. Union activists, protesting what they call a lack of transparency in Congo's privatization plans, cut off power, water, and telephone services. Demonstrations in the streets of La Paz delayed the privatization of Bolivia's oil industry in early 1996.

ADRs AND PRIVATIZATIONS

ADR issues are widely used as part of global offerings of privatized companies. For example, in 1996, governments sold $5.7 billion worth of ADRs in state-owned enterprises in 19 countries. Some privatizations came from developed nations such as Germany and Italy. But emerging market privatizations were major participants, accounting for around $2.5 billion:

Privatization	Country	$ Millions raised through ADRs
CANTV	Venezuela	$904
Gazprom	Russia	$429
Telefonica de Peru	Peru	$918
Commercial International Bank	Egypt	$117
Suez Cement	Egypt	$114

Table 6–1. Major privatization deals issuing ADRs in 1996. *Source:* The Bank of New York.

DIRECT INVESTMENT IN PRIVATIZATIONS

Most privatizations don't involve public offerings or even investors outside the domestic market. According to a recent survey of 530 recorded privatizations in 90 countries, the most popular method of divestiture is the sale of shares or assets directly to a single buyer, perhaps a multinational or a local competitor. There are very practical reasons for this.

1. **Unviable markets.** Some countries haven't had access to the global equity markets and their local stock exchanges can support an IPO. This is especially true in sub-Saharan Africa.

2. Company weakness. Some of the companies are not "investable" in the eyes of international traders. They may have poor balance sheets, poor market position, poor management, or any combination.

3. Small size of company. Not every privatization involves the sale of a large quasi-utility.

4. Dealing with a single private owner is easier. When a government parts with a company, it may want the assurance of knowing the buyer and wielding some influence after it has transferred the assets.

Some deals are privatizations in name only. The government signs a long-term management contract with a private party, but retains ownership and control.

PRIVATIZATION AROUND THE WORLD

Various studies have concluded that privatization usually proceeds in stages. For example, in Latin America, the usual route is commercial companies, followed by infrastructure, and finally, the social sector. Some countries begin their programs by privatizing companies that will meet with the least opposition. Others would prefer to start with their biggest and best firms. Before investing in a privatization, it is a good idea to put the deal in the context of the home country's privatization history and the nature of its overall program.

Bolivia

Bolivia was second only to Peru in major privatizations in Latin America in 1995. Extensive restructuring of the privatized companies has begun, with the aid of outside experts. Foreigners can buy up to 51 percent of the privatized firms.

Brazil

Brazil is a very important investment arena. Its large, growing population, ethnic diversity, and dominant position in Latin America make it a vital strategic linchpin for any company with a truly global strategy. There is worldwide interest in investing in Brazilian privatizations, whether through direct investments, public offerings, or auctions.

As of this writing, Brazil is planning to raise billions through privatizations. The centerpiece is the sale of Vale do Rio Doce Company (CVRD), one of the largest ever.

Many experts expect the CVRD sale to trigger a new wave of Brazilian privatizations. The government has "inventory," that is, other huge companies to sell. For example, telecommunications and petroleum are still run by the state.

In the past, Brazil divested its SOEs mostly through auctions on local exchanges rather than through global offerings. Many of the companies sold were money losers that didn't attract many foreign investors, because the market does not look kindly on home-grown programs. The Brazilian government must get with the program, working with privatization experts around the world and paying the appropriate fees.

CVRD was an important test of the nation's commitment, and while the deal has gone through, the shares fell over 8 percent the day after the privatization. Some analysts believed the company was overvalued, while others expressed dissatisfaction with the new controlling shareholder, a Brazilian consortium known as CSNNY.

The market will be watching to see if Brazil keeps its reform program on track. There seems to be little political opposition to the sale of SOEs in general, but constitutional changes will be required to legitimize them.

One sign of sincerity: Banco do Brasil, the government-run bank that is Brazil's biggest, started a new fund that allows ordinary citizens to participate in privatizations for a minimum of 200 reals.

Central America

Central American nations such as Panama, Honduras, Nicaragua, and El Salvador have already sold millions of dollars worth of state investments. In spite of local opposition, Panama is planning a wave of privatizations, including the state-owned telecom, sports facilities, casinos, and sugar mills.

Chile

Chile sounds like a model of privatization when you consider it has reduced state-owned companies from 500 to 15. But among those 15 is Codelco, the state-owned mining giant that is currently responsible for 40 percent of the country's foreign earnings. The current right-wing opposition would like to see Codelco privatized, but this would be a big step, even for Chile. Still, in the near future we may see some of Codelco's holdings, such as power generation, spun off and privatized.

Chile is proceeding with the sale of its remaining shares of airline Lan-Chile and shipping company Empresa Maritima.

China

For all the excitement about China, its privatizations to date have been disastrous. Many of the privatized companies are trading below their offering price. There are, however, scores of companies waiting in the wings, and eventually they will have their day. Sixteen are currently slated for overseas listings.

Clearly, China has been held back by its SOEs. The Chinese people are getting less for their money from the state-owned companies. With access to almost 75 percent of the government's industrial investment money, annual growth in output was only 7.4 percent between 1989 and 1993, while non-SOE growth was 31 percent for that period. The SOE share of industrial output fell from 74.4 percent to 48.1 percent from 1982 to 1992, while the SOE share of industrial investment fell less than 10 percent.

Chinese SOEs are plagued by waste, mismanagement, and the danger of bankruptcy, which is unthinkable by Chinese standards. Declining revenues mean the state will have to bear more of the burden of providing for these workers when they retire.

One solution is to transfer SOE assets directly into new pension funds. Another is outright privatization. For now, such alternatives are politically anathema. Nevertheless, this writer predicts that Chinese privatizations will begin to roll out before the end of the decade.

On the plus side, China has been making quiet progress, restructuring SOEs on the local level for some time, and thousands of small SOEs have been sold to employees or private investors. Recently, the government announced plans to retain only 1,000 of the roughly 80,000 SOEs, creating excellent prospects for mergers, acquisitions, banking, and investment.

Czech Republic

Since the so-called "velvet revolution" of 1989, the Czech Republic has managed the transition from communist regime to free market capitalist nation with relative grace. However, its growth has lagged behind that of some of its neighbors.

The country has already implemented what Prime Minister Vaclav Klaus termed "the fastest and most comprehensive privatization process." More than 50 percent of former government holdings have been sold, and the public sector now accounts for more than 70 percent of the GNP. Almost all service businesses have been privatized and many industrialized companies as well. New part-owners include Volkswagen, Nestle, and Philip Morris, to name a few.

The Czech Republic is now entering its second round of post-communist privatizations, which will lead to an increase in restructurings and unemployment. It has already privatized more than 7,000 companies, and has done so in less than two years.

Egypt

Egypt is a pleasant surprise. The government has clearly impressed the IMF, and global investors, with its commitment to privatization. Between 1993 and early 1997, Egypt sold 17 state companies through the stock market, raising more than $700 million, and another 6 companies through private sales. In all, 314 companies are to go on the block, with an estimated worth of $25 billion.

Look for Egypt to send investors a stream of interesting companies. Commercial International Bank (CIB) and Suez Cement Company floated GDR issues in London. CIB's issue was five times oversubscribed, raising $119 million. These two stocks comprise more than 16 percent of the capitalization of the Cairo bourse. The IFC has admitted the exchange to its IFC indexes, and the stock market has begun to take off.

Hungary

Unlike the neighboring Czech republic, which allowed for privatizations en masse through the issuance of vouchers that could be exchanged for shares in a variety of companies, Hungary proceeds on a case-by-case basis.

As disputes between Hungarian and foreign bidders mount, Hungary's once-promising privatization program has slowed. A scandal involving the Privatization Agency has added to the uncertainty. On the positive side, the privatization of Magyar Hitelbank went smoothly, adding U.S. $89 million in revenues to government coffers. Privatizations brought in around U.S. $2 billion in revenues in 1996, three times the government target. However, that was down considerably from U.S. $4.5 billion in 1995.

The energy sector has been targeted for privatization. It is in dire need of modernization, and the government has concluded that the only practical source of capital is to privatize. Expect this program to be an auction process, with the world's energy companies bidding against one another. The results will yield very few—if any—pure Hungarian energy plays.

Indonesia

The botched privatization of PT Telkom did not deter the Indonesia government from staying the course on privatizations.

As of this writing, the Indonesian stock exchange is starved for new issues, and this lack of supply has sparked a rally in Indonesian shares. The government will be watching the market carefully for signs of receptivity to privatizations.

Malaysia

Malaysian privatizations have garnered a great deal of media attention, even though it has divested only about 14 companies as of this writing. The program dates back to 1983, when the government, disgusted with the poor performance of SOEs, committed itself to close cooperation with the private sector.

Peru

World Bank privatization consultant Gerver Torres rates Peru's program as one of the world's best. In 1995, Peru led the continent with 30 of Latin America's 65 privatizations. In the three years prior to 1996, the Peruvian government privatized 71 firms. Peru is expected to continue the trend of increasing privatizations every year.

Poland

Poland's program is showing signs of life with a commitment to privatize the nation's energy sector. The centerpiece of the energy sell-off is the sale of a minimum 20 percent stake in Warsaw's Elektrocieplownie Warszawskie S.A., Poland's major domestic producer of energy. The privatizations of telecom TPSA, Nafta Polska, an oil concern, insurer PZU, and copper giant Polska Miedz are all in progress.

Privatization is expected to proceed via a public offer of shares on the Warsaw Stock Exchange, in part to avoid the political fallout from a direct sale to foreign owners. More than 3,500 companies remain under state control.

Poland's privatization programs appear to be working. Before glassmaker Krosno, S.A. was privatized, it was hampered by crushing debt. Losing money, it was forced to close three of its five plants and had only one working telephone line. Since its privatization in 1991, executives have acted swiftly, renegotiating debt, improving management techniques and working conditions, cutting costs, instituting financial controls, and winning back sales. In 1994, Krosno was profitable, and earnings doubled in 1995.

Four banks have been partially privatized, with complete privatization of the sector planned for the year 2000.

Portugal

Portugal is in the midst of a sweeping privatization program. Through 1996, the program had raised more than U.S. $3 billion, more than 2.5 percent of the national GDP. The largest privatization to date is Electricidade de Portugal, the national power utility.

In the past, banking privatizations have dominated. The coming wave will include industrial and service businesses. Much of the proceeds will go toward reducing the country's deficit.

The plan should give the Lisbon stock exchange a boost, as the government will turn to the local stock market to float many of these companies.

Romania

Romania has been auctioning equity in state-owned companies as part of a mass privatization program. The auctions, to take place at privatization agency offices around the country, including Bucharest, are open to bids from Romanian or foreign citizens or companies.

Companies on the auction lists vary in activity, from construction to tourism services, and list registered capital of amounts between 64 million lei and 36 billion lei. (As of this writing, one dollar equals approximately 2,730 lei.) Starting prices for shares vary between 25,000 lei and 102,783 lei per share, depending on the company.

Romania's privatization plan calls for the sale of up to 60 percent of approximately 4,000 companies. The ultimate goal is a near-total privatization, but the State Ownership Fund will retain a controlling interest in about 200 companies deemed to be of strategic importance to Romania. The top 550 companies have been reserved for "strategic investors." A U.S.-funded electronic trading system, dubbed "Rasdaq," has been set up to provide liquidity.

Russia

More than any other nation, the newly re-formed Russia embraced privatization as a symbol of its transformation. The bulk of Russian industry has been transferred to private ownership. It's been messy, it's been unfair, but from November 1991 to summer 1994, 130 million Russians took part in the privatization of 16,000 companies.

The good news is that Russia now has its own version of a market economy, which is likely here to stay. The bad news is that it has perpetuated the cronyism that existed under the old regime, since large segments of industry were handed over cheaply to Russian insiders.

The rape of the nation's oil and gas industry, which created a small group of newly minted billionaires, is the most glaring example. The sector accounts for 17 percent of the GDP and is controlled by an elite group of insiders, political operatives, and "banks."

Not many outsiders are in the game, as Russian privatization has been largely an internal affair. Two-thirds of the shares are held by managers and workers.

As the average Russian citizen finds him- or herself with yet another type of tyrant at the neck, privatization itself could take the blame, and that would be a tragedy.

Sri Lanka

Sri Lanka has one of the largest public sectors outside the centrally planned economies, and its privatization efforts have been disappointing. There has been lots of rhetoric but not much privatization. One hundred eighty SOEs account for about 40 percent of gross manufacturing output, and only 11 enterprises have been privatized. Five others are now managed but not controlled by the private sector.

Politics on the Indian subcontinent has always been filled with passion, so it is hard to predict which road Sri Lanka will take. This writer assumes that international pressures to reduce the SOE drain on the government budget will result in an increase in the number of privatizations. Political opposition is strong, however, and the economic consequences of large-scale privatization are likely to be painful.

Turkey

The privatization agency's sales totaled only $670 million in 1995, far short of the goal of $2.7 billion. Political uncertainty clouds the future of the program.

Venezuela

As Venezuela continues to turn away from its populist policies, the privatization movement is gaining momentum. The government has decided to cooperate with the IMF and has unveiled "Agenda Venezuela," a plan for sweeping reforms. Several earlier privatizations, including the national airlines, Viasa and LAV, did not go well, but CANTV, a telecom provider still controlled by the state, is a popular stock among many Latin fund managers. The real test of resolve will come when the government confronts the issue of whether to privatize part of the state-owned oil company, which could provide badly needed revenues for the government and an exciting stock for investors.

THE CURRENT OUTLOOK FOR PRIVATIZATION

BETTER DEALS FOR INVESTORS. The peak year to date was 1994, when transactions totaled $80.3 billion. In 1995, there was a 40 percent decline, although still respectable it disappointed many. Most blame the Mexican crisis for this wake-up call. Investors began taking a harder look at terms and valuations and saying no to deals that were too rich. They are now demanding more from privatization deals, and they are likely to get it.

To date, the track record for many privatizations has been mixed. The Mexican and Argentine telecoms and some utilities have gone fairly well. The airlines, such as Aeromexico, Mexicana, Aeroperu, Aerolineas Argentinas, Viasa, and others, have been a disappointment. They have been downsized, but still lose money.

Many companies are trading below their offering price, and others have not produced the returns sufficient to justify the risks. The markets are more sober now, placing more realistic valuations on privatization deals.

GOVERNMENTS ARE RECONSIDERING THEIR PROGRAMS. Emerging market governments have been reevaluating their privatizations in light of the lower prices they might receive. Is there enough revenue in the deal to justify a political fight at home? Many consider it more politically and financially feasible to turn to private auctions, bypassing the public equity markets.

SOME COUNTRIES HAVE FEW "QUALITY" DEALS LEFT. The best companies have been sold off, leaving those that are left less attractive and more difficult to float.

Company	Country	Year	Buyers
Telecommunications ENTel	Chile	1986–1988	Telefonica (Spain) Citibank, local bank employees
CTC	Chile	1987–1988	Australian investor (Bond Group) and employees
ToJ	Jamaica	1989	Cable and Wireless (U.K.), local investors
Jamaica Intl. Telecom	Jamaica	1989	Cable and Wireless (U.K.)
ENTEL	Argentina	1990	Northern portion bought by a consortium of STET (Italy), France Telecom, J. P. Morgan, local co.; Southern portion by Telefonica (Spain), Citicorp, and local co.
TELMEX	Mexico	1990	Southwestern Bell, France Telecom, local co., workers.
BTC and BETL	Bermuda	n.a.	Cable and Wireless (U.K.)
St. Kitts Telecom	St. Kitts	n.a.	Cable and Wireless (U.K.)
BTL	Belize	n.a.	British Telecom (25%)
CANTV Airlines	Venezuela	1991	Consortium of local group, AT&T and GTE
Austral	Argentina	1987	Private sale to a local group
Lan Chile	Chile	1989	Scandinavian Airlines (35%)
Compania Mexicana de Aviacion	Mexico	1989	Local investors
Aeromexico	Mexico	1988	Local investors
Aerolineas Argentinas	Argentina	1990	Iberia (30%), workers (10%)
Ladeco	Chile	1990	Iberia (35%)
VASP	Brazil	1990	Local investors
VIASA	Venezuela	1991	Iberia with a local bank (60%)
Energy ENDESA	Chile	1986–1989	Public offering
Peterobras	Brazil	1985–present	Domestic public offering (minority shares)
Bahla Bianca (railroad)	Argentina	1991	Consortium of local company and a foreign railroad

Table 6–2. Core SOEs Privatized in Latin America and Caribbean Region in the Late 1980s. *Sources:* Latin American Regional Reports (various issues); Latin American Weekly Report (various issues); Latin Finance, 1991d; Ambrose et al., (1990): appendix 3, 47; Tironi (1991). As of December, 1991.

WHILE THERE ARE MANY MORE PRIVATIZATIONS TO COME, THE MARKETPLACE IS DIVIDED ON THE LONG-TERM PICTURE. Is the pool of capital shrinking, or is the market becoming more selective?

As of this writing, some experts believe that the privatization market has peaked, while others believe that it will strengthen as market conditions and the political situation in key developing countries improve.

Rest assured, privatizations have plenty of life left in them. The global capital markets are always hungry for new listings of large companies, and there are many waiting in the wings all over the world.

No emerging market book is complete without a discussion of bonds, which have enriched many investors over the past decade. The subject of the next chapter is emerging market debt.

Bonds: Investing in Emerging Market Debt

There is a hardly a sovereign government in the world today that does not borrow, and borrow heavily. Every emerging market analyst likes to see deficit reductions and balanced budgets, but few would argue that emerging market nations needn't borrow in order to emerge. Whether it be to meet infrastructure needs, to provide social services, or to make the transition from communism to a free economy, these nations are like start-up businesses—they need money to fuel growth.

The sea change in the way emerging market nations borrow money was the shift away from using large banks to issuing bonds. Years ago, it was simply not feasible for emerging market nations to issue their own bonds. But the globalization of the markets, plus the pursuit of higher yields has changed all this. Sovereign governments are less likely to default on their bonds than on private sector bank loans. This is analogous to the difference between not paying one's rich uncle and not paying one's taxes: The consequences are very different.

Emerging market debt is more familiar to capital markets than are equity issues, because the world has been lending to these countries longer than they have been buying stock in their local companies. In general, the borrowers are stronger, economically and politically, than they were a decade ago. While there have been ups and downs in recent years, few emerging markets are likely to devolve into banana republics.

The market for such debt has exploded during this decade, although it is still considered a specialized investment. In 1990, emerging market trading volume was about $100 million. In 1996, trading volumes approached $5.3 trillion, according to a volume survey by the Emerging Markets Traders Association. The debt market is dominated by professional traders at large international banks, mutual funds, hedge funds, pension funds, and investment banks.

WHOOPS! THE BANKS AND EMERGING MARKET DEBT

Tradable emerging market debt is began as a result of missteps after World War II escalating in the sixties and seventies. Large banks lent huge sums of money to sovereign nations in Latin America and elsewhere. The bankers figured that a sovereign nation was an excellent credit risk, even in the Third World. It could print its own currency or tax its own people to get the money to repay the debt. "Countries don't go bankrupt," said Walter B. Wriston, then CEO of Citibank.

The banks were wrong. Often, the loans were made to totalitarian regimes that used the money to prop up their governments instead of investing in infrastructure. As political tides shifted, crafty politicians turned the loans into causes célèbres, rendering them symbols of American imperialism. Refusal by a government to repay a loan to an American bank was cheered by the citizens the way the Boston Tea Party was cheered by the colonials in 1775.

What's a bank to do? It's hard enough to foreclose on a house, but foreclose on a *country*? Banks are just private businesses, so they couldn't call in the U.S. military or even call for trade sanctions.

At first, it appeared that many debtor nations would get off nearly scot-free. But it soon became obvious that without reaching some form of compromise, the deadbeat countries would have trouble borrowing again. And they were going to need even more money in the future to shore up and develop their economies.

Bankers and ministers used several methods to repair the damage, including debt buybacks, conversion of debt into local currency that could be used for equity investment, and exchanging the loans for some form of bonds.

SELL IT TO THE STREET

The magic bullet turned out to be a financial concept called *securitization*. Why not convert a debt into a bond that could be sold and then traded on capital markets around the world?

Long a tool of mortgage bankers, securitization—the process of converting an asset to a tradable security—had already taken Wall Street by storm. Mortgages, car loans, credit-card debt, and leases are analyzed, purchased and packaged as securities, and resold in the market. Why not emerging market debt?

Why not indeed? This particular form of financial judo required a different spin: Nonperforming debt had to be transformed into debt that performs, or at least is likely to perform. To accomplish what Wall Street calls "credit enhancement," two strategies were used. First, get the banks to take less money, which, under the circumstances, was a no-brainer. Second, provide some form of guaranteed payment.

Securitization carries risks, and would-be investors were concerned with the future, not with past mistakes. It was clear from the start that if securitization of emerging market debt were to have a chance, sponsors were needed to furnish guarantees.

The sponsors would provide stability by standing behind the bonds, force the debtor to shape up in terms of economic, fiscal, and political policies, and promote the bonds to the financial community. Two principal players stepped forward—the United States government and the International Monetary Fund—to establish the Brady Bonds program.

The securitized loan is issued as a bond. The proceeds from the sale of the bond are used to pay the bank. The borrower has then replaced the old bank loan with a bond that offers more liberal repayment terms. With the debt in the market as a bond issue, there will be hundreds, perhaps thousands of "lenders" shouldering the risk rather than one or two banks.

The nation that issues the bond has an incentive to honor its commitment. In the event that a country defaults on its bond payments, its cost of future borrowing would be very high. A pattern of default would make significant future borrowing virtually impossible.

EMERGING MARKET DEBT: AN OVERVIEW

Perhaps the first debt crisis of the modern era occurred in August 1982, when Mexico defaulted on its loans, triggering a wave of loans gone bad across Latin America. Mexico announced a temporary moratorium on interest payments, and other emerging markets followed its lead, leaving a string of commercial banks with huge defaults.

This crisis culminated in a watershed event in the history of emerging market debt—the "Brady Agreement," first signed in 1989. "Brady Bonds," named for Nicholas Brady, treasury secretary under President George Bush, were the direct result of the attempt by Citibank, J. P. Morgan, and other lenders to salvage their loans to Mexico and other troubled borrowers.

The 1989 agreement restructured Mexico's debt. Under the plan, U.S. banks forgave 35 percent of Mexico's loans and the Mexican government agreed to convert the balance into new giant 30-year bonds. These bonds are denominated in U.S. dollars, so there is no currency risk to U.S. investors, and the principal is backed by zero-coupon U.S. Treasury bonds, often with partial collateral.

Since the first issues, the Brady Plan has been used to restructure debt in other Latin American nations, such as Argentina and Brazil, and other countries around the world, such as Poland, Nigeria, and the Philippines. In each case, the country exchanges its sovereign debt for Brady Bonds in concert with a reduction in the principal and/or interest and arrears owed. The debtor nation gets a break on the amount it owes, the bank gets some of its money back, and the new investors get some form of guaranteed payment. "Par Bradys" have the same face value as the debt they replaced; "discount Bradys" have a face value that reflects a discount on the amount originally owed. Both types trade at sizable discounts to their par value.

Bradys were issued in conjunction with a promise by the debtor nations to behave more responsibly in the future. To qualify, the country has to agree to undertake certain economic reforms in the areas of budget deficits, taxation, and inflation controls.

Venezuela followed soon after Mexico, then Costa Rica, Uruguay, Nigeria, the Philippines and Argentina. Today, the total Brady market is in excess of $150 billion, and Brazil, Poland, Bulgaria, the Dominican Republic and others have joined the program.

In the early years, the investor base for Brady Bonds was almost exclusively Latin "flight capital," often housed in Miami banks. Chartered WestLB of London estimates that Mexicans repatriated approximately $10.7 billion back into Mexico from offshore in 1989 and 1990, in part through the purchase of bonds. The Venezuelans and the Chileans reportedly sent about $2 billion and $1.4 billion respectively.

Other early players included hedge funds looking for a quick hit and a few dedicated country funds. Ironically, some of the buyers were the "original holders," banks that were responsible for creating these bonds, by allowing their defaulted loans to be securitized.

The yield-hungry mutual funds, including junk bond funds, insurance companies, and pension funds, have now entered the market in a big way. They like the yields, the spread, and the capital gain potential of emerging market bonds. Estimates put these institutional holdings at around 30 percent of the overall market.

In recent years, institutions have legitimized the market for emerging country debt. As the markets have gained in popularity and profit potential, banks and other financial institutions have been injecting capital into their emerging market operations, expanding their trading desks and building capital markets departments that, in some cases, rival those of their developed markets operations.

Unlike the debt crisis of the eighties, when LDCs (lesser-developed countries) ruined careers, the emerging market debt sector of today has attracted top talent, who, in many cases, have moved on to run the entire global operations of their respective institutions, an indication that both employers and employees consider emerging market debt to be where the action is.

Today there are more than 125 members of the Emerging Market Traders Association. The market, however, is lorded over by Salomon and J. P. Morgan, trading a full range of bonds and providing a full range of services, including research. Chemical, Chase, and Morgan Grenfell are also major players. Overall, in spite of the large membership, a half-dozen full-service market makers dominate the business.

In 1994, trade in emerging markets debt reached $2.76 billion, spreading from Latin America to Eastern Europe, Asia, and Africa. The market is still predominantly Latin, however, with Mexico, Argentina, Venezuela, and Brazil accounting for about 60 percent of tradable bonds and loan paper.

In spite of the overall strengthening of emerging market nations, the Mexican peso devaluation of 1994 and the Asian banking crisis of 1997 are signs that these nations are not out of the woods yet. For the near future, these nations will continue to pay a premium for access to the capital markets. That means continued high returns on their debt issues.

Most emerging market debt is not rated "investment grade" by the major rating services such as Moody's and Standard & Poor's. This deprives these nations of a significant portion of the investor pool. In most of these countries, economic and fiscal reforms are only a few years old.

Their payment histories are too short or uneven to give comfort to the rating services.

Fund managers include them in asset allocation models. Several mutual funds are devoted solely to emerging market high-yield debt. Emerging-country funds not limited to equities often take on sizable debt positions.

Financial innovation didn't stop with the Brady Plan. New financing techniques that protect investors from emerging market sovereign risk include securitization of future cash flows and IFC B-loans, in which the IFC lends money to a corporation and simultaneously sells a portion of the loan to investors. Since the IFC is still the lender of record, sovereign risk is reduced.

A BRADY BOND PRIMER

The goal of any Brady Bond program is to make emerging market debt more serviceable and to spread the risk among a larger number of players. The debt is more serviceable because the plan usually calls for a reduction in interest and principal and longer maturities. The risk is transferred to a large number of institutions and individuals who freely trade the bonds.

While Brady Bond negotiations have in the broad sense followed the pattern of the original Mexican deal, the terms and options have varied. The required reforms are usually the result of negotiations not only with the United States, but with the International Monetary Fund as well. The IMF's role is to ensure that the country's economic policy is healthy by the time the exchange of loans for Brady Bonds is made.

In strictly financial terms, a Brady Bond is sovereign debt (backed by a sovereign national government) packaged as long bonds (in this case 30 years), backed by collateral (generally assets provided by the sovereign, plus the T-bill guarantee). This makes it a unique risk cocktail of U.S. securities and developing country risk. The bond's value isn't based only on the country's ability and willingness to pay. The relative movement of T-bills will also have an impact on the value of the security, because they are part of the collateral.

Collateral is maintained in an account on deposit at the Federal Reserve Bank in New York. This account is typically invested in high-grade securities for the purpose of generating interest to cover a missed interest payment by a debtor country.

Rolling interest guarantees typically cover the next two to three interest payments (usually 12 to 18 months). As each payment is made by the debtor country, the guarantee "rolls" forward, so if all goes well, the bondholder has the next several payments guaranteed. If the collateral is used to cover missed payments, the sponsor is not obligated to replace it.

In the worst-case scenario, the investor is left with U.S. Treasury bonds that cost more than they should have. In other words, if a country defaults, say five years into a 30-year bond, and doesn't pay a cent after that, the Treasury collateral over the next 25 years will provide you with a positive yield to maturity. For example, even if Brazil defaulted on its Series Z Par Bond, the investment still would yield around 2–3 percent. That's not much of a risk when you consider that the bond pays over 11 percent as of this writing.

BRADY BOND BASICS

- Coupon-bearing bonds with a 10- to 30-year maturity
- Fixed, step, floating rate, hybrid, or combination of each
- Semiannual interest, generally amortizing
- Principal and certain interest collateralized by U.S. zero-coupon T-bonds and other high grade financial instruments
- Issued as both Bearer and Registered Bonds
- Certain Par and Discount Bonds may include value recovery rights or warrants
- Brady Plan countries: Argentina, Brazil, Bulgaria, Costa Rica, Dominican Republic, Ecuador, Mexico, Morocco, Nigeria, Philippines, Poland, Uruguay
- Potential future Brady participants: Nicaragua, Panama, Peru and Russia (Vneshekonobank)
- Currencies: mostly U.S. dollars; some Bradys denominated in deutschemarks, Dutch guilders, French francs, lire, pounds sterling, Swiss francs, and Canadian dollars

---

In practice, most experts believe Brady defaults to be unlikely. But suppose it did happen. Chances are, you would have received some interest payments from the country, which would then be added to the return from the Treasuries. In that case, you might make a very good return overall even if there were a default. As columnist David Goldman wrote in *Forbes* in April 1995, "If Latin countries pay only half their coupons, their Brady bonds will outperform any high-grade U.S. bond by a wide margin." And in the best-case scenarios, such as one described in the February 1996 issue of *Worth*, all the coupons on the Brady are paid; you rake in an extra 7 percent to 10 percent of yield beyond what you could have earned holding a pure U.S. Treasury portfolio.

Bradys now dwarf sovereign loans. Perhaps the most telling statistic regarding the switch from banks to bonds, the ratio of bond to loan trading was 1:1 in 1992; today, it stands at 7:1. The Brady program has served its purpose well, transforming bad loans to salable, liquid securities.

Brady Bonds are the functional equivalent of the emerging market Good Housekeeping Seal of Approval. When Bulgaria created Brady Bonds from its debt, the resulting paper became one of the most heavily traded vehicles. Trading volume sprinted from a mere $1 billion to more than $25 billion, breaking into the top ten in overall trading volume. Brady Bond deals have become so credible that there is now a market for "pre-Bradys," loan pools awaiting conversion to Brady Bonds.

THE MECHANICS OF BRADY BONDS

The Brady plan calls for the minimum purchase of Brady Bonds in lots of 100 with $1,000 face value per bond, or a single bond with a $250,000 face value. Since the bonds typically trade at a deep discount to face value, often 40–50 percent, the cost of a Brady Bond purchase can be considerably less than $100,000.

Brady Bond Terms

- **Principal Collateral:** The market value of the zero-coupon U.S. Treasury collateral used to secure the Brady Bond principal.

- **Stripped Yield:** The semiannual yield of the country cash flow that is not collateralized.

- **Stripped Spread:** The difference in basis points between the stripped yield and the U.S. Treasury yield, calculated as a spread over the U.S. curve.

- **Interest Collateral:** The calculated value of the rolling interest guarantee based on the probability of default as reflected in the stripped spread.

- **Stripped Duration:** The duration of the noncollateralized country cashflows.

Types of Bradys

Brady Bonds come in a variety of flavors; it seems that every negotiation culminates in a different variation. The bonds are designed to benefit the country in question while offering the investor something in return. For different countries, this means different things. Interest rate levels vary. The level of debt forgiveness varies, as does the payback schedule. This has given rise to a wide variety of names and labels for these bonds, which can confuse the investors.

- **Par bonds (PARs)** are registered 30-year bullet amortization bonds issued at par (or exchanged dollar for dollar at the face value of the original loan) and typically carry a fixed-rate semiannual coupon below market rate at time of issue. Interest is usually, although not always, fixed and is secured by a rolling interest guarantee from 12 to 18 months until maturity. Collateral generally consists of U.S. Treasury zero-coupon bonds.

- **Discount bonds (DISCs)** are exchanged at a discount to the face amount, usually carrying a market rate coupon. They are registered and carry a 30- year bullet amortization, a floating semiannual LIBOR+ rate and a 12- to 18-month rolling interest guarantee, collateralized by U.S. zero-coupon T-bonds.

- **Front-loaded interest reduction bonds (FLIRBs)** employ a fixed "stepped-up" rate for a certain number of years to "front load" the bond payment. After the initial period, they turn into floating-rate bonds, earning a LIBOR+ market rate until maturity. Interest payments are usually guaranteed at least through the step-up periods. They are typically 18-year semiannual amortizing bearer bonds.

  For example, Venezuela FLIRBs, issued in 1990, carried a fixed coupon of 5 percent that year, stepping up to 6 percent two years later, then 7 percent in 1994. In 1995, it went to LIBOR+ 7/8 percent until maturity in 2007.

- **Debt conversion bonds (DCBs)** are 18-year bearer bonds, issued at par, amortizing and carrying a semiannual LIBOR+ market rate. Because these bonds have no collateral, they are almost a pure play-on-country risk.

- **New Money bonds (NMBs)** are bearer-amortizing bonds with a floating rate, typically LIBOR+ 7/8 percent, amortizing over a 10- to 15-year life. Like DCBs, they are not collateralized.

- **Past-due interest bonds (PDIs)** are bonds that pay off interest arrears. Variations are sometimes called Eligible Interest Bonds (EIs) and Interest Due and Unpaid Bonds (IDUs). They are typically 12-year amortizing bonds that carry a LIBOR+ market coupon and are issued at par.

- **Capitalization bonds (C-bonds)** were issued in 1994 by Brazil as part of its Brady Plan. C-bonds are registered 20-year amortizing bonds issued with a then-below-market fixed-coupon rate, stepping up to 8 percent over the first six years and holding at that rate until maturity. In addition, these bonds include "capitalized" interest—the difference between the current rate and 8 percent is accrued and paid after a ten-year grace period.

To date, all Brady Bonds have a perfect servicing record on all interest and principal payments. As an added incentive, some Brady Bond issuers have attached to par or discount bonds rights or warrants that provide the bondholder with an opportunity to recover some of the debt or debt service that was forgiven under the Brady Plan, should conditions improve. These rights or warrants are linked to an improvement in the debt servicing capability of the bond issuer. For example, some are known as Oil Warrants and are linked to an improvement in oil prices or oil export receipts.

How to Value Brady Bonds

Only experienced bond investors should attempt to value Bradys. Others should rely on a capable financial professional.

1. Value the principal by computing the present value of the principal of Par and Discount bonds using the strip yield of a U.S. Treasury security with a comparable maturity.

2. Value the collateralized interest using a comparable Treasury security for interest backed by a rolling guarantee; for LIBOR+, a comparable asset-backed security.

3. Then value noncollateralized cash flows by computing the Internal Rate of Return or the strip yield.

4. *The difference between the current market price of the Brady Bond and the value of the collateral is an indication of the "sovereign risk,"* that is, the size of the premium that the market is demanding to assume debt issued by the debtor country. In considering the likelihood of default, analysts use probability models. They also consider the worst case, in which the debtor defaults and the guarantee is activated.

5. No value is assigned to rights and warrants.

OTHER TYPES OF EMERGING MARKET DEBT

PERFORMING LOANS. Some loans have been restructured to trade as bonds, but have not been part of a Brady plan. This usually occurs when the loan is current and the country is not seeking a break in interest or principal; it just wants to turn the loan into a tradable instrument. An example is Moroccan Tranche A loans, a bundle of restructured commercial bank loans. This tranche has a perfect payment record.

NONPERFORMING LOANS. Nonperforming loans are sometimes restructured and placed in pools, which can then be traded. Most of the liquid nonperforming loans are awaiting Brady Bond status. The first nonperforming loans to trade were Mexican and Brazilian loan pools exchanged for bonds in 1988.

Sometimes called *impaired* debt, these loans attract interest in their pre-Brady stage. In 1993, Peruvian impaired debt rose from 20 cents on the dollar to 67 cents, a gain of almost 240 percent.

The most liquid of the nonperforming loans that are not pre-Bradys are the Russian Vneshekonombank loans.

EUROBONDS. Emerging market bonds, usually launched in Europe and denominated in dollars, provide emerging market nations access to the international markets for the raising of new capital. They are often less volatile than Brady Bonds and carry an attractive yield.

The universe of actively traded Eurobonds is very limited, and the issue size tends to be relatively small. They are often distributed by the creditors that originally held the defaulted loans and don't usually enjoy as wide an investor base as Brady Bonds do. In general, stay away from Eurobonds.

Rather than settling old loans, some Eurobonds are typically used to provide infrastructure financing or funds for privatizations or other improvements for countries in the midst of economic reforms. Maturities are short, typically three to ten years. Deal sizes are in the $40 million to $1 billion range.

Corporate Eurobonds, those issued by emerging market companies, have outpaced sovereign Eurobonds. Yields are high, since these companies pay a premium for the risk associated with their country, plus the corporate risk.

Servicing of Russian Eurobonds has been consistently timely, and maturing issues were redeemed on time. This segment of the Russian foreign debt market is considered sacrosanct by the government since the Eurobond market is expected to be an important continuing source of funding.

LOCAL INSTRUMENTS, such as local treasury bills of short-term maturities (90, 180, or 360 days), carry both currency risk and market risk. Local bonds are not for the faint of heart, due to liquidity, volatility, and settlement problems. However, some local bonds, such as Argentine dollar bonds and Russian Ministry of Finance bonds, are worth a look.

DERIVATIVES FOR EMERGING MARKETS

Emerging markets make up one of the fastest-growing sectors for derivatives, namely futures, options, and forward contracts. There are contracts for several emerging market currencies, for stock-index contracts, and for country baskets, which we will cover later in the book. Investors in dollar-denominated debt don't need to be concerned with hedging against local currencies and neither should investors in bonds denominated in deutschemarks and Japanese yen.

The Chicago Mercantile Exchange has been especially aggressive in developing emerging market financial products. The CME offers four different Brady Bond options and futures contracts. Each tracks the value of a specific Brady issue, one each for Argentina and Mexico and two for Brazil. Each Brady contract is dollar denominated and cash settled.

The CME contracts provide Brady Bond investors with additional flexibility. Investors can assume "synthetic" emerging markets exposure, speculating on a Brady Bond's price and maximizing leverage, with easy entry and exit. This type of investing is speculative and high risk, but suitable for aggressive investors. These contracts can be used to hedge a Brady portfolio, "locking" in a yield on Latin American sovereign risk issues; they can be used to trade the difference or "spread" between Bradys and Treasuries (which also have contracts). Brady futures and options are an excellent, if risky way to add emerging market debt to your portfolio or to increase or decrease the risk associated with bonds or bond funds held.

As noted earlier, this is a way to approximate the country risk component. If the market believes Brazilian country risk is increasing, the spread between Brazilian Bradys and Treasuries is likely to increase; if risk is less, the spreads should narrow. Derivative contracts are an interesting way to invest in a country's creditworthiness.

The CME has created a new division, the Growth and Emerging Markets Division, or GEM, to create emerging market products. While they are currently restricted to Latin America, the exchange is expected to create derivative contracts for Asia and Eastern Europe.

THE RISKS OF EMERGING MARKET BONDS

Regardless of the investment vehicles, emerging market investments carry similar risks, which are best covered in Chapter 13 on risk and risk analysis. In this section, let's look at the two risks specifically associated with emerging market bonds.

LIQUIDITY AND VOLATILITY. Only about half the total emerging market debt can be considered liquid. Much of the liquid half is very liquid indeed, especially Brady Bonds, which sometimes trade $50 million or even $100 million at a time. Sometimes the spreads are narrower than those of the U.S. corporate bond and Eurobond markets, an indication of liquidity. The Mexican par bond market is one of the most liquid in the world; the Argentine par Series L bond is at times the most liquid bond trading in the Euroclear system. The bigger trading houses typically handle volumes of $300 million to $1 billion a day, even more on certain days.

Liquidity is critically important in emerging markets because they can be volatile. You need a liquid market so you can get out if you make a mistake. For example, in 1993, Venezuelan debt-conversion bonds sold off from 60 down to 48, then rebounded to 75 cents. In the weeks before the Congressional vote on NAFTA, the Mexican bond market was jumpy, but the big market makers, J. P. Morgan, Salomon, Merrill, Chemical, Citibank, and so forth, continued to quote and maintain liquidity.

Other Risk Factors

Much of the confidence in emerging market bonds is based on the notion that these governments cannot afford to let the capital markets lose confidence in them, since they are so dependent on them. That doesn't mean, however, that foreign investors won't head for the exits at the first sign of political or economic turmoil. In spite of collateral and other guarantees, there is always some sovereign risk.

The biggest risk, however, is market risk. Since Brady Bonds are linked to U.S. Treasuries, U.S. interest rate movements do affect their value. A run-up in U.S. interest rates would make emerging market debt less attractive, as the risks appear less attractive relative to the return.

Then there's the "group" effect. Emerging market debt tends to move in tandem, especially by region. The Mexican devaluation pulled every Latin issue down with it, although they later bounced back.

INTERNATIONAL CREDIT RATINGS

Every emerging nation would like to secure internationally recognized credit ratings for its paper. Such a credit rating provides wider access to the credit markets, and this usually means reduced funding costs, especially for those that earn higher ratings.

A credit rating is basically an opinion. According to John Bohn, president of Moody's Investors Service, "This opinion is defined as the future ability and legal obligation of an issuer of debt to make timely payments of principal and interest on a specific fixed-income security." The rating measures the probability of default over the life of the instrument, but not the risk of loss of market value due to changes in exchange rates or interest rates, or because the debtor exercises an option to prepay.

An unwillingness to grant a rating is, in a sense, an unwillingness to render an opinion.

EMERGING MARKETS BOND INDEX

J. P. Morgan has created an emerging market bond index to reflect the overall performance of this investment class. To qualify for inclusion in its EMBI+ (Emerging Markets Bond Index Plus), a bond must meet specific criteria:

1. A minimum of $500 million outstanding.

2. A credit rating that defines it as an "emerging market": a BBB+/BAAL rating or below.

3. The instrument must have more than a year remaining to maturity.

4. The ability to settle internationally, such as via Euroclear.

More important, Morgan requires that these bonds meet liquidity requirements, and they have applied ratings to them, from L1 to L5, as described in Table 7–1.

L1	Benchmark	Average bid/offer <3/8, and bond quoted[1] by all designated brokers[2]
L2	Active	Average bid/offer <3/4, and bond quoted[1] by at least half of designated brokers[2]
L3	Traded	Average bid/offer <2, and bond quoted[1] by at least one designated broker[2]
L4	Mostly illiquid	Average bid/offer <3, and bond quoted[1] by at least one designated broker[2]
L5	Illiquid	Bond rarely or never quoted by designated brokers[2]

1. A bond is considered quoted in categories L1, L2, and L3 if it is priced 75 percent of the time; it is considered quoted in category L4 if it is priced 25 percent of the time.

2. The list of designated brokers, which changes as the market develops, currently is Eurobrokers, Tullets, Tradition, Cantor, Chapdelaine, and RMJ.

Table 7–1. EMBI+ Liquidity Ratings. *Source: Introducing the Emerging Markets Bond Index Plus,* J. P. Morgan & Co., Inc. July 12, 1995.

A look at the highly regarded EMBI+ index is revealing with respect to the most important emerging market bonds. Bonds with an L1 rating make up 41 percent of the market value of the index, even though only 8 of the 49 (16.33 percent) are rated L1. Nineteen issues are L2 (38.78 percent), but they make up 35 percent of the market value. In most cases, L3s are not Brady Bonds or are Brady Bonds with face values under $1 billion. Conclusion: The larger issues tend to be the most liquid, and most are Bradys.

Emerging market debt is a sensible way to invest in emerging markets. In most cases, however, individual investors lack the capital and the time to trade in this arena. Emerging market bond funds are the wiser course. The returns have recently been excellent.

Devaluations and currency fluctuations affect every emerging market investment vehicle. Chapter discusses the role of currencies in emerging market investing.

Currencies:
The Hidden Emerging
Market Investment

The exchange rate—the price of one country's money expressed in terms of another's—is the ghost in the emerging market machine, sometimes turning losing investments into winners and vice versa.

Currency rates have a direct effect on the returns on international investments in both developed and emerging markets. When the dollar (if you live and work in the United States) goes down against the foreign currency, the returns from holding assets dominated in that currency will benefit. When the currency sells off, your investment will be negatively affected.

Suppose you buy an emerging market stock, say Telekom Malaysia. Technically, your dollars are converted to *ringgits*, the Malaysian currency, at a specified rate. When you sell and want a check from your broker, the ringgits are converted back into dollars. You pay about 11 ringgits per share for Telekom Malaysia, and each ringgit is worth about $.25 U.S. Your cost per share is $2.75.

Two weeks later, the U.S. dollar falls in value against the Malaysian currency. The ringgit is now worth $.40. Even if the price of Telekom Malaysia hasn't moved—it is still 11—you would make a profit if you sold at that price, because the 11 ringgits are now worth $4.40. That's a profit of $1.65 per share—60 percent—on a stock that was bought and sold at the same price in ringgits. So, if the dollar goes down against the emerging market currency, it has a positive effect on your return.

But wait. You invested in Telekom Malaysia because you believe it's a good company and that the stock will rise. You're happy to take your 60 percent profit, but it came as a result of a lucky accident.

Let's consider a different scenario. In this one, Telekom Malaysia's share price rises. Two weeks later, it stands at 26. The dollar rises in value against the ringgit, however, which is now worth only about $.36. You sell your Telekom stock on the Kuala Lumpur exchange, where your account shows a profit of 2 ringgits (let's forget commission and transaction costs in this example). When converted to dollars, however, you have realized only $9.36 per share. So instead of making money, you have actually lost $.24 per share. Your expectation regarding the company was correct, but the falling ringgit rate erased your gains.

The strength of the currency will also affect the valuation levels. If investors expect the local currency to weaken, they will usually demand a higher rate of return to make up the difference. That typically requires a lower price for the stock, which leads to lower price-earnings ratios.

EXCHANGE RATES AND EMERGING MARKET INVESTING

Currency risk is part of global investing in nearly every country that doesn't have an exchange rate linked to the dollar. The problem is stickiest in emerging markets, because there is often little you can do about it. In addition, emerging markets tend to be more sensitive to a decline in exchange rates than are developed stock markets. A weakening of a local currency might trigger a sell-off in the stock market, compounding your losses. The Asian currency crisis of 1997 brought this point home to investors. The collapse of the currencies made Asian stocks less attractive, forcing the local stock markets down in sympathy.

Emerging market investors usually seek to protect the share value of their investments, that is, to make sure the investment in a company is not severely affected by currency movements. The ultimate goal is a *real* return, after the effects of inflation and currency changes.

Currency Speculation in Disguise?

Indeed, it can be. Pareto Partners studied the contribution of currency returns to the overall investment return on international investments from 1987 to 1993. The currency component for the international returns was 57 percent on an EAFE index basket of international stocks. So for that period, over half of the return was the result of the currency play on the U.S. dollar, rather than a neutral rise in the value of the investment.

An analysis of the Argentine stock market returns from 1970 to 1990 reveals a compound annual return of 415.3 percent, measured in local currency (the peso, formerly the austral); when measured in U.S. dollars, the return is only 22.6 percent. The primary reason for this divergence was the depreciation of the peso resulting from chronic high inflation in Argentina.

Did the Currency Rate Fall or Was It Pushed?

Changes in exchange rates fall into two basic categories. Changes that occur when a free-floating currency moves up or down are called "appreciation" or "depreciation." When a country adjusts its currency rate through a policy change, the currency is "devalued" or "revalued."

As an emerging market investor, you must be concerned about both the fluctuation in exchange rates and the risk that a country might devalue or revalue.

Devaluations and revaluations are difficult to predict, because governments don't always do the logical thing. Even the best prognosticators have called it wrong. Consider George Soros's play on the Malaysian ringgits in late 1993. Economic analysis strongly indicated that the currency was undervalued at the time, so Soros's hedge fund bought ringgits. In January 1994, the Malaysian government indicated it would stand firm and adopted capital controls, restricting the flow of money into the country in an effort to avoid revaluing the currency. The hedge funds retreated. Currency rate forecasts—and the speculative plays that follow—are a regular part of the emerging market investment scene.

THE CURRENCY MARKET: A GLOBAL WEATHER MAP

The currency market can be compared to the weather map in the sense that exchange rates—like the current weather—are the culmination of many different patterns originating all over the world and changing constantly.

Currency rates fluctuate because they reflect so many different factors and serve to connect all nations. A change in U.S. interest rates may well affect every currency in the world.

Economic forces affect the supply and demand of currencies. If overall demand for U.S. dollars increases, the dollar's value will rise. A currency may increase in value relative to another—say the dollar strengthens against the Mexican peso—while falling against another—say the Japanese yen. That would, of course, make pesos even cheaper for the Japanese than for Americans.

The result of all these factors is a price that expresses one currency's value in relation to all others. In spite of professional speculators, many experts maintain that currency rates are the reflection of the most efficient market that exists in the world and therefore the most accurate distillation of what is going on in the world from a financial perspective.

The average daily turnover in the foreign exchange market (fx for short) today often exceeds $1 trillion. It is the world's largest and most liquid financial market, much larger than the combined world stock markets. Currency exchange volume related to daily world trade in goods and services accounts for perhaps 2 percent of total volume, which means that most of the currency trading involves the financial markets. The fx market is open 24 hours a day and includes asset transfers, international trade, hedging, speculation, and other financial transactions.

When you invest in emerging markets, you are trading currencies. You must make a decision about what to do about currencies, even if the decision is to do nothing at all.

PURCHASING POWER: INDICATOR OF VALUE

Purchasing power is a useful concept for determining a currency's value in relation to others. The principle is simple: If a basket of goods and services costs much more in one country than in others, that currency is likely overvalued. If it costs much less, the currency is undervalued. Of course, creating equivalent baskets isn't always easy. Circumstances in countries differ. Nevertheless, the concept of purchasing power is widely used.

To understand the concept, let's consider an example. Rice is a commodity produced around the world. Apart from variations in grade and variety, it fetches approximately the same price in free markets everywhere. The concept of purchasing power parity dictates that commodities be priced in exchange rate equivalents.

What does rice cost in Cuba? As of September 1995, four pounds of rice cost just one Cuban peso. Since the official exchange rate is two Cuban pesos to the U.S. dollar, that's only 13 cents per pound. But on the black market, you can get 40 pesos to the dollar, which means you can get 80 pounds of rice for a buck, which is about as close to free as it gets. Now, if this were to occur in a free economy, the situation wouldn't last long, because many folks would do their rice buying in Cuba. People might even sail from Key West in ships, fill them with rice, and bring it back to the United States to sell at a profit.

To do this, they would have to buy pesos to purchase the rice. With so many people buying, the demand for Cuban rice would rise, and so would the price. But currency, like any commodity, is also subject to the effects of supply and demand. As demand for the Cuban peso increased, its value, or exchange rate, would rise too. Perhaps rice prices in the Miami area might fall as sellers cut their price to avoid losing business to Cuba. In theory, the price of rice and pesos would continue to rise until "parity" with the price of rice in other countries was achieved.

But Cuba is not a free economy, and there is certainly something wrong with this picture. For one thing, rice is rationed in Cuba, so you can't buy all the rice you want at this price. For another, the Cuban regime is quietly allowing some "dollarization," meaning you can buy certain goods with dollars. Thus, unsubsidized goods that are in demand are more likely to be priced in their dollar equivalent.

Keep in mind that most Cubans don't earn much more than a dollar a week. So, if they spent their entire paycheck on rice, they could buy about eight pounds. A U.S. worker could buy hundreds of pounds a week at the supermarket price of roughly 50 cents per pound. So who's better off? You can see why simple exchange rates don't tell the whole story and why monitoring them is important.

The standard of living of two countries may be compared using purchasing power parity (PPP) exchange rates. The per-capita GDP of a country may be converted from local currency to U.S. dollars, but that figure doesn't reflect what it will *buy* in that country. PPP attempts to address this.

An emerging nation's per-capita GDP, when converted to dollars, might be only $3,000 per year, but this doesn't necessarily mean that its citizens are starving. The cost of basic human needs, such as housing and food, are probably much lower than in the U.S. PPP exchange rates attempt to account for these disparities by measuring the number of units of the local currency that would buy the same quantity of goods and services as one dollar buys in the United States. For example, in 1995, the Mexican per capita GDP, expressed in U.S. dollars, was $4,011 at the quoted exchange rate. In terms of the PPP exchange rate, per-capita GDP was $7,040, because a dollar buys more goods and services in Mexico than it does in the United States.

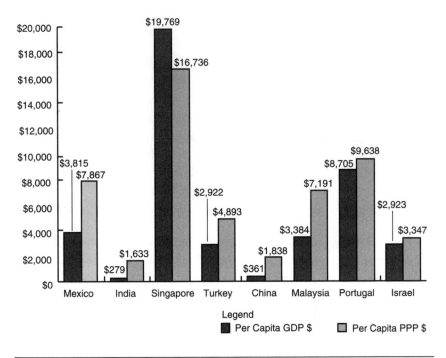

Figure 8–1. Selected Purchasing Power Parities

WHAT MOVES THE CURRENCY MARKETS?

The following factors are usually cited in economic reports. They have an impact on a country's exchange rates, not only in the actual levels, but in the trends they suggest to the market.

INTEREST RATES. The interest rate that a government will pay to borrow its own currency is a simple and direct way to affect supply and demand. If all other factors were equal, professional investors would buy the currency with the highest yield and sell all the others. Fortunately, all other factors are not equal. When it comes to emerging markets, the currencies offering the highest interest rate often carry higher risks. Higher real interest rates will always attract capital flows, especially if the investors believe that country risk is declining.

DEFICITS AND SURPLUSES. The national budget has a direct effect on the perception of the currency's overall strength. Surpluses are good; deficits are not so good.

BALANCE OF TRADE. Relative demand for a country's goods and services is reflected by the balance of trade. A surplus implies that the country is selling more than it is buying, which suggests a net demand for its currency to pay for those goods. In short, a trade surplus is good; a trade deficit is a negative.

INFLATION. High inflation causes a currency to lose value for several reasons. For one thing, it is an indication of certain problems in the economy. For another, inflation erodes purchasing power, and if a currency buys less, there will be a reduction in demand for that currency.

Inflation can also disguise an appreciating currency. The Mexican peso stabilized in 1996 after a steep drop triggered by the December 1994 devaluation. Mexican officials had reason to be happy, right? They were not. Mexico's inflation rate was much higher than that of the United States, and the peso, by holding the same exchange rate, was actually rising in value. In the first four months of 1996, Mexican inflation was about 30 percent. In inflation-adjusted terms, the peso rose 15.5 percent against the dollar.

Suppose it takes 74 pesos to buy a steak in Mexico City. At the exchange rate at the time of this writing, that's about $10. Four months later, it costs 85 pesos. If there has been no change in the exchange rate against the dollar, the steak would cost $11.50. Mexican goods would cost U.S. buyers about 15 percent more than they did four months earlier. The Mexican government must fight inflation with a fury, or face another devaluation. It cannot risk an overvalued peso.

OVERALL ECONOMIC OUTLOOK. Economic indicators—rate of GDP growth, employment, retail sales, capacity utilization, and so forth—are considered predictors of the "state of the nation." The overall perception of a country's economy will affect its exchange rate.

POLITICAL ISSUES. The currency markets loathe political instability because it implies uncertainty. A new finance minister with a history of opposition to reform can send a currency down. So can a violent outbreak in a neighboring country.

CREDIT RISK. This is essentially the net result of all of the above, in that it is the perceived degree of risk that a country will be able to pay its bills in a timely manner.

PARALLEL MARKETS. In many countries, there are two exchange rates—the "official" and the "black market" or unofficial rate. If the official rates are set by the government, the street or black market rate is often a more accurate reflection of the currency's true value. A large gap between the official and parallel market rates exerts great pressure on the government to reevaluate its exchange rate policy. Should the situation continue, it is likely that the exchange rate will eventually be adjusted if the country seeks to move toward free market reform.

These factors are not equal. In some countries, inflation will have more of an impact on exchange rates than in others. In some countries, budget deficits are most important.

CURRENCY AS AN ASSET CLASS

Currencies comprise less than 1 percent of U.S. investment portfolios. This is because, as an end in itself, currency trading is very risky, very volatile, and very speculative. The sole advantage of such an investment is a high return. The best way to make money in currencies is with high leverage, and it is not generally considered a long-term play, but rather a short-term tactic. Fund managers who do play currencies, such as several of the leading hedge funds, are in and out quickly, often taking or liquidating a position in a matter of hours or days.

This kind of investing has its place. Currencies have bull and bear markets and trends, just like any other financial market. However, emerging market currency investing is very difficult, and it requires large pools of speculative capital and high level trading relationships around the world. The exception is the exchange-traded currency contract, such as the Brazilian real and the Mexican peso contracts traded on the CME.

TOWARD A "CONVERTIBLE" CURRENCY

Emerging markets have a history of currency restrictions that set them apart from the international community. When a country restricts the amount of currency that can leave a country, trade is stifled. For example, if Coca-Cola sets up a bottling plant in an emerging market, it may someday wish to take its profits back to Atlanta. For many years, countries restricted this ability.

Convertibility—the ability to freely convert one nation's currency into that of another—is an essential part of the multilateral trade and payments.

The International Monetary Fund counts convertibility as one of its principal missions, as stated in its Articles of Agreement: "To assist in the establishment of a multilateral system of payments in respect of current transactions between members and in the elimination of foreign exchange restrictions which hamper the growth of world trade."

When a country joins the IMF, it is often granted a transitional step. It may be allowed to maintain currency restrictions that were in effect, but it must agree not to reimpose restrictions once they have been eliminated, or to impose new ones. As soon as the balance-of-payments situation allows, the new members are expected to eliminate all restrictions.

Under Article VIII, all members are enjoined from (1) restricting payments or transfers for current international transactions, or (2) engaging in currency arrangements that are discriminatory, unless the measure is authorized under the IMF Articles of Agreement or approved by the IMF.

After the "transition period," all members are eventually expected to accept the Article VIII obligations. As is the case with other signs and signals—such as stock market regulation and a Brady Bond plan—acceptance of Article VIII sends a message to the international financial and trade community that the country will manage its affairs without resorting to exchange controls.

Taken together, the emerging market nations have lifted their restrictions quickly and cleanly, admittedly with some prodding by the IMF. For example, from 1991 to 1993, 11 developing countries liberalized exchange controls on capital movements, while 5 eased or eliminated controls on capital outflows. In almost every case, these changes were part of an overall arrangement with the IMF, which often involved the rescheduling of debt. However, the benefits of convertibility are now widely accepted because of the following reasons.

1. Exchange restrictions are generally regarded as inefficient and ineffective methods of protecting the balance of payments.

2. Countries have found better ways to keep their balance of payments manageable, such as sounder economic and fiscal policies and greater flexibility in managing exchange rates.

3. In the short run, at least, liberalized exchange rates increase capital inflows, which usually improve the country's financial condition.

Convertible currencies and unrestricted exchange are an excellent step in the right direction, but they don't eliminate all currency risk. A nation may impose other restrictions on financial transactions. In addition, currency *devaluation* remains a possibility.

DEVALUATION AND THE MARKET

Devaluation would appear to be a quick and easy way to fix an economy plagued by a growing trade deficit and declining exports. If a currency is cheaper, that country's goods will cost less around the world, and this will help exports and reduce the trade deficit. At the same time, imported goods will be more expensive, so consumers will be more inclined to buy local goods, further reducing the trade deficit.

This doesn't work in the long run, however, because of purchasing power parity, which predicts that the price of tradable goods should be the same. In other words, if you devalue one currency, the price of a locally produced VCR may be cheaper than a foreign import, but sooner or later, the price will rise, or the imported VCR's price will come down. If, as in many cases, the domestic product's price rises, the effect is inflationary. So the effect of devaluation is offset by higher prices, and all you get for your trouble is inflation.

More important, devaluation—unless part of an overall restructuring and sanctioned by the IMF—sends the wrong message. It undermines confidence not only in the currency, but in the economic health of the nation, and it encourages flight capital. International and local investors and traders are willing to accept fluctuations, but they rely on the government's commitment to protect the value of its currency. When that faith is lost, so are the players. The loss of credibility almost always results in higher interest rates on the world capital markets.

For devaluation to be effective in reducing a trade deficit and making a country more competitive, it must go hand in hand with other fiscal policies to reduce domestic demand. While it works better in some economies than in others, the prevailing wisdom is that devaluation is not a good move. And that attitude is good for emerging market investors.

Consider the difference in how Mexico and Argentina faced similar economic circumstances, when a great deal of local currency was flowing into their central banks, demanding dollars in exchange. Mexico's problem came first, and it responded with a 15 percent devaluation. Argentina's central bank pledged to maintain its convertibility to the dollar at parity.

Both countries went into serious recessions shortly after. Argentina bounced back quickly, however, because the international community was more impressed with the nation's will to protect its currency. True, there were more dollars in circulation in the economy, but since there is exchange-rate parity with U.S. dollars, the only effect was the "dollarization" of the economy.

REVALUATION

On the other side of the market are those seeking to protect themselves against devaluation. A currency may be revalued, the opposite of devaluation. The currency appreciates due to official economic policy.

Most governments have resisted, however, in part because they want to keep their exports cheap. But as the capital flows in from the sale of exports and cross-border investment, inflation could be the result. An appreciation would force producers to become more efficient and more competitive, since their exports would cost more. This would serve to dampen inflation.

What to Watch For: Devaluation Alert

INCREASE IN FOREIGN DEBT. A ballooning debt may require some form of government intervention to shore up the currency, and devaluation may be considered.

TRADE DEFICIT. Devaluation is a quick and direct method of dealing with this problem.

HIGH OR INCREASING INFLATION. If inflation is driving domestic prices above comparable levels in other countries, the government may devalue to regain economic equilibrium.

WEAKENING ON WORLD MARKETS. The professional traders speak through their buy/sell orders. If they lack confidence, they will dump or short the currency. The market may then be signaling that the currency is overvalued, prompting the government to respond.

HOW TO DODGE THE FLUCTUATION BULLET

It should be clear by now that it is a good idea to reduce or eliminate the effect of currency fluctuations on your emerging market portfolio. What can be done? The most common approach is hedging.

Few words in modern finance have been more overused and misused than is "hedging." A hedge is simply protection from financial uncertainty. Hedging almost always involves buying or selling something (a financial instrument or asset) that moves counter to that which you wish to protect.

For example, you are in the business of selling computers to Mexico, and you will be paid in pesos. At the promised sale price, and the going exchange rate, you will make $200 per computer. But the order won't be filled for another six months, and if the peso goes down against the dollar by, say 25 percent, you will earn only $150 per computer. Of course, if the peso gets stronger, you could make more than $200. But you are in the computer business, and your goal is to make $200. You'd rather not speculate on currency. So, you sell the peso forward on the futures market, in essence, selling the pesos you will receive in six months at today's prices. This locks in, or **hedges**, your position against a fall in the peso.

Hedging through exchange traded futures and options is feasible for several currencies. The Chicago Mercantile Exchange has been trading the Mexican peso and the Brazilian real. The Mexican peso, launched in April 1995, was—until eclipsed by the real contract—the fastest growing contract in CME history.

U.S.-managed Latin funds have been using these currency derivatives, and not only for hedging. In some cases, the fund manager might seek to "take a position," that is, speculate on the exchange rate in the hope of making a profit, rather than eliminating risk. Many funds are not permitted to trade futures, but it pays to check with the fund sponsor to see if it hedges or speculates in currencies.

Most emerging market currencies are very illiquid and don't lend themselves to hedging. In order to create forward positions, you need speculators who are willing to accept the exchange rate risk you are transferring to them. Recently, market makers have begun creating forward contracts of two to six months, or even longer, in response to those who wish to hedge against devaluation risk. In spite of such contracts, hedging can be difficult in emerging markets.

Many countries have restrictions that make such contracts difficult to buy or sell. In some cases, hedging is simply too expensive.

The over-the-counter market has been growing by leaps and bounds, as investment bankers such as J. P. Morgan, Merrill Lynch, ING Bank, and

Salomon Brothers are creating "custom" hedges structured to meet the needs of a specific client. The client is usually a corporation doing business in an emerging market and seeking to limit its exposure. Recent estimates suggest that 75 percent of the emerging market currency hedging activity is handled by U.S. and European banks.

Hedging in this manner is risky. In illiquid emerging markets there are few counter-parties—the party on the other side of the transaction—to lay off the risk if one party wishes to unwind the deal. That is why such hedges are unsuitable for most mutual funds.

Technically, you can take a position in more than 130 currencies, but practically speaking, less than a dozen are required, since most emerging market currencies track a major currency.

Currency Overlay

A variation of hedging is sometimes called a currency **overlay**. Overlay positions treat the currency investment as a separate and distinct position. The purpose is not a simple attempt to prevent loss, but an attempt to create an optimal investment—offering the most favorable risk or reward and acknowledging that currencies play a role. Thus, overlay investors establish currency positions independent of their stock or bond positions, building a core portfolio of currencies. The result is ideally an overlay that protects against adverse currency movements while capitalizing on long-term currency trends.

To Hedge or Not to Hedge?

If you are a long-term investor, you should be a bit more comfortable in a portfolio or fund that lacks a hedging mechanism.

Short-term investors may do better to seek a hedged fund. If you are investing on your own, hedging makes sense only if you are carrying a large position. If not, consider exchange rate to be part of any decision to buy or sell, just like earnings reports or country risk. Monitor the situation carefully.

A recent study concluded that in emerging markets, unhedged portfolios performed better than hedged ones. One theory is that if an emerging market does well, its currency strengthens along with the stock market. Many emerging markets are in a delicate stage of their economic life cycle, however, and their currencies are especially vulnerable. While they may offer more mature, fast-growing companies, the currency risk may be greater.

1. **Confront it.** Hedge, or use an "overlay" that hedges some, but not all, the risk.
2. **Ignore it.** "Go naked." The most common approach.
3. **Avoid it.** Use dollar-denominated instruments, for example, Brady bonds.

Table 8–1. Three ways to deal with currency risk

To date, few emerging market mutual funds have hedged, in part because it is often too difficult or too expensive. John Templeton, creator of the Templeton Funds and a pioneer in emerging market investing, believes that a well-chosen portfolio will offset the risk of currency fluctuations, since the stocks in the portfolio will be in currencies not subject to the same market forces. This may work for a global fund, but it won't always work in regional funds, which are often highly correlated.

HEDGING FOR "EVERYMAN"

The easiest way to hedge is through exchange-traded contracts such as those traded on the principal commodity exchanges around the country. These contracts are liquid and regulated. The exchange assumes the responsibility that the counter-party will honor the commitment to deliver or accept delivery at the specified time. The Chicago Mercantile Exchange has made a commitment to emerging markets by creating a new Growth and Emerging Markets (GEM) division and awarding seats to financial institutions from emerging markets. In forming GEM, the CME is making a commitment to exchange-listed risk-management products for emerging-market investing, a further sign of maturity in the marketplace.

Since the Exchange "matches" buyers and sellers and then clears, settles, and guarantees all matched transactions, it virtually eliminates counter-party risk. The Exchange "marks to the market," keeping track of losses and gains in a particular trading position and compelling proper margin maintenance.

Currently, the CME offers currency options on the Mexican peso and the Brazilian real, as well as the South African rand.

The response has been better than expected. Look for the CME to introduce other emerging market currencies in the future. Ironically, the Merc has sold peso futures before, from 1973 to 1985, until the Mexican central bank, in an effort to quell peso speculation, prohibited such contracts. So it goes with hedging: You can't have hedgers without speculators. If you seek to limit the speculation, you also limit the ability to manage the risk.

HEDGING IN LATIN AMERICA

Emerging market investors will find Latin America among the more accessible markets to hedge a local currency.

ARGENTINA, for which four- to six-month forward contracts are available. Liquidity is moderate.

BRAZIL has one- to two-month contracts, and the market is relatively active. Brazilian currency options are available in Europe. The Bolsa de Mercadorias e Futuros—of the few viable EM futures markets—often trades 30,000 real contracts, although they are much smaller than CMEs. The U.S.-dollar contract size is $10,000, and the Brazilian stock-index futures contract size is $7,000.

CHILE is doing well, and you can purchase or sell Chilean currency up to five years forward.

MEXICO has a very active forward market, and the U.S. exchanges are now reintroducing exchange-traded forward contracts.

VENEZUELA has a small forward market for commercial transactions.

Some emerging market currencies move in tandem with that of a major country to which it is politically or economically linked. Some Asian currencies seem to follow the Japanese yen or the Hong Kong dollar. The Argentine peso is linked to the U.S. dollar by law. Emerging market investors can sometimes limit currency exposure by hedging the dominant currency in the region.

A MORE PRUDENT ALTERNATIVE: FOREIGN CDS

Some American banks will arrange for the purchase of Certificates of Deposit (CDs) denominated in foreign currency. The minimums range from $10,000 to $50,000. Currently, Citibank and Merrill Lynch have such programs, but the broadest is offered by St. Louis-based Mark Twain Bank, which offers CDs for every tradable currency in the world.

Most emerging market currencies require a $20,000 minimum. You earn interest based on the prevailing equivalent of the T-bill rate in the currency of choice, and the value of your investment fluctuates relative to its exchange rate. Unlike futures, you are never at risk for more than your equity. I expect foreign CDs will become more popular in the future. They are an excellent way to hedge against a falling dollar or to speculate on the rise of your favorite emerging market currency.

Country & Currency	Official Deposit Protection	30 day APY	90 day APY	180 day APY	270 day APY	365 day APY
Argentine peso	YES	6.25	6.40	6.50	6.75	7.00
Australian dollar	YES	5.00	5.00	5.00	5.00	5.50
Belgian franc	YES	1.75	1.75	1.75	2.00	2.75
Canadian dollar	YES	2.35	2.35	2.75	3.00	3.75
Danish krone	YES	3.30	3.30	3.30	3.30	3.30
ECU	YES	2.60	2.60	2.60	2.65	2.75
German mark	YES	2.80	2.85	2.85	2.87	2.90
Greek drachma	YES	8.55	8.60	8.75	8.85	8.85
Irish pound	YES	5.65	5.75	5.75	5.60	5.60
Israeli shekel	NO	12.50	12.20	12.60	12.60	13.25
Italian lira	YES	6.60	6.60	6.50	6.50	6.45
Malaysian ringgit	NO	6.95	6.95	7.00	7.00	7.00
Mexican peso	NO	16.50	17.45	17.20	15.25	17.35
Dutch guilder	YES	2.00	2.10	2.20	2.25	2.35
New Zealand dollar	NO	4.25	7.00	6.85	7.00	7.25
Norwegian krone	YES	2.90	3.05	3.15	3.25	3.45
Philippine peso	YES	8.00	8.25	n/a	n/a	n/a
Portuguese escudo	NO	4.75	4.70	4.25	4.80	4.80
South African rand	NO	14.25	14.25	14.75	14.75	14.25
Spanish peseta	YES	5.10	5.05	5.00	5.00	5.00
Swedish kronner	YES	3.75	3.85	3.85	3.95	4.10
Swiss franc	YES	1.35	1.42	1.45	1.52	1.65
Thai baht	NO	n/a	n/a	n/a	n/a	7.75
U.K. sterling	NO	5.05	5.30	5.30	n/a	5.80
U.S. dollar	YES	4.835	5.063	5.302	5.614	5.771
Venezuelan bolivar	YES	7.50	8.50	9.50	9.75	10.00

Table 8–2. Worldwide CD rates as of April 30, 1997 © Copyright 1997 Treasury Worldwide. Foreign CDs are not FDIC insured. Courtesy of Treasury Worldwide, LLC.

A FEW WORDS ABOUT CURRENCY SPECULATION

This book is about making money in emerging markets, and speculating on emerging market currency movements is a legitimate—if risky—way to do so. The risks and rewards of trading financial futures and options are beyond the scope of this book. If after reading this book, however, you are convinced that you have the tools and staying power necessary to trade based on your expectation of currency-price movements, you can use the exchange-traded futures markets to do so. In fact, this is a major reason for the CME's creation of GEM. An excellent place to start your education is CME's Web site (see Appendix C).

Emerging Market Indexes

An index is a mathematical measure of relative value. In use since the eighteenth century, indexes are used primarily to compare the changes in various economic phenomena such as inflation and stock market performance.

You are probably familiar with indexes, because they have a direct effect on your finances. The Consumer Price Index is often used to quantify cost-of-living raises and rent increases. The Dow Jones Industrial Average, 100 years old and still going strong, and the S&P 500 are used by millions to get a snapshot of the U.S. stock market performance.

A good market index measures the "mood" of the marketplace, serves as a "benchmark" for evaluating investment performance, and guides portfolio selection.

The choice of a benchmark depends on the purpose of the user. An economist tracking general conditions in a market and their effect on the local population would use an index different from a foreign investor whose sole interest is in maximizing return.

Indexes are an important tool for monitoring and analyzing emerging markets. In the United States, stock market performance is now part of even the most abbreviated news reports, and most people have at least a passing familiarity with our largest and fast-growing companies. Most of us are less familiar with local listings and stock markets around the world, and the emerging market indexes provide a window into these markets and insights into their performance.

Local-country indexes are computed in a variety of ways. In direct response to the need for conformity, several financial institutions have constructed indexes that measure performance in countries according to standardized criteria for inclusion of countries and local stocks. For example, the Morgan Stanley Capital Emerging Markets Index (MSCI) includes 739 stocks in 18 countries.

The three most important emerging market index series have been devised by the IFC, Morgan Stanley International, and Barings Securities, but there are many others, and new ones are on the horizon.

HOW TO TELL IF AN INDEX IS USEFUL

1. Does it reflect what the typical investor can achieve in the market? In other words, is the index relevant? Can you buy and sell the stocks in the index? Does it provide a useful measure of the results?

2. Is it comprehensive? Ideally, every class of security and every industry group should be represented. In some emerging markets, however, the industrial base isn't sufficiently broad to include all sectors without biasing the index.

3. Does it have an historical basis? A good index has a history, which is useful for analytic and comparison purposes. Newer indexes often "reconstruct" the data, creating an historical index even though it didn't exist at the time.

4. How often is it updated? We are accustomed to the Dow Jones Industrial Average (DJIA), an index that is recalculated every 30 seconds. This is meaningful, since a lot can happen to the stocks in the DJIA in half a minute. Don't expect such "real time" index calculations in emerging markets. Most of these markets are not sufficiently liquid to create dramatic fluctuations in so short a time. We may see hourly updates of emerging market indexes in the future, but at the moment, daily is the best we can get, as Table 9-1 shows.

5. Is it computed in both local currency and dollars? Indexes should reveal the role of currency in the securities' market performance.

Barings Main EMI Benchmarks	Frequency
Baring Securities Emerging Markets World Index (BEMI)	Daily
Baring Securities Emerging Markets World Index (BEMI NY)	Daily
Baring Securities Emerging Markets Extended World Index (The Extended BEMI)	Daily
Baring Securities Emerging Markets Regional Indices (Asia, Europe, and Latin America)	Daily
Baring Securities Emerging Markets Extended Regional Indices (Asia, Europe, and Latin America)	Daily
Baring Securities Emerging Markets Country Indices (Argentina, Brazil, Chile, Greece, Indonesia, Korea, Malaysia, Mexico, Pakistan, Peru, Philippines, Portugal, South Africa, Taiwan, Thailand, and Turkey)	Daily
Baring Securities Emerging Markets Extended Country Indices (Argentina, Brazil, Chile, China, Colombia, Greece, India, Indonesia, Jordan, Korea, Malaysia, Mexico, Pakistan, Peru, Philippines, Poland, Portugal, South Africa, Taiwan, Thailand, and Turkey)	Daily
Baring Securities Emerging Markets Standalone Regional Indices:	
(BEMI plus China, Colombia, India, Jordan, and Poland)	
(BEMI Asia plus China and India)	
(BEMI Latin America plus Colombia)	
(BEMI Europe plus Jordan and Poland)	Daily
Baring Securities Emerging Markets Standalone Country Indices (China, Colombia, India, Jordan, and Poland)	Daily
Baring Securities Emerging Markets Sector Indices (BEMI and Extended BEMI Sectors) (Agriculture/Food, Basic Materials, Capital Equipment, Consumer Goods, Energy, Financial, Multi-Industry, Real Estate/Property, Services, Transport, Utilities)	Monthly
Baring Securities Emerging Markets Equal Weighted Indices (Equal weighted with annual rebalance) (Equal weighted with quarterly rebalance)	
Baring Securities Emerging Markets Single Country Indices (Hong Kong and Singapore)	Daily
Baring Securities Asian CB Index	Daily
Baring Securities Brazil Mid-Cap Index	Daily

Table 9–1. **Barings Emerging Market Benchmarks** are updated daily. *Source:* Barings Securities (www.barings.com).

WEIGHTING

The IFC Global (IFCG) Argentina Index currently has 31 stocks. Suppose each stock were treated equally. If half went up 10 percent while the other half went down 10 percent, the index would remain unchanged. But in reality, a 10 percent rise in shares of YPF—Argentina's largest company—would have a much larger impact on the Argentine bolsa than would a 10 percent sell-off in the much smaller company, Polledo.

To make an index a more accurate reflection of the market, it often must be adjusted so that all stocks are *not* treated equally. The index must be adjusted to reflect the included stocks' role relative to the overall market. Indexes that don't assign equal values to the included stocks are called *weighted* indexes. Virtually all emerging market indexes are weighted indexes.

Market Indexes

The most common method of weighting is by market capitalization, sometimes called market-value-weighted or market indexes. This is basically a simple approach that consists of multiplying all the stock prices in the index by shares outstanding, and determining the percentage of overall market cap for which each company accounts. The greater the market cap of a company in the index, the heavier the impact on the index. This keeps smaller companies from exerting the same influence as do larger ones.

In our Argentina example, YPF is one stock among 31, but it accounts for 21.43 percent of all the money invested in tradable stocks in the Argentina index. Polledo carries a market weight of just .10 percent. YPF's market cap is over $4.7 billion; Polledo's is $21.3 million.

Company market caps change with each tick, so market weights change constantly. Before the age of cheap computers, few institutions could afford the required number-crunching power to calculate and recalculate market-weighted indexes.

Local market caps often differ from index calculations of market cap. In some cases, governments own large amounts of privatized stock. In Argentina, such shares aren't listed for trading, but the local exchange considers them part of the market capitalization.

Indexes weighted by market cap require a little tinkering to account for dividend reinvestment and changes in the composition of the index.

Market indexes aren't a perfect reflection of overall market performance. If *all* the listed stocks in the country are in the index, it is bound to include some that are illiquid, have a small float, hidden subsidiaries, and so forth. To correct this anomaly, companies might be excluded due to lack of liquidity or cross-ownership. The indexes try to include all major industries even when most of the market cap is in just a few sectors.

As we will see, market indexes can sometimes fall short as a method for allocating investment funds, because they lead investors to favor countries and stocks with large market capitalizations, which can mean missed opportunities.

A good market index:

- **Is thorough,** providing a mirror image of all the stocks in the market.
- **Measures both capital appreciation and dividend income.** Dividend income should be recorded immediately when received and reinvested proportionately.
- **Includes final returns** of delisted and/or bankrupt companies to eliminate any inclination to favor successful companies.

How a Market Index Works

Let's construct a simple—if not oversimplified—market-value index for the emerging market of Freedonia. The Freedonia Stock Exchange has only three stocks: Harpo, Inc.; Groucho, Inc.; and Chico, Ltd.

	Date	*Shares* Outstanding	Price	*Total* *Market* *Capitalization*	*Percent of* *Market* *Value*
Groucho	1/1/98	100	10	$1,000	61.54
Harpo	1/1/98	100	10	$ 500	30.77
Chico	1/1/98	25	5	$ 125	7.69
Total	1/1/98			$1,625	100.00

The total market cap for Freedonia is $1,625, so let's initialize our Freedonia Index at 1.000 on January 1, 1998.

At the end of the month, we look again:

	Date	*Shares* Outstanding	Price	*Total* *Market* *Capitalization*	*Percent of* *Market* *Value*
Groucho	2/1/98	100	10	$1,000	52.63
Harpo	2/1/98	100	8	$ 800	42.11
Chico	2/1/98	25	4	$ 100	5.26
Total	2/1/97			$1,900	100.00

The total market value has risen $375 to $1,900, a 23.08 percent increase. Our Freedonia Index would then be 1.2308. Suppose, however, that it is the end of Harpo's fiscal year, and Harpo pays a dividend of $1.50 per share, for a total dividend payout of $150. Since dividends are included in market-value indexes and are reinvested in proportion, we would reinvest the $150 in direct proportion to the segments of the index as follows:

Invested in Groucho: 52.63% of the $150 dividend = $78.945

Invested in Harpo: 42.11% of the $150 dividend   = $63.165

Invested in Chico: 5.26% of the $150 dividend   = $7.89

The dividend payout will then alter our Freedonia Index as follows:

	Date	Shares Outstanding	Price	Total Market Capitalization	Percent of Market Value
Groucho	2/1/98	100	10	$1,078.945	52.63
Harpo	2/1/98	100	8	$863.165	42.11
Chico	2/1/98	25	4	$107.890	5.26
Total	2/1/98			$2,050.00	100.00

The Freedonia Market Index is now 1.3231: 23.08 percent of the total return is due to stock appreciation; 9.23 percent is the result of dividend income.

GDP Weights

GDP- or GNP-weighted indexes contain countries weighted according to economic size. While smaller economies often grow faster, Brazil, a very large country, is expected to grow very fast in the next few years. I believe that size is irrelevant and that GDP-weighted indexes are not as useful for emerging markets as are market-cap weights. The degree of maturity of an emerging market plays a larger role in growth rate than does the size of the economy.

In spite of the apparent illogic, from June 1985 to June 1993, GDP weights yielded very similar results to market-cap weights, which may mean that the larger the economy, the greater the market cap, at least during that period. But China has the third-largest economy today and is ranked only thirtieth in market cap.

I suggest that you monitor GDP weights because GDP weights complement market weights by accounting for factors neglected by market indexes. Market-cap weights favor size, not growth, and they don't reflect the performance of private companies.

Trading Weights

Indexes that are weighted strictly on liquidity, or the total trading volume, are called trading weights. The theory here is that the more liquid the stocks and the market, the greater the return. There might well be something to this, as capital inflows from foreign investors increase liquidity and can have a positive impact on the price of popular stocks. The inverse may also be true, because liquid stocks, especially those heavily dependent on foreign investors, may be vulnerable to a large-scale sell-off if the stock or market loses favor.

For the five-year period ending in June 1993, investing according to trading weights would have produced disastrous results: Korea and Taiwan, the most liquid markets, did very poorly. Your portfolio would have been heavily concentrated in Korean and Taiwanese stocks, not only dragging down your return but reducing diversification.

Liquidity indexes are useful, but consider them in light of degree of dependency on foreign capital. Since the major issuers of emerging market indexes take liquidity into account in their stock selection process, some trading weighting is already built in.

Equal Weights

What could be simpler than taking the total number of constituents of an index and giving each one an equal weight? Actually, most equal weight indexes are not literally equal. They allow adjustments for great differences in population, for example, assigning greater weights to Brazil, Mexico, Malaysia, Argentina, and Turkey.

Equal-weight indexes don't tell the investor enough about market behavior, but historically, they have produced returns similar to market cap.

Risk Weights

The idea here is to weigh the index constituents in favor of those that have a minimum variance from the investment benchmark you are using. For example, you know of a stock that has moved in the same direction as the DJIA, going up when it goes up, down when it goes down, and by nearly the same percentage, for five years. If you were constructing a risk-weighted index of DJIA stocks, such a company would receive a higher weight than, say, a company that was less highly correlated with the Dow.

Which Type Works Best?

An analysis undertaken by Boston International Advisors of the different weighting methods in emerging markets appears to conclude that the indexes that were diversified performed better than indexes that were biased against diversification. So, GDP, equal weights, and any indexes that spread money around did well, while trading weights and, to some extent, market-cap weights did not perform as well.

OVERVIEW OF THE MAJOR EMERGING MARKET INDEXES

Indexes by Morgan Stanley, the International Finance Corporation (IFC), and Barings Securities are the most widely followed by active and passive fund managers, securities firms, research departments, and investment consultants. However, timely access to this data is too expensive for most investors. Many brokerage firms have access to daily closing indexes and analysis through Reuters, Bloomberg, Telerate, and other data services. Some highlights are available on the Internet and in the business press. As of this writing, Morgan Stanley, Barings, and the IFC distribute limited daily index data to the public via the Internet.

IFC INDEXES

The IFC indexes were created in 1981 in a response to the need for evaluating stock market performance in developing countries. Local stock market indexes vary in computation and stock selection methods, and the IFC wanted to create a standardized approach, that would allow them to link all the developing markets into a composite index.

The IFC Global and Investable Indexes are constructed to measure the day-to-day performance of developing stock markets. Currently, IFC calculates more than 225 indexes as standard practice, providing a variety of perspectives on emerging market performance. Indexes are calculated on a regional, composite, and individual country level, and by industry. The IFC Investable indexes are the ones most commonly used by investors who wish to benchmark performance.

The indexes are based on the IFC's Emerging Markets Database (EMDB), which began collecting data on the emerging markets in 1981 and offering its indexes and data as a commercial product in 1987.

Originally, the IFC indexes were calculated once a year using end-of-the-month prices and the top 10-20 stocks in each market. The stocks were weighted equally. In 1985, the IFC revamped the indexes to use market-capitalization weighting, began computing indexes monthly, and introduced regional indexes as well.

The IFC is more forgiving than most in its definition of emerging stock markets: "All stock markets in developing countries are considered to be 'emerging.' Developing countries are those classified as either low- or middle-income economies by the World Bank, regardless of their particular stage of development." (See the "Emerging Markets Database Frequently Asked Questions" on the IFC EMDB Web site, [www.if.org/EMBD/faq.htm])

IFC's Global and Investable index series currently include 44 and 26 markets, respectively. On November 1, 1996, the IFC Global Composite Index, which excludes IFC "frontier markets," included about 1,780 stocks from 27 markets; the IFC Investable Composite Index included about 1,125 stocks from 26 markets. The "price" indexes reflect adjusted share-price changes, while the "total return" indexes also include reinvestment of gross pretax cash dividends.

Today, with the exception of the IFC "frontier markets," which are calculated monthly, the IFCG, IFC Investable (IFCI), and IFC Tradable (IFCT) indexes are calculated on an end-of-day basis, with data posted electronically by 7:00 P.M. EDT each day.

"Frontier markets" tend to be relatively small and illiquid even by emerging market standards, and information is generally less available than in other markets. For these reasons, IFC calculates these indexes on a monthly rather than on a daily basis. Frontier markets are not currently included in the IFC Global Composite and are not considered "investable" under the IFC's definition, although they may be open to foreign portfolio investment.

The IFC actively maintains its indexes, adding and dropping stocks and countries. It screens for cross-ownership, although not to the extent that might eliminate very large or very liquid companies from the index. As of November 1997, all government stock holdings have been excluded.

For example, in April 1996 the IFC increased the investable weight factor for Korea from 15 percent to 20 percent, following a decision by the Korean government to range the foreign ownership ceiling on Korean stocks from 15 percent to 18 percent and to further increase the limit to 20 percent in the second half of 1996. This meant a rise in Korea's weight from 2.8 percent to 3.6 percent in the IFCI Composite Index, and a rise to 8.1 percent in the IFCI Asia Index.

The ownership change affected the investability of certain stocks, and their place in the Korea index was also adjusted.

Security	IFC Code	Current Weight	Revised Weight
Hana Bank	542380.1	23.20%	23.20% (no change)
KEPCO	542530.1	10.00%	12.00%
KLTC	542550.1	20.40%	20.40% (no change)
POSTCO	542760.1	10.00%	12.00%
Shinhan Bank	542830.1	17.00%	18.00%
Trigem	542917.1	18.00%	18.00% (no change)

Table 9–2. **Adjustments to weights of Korean stocks** following rise in ownership ceiling, April 1996. *Source:* EMDB bulletin.

The IFC takes its work very seriously and has made an important contribution to the development of emerging markets. It has created two "families" of indexes, the IFC Global Indexes and the IFC Investable Indexes.

IFC Global Index

The IFC Global Index includes all stocks selected by the IFC for inclusion in the emerging markets database. That means that if a stock isn't part of the IFCG, it won't be included in any index the IFC computes.

The IFCG is democratic. It is a broad index, including the most active stocks in all the markets it tracks. The main drawback is that, practically speaking, it is difficult to emulate this index because it includes stocks that foreigners are not permitted to own or that have limited "investability," meaning that there are restrictions on ownership. So the

IFCG is meant to provide an overview of broad market activity, but it is not for use to guide portfolios. Preparation of the IFCG does, however, include calculations of valuation ratios such as price–earnings, price–book value, and cash dividend yield.

Stocks must meet certain criteria to qualify for the IFCG index, and the IFCG tries to include capture coverage of between 70 percent and 75 percent of the aggregate market capitalization, drawing on stocks in order of liquidity.

IFCG indexes are built from "the bottom up," that is, on a country-by-country basis, without attempting to produce a composite index that balances by region or sector. An oil company is represented in terms of the local stock market, not in terms of the emerging market's energy sector.

IFC Investable Index

The IFC recognizes that the IFCG includes stocks that are not "investable," so in 1992 it created the IFCI or "investable" index, which adjusts for float, liquidity, and minimum market cap, weighted according to the amount of shares investors may buy by virtue of foreign investment restrictions. According to the IFC, "These indexes have been designed to measure more precisely the returns foreign portfolio investors might receive from investing in baskets of stocks that were legally and practically available to them." The basic IFCI index does not adjust for industry weights.

Investability has a dramatic effect on the composition of an index. For example, Korea and Taiwan have large emerging stock markets, so at 8.4 and 13.5, they carry among the largest country weightings in the IFCG index. Both of these countries restrict foreign investment, however, so their weights in the IFCI index are 2.9 and 6.9, a much smaller role.

By contrast, Malaysia and Mexico—wide open to foreign investment—comprise more than 31.9 percent by weight of the IFCI, but only 22.1 percent by weight of the IFCG. So market weights in the IFCI will change not only as the markets go up and down, but as markets open themselves to foreign investment.

IFCI indexes are popular; the IFC estimates that 75 percent of passively managed emerging market index funds are managed against the IFCI series.

Market Capitalizations and Weights

(as of November 3, 1997)

	IFCG Index Series			IFCI Index Series		
	Number of Stocks	Market Cap US$ mn.	Weight in Composite (%)	Number of Stocks	Market Cap US$ mn.	Weight in Composite (%)
Composite	1,987	1,071,631	100.00	1,426	769,711	100.00
Latin America	334	311,583	29.08	271	289,163	37.57
Asia	1,079	465,474	43.44	758	226,047	29.37
EMEA	-	-	-	397	254,501	33.06
Argentina	35	32,312	3.02	32	32,184	4.18
Brazil	88	101,977	9.52	76	88,894	11.55
Chile	53	48,194	4.50	50	47,609	6.19
China	195	51,210	4.78	43	6,669	0.87
Colombia	27	12,092	1.13	15	9,692	1.26
Czech Republic	41	5,356	0.50	6	2,036	0.26
Egypt	54	8,391	0.78	28	6,654	0.86
Greece	56	17,147	1.60	54	17,105	2.22
Hungary	14	5,683	0.53	12	5,403	0.70
India	133	56,477	5.27	72	16,360	2.13
Indonesia	62	31,078	2.90	61	30,096	3.91
Israel	49	18,568	1.73	46	18,458	2.40
Jordan	44	3,300	0.31	6	1,119	0.15
Korea	195	56,198	5.24	184	20,190	2.62
Malaysia	157	73,351	6.84	157	69,320	9.01
Mexico	75	97,172	9.07	62	92,424	12.01
Morocco	17	7,559	0.71	11	6,537	0.85
Nigeria	31	2,363	0.22	.	.	.
Pakistan	55	6,292	0.59	24	5,593	0.73
Peru	37	9,885	0.92	24	9,280	1.21
Philippines	60	21,066	1.97	49	10,001	1.30
Poland	30	6,445	0.60	30	6,445	0.84
Portugal	23	23,007	2.15	23	20,587	2.67
Russia	37	63,901	5.96	31	39,559	5.14
Slovakia	20	1,425	0.13	5	1,211	0.16
Sri Lanka	50	1,411	0.13	5	447	0.06
S. Africa	78	98,935	9.23	77	98,372	12.78
Taiwan, China	98	151,512	14.14	98	59,927	7.79
Thailand	74	16,880	1.58	65	7,443	0.97
Turkey	58	30,061	2.81	58	30,061	3.91
Venezuela	19	9,951	0.93	12	9,080	1.18
Zimbabwe	22	2,435	0.23	10	955	0.12

Table 9-3. Market Capitalizations and Weights. *Source:* IFC. Note: As of February 1997, the IFC added Investable Indexes for Egypt, Morocco, and Russia.

While many experts believe that countries should be weighted by market capitalization, it can create problems when comparing the different emerging market indexes.

IFC Industry Indexes

IFC publishes 9 sector indexes and 23 industry indexes for both the IFCG and the IFCI industry index series. The nine sector indexes capture all the stocks in the IFCG and IFCI composite indexes, covering agriculture, construction, manufacturing, mining, transportation/communications/utilities, wholesale/retail trade, finance/insurance/real estate services, and other/diversified holding companies.

The 23 industry indexes focus on the most significant industries represented in those indexes, each having typically 1 percent or more of a composite index's total capitalization.

IFC Tradable Indexes, the Latin50, Asia50, and IFC100 are also subsets of the IFCI and consist of the largest and most liquid stocks in the IFCI Composite Index. They are calculated in U.S. dollars.

MORGAN STANLEY EMERGING MARKET INDEXES

Morgan Stanley Capital International offers the MSCI Emerging Market Indices to serve the needs of investment managers worldwide.

Like the IFC, Morgan's emerging market indexes are calculated daily and of two basic types. The MSCI Free Indices, akin to the IFCI series, contain only shares that can be purchased by nonlocal investors; the MSCI Global Indices are broader, including MSCI Free shares plus shares than can be purchased locally.

Morgan Stanley selects stocks from all securities available in the market, excluding stocks owned by other companies, nondomiciled companies, and investment trusts. The goal is to capture 60 percent of the investable market capitalization in terms of both country and industry. If it is unable to achieve that 60 percent goal—in Turkey and South Africa for example—it underweights that country in the regional indexes.

Morgan Stanley collects data on all shares, both listed and unlisted. The company believes that going beyond 60 percent would require it to include stocks with low liquidity and/or low float, making the index less valuable to investors and creating an "uninvestable index." Morgan estimates, however, that it follows stocks that make up about 80 percent of the market and also keeps tabs on the "next generation"—stocks that are candidates for coverage and possible inclusion in the index.

The MSCI Global differs from the IFCG in that it does not include closely held companies and certain classes of companies, such as multiindustry companies, nondomiciled companies, investment trusts, and stocks owned largely by other companies, and it adjusts for industry coverage so that each industry is represented in the same proportion as it is in the market. For example, if 6 percent of Malaysian stocks are in the agricultural sector, 6 percent of the Malaysian index will be in agricultural stocks.

In adjusting for industry coverage, Morgan Stanley is making a trade-off, preferring to be a little more accurate on industries than on total stocks. The IFC, on the other hand, cares only about the total universe of stocks. It appears that Morgan Stanley has concluded that in emerging market investing, industry groupings are an important consideration. (I am inclined to agree.) The IFC does provide extensive industry grouping data, but it doesn't use industry as a screen for company inclusion in the index.

Morgan Stanley uses six basic criteria to define countries for inclusion in its emerging market indexes:

1. Gross Domestic Product (GDP) per capita substantially below the average for developed economies. GDP figures must be approached with caution, however, because they can be distorted by inflation and exchange rates.

2. Substantially greater government regulation limiting or banning foreign ownership in industries and companies than that which prevails in developed markets.

3. A lax regulatory environment, irregular trading hours, and/or less sophisticated back office operations, including clearing and settlement capabilities.

4. Restrictions on repatriation of capital, dividends, interest, and/or capital gains.

5. Greater perceived investment risk than in the developed markets.

6. A general perception by the investment community that the country should be considered emerging.

MSCI Optimization Goals

Mirror Industry Representation in the Local Market. MSCI tries to capture 60 percent of the total market cap of each industry group. It bases the selection not only on market cap, but on sales, net income, and industrial output. It may also take into account the significance of a company in the industry, that is, if it is an industry leader in the country or region. Once selected, the stocks are reclassified to MSCI's standard classifications of 38 industries and 8 sectors to facilitate international comparisons.

MAXIMIZE LIQUIDITY. Liquidity is important to emerging market investors. While trading value is measured over time to determine long-term liquidity, MSCI does not rely solely on trading value, since this would distort the indexes. In addition, MSCI measures liquidity relative to market cap, industry representation, and average liquidity for the country's market. MSCI does not exclude stocks based alone on lack of liquidity. (Some stocks may be relatively illiquid because they are out of favor with investors.)

MSCI takes liquidity into account, but points out that selecting stocks on the basis of liquidity alone can distort country weights, neglect cross-ownership, bias the index against stocks that are countercyclical, and skew industry representation. Since liquidity is constantly changing, an index that is very dependent on liquidity measures would have to be revised quite often.

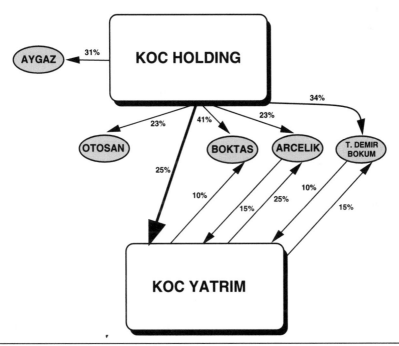

Figure 9–1. CROSS-OWNERSHIP. AN EXAMPLE OF AN INTERLOCKING OWNERSHIP REVOLVING AROUND TWO TURKISH COMPANIES, KOC HOLDING AND KOC YATRIM. KOC HOLDING HAD PARTIAL OWNERSHIP OF 70 COMPANIES INCLUDING 12 PUBLICLY TRADED SUBSIDIARIES, SUCH AS KOC YATRIM, WHICH IN TURN HAS EQUITY INTERESTS IN 16 OTHER COMPANIES. MSCI EXCLUDED BOTH KOC YATRIM AND KOC HOLDING FROM ITS TURKEY INDEX, WHILE LISTING MANY OF THE SUBSIDIARIES, SHOWN HERE AS SHADED. IN LATE 1997, KOC YATRIM AND KOC HOLDING MERGED, WITH KOC HOLDING THE SURVIVING ENTITY. THE IFC NOW INCLUDES IT IN ITS IFCI INDEX. SOURCE: MORGAN STANLEY, IFC.

MAXIMIZE FLOAT. MSCI monitors float—the percentage of stock that is actually freely tradable—for every constituent. If a stock's float is too low, it might be excluded from MSCI's indexes. Float is not always easy to determine in some emerging stock markets, where government holdings and changes in cross-ownership aren't always made public.

A full description of Morgan Stanley's index methodology and construction is available on their Web site. See Appendix C for more information.

BARINGS INDEXES

Barings Brothers, now part of the ING Bank Group, has long been a player in emerging markets. The Barings Indices are generally more selective and less comprehensive than either the MSCI or IFC indexes. They cover the large, liquid companies in countries that must meet strict standards of investability.

Barings Indices emphasize investability or "foreign institutional availability." They are market-cap weighted using only the investment universe available to foreign investors. They are quoted twice daily, in London and New York. As ING Barings has an extensive presence in the emerging world, much of the data are gathered by its own offices. It is especially noted for its liquidity expertise and its knowledge of share structure, trading patterns, and the true float in many emerging markets.

To be included in the Barings Indices, a country must have the following:

- A minimum GDP per capita of U.S. $400.
- A minimum of 100 listed companies.
- A minimum market trading value of U.S. $2 billion per year, attained in at least one of the last three years.

Barings selects individual stocks by screening them according to the following criteria:

- Capitalization value greater than 1 percent of the ING Baring Securities database for that country.
- Minimum free-float of 10 percent, minimum average daily trading value of U.S. $100,000.

In addition, shares that rank first or second in their industry sector may be included if they have a minimum capitalization of 0.5 percent of the ING Baring Securities database for that country and meet the normal free-float and daily trading value rules.

The only difference between the rules for Barings Emerging Market Index (BEMI) and Extended BEMI are that the first (cap) rule for BEMI has a cutoff at 1 percent whereas the cutoff for the Extended BEMI is 0.5 percent.

Additional information on Barings Securities Emerging Markets indexes, including data on economic sector classifications, is available on its Web site. (See Appendix C.)

CORRELATIONS

Emerging market "investable" stocks move in the same direction as the overall market. Analysis by BARRA indicates that for most emerging markets, the fundamental beta of the IFCG and IFCI indexes are similar, indicating that overall market direction is not affected by the inclusion or exclusion of stocks in the index.

Returns are another matter. BARRA compared predicted tracking errors, to determine the difference in return between the two indexes in any given year. If the tracking error is zero, the implication is that they will move in lockstep. The higher the number, the greater the difference. BARRA's conclusion was that, taken together, the returns on the IFCG and the IFCI could differ by more than 11 percent.

By far the largest factor contributing to the difference in returns is country weights. Industry differences, P/E ratios, and so on, accounted for only a small part of the difference.

	BARRA Emerging Markets Model	Barings	IFC Global	IFC Investable	MSCI
Brazil	8.16	15.67	9.34	11.39	9.63
Korea	4.82	4.97	13.62	2.93	15.97
Malaysia	15.73	19.76	15.35	23.54	14.74
Mexico	12.71	31.54	15.18	29.6	217.78
Taiwan	15.86	2.59	13.70	0.93	11.81
Thailand	8.72	7.53	7.62	4.64	5.99

Table 9–4. Weighted indexes compared for six countries that generally are the most heavily weighted in the index. Note that there are some marked differences. This is due to the fact that some indexes reduce the weighting for countries that limit foreign investment, such as Korea and Taiwan.

INVESTING WITH INDEXES:
PASSIVE MANAGEMENT

Indexes have practical value. You can use them to gauge the performance of a country or an emerging market portfolio in the same way that you measure your portfolios or mutual funds against the Dow Jones and S&P indexes. They also provide a good method of monitoring emerging stock markets in search of opportunities. For professionals, they form the core of a strategy known as *passive management,* which is based on the notion that the best way to invest is to create a portfolio that behaves identically to an index.

Passive managers do not use securities analysis to determine if a stock is overvalued or undervalued, or try to forecast a company's earnings growth. Instead, they employ methods—some of them very sophisticated—to create a portfolio (often called an index fund) that will emulate the index of choice. An emerging market index fund that is based on the MSCI Free Index seeks to achieve returns identical to those of this index.

Passive money managers are not out to beat the index, but to *track* it. They hope to replicate the index returns as closely as possible. For example, the goal of a Latin Index Fund might be to track the IFCI Regional Latin America Index; if the index was up 8 percent, the manager would hope to gain 8 percent as well. No more and no less. The passive manager seeks to place its bets on the outcome of the index, pure and simple.

This method requires no insights into individual stocks. It is akin to buying a basket of stocks in the hope of emulating the direction and returns of the Dow Jones Industrial Average or S&P. In fact, many such index funds do exist, emulating a wide variety of indexes for different markets and sectors.

Passive management has been a popular method of emerging market investing. It requires less money, personnel, and resources than does active management. It is also much easier to follow an index compiled by others than to search for growth or value stocks in markets halfway around the world.

Another reason for the popularity of this style is that it allows investors to play countries rather than stocks. If a country's economy is growing, corporate profits are up, and funds are flowing into its stock market, the major indexes that track it will rise as well. Why bother with individual stocks when you can trade a basket of stocks that emulates the index?

Unfortunately, this approach requires too much capital for the average investor. Unless you are extremely wealthy, you won't be able to "buy the index," that is, purchase the stocks that are components of the index, and in the proper proportions. Even if you could, why make the effort? There are mutual funds that do this very thing, and it is unlikely you will be able to improve on their results. These "index funds" are a viable option for emerging market investing.

Such funds usually aren't a perfect replication of the index. It is often impractical and expensive to buy every stock in the index. Managers rely on a statistical sampling technique called portfolio optimization to create a custom portfolio that closely—but not exactly—mimics the index.

All index funds bear the risk of the index. That is, if the overall stock market falls, the index based on it will fall too, and the index fund along with it. So the index fund does not reduce market risk. It simply reduces the risk that your investment returns will be very different from the returns on the index.

Emerging Market Mutual Funds

Mutual funds have been the method of choice for investing in emerging market stocks, based on the argument that such funds require knowledgeable, experienced professionals with substantial resources. The results have been mixed, however, due in part to a shortage of professional fund managers with emerging market experience.

Among emerging markets, there are index funds, actively managed funds, income funds, and open- and closed-end funds. Many of the big mutual fund players—Vanguard, Fidelity, Templeton, and the like—offer some type of emerging market fund. Emerging market mutual funds can narrow your investment focus even further, to a single country or region.

Overseas stock mutual funds can be classified into several basic categories. Since the categories aren't mutually exclusive, some funds fall into more than one group. Nearly every fund that buys emerging market stocks fits into the matrix below.

REGIONS	INVESTMENT APPROACH			
	GENERAL	SMALL CAP	INDEX	SECTOR
GLOBAL				
INTERNATIONAL				
REGIONAL				
SINGLE COUNTRY				
EMERGING MARKET				

Table 10–1. A mutual fund matrix.

WHICH MUTUAL FUNDS BUY
EMERGING MARKET STOCKS?

Mutual funds make money by making money for their investors, so they will often use every opportunity open to them. Therefore, some funds seek out emerging market opportunities even if they aren't mentioned in the brochures.

Little or No Emerging Market Investment

GLOBAL FUNDS invest in stocks around the world, including the United States. While they offer some diversification, they may have as much as 30 percent to 50 percent in U.S. securities and are likely to include Japanese and some Western European stocks. Little capital remains for emerging market investment.

INTERNATIONAL FUNDS invest only in non-U.S. securities, so emerging market participation is more likely. Emerging market holdings are by no means a sure thing, however, nor should they be, because the "international" category does not require it. Many of these funds are designed to provide U.S. investors with a way to diversify their portfolios, while avoiding high-risk investments. Therefore, they probably won't be heavily weighted toward emerging markets, but usually include some emerging market stocks if only to optimize the portfolios.

SMALL-CAP FUNDS, very popular in the U.S. markets, invest in smaller companies that statistically offer better returns under certain market conditions, and above-average growth potential. It is unclear whether this small-cap fund approach will yield similar results in emerging markets. Currently, there are few emerging market small-cap funds to choose from, since most of the liquid emerging market stocks are larger companies. Undoubtedly, second-tier and small-cap stocks will receive greater attention as funds are fully invested in larger companies and if valuations of larger companies become so high as to make them unattractive.

Significant Emerging Market Investment

REGIONAL FUNDS include many with significant emerging market investments. Obviously, the extent and nature of emerging market exposure depends on the region. Latin American regional funds will be solidly invested in emerging market stocks, while a Western Europe regional fund—with the possible exeption of Portuguese and Greek stocks—will not. The entire continent of Africa qualifies as emerging, as does the Middle East.

Regional funds can be an excellent method of investing in emerging markets, but bear the following points in mind:

1. Regional funds may combine developed and emerging market stocks. Scrutinize the portfolio, country allocation, and weightings to determine emerging market exposure. For example, if a "Pacific Basin" fund includes Japan—which comprises about 80 percent of the region's market cap (also including Hong Kong, Malaysia, Australia, and Singapore)—the portfolio could be heavily weighted toward Japanese stocks.

2. Regional definitions are broad. Which countries are in the fund? Some managers stick to countries included in the MSCI indexes, while others do not. For example, an Asian fund might have no emerging stocks at all.

3. Regional funds are less diversified than global and international funds. By definition, diversification choices are limited to countries in a single region. Therefore, they are likely to be more volatile. If the countries within the region are closely correlated, portfolio diversification will be even lower. For example, Mexico dragged all Latin markets down during the peso crisis, so Latin regional funds—with money in Brazil, Argentina, Venezuela, and Peru—didn't benefit much from diversification. Both index and traditional funds were clobbered.

4. Regional funds covering the same region vary widely. Funds often differ in country weightings, allocation, degree of risk, and performance.

5. Regional funds carry currency risk. They are usually unhedged. Sometimes managers hedge individual positions or use derivatives to hedge or partially hedge the entire portfolio. Investors may find it difficult to monitor and assess a fund's hedging activity.

6. Regional index funds can be problematic. Most fund sponsors don't create regional index funds because of the high risks. Indexes work best with a large number of components. Regions with fewer than a dozen stock exchanges, only a few hundred investable stocks, or one or two dominant markets are especially vulnerable. For example, a market-cap index that allocates funds among the seven investable stock markets in Latin America will be heavily weighted toward Mexico and Brazil, making for a portfolio that is not widely diversified. Note that many active managers create the same risky scenario without indexing by actively *choosing* to overweight Mexico and underweight Brazil and Chile.

Pure Plays in Emerging Markets

General-purpose emerging market funds consist of a basket of stocks from a broad base of emerging markets. Since these funds must react to the normal inflow and outflow of investors, their holdings must be sufficiently liquid. Managers "screen" stocks according to volatility and liquidity by using an index or by examining the data on individual stock selection. Some funds restrict themselves to the top 25 markets, others to the funds in the IFCI "investable" index.

Generally, the larger funds prefer higher profile, large stocks, because of the sheer size of the positions they must take. Managers can also create liquidity by purchasing shares in single-country or regional closed-end funds. Closed-end funds trade on the major world stock exchanges, and it is often easier for a manager to buy and sell the fund than an individual stock.

Emerging Market Index Funds

As emerging market indexes have proliferated, so have emerging market index funds. There is no room for ambiguity in investment style here, and investors can monitor the fund holdings with little difficulty.

There are arguments for and against index investing in emerging markets. Here's a quick look at the pros and cons:

Cons
1. Index funds might not reflect your overall objectives. Index funds might fall short of the mark if your goal is more than simple exposure to an emerging market or region.

2. Indexing does not seem to work as well internationally, especially when the indexes are market-weighted. Active managers can move quickly to reduce their investments in a market that has gone sour. By contrast, the index fund is chained to the country and company weights determined by the index.

In 1997, active managers underweighted Malaysia, with a 5.9 percent weighting, as opposed to the MSCI EMF weighting of 12.2 percent, for in spite of its economic might, its stock market was in a slump. In 1997, most emerging market equity fund managers outperformed the MSCI EMF Index. According to Intersec, the median manager betterd the index by more than 10 percent.

3. Indexes tend to "follow" rather than lead in emerging markets. Selection factors for index constituents reflect past performance.

Companies are often included based on how large they are rather than how large they might become. Many emerging market companies are growing faster than the indexes that track the home market.

4. Indexes offer less of an edge in inefficient markets. In emerging markets, exhaustive research, travel, and insights can make a difference in picking stocks. Investors can still gain an advantage with superior information.

By contrast, developed stock markets offer so much data to so many in so little time, it is difficult to gain an edge. Trading is automated; analysis is widely available; financial reporting is standardized. It is hard to learn something that the rest of the market doesn't know as well. Indeed, indexing arose out of the perception that attempting to beat the market over time was futile. It is *not* futile in emerging markets.

5. Stocks benefit from index membership, but you might not. Research has shown that stocks that are included in indexes sell at higher valuations. This is not surprising, given that inclusion in an index will increase liquidity, which often means a higher price. Statistically speaking then, the stock is more likely to be overvalued.

6. It is difficult to outperform the index. Index funds are an efficient form of investing, but they rarely do better than the index they track and quite often don't perform as well.

Pros
1. Passive funds cost less. Index funds are known for their lower operating, management, and transaction costs. Active managers, by contrast, demand high salaries and incentives. Operating expenses, advisory fees, and travel costs tend to be higher in traditional funds. And because active managers trade more frequently, commissions are higher.

2. Index funds offer a tax advantage. The index constituents don't change frequently, so there is relatively little portfolio turnover. Consequently there are fewer transactions and fewer "realized" gains. As such, index funds tend to generate only modest taxable short-term capital gains to investors.

3. Index investing works better as a long-term strategy. Emerging markets will continue their inherent volatility for quite some time. Since the fund is at the mercy of the index, a political or economic crisis might well reduce or eliminate gains in any given year. Since these markets are expected to trend upward over the long term, however, the indexes will rise over time. An index fund should capture those gains.

Selecting an Index Fund

1. Determine whether the index serves your investment purpose. What index does the fund track? Does this benchmark reflect your risk objective, allocation, portfolio, and mix of countries?

2. Look at the expense ratio. Index funds don't typically charge sales fees, so you should never pay a load. In principle, larger funds have lower expense ratios, because they can spread fixed costs over a larger number of shares, and because transaction costs per share go down with the size of the trades. Watch for fee waivers, which keep expenses low until the waivers expire and the fees kick in and the expenses rise.

The expense ratio for a typical domestic index fund should be less than 0.5 percent, but expect to pay as much as 2 percent in emerging markets.

Some index funds charge an up-front transaction fee, but since it goes back into the fund it isn't considered a load.

3. Look at the turnover rate. Asset turnover in the portfolio means more trades and higher transaction fees. A high turnover is a bad sign in an index fund, especially for long-term investors.

4. Determine how often the fund "rebalances" and "switches." Passive though they may be, index managers buy and sell stocks to stay fully invested in proportion to the money in the fund, which changes constantly.

A large privatization may cause a change in a country's index composition and usually requires an adjustment to the portfolio. This trading is called "switching," as the portfolio stocks are "rebalanced" by replacing certain stocks to reflect changes in the index, or to lessen the portfolio's tracking error with the index. To some extent, this is unavoidable, even desirable, as the portfolio should always aspire to track the index as closely as possible.

On the other hand, switching increases fund expenses, so long-term investors would do better to seek out funds that discourage excessive switching. Some funds design their indexes to discourage short-term switching.

Bond Funds

Emerging market bond funds cover a lot of territory, investing from Argentina to Russia to Botswana. The bulk of the money is in Latin

America, the birthplace of the Brady Plan. For more on the types of investments these funds make and how to evaluate them, see Chapter 7.

This little-known category had a breakthrough year in 1996. The J. P. Morgan Emerging Markets Bond Index Plus was up 27 percent in 1995, followed by a 39 percent gain in 1996, outperforming even the roaring U.S. stock market. One of the driving forces was the rebound of certain Latin debt instruments in the aftermath of the peso crisis. Another was renewed confidence in the creditworthiness of Russia, whose bonds rose over 110 percent. In Latin America, Ecuadoran bonds led with a gain of 60 percent.

This performance is also a striking example of negative correlation, since emerging market bonds took off during a bear market in U.S. treasuries. The returns were attributable to two factors: First, the bonds typically pay high yields; second, the market price is affected by investor confidence in the health of the country and the creditworthiness of the government. Any increase in confidence will raise the price of the bonds.

In spite of this performance, only a small amount of capital—about a half billion dollars—has flowed into such bond funds, mostly from institutions and the super-wealthy. Memories of the peso crisis are still fresh in the minds of most investors, and the recent Asian crisis has exacerbated the problem.

Many experts believe that the risks will continue to decrease as emerging nations become committed to servicing their debt. Without Cold War patrons with generous aid packages, or willing banks, they have little choice.

These markets are still dangerous. For example, a recent political crisis in Ecuador quickly erased some of the gains there. Asia is in the midst of a banking crisis. On the other hand, relative newcomers to the international debt markets, such as Egypt, have been coming on strong. In addition, many forms of Brady Bonds can be redeemed when they reach par. With many trading near 90 or better, further upside potential is limited.

One problem with emerging market bond funds is a shortage of qualified management. Many of the current fund managers have crossed over from the U.S. high-yield bond asset class or other form of investment-grade debt instruments. While they may be adept at traditional bond analysis, they are ill-equipped to deal with the special circumstances of emerging markets.

There are several excellent emerging market bond funds, but selecting one will require more than the usual due diligence. Pay particular attention to the expertise of management and its investment philosophy.

Some emerging market funds are authorized to invest in both equities and securities, so you may already be holding some of these bonds.

Special Purpose Funds

Several types of specialty funds have been formed to exploit special situations in emerging markets.

1. Privatization funds invest in privatizations around the world. One, the Global Privatization Fund, is listed on the NYSE. These funds may not be heavily invested in emerging markets, because privatization programs have also gained favor in Italy, France, and other developed countries. You would do well to check the portfolio.

2. Infrastructure funds are really special-sector funds that invest in a variety of industries with the proviso that they are direct plays in building or rebuilding infrastructure. So, an infrastructure fund might invest in telecommunications, utilities, construction, financial services, and so forth. Emerging market sector funds covering electric power, telecommunications, and construction are infrastructure plays as well. However, a dedicated infrastructure fund will cover them all.

It is likely, although not assured, that global infrastructure funds will be heavily invested in emerging markets because that's where much of the action is. Again, you should check the fund's holdings before investing.

Closed-End Funds

Closed-end funds are an unusual class of mutual funds that are often overlooked by investors. These funds have been around for more than a century, but were long ago eclipsed by conventional mutual funds.

Emerging market investors should give closed-ends serious consideration. They are a surprisingly simple way to invest. "If you are not managing huge amounts of money the most compelling way to invest in this area has to be closed-end funds," says Morgan Stanley's global strategist Barton Biggs.[1]

Country fund expense ratios should never exceed 2 percent, and should rarely exceed 1.25 percent. Many managers cap their expenses, deducting any overages from management fees.

How closed-end funds work. The sponsor decides to create a closed-end fund and begins by raising a specific amount of cash by selling a fixed number of shares. This capital is invested according to the objectives and restrictions of the fund, in the country, region, or sector the charter specifies. The stock is listed and traded, with bid and ask, just like any other.

Since the fund is "closed," no additional cash is taken in. (In response to investor interest, fund managers can "open" closed-end funds through rights offerings or secondary public offerings, or they can simply start a new fund.) So if you want to place money in a closed-end fund, you buy the existing shares in the market, or do so in the initial public offering.

Shares of a typical mutual fund are priced according to their net asset value (NAV): the market value of all the stocks held by the fund. This number is easily calculated, and what you pay is roughly what the fund is worth on that day. But shares in closed-end funds are priced like any stock: strictly according to supply and demand. Just as certain companies may be undervalued, trading at less than the breakup value of their assets, shares in closed-end funds may trade for less than the value of the underlying investment holdings they represent. For example, a closed-end fund's NAV might be $5 per share, but the stock might be trading at $4. You can therefore buy five dollars' worth of stock for only four, a discount of 20 percent.

Closed-end fund shareholders may fare better or worse than the actual returns generated by the funds. A fund may be up 10 or 15 percent, but if the host country has fallen out of favor, the stock may trade at a discount, erasing part or all of the shareholders' gains.

What causes the share price of a closed-end fund to rise? Greater demand for the shares, which could be the result of a more favorable view of the host country or an improved fund performance. Sometimes, professional investors attempt to buy a controlling interest in order to make a quick profit by converting the fund to a open-ended conventional mutual fund, or by dissolving the fund and selling its assets.

CLOSED-END SINGLE-COUNTRY FUNDS

Emerging market single-country funds are just what the name implies. Since their focus is narrower than a regional fund, they are typically more volatile than regionals. They are the riskiest of all funds that use geography to define their stock selection. Country funds have existed since the end of the nineteenth century, traditionally as closed-end funds.

There are seven key ways in which closed-end country funds differ from standard mutual funds:

1. **The share price is set by the market according to supply and demand.** Closed-end share prices can trade at a premium or discount to the NAV, impossible to do in open-ended funds. Indeed, that is why some mutual fund managers buy and sell closed-end funds for their portfolios. Prices can be volatile. Mutual funds are priced according to their NAV.

2. **Closed-end fund shares are traded on major exchanges** such as the NYSE and the London Stock Exchange.

3. **Once the fund is closed, no new monies are taken in.** Mutual funds, on the other hand have continuous cash inflows and outflows, because investors are permitted to purchase and redeem shares any time they like.

4. **Closed-ends aren't affected by large-scale redemptions.** A crisis in an emerging market will probably generate some panic selling of open-ended funds, forcing the fund manager to liquidate certain holdings at the worst possible time, often at market lows. Closed-end funds will react to a crisis, but they can't be forced to sell stocks to allow investors to cash out. Managers can follow the best course of action, and they needn't keep large amounts of cash for possible redemptions.

5. **Closed-end funds are more suited to market timers, trend watchers, and short-term investors than are open-ended funds.** Because they are volatile, reflecting the volatility of the host country, there are many opportunities for investors to enter and exit closed-end funds. Premiums and discounts to NAV add to the entry and exit opportunities. By contrast, a well-timed entry into an open-ended fund is much more difficult. On the other hand, closed-ends are stocks, so the purchase and sale will always incur commissions.

6. **Closed-end funds offer unique ways to play emerging markets.** In spite of the increase in the number of emerging market mutual funds, closed-end country funds are still an important vehicle in this asset class. Sponsors will continue to devise new and innovative funds. Competition and increasing volume on world stock markets will reduce costs. There are country funds for every major and many minor markets. There are even frontier single-country funds, such as one devoted to Pakistan. Beta Funds of London offers closed-end funds for Poland, Myanmar, and Vietnam. Morgan Stanley offers an Africa Fund and a Turkey Fund. Scudder runs a Brazil Fund, BEA a Chile Fund. Templeton has a Russia and a Vietnam Fund, among others. Four closed-end India Funds trade on the NYSE.

7. **Closed-end funds carry two types of risk and return.** The first risk is the increase or decrease in the value of the fund (NAV). The second is the change in the share price.

Selecting Closed-End Funds

1. **Learn to resist a bargain.** Closed-end discounts of around 10 percent to 15 percent are fairly common and are not compelling reasons to buy. Fortunately, the market tends to overreact to changes in market conditions. You will often see discounts of 20 percent or more, which does offer an excellent opportunity, even if the fund were to snap back only to its "normal" discount of 10 percent. Expectations of the market's future are reflected in the share price as much as in the current value of the underlying portfolio. The closed-end country fund premiums tend to be greatest at market tops and the discounts are largest following market sell-offs. Base your investment decision on market fundamentals as well as the fund's price.

2. **Perception of quality counts.** Funds considered "higher quality" trade at higher prices than do similar funds with similar investment policies and performance. The spread between a highly regarded fund and one with a lesser reputation can be as much as 30 percent. The difference is readily apparent when one compares the prices of many London-based funds with similar funds in the United States. U.S.-listed funds tend to trade at higher prices.

What accounts for this difference? The reputation and objectives of the fund's sponsor, the domicile of the fund, and the nature of the tax and regulatory environment.

3. **Regulations can affect liquidity.** Two thousand investors are required by the NYSE, while London requires fewer than 200.

4. **Watch for conflicts of interest.** Some funds are hatched by a single financial institution that acts as sponsor, underwriter, investment manager, custodian, administrator, and broker. A quality fund will avoid such conflicts of interest by dividing these tasks among independent institutions and/or constructing "Chinese walls," which prevent such conflicts.

5. **Determine organization and structure.** Is the board of directors independent and diligent? Does it carefully monitor the fund and protect the interests of the shareholders, making sure that the costs are reasonable? Does it act as shareholder advocate when negotiating contracts with

the fiduciary and management? Does it monitor portfolio turnover and commission rates? Since directors are nominated by those associated with the fund (sponsors, underwriters, and so forth), they aren't truly independent.

6. Compare with similar country funds. This is usually a better indicator of performance than comparing it to an index. Be wary of country funds that compare themselves favorably to an index, because they sometimes choose an index that makes their fund look good but is of little relevance.

7. You may already be invested. As I noted earlier, some open-ended fund managers will in turn buy shares in closed-end country funds as a way to gain exposure to less liquid stocks and frontier markets. Check the holdings of all your emerging market mutual funds.

USING MUTUAL FUNDS TO BUILD AN EMERGING MARKETS PORTFOLIO

You can do your own allocation by owning several kinds of mutual funds. You can even diversify among emerging markets through ownership of country and/or regional funds. If you are comfortable with high potential volatility, you can concentrate your exposure in a single emerging market through a single-country fund.

Emerging market funds are valuable tools in a portfolio strategy. Here are some important tips for setting up an emerging market mutual-fund portfolio:

1. Buy several funds. Since no two emerging market funds are exactly alike, you diversify among several funds. Each fund reflects the individual style and skills of the fund manager.

2. Combine country or regional funds. You create your own country allocations by combining several dedicated funds. For example, you can create your own Latin portfolio by allocating your capital among seven closed-end country funds. Establish your own allocation program by deciding the percentage of total capital in each fund.

3. Don't rely on fund labels. In the drive to stay competitive, funds often switch categories or styles. This may seem unethical, but it is rarely illegal. You invest in an emerging market fund that is supposedly restricted to large-cap stocks, only to find out later that the fund manager has put money into some high-risk small caps in the hopes of increasing the return. The best way to protect yourself is to monitor the fund's holdings through research publications or software provided by Morningstar, Value Line, and CDA Weisenberger, among others.

4. Combine styles. Some investors mix index and active funds. This strategy allows you to track the index and try to outperform it at the same time.

5. Buy one fund and stick with it. Emerging market funds are most promising over the long view. The best managers try to stay nimble while keeping a long-term investment horizon. If you like a fund, be prepared to stay with it for more than a few months.

6. Make sure your investments are liquid. If you actively manage your portfolio, the funds you select should allow telephone transactions at no charge and without restriction. You may be increasing or decreasing your investment in the fund periodically, and you don't want to lose time and effort.

7. Regularly check the allocations of countries in multi-country or regional funds.

8. Don't invest in funds that do a lot of currency hedging unless you have a great deal of currency exposure in your overall portfolio (that is, a large percentage of foreign stocks and little or no currency hedges).

9. Stay current. Don't go to sleep after you write the check. Keep up with changes and trends in emerging market economies and stock markets through periodicals (for example, *The Wall Street Journal, Barron's, The Economist, The Financial Times*), government publications, and data available on the Internet.

10. Don't sell on weakness. In emerging markets, time is on your side. Short of a major coup or revolution, these countries will continue to grow. So accept the volatility and don't sell when the news is bad. If this kind of volatility rattles you, pick a fund with a broader focus (that is, an emerging markets fund) that has greater diversity.

11. Check the resources of the fund and the credentials of the manager. Many of these funds are "young," so their track records will not be historically significant. Get a feel for the manager's background, and how he or she goes about the business. Does the manager make site visits?

How often? Does this person have a network of analysts and advisers in local markets?

12. Consider the tax implications. Mutual funds that own emerging market stocks are subject to certain tax regulations of the home market, including withholding taxes on dividends, and in some cases, on capital gains and interest. Foreign-based mutual and closed-end funds are subject to special U.S. rules, and can sometimes trigger tax liabilities on income not actually received by the investor. Check with the fund sponsor.

Mutual funds mutate like viruses. They follow the capital flow, they follow fashion, and they follow the headlines. If the market so dictates, several "emerging market small-cap" funds will spring up. "Global emerging market" funds, which combine U.S. and emerging market stocks (but exclude the rest of the world) are also a possibility, especially if such a portfolio appears optimal for a significant number of investors. As they used to say at the five and dime, "If you don't see what you want, ask for it." The mutual fund families may have what you are looking for.

ENDNOTES

1.   Andrew Bary, "Overseas Bargains?" *Barron's* (New York), August 19, 1996.

Constructing an Emerging Market Portfolio

Frankly, many tried and true investment techniques have yet to prove their worth in emerging markets. Most professionals believe that, in the end, world stock markets will grow more alike and the principles of portfolio theory and stock selection eventually will apply everywhere. Until that day comes, however, emerging markets should be regarded as special situations and the basic strategies require some tweaking.

In recent years, portfolio managers have embraced the concept of asset allocation, which is partially responsible for their keen interest in emerging markets.

ASSET ALLOCATION

You may already be familiar with the asset allocation concept. The basics are simple. Investments are grouped in major investment categories or *asset classes*, reflecting similar fundamental risks and market forces. A commonly used list of asset classes includes stocks, bonds, real estate, and international investments. Each asset has an expected level of return, risk, and volatility associated with it.

According to the theory, the asset allocation decision—how much money you *allocate* to each category—is more important than the *choice* of individual investments within that category. An investor with *all* his or her money in U.S. stocks will suffer in a bear market, regardless of stock-picking skills.

The aim of *asset allocation* is to properly apportion capital among these asset classes to create a portfolio that will achieve given investment

objectives. You attempt to build the portfolio that best matches your individual situation and goals, expressed in terms of optimal returns against
maximum acceptable risk. If the objectives change, so should the asset
allocation.

Ideally then, investors should shift their allocations as they grow older,
change jobs, raise a family, retire, and so forth. A retiree would likely have a
different ideal asset allocation than would a 30-year-old with two children.

An in-depth analysis of asset allocation theory and practice is
beyond the scope of this book, but emerging markets are important to
adherents of the allocation approach. Portfolio managers now regard
emerging market stocks as a unique asset class, distinct from international stocks. Wall Street investment strategists are recommending that
investors allocate a portion of their portfolio capital to emerging markets,
and many large institutions have followed suit.

In order to determine the optimal asset allocations, technicians combine assets in different proportions and combinations to generate a set of
alternative portfolios. Using data on the expected annual returns and the
volatility or risk (usually as measured by standard deviation[1]) of each asset
class, they compare the portfolios to arrive at those that offer the best
combination of potential risk and reward.

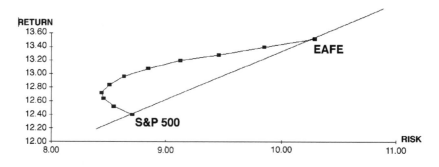

Figure 11–1. EFFICIENT FRONTIER CURVE. A SET OF OPTIMAL PORTFOLIOS, WHEN
PLOTTED, DESCRIBES A CURVE CALLED THE EFFICIENT FRONTIER. IT SHOWS
THAT A PORTFOLIO WITH BOTH U.S. AND INTERNATIONAL STOCKS
OFFERS THE BEST COMBINATION OF RETURN AND RISK.

Clearly, emerging market investments are at the outer edge of the
risk spectrum. When seen as part of an overall portfolio, however, they can
actually *improve* risk while increasing returns. The most promising emerging markets offer the best combination of high returns, low volatility, and
a low correlation with other asset classes in a portfolio.

The Emerging Market Asset Class

According to data compiled by Pioneering Management Corporation, emerging market equities yielded average annual returns of 16.0 percent for the 47-year period through 1992. The S&P 500 and the EAFE Index, by contrast, showed returns of 11.7 percent and 11.12 percent respectively.

EMERGING MARKETS AREN'T HIGHLY CORRELATED WITH DEVEL-OPED MARKETS. Historical evidence suggests that many emerging markets go their own way, making them excellent candidates for portfolio diversification. Even as the globalization of finance links stock markets around the world, local factors such as interest rates and economic policy and growth work against high correlations with the U.S. markets. Investing in several emerging regions and countries also makes sense, since correlations are low *between* many emerging markets. For example, from December 1984 to December 1990, the correlation between Argentina and Malaysia was zero. Between Thailand and Korea, correlation was .001. In 1997, many emerging Asian stock markets dropped sharply due to banking and currency crises, while Latin American markets posted solid gains.

I believe that emerging market investing is best understood when viewed as two basic tasks: *process* and *style*.

Process refers to the procedures used to define your emerging market universe, that is, the methods you use to determine how and where you will look for your emerging market investments. Style refers to the investment approaches or styles commonly employed in portfolio management. Styles are the methods you use to select and manage investments in specific stocks. I discuss process in this chapter and styles in the next.

THE SELECTION PROCESS

Top-Down Investing

Selecting a country or region is similar to selecting a stock based on an analysis of the company's fundamentals. Country allocation investors select countries based on macroeconomic factors. Since diversification is an important way to limit risk, these investors rarely narrow their choices to just a few countries. Rather, they assign relative weights among a group of markets, favoring those that seem most in line with their investment objectives. Portfolios may also be weighted by sector, industry, or region.

This brand of active analysis is sometimes called *top-down*, because the selection begins with a broad macroeconomic analysis of the emerging market universe and progresses to a final, narrow selection of stocks. The top-down approach is based on the assumption that important stocks in each emerging market are highly correlated and move together. What counts, then, are the *countries*, not the individual stocks.

Just as a securities analyst might look at P/E ratios, growth rates, and other factors when selecting stocks, the top-down investor looks at GDP, inflation rates, balance of payments, and other indicators to decide which countries to invest in.

Die-hard top-down investors believe the single most important factor determining the return on an emerging market portfolio is country selection and country weighting. Everything else, including industry sector and fundamentals of the individual companies, is secondary.

Many top-down investors are passive: Once they decide on the country allocations, they use optimizers to select stocks that emulate the index for each country they have chosen. The result is a portfolio that behaves like a portfolio of country index funds.

Other top-down investors prefer to make their own stock choices once they have made the country allocation decision. Since stock selection is a secondary concern, however, they tend to choose larger, liquid stocks, or those that are highly correlated with the indexes.

Selecting Countries

When selecting countries, your fundamental task is to determine the relative value and upside potential of the local stock market. Readily available emerging market data will provide a solid overview of the market. Look at the historical data and that of comparable markets. Is the market overvalued? Undervalued? Are the expected earnings growth rates of the important listed companies unusually high or low?

Some of this information is available to investors from public institutions such as the World Bank, the IMF, and the United Nations. Your stockbroker of choice may provide some information courtesy of its emerging market analysts. The major emerging market mutual funds make their country allocations public, providing models against which to measure your own choice of countries and weights.

The tools you need for top-down analysis are widely desseminated, such as news, leading emerging market indexes, the business press, risk analysis, and the country data flowing onto the Internet and into the business press daily, weekly, monthly, and quarterly. There are also private firms that provide this kind of analysis to institutions and money managers, but their fees tend to be quite high. As the customer base—emerging market investors—increases, the cost of information will fall.

Your investment universe is as much a personal decision as it is a technical one. Do you have a special interest in a particular country or region? How much capital are you willing to put at risk? Will you spread it across several countries or regions or concentrate on one? How risky is your overall portfolio?

Seven Signs of Promising Emerging Markets

1. **Improving finances,** with the government moving toward a balanced budget or even a surplus.

2. The country should be moving toward **a free and open market,** instituting regulations that are favorable to foreign investment. A recent study by the Fraser Institute showed that countries that rated high in economic and political freedom and openness had much better growth rates. Where the data was available, the study covered a 20-year period from 1975 to 1995.

3. **A privatization program** should be in the planning stages or well underway. Look for participation by recognized investment banks as advisers to privatizations or underwriters of upcoming IPOs of newly privatized companies.

4. **A working stock market.** Not simply one that trades, but one that provides what all honest investors expect: a mechanism for getting a fair price, ease of trading, liquidity, and investor protection. See "Is the Local Stock Market Safe?" later in the chapter.

5. **A lightening debt burden.** Organization for Economic Cooperation and Development (OECD) countries have debt-to-GDP ratios that run as high as 60 percent or more, but emerging market ratios should be much lower. Poland, for example, had a debt-to-GDP ratio of 34.6 percent in 1996; Brazi's was 24.8 percent.[2]

6. **A favorable economic cycle.** At a given point in time, emerging markets will be at different stages of their economic life and credit cycles. You should be able to tell the leaders from the slackers.

7. **Economic freedom.** Economic freedom is one reliable predictor of growth.

	Emerging Market Leaders	*Emerging Market Slackers*
Public finance	Stable, balanced budgets, often surpluses	Deficits or declining surpluses
Inflation	Single digit or low teens	High double-digit, often 30% or more; hyperinflation running a few hundred to a few thousand percent.
Growth rate	GDP growth 4-6% or more	Anything less than 4% may be symptomatic of a recession, inconsistent economic policies, or other increasing risk factors. Risk/reward may be unfavorable.
Indebtedness	Should have debt/GDP ratios that are 30-40% less; or declining significantly because of Brady Bond restructurings and/or privatizations	High debt/GDP ratios, increasing budget deficits
Interest rates	Stable interest rates preferably declining, moving closer to rates for OECD nations	High real interest rates, typically exceeding 20%
Corporate performance	A stable economy and rising consumer confidence usually spurs rising corporate profits.	Corporate profits are depressed, often declining markedly from previous years; often accompanied by excess capacity.
Investment opportunities	Companies with sustainable growth rates of 15-25% or even higher. Leader countries are also ideal places to look for second-tier small-cap stocks benefiting from the "trickle-down" of a growing economy. Many such companies may be suppliers to the larger, often newly privatized giants. Others may be positioned to take advantage of the rise in consumer demand.	Often, stock picking in a slacker country is a country bet, because the company's prospects are likely to be dependent on an improvement in market conditions. Slackers are for those who are willing to bet on a recovery or reforms and have the stamina to wait it out.

Table 11–1. How to tell market leaders from poor performers.

We are not suggesting that you look only at stocks in leader markets and shun the laggards. Often, there are bargains to be found in laggard nations, and for that reason, they can spark investor interest and a rising stock market. A recent example was Lehman Brothers and SBC Warburg's recommendation on Venezuela's Cia. Anonima Nacional (CANTV), which in part reflects their view that Venezuela's economic reforms will turn the country around. In the wake of the Asian currency crisis in mid-1997, investors combed the exchanges for bargains among fiercely competitive Asian tiger companies, in the belief that they would rise again.

Is the Local Stock Market Safe?

Don't assume foreign stock markets function just like our own. Before investing, learn the answers to the following questions:

- Are there minimum requirements for broker dealers? Minimum capital requirements, net capital requirements, and professional standards?

- Are the investor protection rules against fraud and abusive practices clear? Are they vigorously enforced?

- Does the government or the local securities industry provide protection in case of default or insolvency of its members, such as an insurance or other guarantee program?

- Do regulators require standardized and accurate record keeping? Do they require standard trade documentation and "marking to the market"?

- Are the financial reporting requirements clearly defined and enforced? Does the regulatory body have the authority to monitor reporting and enforce the rules? Does it have the staff and technical capability required to analyze and understand the financial condition of the listing companies and member firms it regulates? Does the regulatory body review all prospectuses, shareholder communications and annual reports? Does it monitor listed companies to make sure they maintain minimum listing requirements (net worth, float, number of shareholders, and so forth)?

- Does the local legal and accounting community have a stake in supporting the regulations? If the stock market community has integrity, securities attorneys who are lax in advising clients of the proper disclosure requirements will suffer a poor reputation and a loss of clients. The same holds true for accountants who are consistently delinquent on timely preparation of financial statements. If these professional communities are consistently lax, it is a sure sign the rest of the securities industry is lax as well.

- Have regulators and the securities industry encouraged the development of a financial advisory and information industry to assist investors in making informed decisions? Advisers and information services strengthen the regulatory environment because they are more likely to pick up delinquent disclosures, misinformation, suspicious trading patterns, market manipulation, and conflicts of interest among insiders. They also make the market more efficient. The more expertise in a market, the more level the playing field.

- Does the stock market's infrastructure meet international standards? Are the trading systems, custodian and depository arrangements, clearing and settlement procedures widely accepted?

- Are there formal or informal limits on foreign investment in the stock market? Limits on foreign ownership of corporations? Rules governing repatriation of profits and capital by foreigner investors?

- How frequent is disciplinary action against brokers? Negligible disciplinary action isn't a sign of a well-behaved brokerage community. In practice, a low number of disciplinary proceedings usually means the market is not well policed.

- Is there recourse if an investor believes he or she has been mistreated? Are there efficient, "investor-friendly" mechanisms for resolving disputes, or do they require drawn-out and costly litigation? Litigation of any type is a nightmare in emerging markets.

Bottom-Up Investing

Some investors ignore country allocation and base their stock selection purely on the merits of the individual stocks. In practice, this bottom-up process doesn't fully ignore country factors. It is impossible to analyze an emerging market stock without factoring in the local economy, income growth, market size, and inflation. However, bottom-up investors look at stocks first and consider countries only after a company provokes their interest. The techniques of emerging market stock selection are discussed in detail in the next chapter.

Top-Down/Bottom-Up: The Combined Approach

A combination of top-down and bottom-up is the common-sense method for the individual investor. The top-down process narrows the investor's focus: Unless you have large resources, you can't practically scour the entire emerging market world for opportunities. Once you've settled on a few favored nations, use old-fashioned bottom-up fundamental securities analysis to find the gems within those markets.

Top-down	Portfolios are constructed primarily by overweighting *markets* that are expected to outperform. Stock selection is typically an active process but is of secondary importance. Frequently, stock holdings within a country are broadly diversified with portfolio returns having a high correlation with local index returns.
Bottom-up	Portfolios are constructed primarily by selecting *stocks* that are expected to outperform. Attention to market allocation may be part of portfolio risk control, but the attempt to identify attractive markets is of secondary importance.
Top-down/ bottom-up	Portfolios are constructed by combining market allocation and stock selection elements. One element may be more important than the other but does not dominate.

Table 11–2. Summary of top-down and bottom-up processes. *Source:* InterSec Research Corp.

SPECIAL SITUATIONS: INVESTING IN FRONTIER MARKETS

Those who are adventurous should consider frontier markets, those countries that have only recently begun to attract outside investors. Some of these countries have only the most rudimentary stock markets, with a few listings and fewer regulations. Some have no stock market at all, requiring direct investment in order to participate. The goal of such investing is a very big score, perhaps a 1000 percent return or more. In order to realize such gains, the investor has to be positioned in the market before the arrival of conventional emerging market investors, who are hardly latecomers themselves. Frontier market investors are pioneers, often making direct investments that provide no liquidity and a long-term commitment. They might purchase an equity interest in a local company, buy real estate, or buy shares on an exchange that is barely functioning.

What Makes Frontier Markets Move?

- *Stability.* Frontier markets have long been inherently unstable. When one such market shows signs of stability, investors respond. An agreement to, say, allow inspection of nuclear facilities or an indication of a willingness to negotiate disputes will attract true frontier market investors to the country.

- *Liquidity.* When sufficient interest builds so that there is genuine buying and selling, the markets reach a level of maturity that attracts institutional investors.

- *Early gains.* Short-term gains of 50 percent, 100 percent, or more attract the attention of global funds, institutions, and the world investment community.

- *Bull markets.* Investors in industrialized nations who are flush with trading profits are more willing to be adventurous.

- *Demand for new opportunities.* Risk capital seeks fresh opportunities. Because frontier market investors are prepared to run big risks, they can go where others won't. As the world economies mature, there are few untapped markets remaining. It's fair to say that every country on earth is now fair game for investors.

Eight Strategies for Frontier Market Investing

1. *Buy shares in a closed-end fund.* For many investors, closed-ends are the only practical way to invest in frontier markets.

2. *Be prepared to do private deals.* In frontier markets the stock exchange volumes are often so thin that the only way to accumulate a sizable stock position is to negotiate directly with private shareholders in off-exchange deals.

3. *Go direct.* Travel to the country, meet the people, or buy into the business or joint venture. In some countries, the only way to invest is to negotiate a private stake.

4. *Invest in a private fund or partnership.* There are several partnerships and funds designed for direct investments in frontier markets. The money managers are hunting big game, so consider this a speculative

investment in spite of the pedigree of the fund sponsor and/or money manager.

5. *Invest in established companies that are active in the region.* Some American and European companies have shown aggressiveness in pursuing market share in frontier markets and in making deals to manufacture or build infrastructure.

6. *Buy everything in sight.* Find a market with little or no investor participation and buy a little of each of the largest stocks on the market. Veteran emerging market investors moved into Indonesia in 1989, buying all 18 stocks on the then tiny Jakarta Exchange.

7. *Stay slightly ahead of the curve.* With the world's money managers running out of new markets to invest in, they will eventually buy into an emerging market as soon as its stock market is workable. Should you find an opportunity to enter a market about to go legit, you may well find your portfolio lifted by a tidal wave of new money entering the market.

8. *Be patient.* Frontier investors don't always guess right. Anticipated reforms and political stability may not materialize according to expectations. The country may not develop at the expected pace and the investment vehicle itself may not pan out. In many cases, however, with the assistance of developed nations, a frontier market eventually rights itself and gets back on course. A one-year investment may turn into five, but may still be very profitable in the end.

ADVICE FROM THE PROS

Here are a few tips from the "front line" on getting involved in emerging market stocks.

- *Set up a local network.* Local contacts are invaluable. Brokers, economists, local officials, political analysts, and local businesspeople can provide useful insights.

  If you can't visit the emerging market, attend one of the many emerging market conferences held in the United States every year in many major cities. They are sponsored by U.S. and foreign-government agencies, trade groups, brokerages houses, and banks, to name a few. Many emerging markets movers and shakers attend. Don't be shy. Introduce yourself at the end of presentations, at cocktail receptions, and at luncheons.

- *Use your computer.* A personal computer is a valuable tool for gathering fundamental, market, and technical information. You can gather data on countries, on local stock markets, and to a lesser degree, on individual companies. You can e-mail local brokers, analysts, and corporate executives. Visit our Web site at *www.emergingmarkets .com* for links to useful emerging market sites.

- *Follow-up is easier than you think.* Correspond via fax or e-mail. Many of the emerging markets have Internet access. I have even received financial statements via the Internet.

- *Before you invest in an emerging market, find out if you are already invested there.* Some funds with names such as "capital appreciation," or "growth," may seem like purely domestic funds, but are invested in emerging markets. Check your mutual fund portfolio. Are any of the mutual funds you are currently holding invested in emerging markets? Pension funds are also increasing their participation in emerging markets; some of your pension money might be invested there.

- *Remember, the best gains come early.* Some emerging markets are in the later stages of their life cycles, so you can expect smaller gains. If you are after near triple-digit gains, you'll have to invest in the newcomers such as Egypt, Kenya, or Vietnam.

- *Consider direct investment.* In 1995, direct investment in emerging markets accounted for over 39 percent of the total capital inflows to emerging markets, more than $90 billion. This is an exciting way to invest. This approach is for sophisticated investors only, or those with a direct and solid relationship with a company or local investment group.

- *Don't assume every analyst and fund manager is an expert.* Demand for emerging market research analysts has been strong, and the ranks include many who are relatively inexperienced. Some are barely out of B-school, while others are covering unfamiliar markets. As recently as 1990, noted one analyst, everyone was an [emerging markets] generalist, and for the most part in Mexico.

- *Consider the relative value of alternative investments.* Investment capital flows toward higher returns, assuming risks are judged roughly equal. If the return on more conservative investments rises relative to emerging market stocks, they tend to gain capital inflows at emerging market's expense. A notable example is a substantial rise in U.S.

interest rates or a booming stock market in the United States, Europe, or Japan. If investors believe they can do as well in the U.S. stock markets, why should they run the risk of devaluations, political instability, and so forth, in emerging markets?

- *Consider the "flush factor."* U.S. investors, flush with cash from big gains made in the U.S. market, will eventually diversify rather than push their luck in the belief that the U.S. bull market will continue to go up forever.

CONCLUSION

As we enter the twenty-first century, stock market opportunities will exist in nearly every country in the world. Few investors can cover every excellent stock in every country. As this chapter has shown, there are several ways to narrow the field, whether by devoting your efforts to finding the countries with the best investment potential (top-down), looking for the best stocks (bottom-up), or a little bit of both (top-down/bottom-up combination). Chapter 12 is devoted to investment styles, including a discussion of emerging market stock selection, the essence of bottom-up investing.

ENDNOTES

1. Investment managers describe investment risk as a variance around the expected rate of return. They measure it with standard deviations. One standard deviation will contain about 68 percent of the expected future returns. For example, the standard deviation of the S&P runs about 20 percent, which means that 68 percent of the time, the results are plus or minus 20 percent, or between -10 and +30 percent. The results will fall outside this range around 32 percent of the time. Naturally, a smaller standard deviation means a smaller range of possible returns and less risk.

   The smaller the variations around the expected result, the smaller the standard deviation, and the smaller the risk.

   It's important to understand that risk doesn't necessarily mean loss. All investments vary a little from year to year, even savings accounts, so they have a measurable risk. But in the case of savings accounts, we would never expect to have a loss.

   Other markets will have different rates of return and different standard deviations.

2. Constantin Vayenas, ed., "New Horizon Economies," *Union Bank of Switzerland* (3rd Quarter 1996).

Selecting
Emerging Market Stocks

Any investor with experience picking U.S. stocks can—in theory—pick emerging market stocks, because stock screening and selection methods should work anywhere. In practice, the fundamental techniques of securities analysis require some adjustments for special conditions in emerging markets.

1. **Emerging markets are less efficient.** They contain numerous undiscovered opportunities because some company information is hard to come by and stock prices don't always reflect the news accurately. Good, solid research can lead to excellent gains, whether from finding a company with an unusual growth rate or finding a "value" company that has a few unique attributes that have gone unnoticed by the market.

2. **Emerging market stocks are more volatile than those in developed markets.** This means they may often be at variance with their fundamental value, creating more buying and selling opportunities.

3. **Independent research can add value.** You have to dig for solid information on most emerging market companies. Investors who do so can gain a valuable edge. In the United States, you're not as likely to gain a leg up on the rest of the market, because most relevant data are widely available.

4. Many companies move independently of their country indexes.
As in the developed markets, emerging markets are home to companies
that outperform the local market. For example, during a run-up in
Thailand in 1992, the banking sector took off, and Thai bank stocks doubled, while the overall market was up only 30 percent.

GROWTH VERSUS VALUE STOCKS
IN EMERGING MARKETS

Let's apply the perennial debate, growth vs. value investing to the emerging markets scene.

The Case for Emerging Market Growth Stocks

IN EMERGING MARKETS, GROWTH STOCKS ARE OFTEN FOUND IN
BASIC INDUSTRIES. In developed countries, it usually takes something special to qualify as a growth stock—innovative technology, innovative marketing, an ability to ride a hot consumer trend, a "superstore" concept, or
some other dramatic advantage. By contrast, emerging market growth
companies are often engaged in businesses, such as beverages, cement, and
autos, that are considered mature, slow-growth, and fiercely competitive in
the United States and Europe. Huge infrastructure projects such as construction, power plants, and road building are spurring demand in many
basic industries.

Emerging markets are rife with stocks such as Tata Engineering and
Locomotive, an important Indian vehicle manufacturer. At this writing,
Tata stock is growing at a rate of over 20 percent per year. Polish cement
maker Gorazdze posted an estimated 17 percent return on equity in 1996.

CONSUMER GOODS AND SERVICES ARE RIDING THE WAVE OF HUGE
DEMAND IN GROWING MIDDLE-CLASS CONSUMER MARKETS. The number
of middle-income workers is increasing around the world, creating emerging market growth stocks in everything from beverages to beepers.
Consumer markets in developed countries are usually more competitive.
Consumer product companies in mature economies are compelled to rely
on costly, elaborate, and risky marketing techniques to sell products.
Competition is fierce, the public is fickle, and picking the market leaders
is often difficult.

Emerging consumer markets are, for the time being, less sophisticated. A well-financed, well-managed brewery with a good product will probably sell more beer as the economy grows. Consumers will purchase more televisions as cable systems expand, more cellular phones as service increases, and more autos as disposable income grows and the highway system expands.

While Kodak, Fuji, and Agfa battle for market share in the United States, Japan, and Europe, racing to introduce state-of-the-art films and digital photography, half the world's population has yet to take even the simplest snapshot.

OPPORTUNITIES ABOUND IN THE EMERGING MARKETS TECH SECTOR AS WELL. Emerging markets are evolving at a faster rate than developed markets, and they are advancing in the same direction. Skyscrapers get built. Huge computer networks are under construction. Middle-class households buy personal computers for consumer banking and schoolwork.

Some consumer segments behave much like those in developed markets. In July 1997, a state-controlled telecom in Rio de Janeiro offered 55,000 new cellular lines. The company finally stopped counting when the number of applicants hit 1.4 million. The average monthly bill of a Brazilian cellular phone user is U.S. $150, twice that of the U.S. average.

THE PRICE OF GROWTH IS OFTEN LOWER. Emerging markets add an additional universe of potential growth stocks. Many are not yet fully priced and are trading at very attractive (P/E) ratios. However, you probably won't read about them in the newspapers (by that time it's often too late); you'll have to do some research. Where can you find a profitable drug maker trading for 14 times earnings? Try the Budapest Stock Exchange, where Richter Gedeon earned 27 percent ROE with an 1997 estimated P/E of 14.4. Czech tobacco company Tabak currently sells for 12 times earnings.

The Case Against Growth Investing in Emerging Markets

TOO MANY INVESTORS CHASING TOO FEW STOCKS. While it is true that money managers are becoming more cautious and looking for value, demand for emerging market growth stocks often drives prices up.

MANY EMERGING MARKET COMPANIES HAVE SHORT OPERATING HISTORIES. Economic reform is less than a decade old in many nations, and numerous companies were formed—or reorganized—only recently. Even the newly privatized giants and the family-controlled firms that have been around for years have changed so drastically that earnings analyses can be difficult. However, these stocks might appear downright conservative when compared with some of the freshly minted high-tech stocks trading in the United States.

HIGH EXPECTATIONS. With rising sales and earnings in booming economies, growth stocks may be vulnerable on the downside should they disappoint.

SK Telecom[1] is a former high-flying stock, riding a wave of booming demand for cellular phone service. But a soft stock market and increasing competition triggered a sell-off in the stock, although the fundamentals remain strong.

MANY EMERGING MARKET COMPANIES AREN'T CLASSIC GROWTH STOCKS. Many are highly leveraged; management depth is often lacking or difficult to assess.

The Case for Emerging Market Value Investing

EMERGING MARKET STOCKS ARE EQUALLY FERTILE FIELD FOR THE CONTRARIAN WHO PREFERS VALUE INVESTING. Value investors are essentially contrarians because they disagree with the market's assessment of a company's value.

Consider the sell-off in SK Telecom. As of early December 1996, the company's enterprise value—determined by stock market value plus net debt—stood at only 4 times earnings (before depreciation and taxes), compared with a ratio of around 10 for other Asian telecoms. SK Telecom holds a 70% share of the Korean cellular market.

INVESTOR REACTION TO EMERGING MARKETS CREATES MANY OPPORTUNITIES FOR MISPRICING. Value investors believe the market is repeatedly wrong, because it frequently overlooks companies that aren't "sexy," favors hot sectors, and moves on rumors, perception, and misinformation. Therefore, they often love bad news, because the resulting panic selling gives them a buying opportunity.

With their share of political crises, scandals, and volatility, emerging economies provide ample opportunities for the market to overreact and get it wrong, thereby creating opportunities for value investors. The quickest way to create value is through panic selling.

THE MARKET OFTEN OVERPRICES THE RISK. Many emerging market companies and economies are more stable and viable than the market perceives them to be. Emerging market listed companies pay a risk premium that is reflected in the stock price, and, often, that premium is too high.

In March 1996, a banking crisis in Venezuela and government wrangling with the IMF prompted several experts to predict "mass unrest," "rioting," and an environment "not favorable for a sustainable rally in stocks." In December, Standard & Poors issued a statement expressing optimism that reforms would solve the banking crisis and that credit ratings were poised to improve. The government reversed the severe fiscal deficit of 1995, posting a surplus in 1996. The stock market (IPC Index) rebounded, and was up over 28 percent for the year ending February 25, 1997.

EVENTUALLY, THE MARKET CATCHES UP. Capital always seeks opportunity and eventually the international community catches on. If your out-of-favor value stock continues to perform well and shows signs of quality, the market will catch on eventually.

The Case against Value Investing in Emerging Markets

RECOGNIZING VALUE IS DIFFICULT. In markets where financial data is suspect and financial health is difficult to diagnose and many companies are new, or newly traded, there is little reliable historical data on earnings and dividends.

MOST EMERGING MARKET STOCKS ARE HELD BY INSTITUTIONS. Value investors look for stocks in which institutional ownership is low or at least declining. Most liquid emerging market stocks have a strong institutional presence.

PATIENCE AND DISCIPLINE ARE REQUIRED. Value investors must have the conviction that the market will eventually price the stock at a P/E that, at the least, approaches the market average. This can be particularly scary in emerging markets, where liquidity might dry up during a period of market decline.

THE EASY PICKINGS ARE OFTEN GONE. Portfolio managers—many of them quite conservative—regularly look for undervalued emerging market stocks to diversify their portfolios. By the time individual investors find such stocks, they are no longer value-priced.

MANAGEMENT PROBLEMS MAY BE HIDDEN. Good companies with bad management might look like value stocks, because they trade at a discount and appear undervalued relative to value-stock criteria. Unfortunately, value analysis can't detect bad management, which is often a bigger problem in emerging markets than it is in the United States and Europe.

WHICH WORKS BETTER IN EMERGING MARKETS: GROWTH OR VALUE?

There is no simple answer. A recent study by Batterymarch Financial Management found patterns that indicated that stocks selected according to "growth" factors or "technical" factors (such as momentum or relative strength) produced higher yields than value. In certain markets, however, value factors have offered higher returns. Stocks screened for value did better in Chile, while stocks screened for growth did better in Argentina. Mexican stocks didn't respond to growth or value, but appear instead to be more influenced by money flows.

Emerging markets will continue to stymie those who wish to apply investment approaches refined in developed markets. The most successful investors have learned to adapt, combining techniques to achieve an approach that suits the country or region and the stage of its economic cycle.

Some years, market opportunities will be found in value stocks. Other times may favor growth. In that sense, emerging markets behave like developed ones.

Batterymarch's CEO Tania Zouikin concludes that "investors should not employ a single style such as growth or value across all markets ... [they] must adapt the growth or value factors to specific markets. It appears that investors can gain incremental returns by implementing different styles in different market environments."[2]

Allocation ("Top-Down")	Actively pick markets to invest in and allocate among them. In essence, a market or region is analyzed much as if it were a country.
Fundamental ("Bottom-Up")	Pick stocks using "bottom-up" approach—traditional security analysis, balance sheet and investment ratios. Requires good data sources.
Growth	Emphasis on stock selection based on growth rate; differences in financial reporting can make it difficult to identify earnings growth using traditional domestic measures.
Value	Managers select stocks that are attractively priced; unlike growth, such measures as p/e, price/book, etc., are widely used.
Currency-driven	Various types of investments designed to mirror currency predictions, e.g., stocks that move with currency rates, etc.
Derivative	Investment decisions are implemented through the use of options, futures, and other derivatives. Examples include currency futures, index futures, and options.
Multi-factor	Evidence indicates that using several styles works better than using only one.

Table 12–1. Summary of emerging market investment styles and processes.

SCREENING EMERGING MARKET STOCKS

Professional investors often "screen" thousands of listed stocks by applying a set of criteria that filters out all but the companies that merit a closer look. Screening criteria fall into five basic categories: growth, profitability, pricing or valuation, risk, and marketability or liquidity. The universe of tradable emerging market stocks is quite manageable, as many of the emerging stock markets have very few listings. Nevertheless, stock screens are widely used there as well.

In emerging markets, the most important screen is growth. Earnings growth is obviously preferable, but if earnings are flat, and there is a justifiable reason, you can allow yourself to be impressed by revenue growth, high profit margins, and increasing market share. The exception is an old, established, lumbering company that represents an ideal acquisition target for a multinational seeking a beachhead in that market. However, picking merger or acquisition targets in emerging markets is usually best left to the experts. Even if you are fortunate enough to pick the right company, such deals often get bogged down in government approvals and union negotiations.

CERTAIN PERFORMANCE AND VALUATION MEASURES WORK BETTER IN SOME EMERGING MARKETS THAN IN OTHERS. Income statement criteria work better in countries where financial statements are held in high regard. In Latin America, there are still some irregularities in financial reporting, so the investment community tends to look at market factors, often relying on technical indicators such as flow of funds. Not surprisingly, P/E works better where there are reliable data and less well where there are not.

Look at the overall track record of companies in forecasting forward earnings estimates. Are they consistently overstated, or are they reliable? Portfolio Manager Punita Kumar notes that *revised* earnings is a useful quantitative factor in most emerging markets.[3]

TRADITIONAL SCREENING CRITERIA ARE SOMETIMES CONTRADICTORY. Screen for both high-growth *and* high-dividend payout, and you won't have many stocks to choose from. It's like demanding fuel economy and sports-car high performance: They just don't go together. Many fast-growing emerging market companies have limited access to financing and reinvest their profits.

P/E MAY NOT BE USEFUL IN MOST EMERGING MARKETS. While P/E enables you to make a rough approximation of a projected return on investment, they work best in situations that are slow and steady. And emerging market companies are anything but. So, emerging market investors tend to pay less attention to P/Es as a measure of overpriced shares. In Asia, stocks have traded as high as 100 times earnings.

Local factors affect the P/E ratio. For example, accelerated depreciation can depress earnings, making the P/Es appear high relative to a similar company, because the local market adjusts for that depreciation.

Noted emerging markets specialist Michael Howell has devised another approach: He compares an emerging stock market's average P/E ratio to the country's five-year real growth forecast. According to Howell, in June 1996, in the developing markets the average P/E was seven times the real growth rate; in emerging markets, the average P/E was only 2.9 times the growth rate. "So as a group," says Howell, "[emerging market stocks] are incredibly cheap."[4]

VALUATION BASED ON EARNINGS CAN BE MISLEADING. Earnings may not be what they seem. Management can, in certain countries, manipulate earnings by moving cash in and out of reserve accounts.

When looking at emerging market valuation ratios, always consider:

1. The industry average for the local market;
2. The averages for the country;
3. Global averages for the industry and region;
4. Ratios for comparable companies in other markets.

Unfortunately, performance benchmarks and ratios aren't always easy to obtain on a timely basis, because some markets don't require frequent disclosure of the data required to compute them. (If earnings are disclosed only once a year, how do you figure a true P/E nine months later?)

Some countries allow more than one type of common stock, complicating the computation of stock ratios based on common shares outstanding.

COMPANY SIZE COUNTS. Consider the size of a company from several perspectives: its ranking in the local stock market; in its sector; on the global scene. Some emerging market stocks, such as Argentina's YPF and Russia's Lukoil, are among the world's largest companies.

Picking one of the "ten largest" in a market is a mixed blessing. You gain liquidity, and usually, greater disclosure, and the benefit of available institutional research. Such stocks are usually at the high end of the valuation scale, however. There aren't likely to be any bargains here. So there had better be significant growth in the company's future to justify the high price.

LIQUIDITY IS A PRIMARY CONSIDERATION. Liquidity is gaining recognition as a valuable selection criterion because emerging market share prices are often determined not by rigid financial measures, but simply by how much investors are willing to pay and how much money is available. As a result, investor sentiment and the resulting capital flows are very important in emerging market investing. This sort of pricing occurs in developed markets as well, whenever there is a hot stock or a hot sector. Nevertheless, with thousands of analysts tracking industries and stocks, alarms usually sound when valuations get too high. This is less true in emerging market investing.

When investing in emerging markets, always try to determine the supply-and-demand situation for the financial asset in which you are investing. You can pay very little for a stock, or you can pay a great deal, but you can't ignore market sentiment. That sentiment is best measured by how much capital is flowing in and flowing out, and who is buying or not buying. Local savings rates, the availability of pension fund investments and lifting of restrictions on foreign ownership also play a role in a foreign stock's liquidity.

In 1996, B-shares trading on China's Shenzen exchange took off. Did companies suddenly begin making much more money? Did events in China reduce the political risks?

No. B-shares were restricted to foreign ownership, but investors snapped them up in anticipation of the lifting of the restrictions. Investors were wagering that the capital inflow from Chinese investors would raise the liquidity—and prices—of these stocks.

FINANCIAL STRENGTH IS MORE FRAGILE. Size counts, but financial health counts more. Examine the standard financial ratios and pay close attention to a deteriorating balance sheet or potential bankruptcies. While there are many excellent managers in emerging market nations, there is less depth, and it is easy for a once-healthy company to go into a tailspin.

Nevertheless, don't set the bar too high. As financially weakened emerging market companies tend to be heavily discounted by the market, you might find some bargains in potential turnarounds or acquisition targets.

GLOBAL COMPARISONS ARE EVEN MORE IMPORTANT THAN LOCAL COMPARISONS. Solid fundamental analysis should be used to compare the company's strength and performance to other companies in the country, region, sector, or specific industry. You might, for example, want to rule out any company with a higher P/E multiple than the industry average.

Developed	Emerging
Both growth and value strategies widely in use.	Most concentrate on finding growth.
Growth opportunities favored in technology and other innovative businesses.	Slow-growth industries in developed countries may be on the fast track in emerging markets, due to the need for infrastructure. Growth opportunities in basic industries such as utilities, energy, telecommunications, retailing, cement, cable TV, and mining.
Local valuations, i.e.,market cap and industry multiples, are important benchmarks.	Absolute valuations more important, as local valuations are often distorted by capital flows (hot money, capital flight, etc.).
Industry trends and consumer buying patterns more important that most macroeconomic forces.	Pure "bottom-up" investment style not practical; you need a lot of top-down knowledge. Country factors must be taken into account.
Growth rate affected by general business environment.	Growth rate markedly affected by a variety of macroeconomic forces.

Table 12–2. Stock-picking compared.

Seven Mistakes Investors Make When Screening Emerging market Stocks

1. Redundant screening. Unless there is a specific reason to screen for price-earnings ratios, price-book value, price-sales and price-cash flow, you needn't track each one. They will usually list the same types of stocks. Favor the most reliable data for the particular market. For example, in countries where book values are suspect, you might be better served by price-sales. In countries such as India and Malaysia, where strict American-style accounting practices apply, financial statement analysis is more worthwhile for screening.

2. Misjudging the liquidity risk. Liquidity risk is often overstated. Before you invest, look at a company's trading volume over the past few years. Find the lowest-volume trading day and the lowest-volume week. What percentage of the "float" changed hands? The number of shares you are planning to buy should be a small fraction of a percent of this figure.

The liquidity situation in emerging markets can vary. Brazil has a growing stock market, but Telebras, a leading blue chip, has accounted for more than 50 percent of the trading volume on certain days.

Obviously, the amount of liquidity you require is somewhat related to your investment horizon. If you are a longer-term investor and you have the resources to stay in a market until liquidity improves, you can be more flexible in your liquidity requirements.

3. Confusing volatility with liquidity. An emerging market stock with lower volatility than the overall market might seem like a more conservative buy. However, its lack of fluctuation could be a sign that the stock is quiet and liquidity is very low.

4. Getting the stock picks right but the portfolio wrong. Your stock selection should make sense as a portfolio. If strict application of your stock screens generates a list that is 75 percent Mexican, adjust your criteria to allow more diversification. A single-country bet is generally unwise over the long term.

5. Ignoring your instincts. What industries and regions do you understand best? Have you done business with the company? Are you acquainted with top management? If you have an opportunity to familiarize yourself with a company, do it.

6. Relying on technical analysis. Market technicians have shied away from emerging markets because they need reliable historical data, and there isn't much available. In addition, technical analysis is more difficult in less liquid markets. There are signs, however, that certain technical *indicators,* such as relative strength, may be useful. Technical analysis may have its day in emerging markets, but that day has not yet arrived.

7. Misjudging rumors. Emerging market stock watchers seem to love rumors. Perhaps it is because information is less accessible to outsiders than in the developed countries. Markets move on rumors such as the pending resignation of a key finance minister, a brewing corruption scandal, local resistance to a privatization, and so forth. If you are interested in emerging markets and have money in them, you won't be able to ignore these rumors. They will find you. However, do not be impulsive. Acting on rumors is often expensive.

STOCK SELECTION CRITERIA

This is the most interesting and enjoyable aspect of emerging market investing and, in my opinion, makes it one of the most level playing fields in the investment world. These markets are moving so fast, companies are growing and mutating so quickly that even the best professional managers can't uncover or price every opportunity.

Keep the following criteria in mind when looking for those emerging market stocks that could turn out to be winners.

COMPETITIVE ADVANTAGES in the current and future environment. Does the country have valuable or scarce natural resources? Does the company have a well-regarded and recognized brand name? Does it possess consumer loyalty? Will the company be hurt, helped, or unaffected by economic and trade alliances affecting the country?

Are the company's advantages sustainable in light of foreign competition and economic reform? Many emerging market companies have grown up in protective environments, shielded from competitive pressures by tariffs, government favoritism and subsidies, the absence of foreign competition and cheap labor. Now that the country is open to foreign investment and free trade, what are the company's prospects? Can it remain or become a low-cost producer capable of competing with high-tech production techniques from abroad? Can it retain market share?

MARKET SHARE is a good benchmark. Well-managed companies tend to consolidate and increase market share when the economy expands.

MANAGEMENT. Good management can require different skills in emerging markets. Managing during a period of economic reform is challenging.

Take a careful look at who is running the company, where he or she has been trained, and whether or not management is really calling the shots. Many emerging market companies are still being run by the founding families, and the founding patriarch or matriarch may lack the vision and drive to take the company forward.

Don't, however, automatically assume that a family business isn't managed well. Many closely held businesses are controlled by savvy managers raised in the business, educated in the finest business schools in the United States and Europe, and well-schooled in productivity innovations.

STRATEGIC RELATIONSHIPS. Does the company have foreign investors or joint venture partners? If so, what are the benefits? Foreign partners might provide technology transfer, management assistance, markets for the company's goods, or simply money.

A foreign firm may even provide a brand, as in the hotel business, where a local company builds a hotel and runs it with help from Sheraton or Intercontinental. The new hotel has immediate name recognition and the benefits of an international reservation system and "frequent-guest" programs.

HIDDEN ASSETS. Finding hidden assets in emerging market companies is hard work, but can be rewarding. Serious investors begin by doing everything short of sleeping with the financial statement under their pillows. The casual investor, for example, might not discover that the subsidiary is worth more than the parent company.

As in the United States, the book values might not reflect the true value of fixed assets such as land, machinery, and stock holdings. Assets such as real estate holdings in an emerging world capital may hold hidden value.

Hidden value may be lodged in "warehoused" assets. An agricultural conglomerate with a large land bank may include acreage with potential residential or commercial value, a site for an infrastructure project, even a mining project. The same is true of banks that hold portfolios of foreclosed properties, and labor unions and pension funds that may own property purchased for investment, awarded by the government, or paid out as a settlement in a labor dispute.

NAME BRAND OR CORPORATE ISSUE IN THE MAKING? Few emerging market companies have succeeded in establishing worldwide brand names. It does happen occasionally: Corona beer from Mexico, Concha y Toro wines from Chile, and Jaffa oranges from Israel. Korea's Goldstar has brand recognition in consumer electronics. There are more to come.

FINANCIAL STATEMENTS. Read the company's annual reports, press releases, and presentations to industry, government, and financial institutions to get a feel for future plans, future capital needs, and sources of capital. Again, these are emerging market companies, so don't be surprised if these data are scarce. You may indeed be obliged to pay the company a visit.

HISTORICAL DATA on price, standard deviations, valuations, correlation with the local market index, and liquidity.

SHARE OWNERSHIP. How much is held by insiders? Are the principal shareholders a founding family? Are any of the shares held by institutions? If so, what is the makeup? Mutual funds? Pension funds? Merchant banks? Money managers? Investors have different objectives and investment horizons. A mutual fund may not be able to hold the position if faced with a run of redemptions caused by poor performance or a market sell-off. During the Mexican peso crisis, many fund managers reluctantly liquidated holdings at bargain prices as panicked investors rushed for the exits and withdrew their money.

COUNTRY RISK. Do not forget to factor country risks into your investment decision. A bottom-up investor must also be involved in country selection. No investor can reasonably be expected to look for stocks in every emerging market. When narrowing your focus to specific countries, you are, of course, engaging in a practice that will affect your risk. See Chapter 13 for a detailed discussion of country risks.

ADVICE FROM THE PROS

Here are some tips from the experts on selecting emerging market stocks.

CREATE A BARGAIN LIST. Use process, style, and screening techniques to generate a list of stocks to follow, not necessarily to buy. Your list might be as small as 25 companies, or as large as 200, depending on the amount of time and capital available. Favor stocks with good long-term prospects that justify the effort, rather than "hot-money" stocks that offer a one-time buying opportunity.

DON'T RELY SOLELY ON BROKERAGE REPORTS. There are often conflicts of interest between research and investment banking departments. Aggressive investment bankers seeking new business and the chance to manage privatizations sometimes put pressure on research departments to avoid critical reports.

Much of the available research is in the "top-ten" stocks. Don't expect the same depth and insight you are accustomed to finding in U.S. and European markets.

DON'T ASSUME EVERY ANALYST AND FUND MANAGER IS AN EXPERT. Demand for emerging market research analysts has been strong, and the ranks include many who are relatively inexperienced. Some are barely out of B-school, while others are covering unfamiliar markets.

MAINTAIN A HEALTHY SKEPTICISM TOWARD LOCAL BROKERS. Local brokers who trade on exchanges that don't forbid "front running" or enforce rules against it will often build inventory in a stock and then begin touting it to emerging market buyers around the world.

WATCH COMMISSIONS. Commissions are generally higher overseas than in the United States. Negotiate and be on guard against double dips—one commission to your broker and another to a foreign affiliate. Ask if there are any other charges.

FIND OUT WHO THE INTERMEDIARIES ARE. An emerging market trade rarely involves a single institution. Custodians and/or other brokers are involved. Firms can and do run into problems, such as the case of the brokerage firm whose failure single-handedly resulted in a crash on the Athens Stock Exchange. Ask your broker about the institution handling the trade and for assurances regarding reputability and stability.

TRADING IS IMPROVING. Custodians are becoming more trustworthy and efficient. Competition is driving fees down, and improving communications means quicker, more reliable executions.

DON'T ASSUME "EVERYONE'S WATCHING." Despite all the time, money, and effort spent looking for emerging market opportunities, many situations are overlooked. You may know something the market doesn't. Look for opportunities where all the positive news is not reflected in the price.

Stocks followed by fewer than eight analysts are called "underfollowed stocks," and they offer the greatest opportunities. Fewer institutions are likely to participate. While this may add to volatility and lower valuations, it also creates opportunity.

LOOK AT CASH FLOWS. Cash flows are less susceptible to financial statement manipulations. EBIDTA, or earnings before interest, depreciation, taxes, and amortization, is one of the best measures when comparing emerging market stocks "cross-border," or historically.

USE SECTOR VALUATIONS FOR COMPARISONS. Although historical data on an emerging market stock may be thin, you can often learn a great deal by looking at its position—and valuation—relative to the stock's industrial sector, locally and globally.

BE PRACTICAL. Don't buy shares in markets and companies that are difficult to follow. If you don't have the time, resources, or money, pass on the opportunity.

GET USED TO WORKING WITH LESS. Emerging market investing demands flexibility. Money managers often make decisions based on much less data than they are accustomed to in developed markets.

DON'T ASSUME ALL INVESTORS THINK ALIKE. In the United States, we are familiar with concepts such as "profit-taking," "tight-money policies," "year-end tax selling," and other market-moving phrases that describe actions taken by thousands of investors. By contrast, local emerging market investors often respond differently. They have less experience, and they often differ in their goals and approach. For example, emerging market investors tend to be "holders"; they don't trade as often as Americans. Many believe the stock should not be sold for less than they believe it is worth, regardless of the market cap.

PRIVATIZATION DEALS OFTEN BEHAVE LIKE HOT IPOs. In theory, privatization should produce opportunities for value investors. Many are bloated, money-losing, and inefficient state-run enterprises. The privatization effort provides the funds and freedom to cut expenses, modernize, and bring in talented management. Government, investors, and the private sector have a stake in the outcome.

Unfortunately, the shares are usually priced to reflect the future value of the company, as if the turnaround had already succeeded. Why? A combination of factors: Prestigious investment bankers conduct high-profile road shows, promoting the shares. These stocks are widely anticipated and followed by many analysts, so there is a great deal of information available. Money managers and institutions prefer widely followed companies.

In general, avoid buying new-issue privatizations. Let them trade awhile.

In certain cases you can take a position *before* a large privatization deal. Some state-owned companies are already public, although the state still owns most of the stock. You can buy and sell shares in anticipation that the government will increase private ownership through an offering.

STUDY THE MARKET CONSENSUS. Do most analysts agree on earnings and growth forecasts? Or is there a wide range of estimates? The answer always reveals something about the market's perception of the company. If there is signficant disagreement among analysts, you may be able to improve on the information available to the market by doing your own research, and you may find a bargain that has been overlooked. While I haven't conducted a formal survey, I have noticed a greater variance in opinions when it comes to emerging market stocks.

If a strong consensus exists, it is likely that the forecast is more reliable and that the share price reflects that consensus. Again, your own research might tell another story.

"DECONSTRUCT" ASSETS. Many emerging market companies have numerous affiliates, a legacy from an earlier era when ruling family dynasties controlled many sources of wealth. Break down the company into individual assets and try to determine what these assets might sell for privately. Private companies are usually priced at lower multiples than public firms, so your valuations are more likely to be conservative. Many of these companies are in the process of reorganizing and will probably sell off some of their divisions, so this information will also help you determine the company's breakup value.

DON'T IGNORE THE TAX IMPLICATIONS. Most emerging market companies withhold tax from dividends, as required by their governments. The rates can be as high as 35 percent, but are often lower in countries that have signed tax treaties with the United States, usually around 15 percent. Tax on interest income and capital gains is less prevalent, but you should check.

Ask two questions before investing: How will taxation affect my return? And how will this investment impact on my U.S. taxes? In most cases, the overall tax implications will be less when buying stocks in "tax-treaty" countries. However, yields are often higher in nontreaty countries.

In addition to the world's major economies, quite a few emerging markets are tax-treaty signatories: China, South Korea, India, Indonesia, Pakistan, and the Philippines in Asia; Egypt, Israel, Morocco, and Tunisia in the Middle East; and Mexico in North America. As of this writing, Thailand, Turkey, and South Africa are in negotiations with the United States. The region with the fewest tax-treaty partners is the one closest to us: Central and South America.

Tax treatment information on ADRs is readily available from the sponsors. Your brokerage firm or custodian should be able to assist you on stocks traded on local exchanges. You can also contact the local stock exchange. Many have Web sites and are quite responsive. If you aren't a U.S. taxpayer, check with your national tax authority on the tax-treaty status and withholding rate of the emerging market in question.

If you plan to buy an emerging market stock that carries potential foreign tax implications, don't use a retirement or other tax-free account. You won't get the benefit of the foreign tax credit against your U.S. tax payment.

If you haven't seen an emerging market company's financial statement, you probably shouldn't buy the stock.

EMERGING MARKET CHECKLIST[5]

Company Background Data

- ❑ When was the company founded? Listed?
- ❑ Number of shareholders, shares issued and outstanding, trading volume, price history?
- ❑ Who are the principal shareholders? In what proportion? Purpose of investment?
- ❑ Lines of business, major and minor. Market share and ranking within industry, in country, region, and worldwide. Does it export?
- ❑ How is the company regarded by emerging market analysts and institutions. Regular coverage? Occasional? Ignored? Emerging market "blue chip"?
- ❑ Pending corporate activity. New capital raising? If so, debt, equity, IPO, secondary? Mergers or acquisitions? Privatization?
- ❑ Subsidiaries?

Financial

- ❑ Operating margins?
- ❑ Key ratios: Return on Equity (ROE), Return on Assets (ROA), current ratio, interest coverage, asset turnover?
- ❑ Ratios improving or shrinking?
- ❑ Adequate capital to finance growth?
- ❑ Historical and current trends in sales, earnings, and receivables?
- ❑ Financial sensitivity to interest rate and inflation changes?

❏ Hidden assets?

❏ Hidden liabilities, income and/or receivables in the form of loans from or to affiliates?

❏ Hidden transactions? Affiliates used to siphon profits, move blocks of cash, or transfer liabilities or assets?

Current Valuation

❏ Valuation ratios: p/e, p/cash flow, dividend yield, p/bv, p/sales, as compared with market, local and worldwide industry, and historical data?

❏ Quality of earnings? How much due to inflation, extraordinary items, revenue from subsidiaries?

❏ Based on above analysis, is company attractively priced?

Growth Potential

❏ Earnings rising? Are sales growing? Is the growth rate accelerating?

❏ Is the growth based on sustainable long-term trends or temporary or short-term situations?

❏ Do the overall conditions in the country and the company's overall market favor growth? Long-term or short-term?

❏ Do earnings follow a cyclical pattern?

❏ Nature of earnings? From operations? Extraordinary items? Accounting "tricks"?

❏ Are profit margins increasing? Is productivity increasing?

❏ Is the company investing in R&D? How much, as a percentage of sales?

❏ Is the company reinvesting its profits?

Possible "Overlooked" Situation

❏ Is there a hidden asset play?

❏ Is the company on the verge of turnaround? Restructuring? Change in management? New product? Change in target market? Fresh capital? A pending deal with the labor unions?

❏ Has institutional research overlooked certain positive factors? A major concession from a provincial government? An alliance or partnership?

Impact of Economic Regulation

❏ Is it part of a cartel or monopoly about to be broken up? Will such a move create more or fewer competitors? How strong will they be?

❏ Is the company dependent on government "protective" measures that are about to be lifted? What will be the impact?

❏ If a government contractor, has the current situation resulted in slow, deferred, or canceled payments? Is there a trend in this direction?

❏ Will free or liberalized trade spur or retard growth? Can the company compete with imports? Do its products have a ready export market?

❏ What is the current and future state of privatizations? Will the privatization create powerful new competitors? Will it create merger-and-acquisition opportunities?

❏ Has there been an increase or decrease in capital inflows to the market? Is the trend positive or negative? Do capital inflows have an impact on sales and earnings?

❏ Are foreign firms establishing themselves in this market? Are they making acquisitions and forming joint ventures? Is the company a potential candidate?

Competitiveness

❏ Does the company enjoy a technological advantage in the market? In the region? Worldwide? Is this advantage increasing or declining?

❏ If the company is lagging technologically, what is being done to close the gap?

❏ What is the nature of its competitive advantages? Low labor costs? Low raw material costs? Proximity to primary markets? Low energy costs? Supplier to growing industrial sector? Government contractor? Holder of valuable license?

❏ Are these competitive advantages becoming firmer or are they weakening? Are labor costs and commodity or energy costs rising? Government contracts to open bid process? Licenses expiring?

❏ How vulnerable to competition? Are imports competitive? Will newly formed domestic competition and foreign subsidiaries enjoy competitive advantages that threaten company's market share?

❏ Are any of the current or future competitors "world class"?

❏ What are the current trends among existing competitors? Are they becoming more efficient? Are they well capitalized? What is their cost structure?

❏ Has inflation, currency, or other economic issues altered the competitive picture?

❏ Can the company compete with others in expansion? Can it borrow or sell equity at comparable terms? Can it generate similar or superior economies of scale?

Management

❏ Is the organizational structure consistent with the best-managed companies in the industry?

❏ What is the depth of management experience and training? Does management have work experience in other markets?

❏ What is the nature of key management training? Academic? Technical? Local or abroad? Degrees attained? On-the-job training?

❏ Is the company managed by the founder? Is he or she a professional manager or entrepreneur? What is the level of family involvement in day-to-day management and key decision making?

❏ Overall reputation of management for honesty, reliability, negotiating skills, and internal management of the firm's human resources?

Labor, Plant and Equipment

❏ Are the plants well designed in accordance with the latest manufacturing techniques and plant-design innovations?

❏ Is the physical plant clean and well maintained?

❏ Is the machinery comparable to that of world-class competitors? If not, how much of a disadvantage does this create?

❏ Is the machinery compatible with world standards? How important? If the company supplies parts and components, this could be very important. If it makes a finished product, it would be less so.

❏ How effective is the company's quality control? Does it equal or exceed industry standards?

❏ Is the physical plant computerized and automated?

❏ What is the overall state of labor relations? Has the company been subjected to strike actions, slowdowns, or "sick-outs"? Have any been threatened? Are any expected?

❏ Any upcoming major labor negotiations? Are labor and management far apart?

❏ What is the skill level of employees? How does it compare with competitors?

❏ Is employee turnover high or low? Reasons?

❏ Is the company reliant on imported labor? Are there any pending regulations that could cut off this labor source?

Regulatory Issues

❏ Who audits the firm's books? Is the firm internationally recognized? Is it an affiliate or a correspondent of an international accounting firm? What is the firm's reputation in its home market? What is its record on accounting malpractice?

❏ Are financial reporting and accounting standards different from the accepted local norm? From the industry? Different from those of the United States?

❏ Impact of local accounting standards and techniques: inflation accounting, valuing assets, definition of book value, treatment of dividends, etc.?

❏ Subsidiaries consolidated? Listed or unlisted? Have you examined available financial statements of subsidiaries?

❏ Any upcoming or recent changes in accounting methods? Impact?

ENDNOTES

1. Much of the data on Korea Mobile Telecom come from Michael Schuman and E. S. Browning, staff reporters, "Heard on the Street: Some Still Wary of Downfallen Korea Mobile," *The Wall Street Journal,* December 4, 1996.

2. Zouikin, Tania, "Do US Styles Work in Other Markets?" Investment Research News, Batterymarch Financial Management, Inc., available on the Batterymarch World Wide Web site.

3. Kumar, Punita, "Quantitative Models in Emerging Markets Stock Selection," *Investment Research News, Batterymarch Financial Management Inc.,* 2/3 (1996).

4. Joan Warner with Dave Lindorff, "Developing Markets Have a Life of Their Own," *BusinessWeek* (June 17, 1996).

5. Based in part on material in *The World's Emerging Stock Markets,* by Keith K.H. Park and Antoine van Agtmael, Chicago, Illinois, Probus, 1993. This is an excellent work by two seasoned emerging market pros.

Analyzing the Risks

While the inherent risks in emerging market stocks are technically no different from those in industrialized nations, they carry the added risks of their locales. Since these nations are less stable, investors must include an additional factor—*country risk*—in their securities analyses.

Country risk and its by-products, such as inflation, organized violence, labor strife and even revolution, create special problems for investors. While such events aren't common, they are much more likely in emerging markets than in developed nations. The United States has racial tensions, labor-management confrontations, and a healthy share of government corruption. It does not, however have hyperinflation, "ethnic cleansing," general strikes that paralyze the nation, and national leaders looting billions from the Treasury.

Emerging market political "disasters" are less probable, because the world of "banana republics" and "outlaw nations" is nearly at an end. In spite of the persistence of hot spots around the world and indescribable cruelties and atrocities, events that destabilize economies and dramatically alter local financial markets are rare. Singular events rarely change investment fundamentals in a single stroke.

Occasionally, the unthinkable happens. In November 1996, the Athens Stock Exchange closed for three days when a local brokerage firm failed to pay $10 million in settlements, a paltry sum by Wall Street standards. The downing of two "Brothers to the Rescue" aircraft by the Cuban government put an end to many plans for American direct investment there. At least one closed-end fund failed to get off the ground, and another had to change its strategy. Investors shuddered when Peruvian

Tupamaro rebels seized the Japanese embassy and took dozens of hostages.

Emerging market country risk can also have an impact on stock prices in advanced nations. A crisis in the Middle East, for example, might result in higher oil prices, triggering a sell-off in airline stocks on fears that those rising fuel prices will cut into profit margins.

This book is about investments, not politics, so we will examine the risks of emerging markets purely from the vantage point of investment opportunities. This chapter covers the political, economic, and social risks that affect investment in a particular country or region. Other risk factors—common to all global investments, such as liquidity, currency, and portfolio risk—are discussed elsewhere.

Rank Dec-9	Rank Sept	Weighting	Total score Dec	Change from Sept	Economic performance	Political risk	Debt indicators	Debt in default or rescheduled	Credit ratings	Access to bank finance	Access to short-term finance	Access to capital markets	Discount on forfeiting
1	1	United States	99.45	-0.55	24.56	25	10	10	10	5	5	5	4.9
2	2	Luxembourg	99.13	0.24	25	24.7	10	10	10	5	5	5	4.42
3	3	Netherlands	98.33	0.35	24.16	24.46	10	10	10	5	5	5	4.71
4	5	Norway	98.2	1.65	24.18	24.37	10	10	10	5	5	5	4.65
5	4	United Kingdom	97.79	0.17	23.07	24.82	10	10	10	5	5	5	4.9
6	7	Germany	96.2	0.84	21.33	24.97	10	10	10	5	5	5	4.9
7	12	Switzerland	96.07	2.38	21.33	24.84	10	10	10	5	5	5	4.9
8	6	Canada	95.94	0.52	23.58	23.91	10	10	8.96	5	5	4.5	5
9	8	Denmark	95.5	0.43	22.79	24.16	10	10	9.38	5	5	4.5	4.67
10	9	Austria	95.12	0.76	21.5	23.91	10	10	10	5	5	5	4.71
11	14	France	94.76	1.81	20.83	24.03	10	10	10	5	5	5	4.9
12	10	Ireland	94.37	0.59	23.58	22.41	10	10	9.17	5	5	4.5	4.71
13	15	Finland	94.18	1.4	22.93	22.92	10	10	9.17	5	5	4.5	4.67
14	16	Belgium	93.18	0.96	21.19	23.41	10	10	9.38	5	5	4.5	4.71
15	21	Sweden	92.94	2.2	22.22	23.01	10	10	8.54	5	5	4.5	4.67
16	11	Singapore	92.66	-1.07	22.07	21.91	10	10	9.69	5	5	4.75	4.24
17	18	Australia	92.16	0.63	21.02	22.69	10	10	8.75	5	5	5	4.71

Table 13-1. Euromoney Magazine's Country Risk Rating, November, 1997. *Source: Euromoney magazine.*

Rank		Weighting	Total score Dec	Change from Sept	Economic performance	Political risk	Debt indicators	Debt in default or rescheduled	Credit ratings	Access to bank finance	Access to short-term finance	Access to capital markets	Discount on forfeiting
Dec-7	Sept												
18	13	Japan	92.15	-0.84	18.61	24.27	10	10	10	5	5	4.5	4.76
19	19	Spain	91.86	0.52	22.12	21.81	10	10	8.75	5	5	4.5	4.68
20	17	New Zealand	91.55	-0.65	20.44	22.03	10	10	9.38	5	5	5	4.71
21	20	Portugal	90.52	-0.53	21.97	21.45	10	10	8.13	5	5	4.5	4.48
22	23	Italy	89.8	2.87	20.22	22.07	10	10	8.33	5	5	4.5	4.67
23	22	Taiwan	88.19	-0.13	21.08	21.16	10	10	8.75	5	5	3	4.21
24	24	Iceland	86.74	0.9	20.73	19.9	10	10	7.81	5	5	4	4.3
25	25	Hong Kong	85.24	-0.26	19.92	20.21	10	10	7.08	5	5	4	4.03
26	26	Cyprus	81.7	0.49	19.29	17.92	10	10	7.5	5	5	3	3.99
27	31	United Arab Emirates	81.4	4.13		10	10	5.63	5	5	3	3.87	td
28	34	Kuwait	81.18	4.98	20.18	18.01	10	10	6.46	5	4.67	3	3.86
29	58	Bermuda	80.45	22.4	18.91	19.08	10	10	8.96	5	5	3.5	0
30	27	South Korea	78.29	-1.96	17.47	17.65	10	10	7.29	5	5	2.5	3.37
31	29	Chile	78.01	-0.22	18.9	18.37	8.7	10	6.04	4.62	3.83	3	4.54
32	30	Greece	77.28	-0.56	17.56	17.02	10	10	5	5	5	3.5	4.2
33	33	Israel	77.27	0.69	17.13	17.31	10	10	6.25	5	4.58	3.25	3.75

Table 13-1. *(cont.)*

Rank Dec-7	Rank Sept	Weighting	Total score Dec	Change from Sept	Economic performance	Political risk	Debt indicators	Debt in default or rescheduled	Credit ratings	Access to bank finance	Access to short-term finance	Access to capital markets	Discount on forfeiting
34	35	Saudi Arabia	76.53	2.28	18.02	17.11	10	10	4.38	5	4.67	3.5	3.86
35	28	Malaysia	76.44	-3	17.29	17.1	9.2	10	7.5	4.09	4.17	3.5	3.6
36	32	Brunei	76.07	-1.15	17.46	20.83	10	10	0	5	4.67	3.75	4.37
37	36	Slovenia	75.15	2.18	17.94	16.33	9.55	10	6.46	3.47	3.92	3.25	4.23
38	39	Mauritius	73.48	2.18	23.28	16.34	9.12	10	5	1.12	3.83	2	2.79
39	40	China	72.81	1.52	19.41	17.5	9.49	10	5.94	0.06	2.83	3.5	4.07
40	50	Bahamas	72.8	8.7	16.87	16.17	10	10	6.25	5	5	3.5	0
41	42	Qatar	72.68	2.85	14.6	16.4	10	10	5	5	4.67	3.25	3.77
42	45	Bahrain	72.06	4.55	16.35	15.38	10	10	3.75	5	4.67	3	3.92
43	48	Oman	71.69	5.04	18.28	17.17	9.38	10	4.69	0	5	3.25	3.92
44	37	Czech Republic	71.23	-0.49	16.6	16.39	9.2	10	6.25	2.41	3.17	3.18	4.04
45	41	Hungary	70.8	0.82	17.88	15.11	7.92	10	4.58	5	2.83	3.5	3.97
46	44	South Africa	70.6	2.77	16.39	14.58	10	10	3.75	5	3.83	3	4.05
47			68.73	-2.65	21.47	18.46	0	10	7.08	0	5	2.5	4.22
48	47	Poland	68.05	1.4	18.3	15.33	9.16	10	4.58	0.28	3	3.25	4.15
49	43	Indonesia	65.45	-3.42	16.11	14.39	8.36	10	4.38	2.88	3.83	2.5	3
50	51	Mexico	65.34	1.9	16.99	13.87	8.37	10	3.13	2.44	3.58	2.75	4.22

Table 13–1. (cont.)

Rank Dec-7	Rank Sept	Weighting		Total score Dec	Change from Sept	Economic performance	Political risk	Debt indicators	Debt in default or rescheduled	Credit ratings	Access to bank finance	Access to short-term finance	Access to capital markets	Discount on forfaiting
51	46	Thailand		65.13	-1.71	13.89	14.08	9.23	10	5.31	3.85	3.83	1.5	3.43
52	56	Tunisia		65.03	5.17	17.25	14.91	8.74	10	4.38	0.14	3.75	2	3.87
53	53	India		64.48	3.1	15.81	15.09	8.84	10	4.06	0.28	3.75	2.5	4.15
54	52	Argentina		64.09	0.93	16.43	13.91	8.59	9.93	2.92	0.68	4.33	3.25	4.05
55	60	Panama		63.2	6	17.09	13.15	8.49	10	4.69	0	3.42	2	4.37
56	55	Colombia		63.14	2.87	14.07	14.6	8.91	10	4.38	1.8	2.17	3	4.22
57	49	Philippines		63.05	-1.57	15.47	14.64	8.84	10	3.75	1.05	3.67	2.25	3.39
58	57	Uruguay		62.24	3.73	14.55	14.54	8.91	10	4.38	0.33	3.67	2.5	3.37
59	69	Turkey		62.23	9.46	12.72	18.82	8.63	10	1.67	0.84	3.58	3	2.97
60	63	Estonia		61.77	5.23	16.08	12.75	9.88	10	5.31	0	2.21	2.5	3.03
61	54	Slovak Republic		61.63	1.27	14.86	13.78	9.28	10	4.38	0.31	2.63	2.5	3.91
62	64	Egypt		60.54	5.12	16.02	14.14	8.59	9.72	3.96	0	2.67	2	3.45
63	67	Botswana		59.54	6.1	18.55	15.96	9.7	10	0	0	3.83	1.5	0
64	59	Latvia		59.06	1.35	14.79	11.89	9.85	10	5	0	2.21	2.5	2.82
65	65	El Salvador		58.53	4.37	15.71	11.48	9.38	10	3.75	0	3.33	0.5	4.37
66	68	Jordan		58.4	4.98	19.01	12.87	7.91	8.93	2.5	0	2	1.75	3.43
67	61	Brazil		58.2	1.48	14.56	12.6	8.63	10	2.08	1.43	2	3	3.91

Table 13-1. *(cont.)*

Rank		Weighting	Total score Dec	Change from Sept	Economic performance	Political risk	Debt indicators	Debt in default or rescheduled	Credit ratings	Access to bank finance	Access to short-term finance	Access to capital markets	Discount on forfeiting
Dec-7	Sept												
68	76	Costa Rica	57.82	7.52	14.98	13.06	8.96	10	3.44	0.09	3.67	1	2.62
69	66	Morocco	57.75	3.96	16.23	13.5	8.14	10	0	0.19	3.42	2.5	3.78
70	62	Lithuania	57.43	0.77	14.29	12.27	9.81	10	3.75	0	2.21	2.25	2.86
71	71	Venezuela	55.74	3.58	12.95	12.43	8.74	10	2.5	0.09	3	2.5	3.53
72	70	Croatia	54.47	1.79	14.55	11.66	9.55	4.36	4.38	1.37	2.19	2.75	3.65
73	74	Lebanon	53.6	2.84	12.58	11.3	9.24	10	2.5	0.34	2.17	2	3.48
74	75	Romania	52.96	2.48	12.42	10.74	9.44	10	2.5	0.42	2.29	1.75	3.41
75	78	Peru	52.52	2.44	12.76	11.45	8.83	9.29	1.25	0.19	3	2	3.75
76	73	Guatemala	52.15	1.18	12.51	10.78	9.4	10	3.13	0	3.42	0.5	2.42
77	77	Vietnam	51.46	1.21	13.28	11.02	8.04	10	2.5	0	1.5	0.75	4.37
78	79	Russia	50.72	0.98	12.66	9.87	9.31	8.73	3.13	0	2.13	2.75	2.14
79	86	Ghana	49.58	4	14.67	10.75	8.05	10	0	0	2.67	0.5	2.95
80	81	Fiji	48.98	0.29	14.84	11	9.65	10	0	0	3	0.5	0
81	80	Paraguay	48.08	-0.71	10.47	11.97	9.39	10	2.5	0.01	3.25	0.5	0
82	85	Kazakhstan	48.04	2.13	10.87	9.36	9.56	10	2.5	0.16	1.78	2.25	1.56
83	84	Sri Lanka	47.78	1.49	10.26	11.51	8.92	10	0	0	2.67	1.5	2.92
84	89	Bolivia	47.67	3.61	13.14	10.63	7.95	9.11	0	0.9	2	1.25	2.68
85		Puerto Rico	47.39	-0.04	0	16.39	10	10	0	5	5	1	0

Table 13-1. (cont.)

Rank		Weighting	Total score Dec	Change from Sept	Economic performance	Political risk	Debt indicators	Debt in default or rescheduled	Credit ratings	Access to bank finance	Access to short-term finance	Access to capital markets	Discount on forfeiting
Dec-7	Sept												
86	95	Jamaica	47.07	7.81	13.82	10.08	7.64	9.41	0	1.36	3.25	1.5	0
87	83	Papua New Guinea	46.86	-0.15	11.78	11.63	8.72	10	0	1.23	3	0.5	0
88	88	Pakistan	46.37	1.86	10.55	9.41	8.58	10	1.56	0.97	1.67	1.25	2.39
89	129	Barbados	45.63	15.72	13.82	13.23	0	10	3.75	0	3.83	1	0
90	101	Uganda	44.97	8.02	18.18	6.55	8.53	8.87	0	0	2.33	0.5	0
91	103	Nepal	43.91	7.3	10.91	8.26	9.04	10	0	0	3.17	0.5	2.03
92	94	Uzbekistan	43.35	3.94	12.87	5.99	9.76	10	0	0	1.78	1.5	1.45
93	87	Bangladesh	42.5	-2.13	8.51	9.4	8.86	10	0	0	2.67	0.5	2.56
94	108	Vanuatu	42.41	7.45	10.18	9.42	9.64	10	0	0	3.17	0	0
95	92	Zimbabwe	42.24	1.36	12.22	9.59	0	10	0	2.9	3.5	1.25	2.78
96	93	Kenya	42.17	1.7	10.09	8.47	7.94	10	0	0	2.67	0.75	2.25
97	100	Cote d'Ivoire	41.8	4.81	13.94	8.68	5.9	9.52	0	0.76	2	1	0
98	104	Gabon	41.4	4.99	13.82	9.97	7.91	7.7	0	0	2	0	0
99	72	Trinidad & Tobago	41.1	-9.91	0	13.9	8.87	10	3.75	0	3.33	1.25	0
100	99	Ecuador	40.84	3.74	11.4	10.13	8.1	0	1.88	0.99	3.25	2	3.09

Table 13–1. (cont.)

THE KEY RISK FACTORS IN
EMERGING MARKET INVESTING

The three principal measures of risk for emerging markets are *political* risk, *economic* risk, and *financial* risk.

1. **Political risk** measures forces such as government policy and leadership, internal and external conflict, tensions, political parties, and bureaucracy.

2. **Economic risk** is concerned with factors that affect and predict the economic health of the country such as inflation, current account balance, exchange rates, national debt, and so forth.

3. **Financial risk** is concerned with the factors affecting financial and business transactions, such as payment history of public and private institutions, the sanctity of contracts, and treatment of loan defaults.

These risk factors are interconnected. For example, if the population of a country is poor, and it is seething with rage against the government, political risk might increase as some advocate forceful overthrow of the government. This occurred in 1996 in Chiapas State in Mexico. If poverty forces increased government spending for welfare programs or a slackening in demand for consumer goods, the effect might be increased economic risk. If the burden of poverty leads to government difficulties in meeting its financial obligations on sovereign debt, the result will be increasing financial risk.

Political risk measurements tend to be subjective in nature. There is no reliable, purely quantitative statistical method with which to measure political risk. Some firms provide opinions based on the work of in-house experts, while others poll a select group and factor in the consensus. One form of political risk analysis might rely on an expert's assessment of the corruption in Asia, while another might poll outside experts and incorporate the results into its risk analysis.

Economic risk measurement involves a more straightforward analysis of economic indicators. Much of the data needed to make a reasonable assessment of the economic condition of a country are readily available in the business press and on the Internet (see Appendix C). Risk experts occasionally rely on polling and use proprietary data.

Financial risk can be assessed by a set of statistics, but certain factors, such as the ease of completing transactions, may require some subjective conclusions.

A Basic Political Risk Questionnaire

The following questions are designed to address issues raised in professional political risk analysis. Take the time to complete the questionnaire and you will be rewarded with a reasonable overview of the country's political risk outlook:

1. How stable is the country's government and political system?

2. Is policy making an orderly process, or is it based on the whim of one or several all-powerful leaders?

3. Is there festering discontent among the population?

4. Are there any religious, ethnic, or linguistic tensions? If so, are they severe? Have they ever or are they likely to result in violence? (Examples: Serb/Croat/Bosnian in Bosnia, Hindu/Muslim in India.)

5. Is the country threatened by terrorism or organized criminal elements?

6. Does the current regime resort to oppressive measures and coercion to maintain power? (Examples: Myanmar, Romania.)

7. How strong is the opposition? Is the electorate divided into many political factions, making it difficult to form coalition governments?

8. How strong is the left-wing element? The right wing?

9. Are labor unions deeply involved in politics?

10. Are the military or organized religious factions involved in politics?

11. Does the government have a history of stability or instability? How orderly has succession been? Does the government have a history of policy continuity and consistency?

12. Does the government have a history of nationalizing private businesses or expropriating private investments? Of privatizing state-owned enterprises?

13. Is the population very nationalistic? Is there widespread corruption or nepotism in government?

14. Is the country dependent on an outside major power? Are regional forces important? (Examples: Islamic fundamentalism throughout the Middle East; Clinton's willingness to brave Congressional opposition and structure a rescue plan for Mexico.)

15. Has the government raised economic expectations? (Example: Russian leaders have promised better times under capitalism.)

16. Are social conditions a source of discontent or do they reinforce the status quo?

17. Consider overall living standards, wealth and income distribution, labor conditions, unionization, literacy, the welfare system, and urbanization trends.

Useful Data for Determining Financial and Economic Risk

Most of this information is widely available on the Internet and in leading financial publications (see Appendix C).

Current account deficit	Export mix (types of goods)
GDP growth	Short-term credit
Reserves	Amount and nature of foreign debt
Exports	Debt in default
Budget deficit	Debt rescheduled
Convertibility of currency	Credit rating–sovereign debt
Inflation rate	Credit rating–provincial
GDP per capita	Credit rating–structured finance
Savings rate	Inflow and outflow of portfolio investment
Budget discipline	Performance of public sector

The following data are harder to gather, but several international law, accounting, and consulting firms conduct surveys to assess the business environment for clients. Many firms distribute summaries to the news media and make copies available to the public on request.

Attitudes toward foreign investors	Bureaucratic delays
Enforceability of contracts	Suspicious loans and grants
Ease of communications and transport	Political pressure on economic decisions
Skill of local management	The role of political pressure in economic policy
Corruption in business and government	

OTHER FORMS OF RISK

CREDIT RISK. Basically, a subset of financial risk, credit risk is a measure of creditworthiness, that is, a country's credit rating. Credit rating is essentially subjective, as it is determined by bankers and underwriters who use a variety of measurements to rate the creditor. *Institutional Investor* determines credit rating by asking a group of leading international bankers to rate each country on a scale of 0 to 100, but it doesn't tell them how to do it. The publication averages the ratings, assigning weights to ratings, based on reliability. Bankers with more at risk in the country are given higher weights, as are those with more sophisticated methods of analyzing credit.

Credit ratings from various rating services tend to agree. Research by Claude Erb, Campbell Harvey, and Viskanta Tadas[1] found a 95 percent correlation between Moody's, S&P, and *Institutional Investor* ratings.

Bankers and stock market investors share the same concerns. Like investors, bankers are concerned with the future and only the future. Their money is at risk, and they must anticipate problems that might occur during the loan period. Their ratings are used to estimate the probability of default, which in turn determines the interest rate that a country will have to pay. Often, tens of millions are riding on their decisions.

Many of the factors taken into account in a credit risk measure are also likely to affect the stock market. Therefore, country credit risk is a solid, useful measurement for emerging market equity investors. It is not surprising that fear of a credit-rating change can cause markets to fluctuate, as when in November 1996 the Thai equity market fell to a 39-month low, largely over concerns of a ratings downgrade.

	Moody's	*S & P*	*Institutional Investor**
Hong Kong	A3	A	65.3
Singapore	Aa1	AAA	83.7
South Korea	A1	AA-	72.1
Taiwan	Aa3	AA+	77.5
Bangladesh	-	-	26.9
China	A3	BBB	57.2
India	Baa3	BB+	46.3
Indonesia	Baa3	BBB	52.2

Table 13–2. Emerging Markets Credit Ratings. *Source: New Horizon Economies,* Union Bank of Switzerland, 2nd Quarter 1997, Institutional Investor, Moody Investor Services, Standard & Poors.

	Moody's	*S & P*	*Institutional Investor**
Malaysia	A1	A+	67.7
Pakistan	B2	B+	29.2
Philippines	Ba2	BB+	40.5
Sri Lanka	-	-	33.7
Thailand	A2	A	63.2
Vietnam	-	-	32.8
Argentina	B1	BB-	38.9
Brazil	B1	B+	39.3
Chile	Baa1	A-	61.2
Colombia	Baa3	BBB-	26.4
Ecuador	-	-	26.4
Mexico	Ba2	BB	41.6
Panama	Ba1	BB+	28.5
Peru	B2	-	30.0
Venezuela	Ba2	B	32.0
Bulgaria	B3	-	23.5
Croatia	Baa3	BBB-	26.0
Czech Republic	Baa1	A	62.0
Estonia	-	-	31.1
Hungary	Baa3	BBB-	44.7
Latvia	-	BBB-	25.7
Lithuania	Ba2	-	25.3
Poland	Baa3	BBB-	44.0
Romania	Ba3	BB-	31.0
Slovakia	Baa3	BB+	41.2
Slovenia	A3	A	49.9
Kazakhstan	-	-	19.6
Russia	Ba2	BB-	21.4
Ukraine	-	-	16.6
Uzbekistan	-	-	16.1
Greece	Baa1	BBB-	50.3
Italy	Aa3	AA	72.4
Portugal	Aa3	AA-	69.2
Spain	Aa2	AA	73.6

Table 13–2. *(cont.)*

	Moody's	S & P	Institutional Investor*
Egypt	Ba2	BBB-	35.1
Israel	A3	A-	52.2
Jordan	Ba3	BB-	33.1
Morocco	-	-	39.3
Saudi Arabia	Baa3	-	55.1
Turkey	Ba3	B	41.1
Côte d'Ivoire	-	-	18.5
Ghana	-	-	29.6
Kenya	-	-	27.9
Nigeria	-	-	15.2
South Africa	Baa3	BB+	46.3
Zimbabwe	-	-	32.5
*100=lowest default risk			

Table 13–2. *(cont.)*

Interpretation	Standard & Poor's Ratings	Moody's Ratings
Investment Grade		
Highest quality	AAA	Aaa
High quality	AA+	Aa1
	AA	Aa2
	AA-	Aa3
Strong payment capacity	A+	A1
	A	A2
	A-	A3
Adequate payment capacity	BBB+	Baa1
	BBB	Baa2
	BBB-	Baa3
Speculative grade		
Likely to fulfill	BB+	Ba1
obligations, ongoing	BB	Ba2
uncertainty	BB-	Ba3
High-risk obligations	B+	B1
	B	B2
	B-	B3

Table 13–3. Interpreting Sovereign Risk Ratings. *Source: New Horizon Economies,* 2nd Quarter, 1997.

Such reactions are becoming less common, as most developing nations honor their obligations. The world is becoming more creditworthy. In September 1996, the global average credit rating compiled by *Institutional Investor* reached 39.6, the highest since 1987; six months later it rose to 40.1, the seventh consecutive increase. Forty-five countries improved by a point or more, while only nine fell by the same amount.

The global rating still has a way to go to reach the 53.5 rating it hit in March 1980, before the era of defaults began. Perhaps today's global bankers are a bit more cautious in their assessments and less generous with their ratings. Nevertheless, Walter Wriston may well turn out to be correct in his observation that countries don't go bankrupt, thanks in part to the IMF.

INFORMATION RISK, or, as it is sometimes called, "misinformation risk." You can count on getting a fair share of faulty information, whether it be a deliberate attempt to mislead, sloppy research, or simply outdated data.

Information risk varies from country to country, in both quality and quantity. The risk is usually greater in countries in which the press is controlled or censored by the government. However, the risk may be just as high in countries where information gathering and reporting is unreliable and communication is poor.

"DISENCHANTMENT RISK." Journalist Walter Mead uses this term to describe the risk of being invested in an emerging market when it is no longer fashionable. It is the risk of being invested in a market that is "cooling off" in the minds of the investment community.

Markets don't fall out of favor without a reason, such as a change in fundamentals, returns that are below expectations, or a political or economic crisis. However, disenchantment shouldn't be construed as an *automatic* sell signal. The investment community can be fickle and ill-informed, and often overreacts.

WHY BOTHER MONITORING COUNTRY RISK?

TO AVOID OVERLOOKING IMPORTANT INVESTMENT FACTORS. Comprehensive country risk analysis rarely forecasts the next disaster, but it does give you a good idea of where the country is headed. A simple look at the GDP growth and inflation figures might not offer much of a warning, but a good country risk report should reveal the conditions behind the figures. For example, strong economic growth rates don't reflect labor strife or political corruption.

COUNTRY RISK ANALYSIS HAS PREDICTIVE VALUE. A study conducted by Professor Campbell Harvey of Duke University and Claude Erb and Tadas Viskanta of First Chicago concluded that country risk measures are highly correlated with future equity returns. In other words, risk measures may be useful in structuring a profitable investment portfolio, in much the same way that investors use P/E ratios and earnings growth.

Harvey and others also discovered that the five different measures they studied—political, economic, financial, "composite," and country credit rating—are highly correlated with one another.

The researchers simulated two portfolios based on the Morgan Stanley Country Indexes (MSCI) and the International Finance Corporation's IFC indexes. One portfolio held only "upgraded" countries, those with improved risk ratings. The other held "downgraded" countries. The researchers then began their study, waiting six months before assigning countries to a portfolio.

At the end of the six-month period, the Harvey team compared the risk ratings for each factor and country. They based their findings on risk ratings produced by the International Country Risk Guide (ICRG) and *Institutional Investor's* country credit ratings. If the risk was the same or lower, it put the country in the "upgraded" portfolio. If the risk was higher, the country went into the "downgraded" portfolio. Every six months, they looked again and switched any country whose risk increased into the "downgraded" portfolio, while placing those with an improving situation into the "upgraded" one.[2] The effect of all this is two portfolios: one in which you buy all the countries that have reduced or equal risk and one in which you buy all the countries with increased risk.

The authors did a simple simulation of a portfolio based on country-risk ratings, buying when a country was upgraded and selling when it was downgraded.

The results were significant: Risk measurements matter in emerging market investing, and economic risk is the best measure. The upgraded portfolio returned 25.8 percent for the year from June 1994 to June 1995. The downgraded portfolio yielded 18.6 percent. One would expect that the higher yield would be associated with higher risk. But in this case, *the lower risk provided the best return.* It appears that the market does not reward rising economic risk, which may include inflation, current account deficit, low liquidity, and so forth. (For a description of economic risk components, see the section on ICRG later in this chapter.) In addition, the upgraded portfolio was less volatile and had lower beta.

When portfolios were constructed using upgrades and downgrades in political risk, the results were less dramatic. The returns were slightly better for the upgraded portfolio, but volatility and beta were higher. In the case of political risk, then, there is a price to be paid for a higher return. When financial risk was used, the downgraded portfolio did better. However, the upgraded portfolio based on the composite index—which factors in all three types of risk—did the best of all.

Can These Risks Be Managed?

Yes and no. Some traditional risk-management techniques, such as hedging and arbitrage, rarely work in emerging markets, primarily because the securities and derivatives needed to devise such a strategy don't yet exist. However, you can do more than simply hold your breath.

ANALYZE THE RISKS EARLY AND OFTEN. Consider the country risk factors before investing in an emerging market company and update your analysis no less than on a quarterly basis.

Many investors prefer to leave risk analysis to professionals. While a great deal of data is widely available, inconsistencies and inaccuracies sometimes arise. Reporting methods might change, altering the interpretation of the data. Finally, financial statistics must be converted to a single currency to be useful for comparison purposes.

Available data are sometimes out of date. While information usually costing thousands of dollars is often found on the Internet free of charge, it may be months if not years behind, so the paying customers don't feel cheated.

Investors can make a reasonable assessment of the risks involved in investing in a given country on their own. In fact, it is more difficult to analyze the risks of investing in Netscape or Apple than to gauge the country risk of investing in Poland or even Israel. While no one can predict the outcome of a battle for market share or that of the Middle East peace process, the average investor has access to virtually all the information needed to assess emerging market country risk. If you lack the time or inclination to do it yourself, there are many services that do it for you (see Appendix C).

In addition, you should scan the international and business news daily for stories relating to the home market. The Internet and other dedicated on-line services offer electronic "clipping" features, which will do customized retrieval of stories relating to topics you suggest.

Daily monitoring is important because big things can happen overnight. While rare, sometimes a single event on a given day can stop an investment market dead in its tracks, especially in frontier markets. In February 1996, the Cuban government shot down two aircraft operated by the "Brothers to the Rescue" Cuban exile group. President Clinton then declared support for the anti-Castro Helms-Burton bill. *Time* magazine ran a headline declaring "This Cold War Is Back," and several embryo market investment managers were left high and dry. The "Cuba Fund" is now called the Caribbean Basin Fund and invests accordingly. The Beta Gran Caribe Fund, a closed-end that had raised millions for investment in Cuba, closed its Havana office.

DIVERSIFY. The more funds you allocate to a single country, the greater the overall risk to the portfolio. Likewise, the more funds allocated to high-risk countries, the greater the risk to the portfolio.

SELECT INDIVIDUAL STOCKS CAREFULLY. A country may be risky, but in some cases the individual stock may be solid enough to withstand deterioration in the risk rating.

DON'T OVERREACT. Monitoring a country's investment risk means just that. A single event or a negative news story is usually not sufficient grounds for liquidating or taking a position.

You shouldn't be overly concerned with emerging market country risk, nor should you ignore it. The key is to approach the subject systematically, monitoring the situation through reliable news or information sources, or relying on a professional risk-analysis service.

KEEP AN EYE ON THE LONG TERM. Emerging markets have the fundamentals on their side over the long term. Most of them are growing rapidly and are quite resilient. Barring a revolution or other disaster, they are likely to rebound from short-term destabilizing influences.

The opposite is also true—short-term optimism can overshadow serious long-term problems. "There is an old investment adage ... the best time to invest is when blood is in the streets," comments Jim Rogers. "But in the former Soviet Union, it is just the calm before the storm."[3]

WATCH THE GOVERNMENT CLOSELY. Emerging market governments are often the instigators of a change in the country's risk rating. The government may create a problem or a solution, initiate or oppose reform, or react to a situation created by the private sector or its citizens. For example, government response to the Mexican peso devaluation (Mexico, Argentina), a revolt (Russia, Mexico), an invasion threat (Taiwan), a drug scandal (Colombia), and a banking crisis (Venezuela) in each case altered the business climate.

Take stock of the government's political will. Is it strong enough—and committed enough—to stay the course? Emerging market economic reforms can be painful. Groups that suffer usually become part of the opposition and put added pressure on the government.

For example, privatization has created a backlash in Russia. Fiscal austerity and currency reform in Argentina have increased unemployment and threatened pensioners. The Brazilian government faces great political opposition to many of its reform measures and privatizations.

CONSIDER THE ENLIGHTENED SELF-INTEREST OF THE POWER ELITE. People in power generally do what is best for *them*, regardless of their political leanings. Arnab Banerji and his emerging market team at Foreign & Colonial, a London-based money management firm, have conducted risk analysis based on the premise that the likelihood of a severe change affecting an emerging market is determined by self-interest of those in power. "In most countries," he says, "ideology is a mask for self-interest."

For an example, consider Taiwan. In early 1996, mainland China conducted military maneuvers in the Taiwan straits, and the United States responded by moving U.S. Navy ships to the area. There was some tough talk from both the Chinese and the Taiwanese.

Banerji analyzed the China/Taiwan conflict and determined that most of the influential groups on the mainland—the Red Army, communist officials, bureaucrats, and entrepreneurs—have benefited greatly from the move to capitalism. In short, many powerful people are getting rich. It is, therefore, not in their best interest to pick a fight with Taiwan, which would surely damage business. Therefore, Banerji concluded that an invasion is not likely. The sabre rattling by the mainland Chinese? Just a way to influence the Taiwanese election, Banerji believes.

This analysis led Banerji to the viewpoint that the sell-off in the Taiwanese market that followed the crisis was overdone. Currently, pundits are concerned about how the Chinese will manage their absorption of Hong Kong now that the British are gone. If Banerji is correct, the Chinese are unlikely to take any actions that would undermine a market that has created so much wealth.

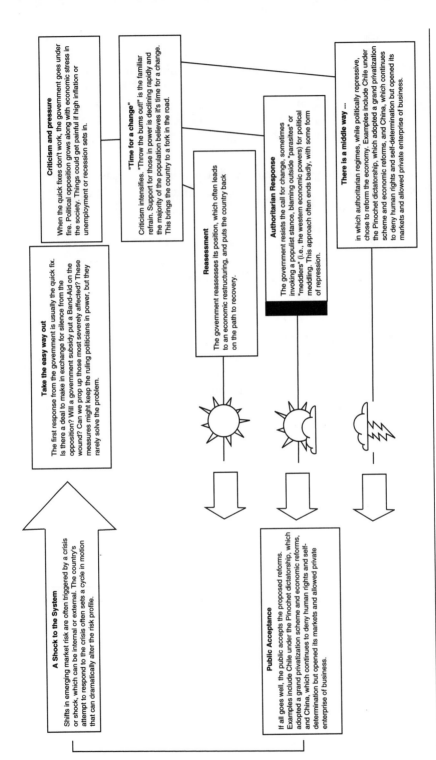

Figure 13–1. GOVERNMENT POLICY CYCLE. A GOVERNMENT'S RESPONSE TO A CRISIS OFTEN DETERMINES THE OUTCOME.

RECOGNIZE THAT THE MARKET OFTEN ANTICIPATES RISK. For example, President Clinton decertified Colombia for not doing enough in the war against drugs, which means a suspension of aid and trade credits. But the market in Colombian debt barely moved, widening by about 15 basis points. Why? The market had already discounted the risk of decertification—the risk was already reflected in the lower share prices. Colombian president Ernesto Samper had been charged with accepting bribes from drug cartels. The coming decertification had been widely reported.

REMEMBER THAT INVESTORS ARE REWARDED FOR EMBRACING RISK. Investors are theoretically given a break—in the form of lower share prices—for buying stocks in high-risk countries. Emerging market analysts at UBS Global Research have described the existence of a "risk premium," which has the effect of reducing the market's valuation of a given stock. In other words, a company located in a high-risk country will get a lower valuation than it would had it been located in a lower-risk market. Theoretically, then, the higher the risk, the cheaper the stock. However, this is not a rule to be applied across the board. Remember the work of Harvey, Erb, and Viskanta cited earlier in the chapter.

TAKE ADVANTAGE OF THE HERD MENTALITY. The market tends to react to news and overlook quiet progress. Around the world, many emerging markets have been upgraded, garnering higher scores (lower risk), but the share prices have yet to reflect this improvement. When the situation in a given emerging market improves, but the stock market does not rise, a buying opportunity may exist.

As a well-informed investor, you might be in a position to take advantage of the herd mentality. The market tends to overreact to bad news. For example, the Taiwanese market sold off when the mainland Chinese began military maneuvers in the Straits of Taiwan; most of Latin American's bolsas sold off in sympathy with the Mexican peso crisis. In both cases, investors overreacted, creating buying opportunities for astute investors.

REMAIN DETACHED. Keep in mind that your analysis should be free of personal opinion regarding human rights and political systems. Your goal is to determine the degree of risk you will be facing when making an investment.

ANALYZE RISK WITH YOUR HEAD, NOT YOUR HEART. Predictability is usually good for investment, and a stable government is favorable for investment, even if it goes against your personal views. You may wish to

COUNTRY	CURRENT RATINGS Political Risk	COMPOSITE RATINGS Financial Risk	Economic Risk	Year	Current Month	Year Ahead
	10/95	10/95	10/95	10/94	10/95	10/96
Argentina	74.0	34.0	31.5	73.0	70.0	70.0
Bahamas	73.0	40.0	37.0	74.0	75.0	75.0
Bolivia	63.0	36.0	33.0	63.0	66.0	63.0
Brazil	64.0	33.0	28.0	67.0	62.5	67.0
Canada	81.0	46.0	39.0	83.0	83.0	84.0
Chile	74.0	43.0	42.0	77.5	79.5	79.0
Colombia	60.0	40.0	35.5	67.0	68.0	67.5
Costa Rica	74.0	38.0	36.0	73.5	74.0	71.0
Cuba	62.0	26.0	20.0	51.5	54.0	58.5
Dominican Republic	64.0	33.0	35.0	65.5	66.0	61.0
Ecuador	58.0	33.0	32.0	62.0	61.5	65.0
El Salvador	68.0	32.0	37.0	65.5	68.5	67.5
Guatemala	60.0	29.0	33.5	59.5	61.5	60.0
Guyana	70.0	31.0	28.5	62.0	65.0	67.5
Haiti	51.0	19.0	28.0	37.0	49.0	46.0
Honduras	55.0	30.0	31.5	58.0	58.5	59.5
Jamaica	73.0	41.0	34.0	71.5	74.0	75.0
Mexico	65.0	37.0	30.0	74.5	66.0	71.5
Nicaragua	63.0	29.0	22.5	55.5	57.5	59.0
Panama	59.0	36.0	36.5	64.0	66.0	70.0
Paraguay	71.0	39.0	31.5	73.0	71.0	70.0
Peru	56.0	31.0	33.0	60.0	60.0	66.5
Suriname	62.0	29.0	20.5	56.0	56.0	58.0
Trinidad & Tobago	63.0	37.0	36.0	66.0	68.0	70.0
United States	80.0	48.0	38.0	78.0	83.0	82.5
Uruguay	64.0	41.0	32.5	70.5	69.0	70.0
Venezuela	65.0	34.0	34.0	65.5	66.5	67.5

Table 13–4. Sample risk assessments and one year forecasts as of October 1995. Highest numbers mean the lowest risk. Note that only Haiti posts a higher composite risk rating than Cuba; Cuba scores lower on economic risk. Obviously, the United States and Canada lead the pack, but Chile is just a tad behind the United States. *Source:* IBC Licensing USA, 1995.

withhold investment dollars so as not to aid and abet a political system you find abhorrent, and it is not my aim to say that you shouldn't. By all means, follow your heart, as long as you fully understand the risks.

DO-IT-YOURSELF RISK ANALYSIS

Do Rely On

In-depth analysis of the market by professionals, such as the IFC.

Country Risk Reports.
They are available by subscription and are expensive, but back issues are available on-line often only a few months old. *The Economist* runs them from time to time in their Economic Indicators section.

The U.S. government.
Okay. So it didn't predict the fall of the Shah or Tiananmen Square. But it provides good information for those doing business or invest-ing abroad. See the Appendices for a list of resources.

Serious, sober publications dedicated to serving the international investor.

Don't Rely On

News media, who are in search of a good story and lack the ability to assess the investment implications.

Anyone with a hidden agenda.
A friend of mine is a widely regarded expert on a certain small Latin American country. Few know that he is on the payroll of that nation's Chamber of Commerce. Enough said.

Banks and brokerage firms.
Doing business in the emerging markets means dealing with the governments. Big brokerage firms and investment bankers are always trolling for business from big companies and the government, which may be privatizing or issuing bonds. The same is true of banks. Local institutions are even less trustworthy. These folks aren't lying; they are just overly optimistic and under pressure to put a positive spin on things.

Publications with a political "point of view." Liberal publications will not be sympathetic to rightist regimes, nor will conservative public-ations look kindly on those run by socialists, regardless of the govern-ment's competency. Chile has been rather soft on former members of the military junta that ruled under Pinochet. Certain publications might tend to exaggerate the problem.

"**Uncle Louie.**" Got a
friend or relative who travels
to an emerging market and
does business there? His or her
insights can be very valuable.
Do not make any investment
decisions solely on this advice, but
it is an important reality check.

Your head. Many of the
world's economic miracles are
in nations governed by despots
who conduct business with
corporations and foreign
governments around the world.
Unless guilty of atrocities and
large-scale human rights abuses,
such nations are included in the
international investment universe.

Your heart. If you
empathize with the people and
culture of an emerging market
and wish to help, there are
many ways to do so. But your
feelings will not convert a bad
investment into a good one.

PROFESSIONAL RISK ANALYSIS

Money managers and institutional investors, as well as large corporations,
that have a great deal at stake in emerging markets solicit the opinions of
informed, unbiased risk experts. They turn to:

RISK ANALYSIS SERVICES, are usually run by former foreign service
officials, intelligence experts, academics, or a combination of all three.
Their strength lies not only in their expertise, but also in their objectivity.

FINANCIAL INSTITUTIONS, on the other hand, often temper their
assessment of country risk to avoid offending the authorities, because they
are often clients. Would you trash a country if you were a candidate to
underwrite a major privatization? In fairness, many international banks
and brokerage houses have talented, well-trained, and well-informed staff
and excellent data gathering resources.

Risk Analysis Services

Institutional Investor surveys leading international bankers and asks
them to rate each country on a scale from 1 to 100, with 100 representing
the highest creditworthiness. *Institutional Investor* averages the ratings of
the group and then applies a weighting system according to each country's

exposure to the international credit markets and the sophistication of the data available for each country.

The user is then relying, ultimately, on a consensus of the subjective opinion of the bankers surveyed. To make the ratings more useful, *Institutional Investor* asks the experts to rank the factors they take into account, in order of importance. Certain factors may be more important in some countries and less important in others.

INTERNATIONAL COUNTRY RISK GUIDE (ICRG) is a leader in the field. A look at the methodology will give the reader some valuable insights into how to size up emerging market risk, as well as an understanding of how to read a professional country risk report.

Compiled, written, and edited in the U.K., the ICRG is a monthly report that provides financial, economic, political, and composite risk ratings for 130 countries. The report is comprehensive. Not only does it provide you with an accessible and clear rating system, but the included data enable you to assess the risks for yourself. In short, you can calculate your own risks by weighting certain factors to reflect your own personal biases or needs. ICRG has been measuring country risk since 1980.

ICRG contains 24 individual ratings, plus a rating for each of the three key risk-factor groups (economic, political, and financial) and an overall score (comprehensive) for each country. The rating system assigns the lowest score to the highest-risk countries. The individual factors are weighted to reflect their importance in the overall risk rating. The highest possible score for each factor reflects the weight it is assigned. For example, the political risk factor, "Economic planning failures" has a maximum score of 12. The financial risk factor "Foreign trade collection experience" has a maximum score of 5 because it is less important to the overall country risk rating.

To allow comparisons among countries, ICRG assigns weights to economic indicators. ICRG computes its composite risk ratings by combining political, financial, and economic risk ratings and then taking half the total.

For example, in October 1995, Algeria's ratings were

Political	Financial	Economic	Composite
45	36	26.5	54[4]

THE COPLIN-O'LEARY RISK-RATING SYSTEM. Developed by William D. Coplin and Michael O'Leary, this risk-assessment model

	Factor	Maximum Score
Political	*Source: Qualitative Data Based on ICRG Staff Analysis*	
	Economic expectations vs. reality	12
	Economic planning failures	12
	Political leadership	12
	External conflict	10
	Corruption in government	6
	Military in politics	6
	Organized religion in politics	6
	Law and order tradition	6
	Racial and nationality tensions	6
	Political terrorism	6
	Civil war	6
	Political party development	6
	Quality of the bureaucracy	6
	Maximum Possible Political Rating	100
Financial	*Source: Quantitative and Qualitative Published Data and Staff Analysis*	
	Loan default or unfavorable loan restructuring	10
	Delayed payment of suppliers' credits	10
	Repudiation of contracts by governments	10
	Losses from exchange controls	10
	Expropriation of private investments	10
	Maximum Possible Financial Rating	50
Economic	*Source: Quantitative Published Data*	
	Inflation	10
	Debt service as a percent of exports of goods and services	10
	International liquidity ratios	5
	Foreign trade collection experience	5
	Current account balance as a percent of goods and services[5]	15
	Parallel foreign exchange rate as market indicators[6]	5
	Maximum Possible Economic Rating	50

Table 13–5. The Key Risks according to ICRG. *Source:* Political Risk Services.

evolved from U.S. State Department and CIA research and 20 years of academic study. It is widely recognized as the first practical system devised to quantify and rate political risk. This program has been serving the private sector since 1979. Reports cover forecast periods of 18 months and a longer term covering five years.

The Coplin-O'Leary Rating System and the accompanying Prince Method of forecasting risk provide investors with valuable insights. While ICRG and Coplin-O'Leary cover much of the same territory, their analysis of risk is somewhat different. Here's a closer look at the Coplin-O'Leary risk-assessment model.

Country Risk Factors

REGIME STABILITY. The risk of change in key government personnel. How high is the risk, and what is the likely method? By authorized political means, for example, an election; or by illegal action?

Regime change is measured as *Regime Stability,* which indicates the government most likely to be in power over the forecast periods. Coplin-O'Leary rates regime stability by probability as expressed in percentages. Notations show any rating and regime changes from previous reports. The regime label signifies the most powerful component of the government, which is not as simple as it sounds. It could be a dominant leader, a political party, or a part of the government such as the congress or the cabinet. It could be an alliance, such as between a labor union and the military.

POLITICAL TURMOIL. The risk of politically inspired violence, such as violent strikes and demonstrations, terrorism, guerrilla activity, riots, or even civil war. Like regime stability, *Turmoil Risk* is expressed as a probability expressing the likelihood that political turmoil will occur. The short-term risk that turmoil will affect international business is rated as low, moderate, high, or very high.

Low risk means that discontent is expressed peacefully. Political violence is extremely rare and rarely affects international business directly.

Moderate risk implies that there are significant levels of unrest and discontent, which could affect international business through occasional acts of political violence, such as terrorism, riots, or labor unrest.

High risk countries are those that experience levels of violence or potential violence that could have a serious impact on international business.

Very high risk is a situation in which conditions are approaching a state of war.

GOVERNMENT POLICY. Official decisions affecting fiscal and monetary policy, trade regulations and/or foreign investment. Government policy is far and away the most important factor. Regimes don't change that often, but policy does, often affecting the investment climate.

EXTERNAL EVENTS. Actions by other countries that affect risk. External events, such as a war or a change in status with a developing nation, such as sanctions against South Africa, can have a major impact, but such occurrences are rare as well.

Business Environment Risks

Coplin-O'Leary have devised a letter-grading system to serve as a guide for investment. They characterize risk as financial transfer risk, direct-investment risk, and export market risk. Ratings run from A+ to D-.

FINANCIAL TRANSFER RISK is concerned with the flow of capital and refers to the risk of converting local currency to foreign, or the transfer of funds out of the country for any business purpose. Two of the biggest concerns are the ability to repatriate profits and to receive payment for exports. Emerging market investors must be concerned with the ability to receive the proceeds from the sale of their stock on local exchanges, including the original investment and any capital gains and dividends.

"A" countries have no barriers to financial transfer and little likelihood that restrictions will appear in the future.

"B" countries have some delays in financial transfers and reasonable chance of delays during the forecast period.

"C" countries are those with modest to heavy delays and even blockage. There is a good chance that barriers will increase and little chance that they will decrease during the period.

"D" countries impose heavy controls on currency exchange and transfer, with little chance of improvement during the forecast period.

DIRECT INVESTMENT RISK applies to foreign direct investment in companies, wholly-owned subsidiaries, and joint ventures. Factors rated include several associated with financial transfer risk, and a few additions.

The long-term rating also takes into account the relative strength of the forces supporting and opposing restrictions on foreign investment.

"A" countries have few controls or restrictions on equity ownership, local operations, repatriation of funds, or foreign exchange. Taxation does not discriminate against foreign business investment and ownership. There is little likelihood that restrictions will increase and little threat from political turmoil.

"B" countries pose some risk to equity ownership, often by requiring some partial ownership by nationals. There are restrictions on local operations, particularly in local procurement. Some currency and repatriation restrictions are possible. There is some threat from political turmoil and a significant possibility that restrictions and turmoil might increase.

"C" countries place considerable restrictions on direct investment. Requirements might include majority ownership by nationals. There are significant restrictions on currency exchange and repatriation. Tax policy may discriminate against foreigners, and there is a good chance that turmoil will remain high or even increase during the forecast period.

"D" countries restrict equity ownership, often with outright prohibition. Local operations are highly regulated, as are all financial transfers. There is likely to be a form of tax discrimination, and political turmoil may pose a serious threat. Things are not likely to get better during the forecast period.

EXPORT MARKET RISK refers to the risks faced by those exporting to a country. Again, part of this risk is attributable to financial transfer risk, which has to do with restrictions and difficulties in getting paid. Other risks include tariffs and restrictions on imports. Even if you are investing in a local company, you should be concerned about export market risk. Some of the best emerging market companies are those that assemble, bottle, and/or market goods from developed nations. Restrictions on certain auto parts would have a direct effect on companies that assemble cars with U.S. or Japanese components.

"A" countries have low trade barriers and adequate foreign reserves, allowing for prompt payment. They are politically and economically stable, and there is little chance that conditions will deteriorate.

"B" countries are those where there is a risk of moderate trade barriers. Conditions include some protectionist sentiment and a poor foreign exchange and current account position. Modest payment delays may result, and there is some chance that business conditions will deteriorate.

"C" countries are those with high tariffs and other barriers to trade. There is often a strong protectionist sentiment and weak foreign-exchange position; the risk of prolonged payment delays or nonpayment suggests conservative credit policies. There is little chance of improvement and a strong chance that things will deteriorate.

"D" countries have high tariff and nontariff barriers. They are strongly protectionist and usually lack foreign currency reserves. There is a high likelihood of long payment delays or nonpayment and little chance of improvement. There is a strong chance that things will deteriorate.

Risk Component	Financial Transfer	Direct Investment	Export Market
Turmoil	✓	✓	✓
Restrictions on equity		✓	
Restrictions on local operations[7]		✓	
Taxation discrimination		✓	
Repatriation restrictions	✓	✓	
Exchange controls		✓	✓
Tariff barriers			✓
Nontariff barriers			✓
Payment delays	✓		✓
Expansionary economic policies	✓		✓
Labor costs		✓	
Foreign debt	✓		✓
Investment restrictions			
Restrictions on foreign trade			✓
Domestic economic problems			
International economic problems			

Table 13–6. Components of the International Business Climate Index (IBC). *Source:* Political Risk Services, Coplin-O'Leary Rating System. *Quantitative data analyzed by staff; qualitative ratings by expert panel.*

ENDNOTES

1. Claude Erb, Campbell Harvey, and Viskanta Tadas, "Political Risk, Economic Risk and Financial Risk," Published on the World Wide Web www. duke.edu/~charvey/Country_Risk/couindex.htm.
2. Ibid. To leave a downgraded portfolio, the risk rating had to rise. If it remained the same, it remained in the downgraded portfolio.

3. Rogers, Jim, "No new money for the old Russian Empire," *Financial Times* (October 5, 1996).

4. Rounded up from 53.75.

5. Current account is defined as:
   Exports of goods and services + inflows of unrequited public and private capital transfers - Imports of goods and services + unrequited capital outflows
   A negative current-account balance indicates that for that period, more capital has gone out than came in.

6. Parallel foreign exchange rate is a euphemism for the existence of an active black market in local currency. Where the country's official exchange rate might be 10 to the dollar at the airport, the local cab driver might offer you 30. This is often an indication that the currency is overvalued.

7. For example, procurement, labor, management.

Emerging-Market ADRs

COUNTRY	ISSUE	SYMBOL	RATIO	S/U	INDUSTRY	DEPOSITARY
Argentina	Alpargatas S.A.I.C.	ALPAY	1:10	S	TEX	MGT.
Argentina	"Banco De Galicia Y Buenos Aires ""B"""	BGALY	1:4	S	BKS	BNY.
Argentina	Banco Frances Del Rio De La Plata Com	BFR	1:3	S	BKS	BNY.
Argentina	"Buenos Aires Embotelladora ""B"" Shares"	BAE	1:2	S	BEV	BNY.
Argentina	Capex S.A. Gdr	CXAPF	1:2	S	UTI	CIT.
Argentina	Central Costanera S.A.	CRCNY	1:10	S	OTH	CIT.
Argentina	"Central Puerto, S.A. 144a"	CEPUY	1:5	S	OTH	CIT.
Argentina	Cresud Common Shares	CRESY	1:10	S	FOD	BNY.
Argentina	Disco S.A.	DXO	1:3	S	RET	CIT.
Argentina	Irsa Common Shares	IRS	1:10	S	RES	BNY.
Argentina	"Manufacturas De Papel, C.A. (Manpa)"	MUPAY	1:25	S	PAP	CIT.
Argentina	Metrogas S.A.	MGS	1:10	S	OGS	CIT.
Argentina	Mirgor S.A.C.I.F.I.A. 144a	MIRKY	1:1	S	AUT	CIT.
Argentina	Mirgor S.A.C.I.F.I.A. Gdr	MRGRY	1:1	S	AUT	CIT.
Argentina	"Nortel Inversora Preferred ""B"" Shares"	NTL	20:1	S	TEL	MGT.
Argentina	"Nortel Invesora S.A. Series ""A"" Gdr"	NOIAG	5:1	S	TEL	MGT.
Argentina	"Nortel Invesora S.A. Series ""B"" Gdr"	NOIBG	5:1	S	TEL	MGT.
Argentina	Perez Companc S.A.	CNPZY	1:2	S	OGS	MGT.
Argentina	"Quilmes Industrial (Quinsa), S.A."	LQU	1:1	S	FOD	CIT.
Argentina	Siderar S.A.I.C. Gdr	SDRPP	1:8	S	MIN	CIT.
Argentina	Siderar S.A.I.C. Reg S	SDRPPREGS	1:8	S	MIN	CIT.

COUNTRY	ISSUE	SYMBOL	RATIO	S/U	INDUSTRY	DEPOSITARY
Argentina	Sociedad Comercial Common Shares 144a	SCDPF	1:1	S	OFI	BNY.
Argentina	Sol Petroleo Common Shares	SLEOY	1:1	S	OGS	BNY.
Argentina	Telecom Argentina Stet-France Telecom	TEO	1:10	S	TEL	MGT.
Argentina	Telefonica De Argentina S.A. Gdr	TAR	1:10	S	TEL	CIT.
Argentina	"Transportadora De Gas Del Sur, S.A."	TGS	1:5	S	OGS	CIT.
Argentina	"Ypf Sociedad Anonima ""D"" Shares"	YPF	1:1	S	OGS	BNY.
Bolivia	Banco Industrial Common Shares	BITSY	1:2	S	BKS	BNY.
Bolivia	Banco Mercantil Common Shares	BMBVY	1:1	S	BKS	BNY.
Bolivia	Banco Nacional De Bolivia	BNBVY	1:5	S	BKS	BT.
Bolivia	Banco Santa Cruz	BSCZY	1:5	S	BKS	BT.
Brazil	Acesita-Cia. Acos Especias Itabir	ATASY	1:1800	S	STE	MGT.
Brazil	Aracruz Cellulose Preferred Shares	ARA	1:10	S	PAP	MGT.
Brazil	"Bahia Sul Cellulose, S.A. ""Ord."""	BHISY	1:20	S	PAP	CIT.
Brazil	"Bahia Sul Cellulose, S.A. ""Pref."""	BHIAY	1:20	S	PAP	CIT.
Brazil	Banco Bradesco SA	BBQCY	1:1000	S	BKS	CIT.
Brazil	Bombril S.A.	BMBBY	1:1000	S	FOD	BNY.
Brazil	Bompreco S.A. Supermercados DO Nordeste	BORPP	1:2	S	MER	CIT.
Brazil	Brazil Realty	BRZD	1:10	S	RES	BT.
Brazil	Celesc-Centrais Ele. Da Santa Catarina	CAIOY	1:100	S	UTI	CIT.
Brazil	Celesc-Centrais Ele. Da Santa Catarina A	CAIAY	1:100	S	UTI	CIT.
Brazil	Celesc-Centrais Ele. Da Santa Catarina B	CAIBY	1:100	S	UTI	CIT.

COUNTRY	ISSUE	SYMBOL	RATIO	S/U	INDUSTRY	DEPOSITARY
Brazil	Celesc-Centrais Ele. Santa Catarina 144A	CEDSC	1:100	S	UTI	CIT.
Brazil	Celesc-Centrais Ele. Santa Catarina Regs	CESSC	1:100	S	UTI	CIT.
Brazil	Cemig-Companhia Energetica De Minas	CEMZY	1:1000	S	UTI	CIT.
Brazil	"Ceval Alimentos, S.A. Common"	CVEPY	1:1000	S	FOD	CIT.
Brazil	"Ceval Alimentos, S.A. Preferred"	CVEAY	1:1000	S	FOD	CIT.
Brazil	Comp. Paranaense De Energia-Copel Common	CXBVY	1:1000	S	UTI	BNY.
Brazil	Comp. Paranaense De Energia-Copel Pref	ELP	1:1000	S	UTI	BNY.
Brazil	Companhia Brasileira De Distribuicao—CBD	CBD	1:1000	S	RET	BNY.
Brazil	Companhia Brasileira De Distribuicao —CBD 144A	CBDDYP	1:1000	S	RET	BNY.
Brazil	Companhia Cervejaria Brahma-Common	BRHC	1:20	S	BEV	BNY.
Brazil	Companhia Cervejaria Brahma-Preferred	BRH	1:20	S	BEV	BNY.
Brazil	Companhia De Fabricadoras De Pecas-Cofap	CFPEY	1:2	S	AUT	BNY.
Brazil	Companhia Energetica De Minas Gerais	CEMCY	1:1000	S	UTI	CIT.
Brazil	Companhia Energetica De Minas Gerais	CEMHY	1:1000	S	UTI	CIT.
Brazil	Companhia Energetica De Minas Gerais	CEMFY	1:1000	S	UTI	CIT.
Brazil	Companhia Energetica De Sao Paulo	CMPSY	1:300	S	UTI	BNY.
Brazil	Companhia Energetica De Sao Paulo 144A	CMPSYP	1:300	S	UTI	BNY.
Brazil	Companhia Siderurgica Belgo-Mineira	CSBMY	1:200	S	OTH	CIT.
Brazil	Companhia Siderurgica De Turbarao 144AA	CSTUY	1:40	S	STE	MGT.
Brazil	Companhia Siderurgica De Turbarao Gdr	CSNIY	1:40	S	STE	MGT.
Brazil	Companhia Siderurgica de Turbarao—CSN	CSNNY	1:1000	S	STE	CIT.
Brazil	Companhia Suzano	CSZPY	1:3	S	PAP	BNY.

COUNTRY	ISSUE	SYMBOL	RATIO	S/U	INDUSTRY	DEPOSITARY
Brazil	Companhia Suzano Preferred Shares	CSZPY	1:3	S	PAP	BNY.
Brazil	Companhia Vale Do Rio Doce (Cvrd)	CVROY	1:250	S	MIN	MGT.
Brazil	Copene Preferred Shares	CPEPY	1:50	S	CHM	BNY.
Brazil	Ctm Citrus Preferred Shares	CTMMY	1:100	S	FOD	BNY.
Brazil	Dixie-Toga Preferred GDR	DTSAREGS	1:10	S	PPP	BNY.
Brazil	Electrobras-Centrais Electricas Ord.	CAIFY	1:50	S	UTI	MGT.
Brazil	Electrobras-Centrais Electricas Pref	CAIGY	1:50	S	UTI	MGT.
Brazil	"Electrolux Do Brasil, SA"	EXDBY	1:5000	S	HCG	CIT.
Brazil	Eucatex S.A.	ECTXY	1:100	S	OTH	CIT.
Brazil	Globex Utilidades S.A. Common	GBXOY	1:1	S	RET	BNY.
Brazil	Globex Utilidades S.A. Preferred	GBXPY	1:1	S	RET	BNY.
Brazil	Industrias Klabin Preferred Shares	IKLBY	1:10	S	PAP	BNY.
Brazil	Iochpe-Maxion Preferred Shares	IOCJY	1:25	S	MAC	BNY.
Brazil	Lojas Americanas Preferred Shares	LOJAY	1:1000	S	RET	BNY.
Brazil	"Lojas Arapua, S.A. 144a"	LJPFF	1:1000	S	MER	CIT.
Brazil	"Lojas Arapua, S.A. Gdr"	LJPSF	1:1000	S	MER	CIT.
Brazil	Makro Atacadista SA	MKRAY	1:10	S	MER	CIT.
Brazil	Makro Atacadista Sa 144a	MKRBY	1:10	S	MER	CIT.
Brazil	Makro Atacadista Sa Reg S	MKRBF	1:10	S	MER	CIT.
Brazil	"Marcopolo, Sa"	MARCY	1:100	S	MAN	CIT.
Brazil	Multicanal Participacoes Preferred	MPARY	1:10	S	MED	BNY.

COUNTRY	ISSUE	SYMBOL	RATIO	S/U	INDUSTRY	DEPOSITARY
Brazil	Oxiteno S.A.	OXTIY	1:1	S	CHM	CIT.
Brazil	Perdigao S.A.	PDGOY	1:5000	S	FOD	BNY.
Brazil	Petrobras Distribuidora S.A.	PTBRY	1:500	S	OGS	BNY.
Brazil	Petroleo Brasileiro S.A.-Petrobras 144A	PBRPP	1:100	S	EES	CIT.
Brazil	Petroleo Brasileiro S.A.-Petrobras Reg S	PBRPPREGS	1:100	S	EES	CIT.
Brazil	Petroleo Brasileiro S.A.-Petrobras-Pref.	PEBRY	1:100	S	EES	CIT.
Brazil	Rhodia-Ster Common Shares 144a	RHODPY	1:10	S	TEX	BNY.
Brazil	Rossi Residencial S.A. 144A	RORPP	1:5	S	RES	CIT.
Brazil	Rossi Residencial S.A. Reg S	RORPPREGS	1:5	S	RES	CIT.
Brazil	São Paulo Alpargatas	SAALY	1:50	S	TEX	BNY.
Brazil	São Paulo Alpargatas Preferred	SAANY	1:50	S	TEX	BNY.
Brazil	Sementes Agroceres Preferred Shares	SMTAY	1:1000	S	FOD	BNY.
Brazil	Teka-Tecelagem Kuehnrich S.A.	TKTPY	1:5000	S	OTH	CIT.
Brazil	Telebras	TBR	1:1000	S	TEL	BNY.
Brazil	Telebras 144a	TBRAYP	1:1000	S	TEL	BNY.
Brazil	Unibanco-UNIAO De Bancos Brasileiros SA	UBB	1:500	S	INV	CIT.
Brazil	Usiminas Preferred Shares 144a	USDMY	1:10000	S	STE	BNY.
Brazil	Usiminas Preferred Shares Reg S	USNSY	1:10000	S	STE	BNY.
Brazil	Votorantim Celulose & Paper	VCEPY	1:500	S	PAP	MGT.
Chile	Afp Provida S.A.	PVD	1:1	S	INV	BNY.
Chile	"Banco BHIF "G" Shares"	BB	1:10	S	BKS	BNY.

COUNTRY	ISSUE	SYMBOL	RATIO	S/U	INDUSTRY	DEPOSITARY
Chile	Banco De A. Edwards	AED	1:165	S	BKS	CIT.
Chile	Banco De Santiago	SAN	1:1039	S	BKS	MGT.
Chile	Banco Santander-Chile	BSB	1:220	S	BKS	CIT.
Chile	Chilgener S.A.	CHR	1:68	S	UTI	CIT.
Chile	"Chilquinta, S.A."	CQNAY	1:3	S	UTI	CIT.
Chile	"Chilquinta, S.A. Gdr"	CLQTY	1:3	S	UTI	CIT.
Chile	Compania Cervecerias Unidas S.A.	CCUUY	1:5	S	BEV	MGT.
Chile	"Compania De Telecom. De Chile ""A"""	CTC	1:4	S	TEL	CIT.
Chile	"Cristalerias De Chile, S.A."	CGW	1:3	S	OTH	CIT.
Chile	Distribuidora Chilectra Metropolitana	DCM144A	1:10	S	UTI	MGT.
Chile	"Embotelladora Andina, S.A. "A" Shares"	AKOA	1:6	S	BEV	CIT.
Chile	"Embotelladora Andina, S.A. "B" Shares"	AKOB	1:6	S	BEV	CIT.
Chile	Empresas Telex-Chile Common Shares	TL	1:2	S	TEL	BNY.
Chile	Endesa-Empresa Nacional De Electricid	EOC	1:30	S	UTI	CIT.
Chile	Enersis S.A.	ENI	1:50	S	UTI	CIT.
Chile	"Laboratorio Chile S.A. ""B"""	LBC	1:20	S	DRU	CIT.
Chile	Madeco Common Shares	MAD	1:10	S	STE	BNY.
Chile	Maderas Y Sinteticos Common Shares	MYS	1:30	S	PAP	BNY.
Chile	Quinenco S.A.	LQ	1:10	S	MUL	CIT.
Chile	Santa Isabel	ISA	1:15	S	MER	CIT.
Chile	"Sociedad Quimica y Minera De Chile ""B"""	SQM	1:10	S	CHM	BNY.

COUNTRY	ISSUE	SYMBOL	RATIO	S/U	INDUSTRY	DEPOSITARY
Chile	Supermercados Unimarc Common Shares	UNR	1:50	S	FOD	BNY.
Chile	Vina Concha Y Toro Common Shares	VCO	1:50	S	BEV	BNY.
China	"Beijing Yanhua Petrochemical Co., Ltd."	BYH	1:50	S	CHM	BNY.
China	China Eastern Airlines Corp. Ltd.	CEA	1:100	S	AIR	BNY.
China	China Southern Airlines Company Ltd.	ZNH	1:50	S	AIR	BNY.
China	Guangshen Railway Company Limited	GSH	1:50	S	TRN	MGT.
China	"Guangzhou Shipyard Int'l.Co.Ltd.""H""""Sh"	GSHIY	1:10	S	SHO	BNY.
China	Harbin Power Equipment Company Ltd 14	HPECYP	1:100	S	EEI	BNY.
China	"Huaneng Power International, Inc."	HNP	1:40	S	UTI	CIT.
China	Jiangling Motors Corp. Gdr	JMCPP	1:100	S	AUT	CIT.
China	Jilin Chemical Industrial Company Ltd	JCC	1:100	S	CHM	BNY.
China	Maansham Iron & Steel Ltd. 144a	MIS144A	1:100	S	STE	CIT.
China	"Qingling Motor Company, Ltd. Gdr"	QINGDR	1:50	S	AUT	CIT.
China	"Qingling Motor Company, Ltd. Reg S"	QINREGS	1:50	S	AUT	CIT.
China	"Shandong Huaneng Power ""N"""" Shares"	SH	1:50	S	UTI	BNY.
China	"Shanghai Chlor-Alkali Chemical Co., Ltd"	SLLBY	1:10	S	CHM	BNY.
China	"Shanghai Erfangji Co. Ltd. ""B"""""	SHFGY	1:10	S	MAC	BNY.
China	Shanghai Hai Xing Shipping Co. Ltd. 144A	SHGXAY	1:100	S	TRN	BNY.
China	Shanghai Hai Xing Shipping Company Limited	SHGXY	1:50	S	TRN	BNY.
China	Shanghai Jinqiao Processing Dev Co. Ltd.	SJQIY	1:10	S	RES	BNY.
China	Shanghai Lujiazui Finance Trade Zone Dev	SLUJY	1:5	S	RES	BNY.

COUNTRY	ISSUE	SYMBOL	RATIO	S/U	INDUSTRY	DEPOSITARY
China	Shanghai Outer Gaoqiao Ftz Dev. Co. Ltd.	SGOTY	1:5	S	MUL	BNY.
China	Shanghai Petrochemical Company Limited	SHI	1:100	S	CHM	BNY.
China	Shanghai Tyre And Rubber Co. Ltd.	SIRHY	1:10	S	RUB	BNY.
China	Shenzhen S.E.Z. Real Estate And Prop.	SZPRY	1:10	S	RES	BNY.
China	Tsingtao Brewery Company Limited	TSGTY	1:10	S	BEV	BNY.
China	Yizheng Chemical Fibre Company 144a	YCF144A	1:100	S	CHM	CIT.
China	Zhejiang Se Electric Power Co Ltd. 144A	ZHJGYP	1:50	S	EES	BNY.
China	Zhejiang Se Electric Power Co Ltd. Reg S	ZHJGYPREGS	1:50	S	EES	BNY.
Colombia	"Banco De Colombia, S.A. 144a"	BDCGF	1:16	S	BKS	CIT.
Colombia	Banco Ganadero Common Shares	BGA	1:100	S	BKS	BNY.
Colombia	"Banco Ganadero S.A. Pref. ""C"""	BGA+	1:100	S	BKS	CIT.
Colombia	Banco Industrial Colombiano S.A.	CIB	1:4	S	BKS	BNY.
Colombia	Carulla & Cia. Preferred Shares 144a	CCIAYP	1:1	S	RET	BNY.
Colombia	Cementos Diamante S.A. 144a	CGLOY	1:3	S	CST	CIT.
Colombia	Cementos Diamante S.A. Gdr	CDTRF	1:3	S	CST	CIT.
Colombia	"Cementos Paz Del Rio, S.A. Gdr"	CPAZY	1:15	S	CST	CIT.
Colombia	Corporacion Financiera Del Valle S.A.	CFVLY	1:2	S	BKS	CIT.
Colombia	Corporacion Financiera Del Valle S.A.	CFDVY	1:2	S	BKS	CIT.
Colombia	Gran Cadena De Almacenes Colombia 144A	GCACYP	1:10	S	RET	MGT.
Colombia	Gran Cadena De Almacenes Colombia Reg S	GRANGDR	1:10	S	RET	MGT.
Colombia	"Papeles Nacionales, S.A."	PAPGDR	1:40	S	PAP	BT.

COUNTRY	ISSUE	SYMBOL	RATIO	S/U	INDUSTRY	DEPOSITARY
Croatia	Pliva D.D Reg S	PLIVREGS	50:1	S	DRU	BT.
Croatia	Pliva D.D 144A	PLIV	50:1	S	DRU	BT.
Croatia	Zagrebacka Banka D.D.	ZGBBY	10:1	S	BKS	BT.
Czech Rep.	Ceska Sporitelna AS 144A	CSSP144A	1:1	S	BKS	BT.
Czech Rep.	Komercni Banka A.S.	KOMBY	3:1	S	BKS	BNY.
Czech Rep.	Komercni Banka A.S. 144a	KBANYP	3:1	S	BKS	BNY.
Ecuador	Banco Amazonas	BCOAMAZ	1:100	S	BKS	BNY.
Ecuador	Banco De Guayaquil	GUAPP	1:100	S	BKS	BT.
Ecuador	Banco La Previsora S.A.	PREVCY	1:50	S	BKS	BT.
Ecuador	"La Cemento Nacional, C.A."	LCNSF	1:1	S	CST	CIT.
Egypt	Al Ahram Beverage Company 144A	ALAHB	2:1	S	BEV	BT.
Egypt	Commercial International Bank (Egypt)	CIBEG	10:1	S	BKS	BT.
Egypt	MISR International Bank-144A	MISRY	10:1	S	BKS	BNY.
Egypt	MISR International Bank-Reg	MISRYREGS	10:1	S	BKS	BNY.
Egypt	Suez Cement Company S.A.E. 144A	SZCCYP	1:1	S	CST	BNY
El Salvador	Compania De Alumbrado Electrico De Ss	ELSAY	1:1	U	UTI	MGT.
Ghana	Ashanti Goldfields Company Ltd.	ASL	1:1	S	MIN	BNY.
Greece	"Boutari & Son, S.A."	BOUOTC	3:1	S	FOD	CIT.
Greece	"Boutari & Son, S.A. Preferred"	BJSPY	3:1	S	FOD	CIT.
Greece	Credit Bank A.E.	CBAEY	4:1	S	BKS	MGT.
Greece	Globe Group S.A.	GLGYP	1:1	S	MUL	BNY.

COUNTRY	ISSUE	SYMBOL	RATIO	S/U	INDUSTRY	DEPOSITARY
Greece	Hellenic Telecommunications 144A	HLTQF	2:1	S	TEL	BNY.
Greece	Hellenic Telecommunications Reg S	HLTOY	2:1	S	TEL	BNY.
Hungary	Borsodchem Rt 144A	BSRTYP	1:1	S	RUB	BNY.
Hungary	Borsodchem Rt Reg S	BSRTYPREGS	1:1	S	RUB	BNY.
Hungary	Cofinec 144A	COFNYP	1:1	S	PPP	BNY.
Hungary	Cofinec Reg S	COFNYPP	1:1	S	PPP	BNY.
Hungary	Fotex Rt	FOTXY	1:5	S	OTH	MGT.
Hungary	Gedeon Richter 144A	CWGRYP	1:1	S	DRU	BNY.
Hungary	Gedeon Richter Reg S	CWGRYPREGS	1:1	S	DRU	BNY.
Hungary	Mol Magyar Olaj-Es Gazipari Rt. 144a	MOLMYP	1:1	S	OGS	BNY.
Hungary	Mol Magyar Olaj-Es Gazipari Rt. Reg S	MOLMYPREGS	1:1	S	OGS	BNY.
Hungary	Otp Bank Reg S Gdr	OTPREGS	1:1	S	BKS	BNY.
Hungary	Pick Szeged Rt. Gdr	PSZ	1:1	S	FOD	CIT.
Hungary	Tiszai Vegyi Kombinat Rt. (TVK) 144A	TZVKYP	1:1	S	CHM	BNY.
Hungary	Tiszai Vegyi Kombinat Rt. (TVK) Reg S	TZVKYPP	1:1	S	CHM	BNY.
Hungary	Zalakeramia Rt. 144A	ZALAYP	5:1	S	CER	BNY.
Hungary	Zalakeramia Rt. Reg S	ZALAYPP	5:1	S	CER	BNY.
India	Arvind Mills Ltd. 144a	ARZMF	1:1	S	TEX	MGT.
India	Arvind Mills Ltd. Gdr	ARVNFR	1:1	S	TEX	MGT.
India	Ashok Leyland Ltd. 144a	ALRPP	1:3	S	AUT	CIT.
India	Ashok Leyland Ltd. Gdr	ALRPPGDR	1:3	S	AUT	CIT.

COUNTRY	ISSUE	SYMBOL	RATIO	S/U	INDUSTRY	DEPOSITARY
India	Bajaj Auto Limited 144a	BAJHYP	1:1	S	AUT	BT.
India	Bharat Hotels Limited	BHL	1:2	S	HOT	BT.
India	Bombay Dyeing & Manufacturing Co. Ltd	BDYMFR	1:1	S	MAC	CIT.
India	BPL Cellular Holdings Limited Reg S	BPL	1:1	S	TEL	BNY.
India	Bses Limited 144a	BSESYP	1:3	S	UTI	BNY.
India	Century Textiles And Indutries Ltd. G	CYTXF	1:1	S	TEX	CIT.
India	Cesc Limited 144a	CESCYP	1:1	S	UTI	BNY.
India	Cesc Limited Reg "'S'" Gdr"	CESCRS	1:1	S	UTI	BNY.
India	Core Health Care Products GDR	CPRINAGDR	1:1	S	CHM	BT.
India	Crompton Greaves Limited 144A Gdr	CGRVYP	1:1	S	ENG	BNY.
India	DCW Limited	DCWLF	1:5	S	CHM	CIT.
India	Dr. Reddy's Laboratories Gdr	REDDSY	1:1	S	DRU	CIT.
India	Dr. Reddy's Laboratories Ltd 144a	REDDYPYP	1:1	S	DRU	CIT.
India	Eid Parry (India) Limited 144a	EIDPYP	1:1	S	MUL	BNY.
India	Eih Limited 144A	EIHMY	1:1	S	HOT	BNY.
India	Eih Limited Reg S Gdr	EIHLF	1:1	S	HOT	BNY.
India	Finolex Cables Limited Gdr	FINGDR	1:1	S	TEL	CIT.
India	Flex Industries Limited	FILOYP	1:2	S	PPP	BT.
India	"Garden Silk Mills Limited Reg "'S'" Gdr"	GSM	1:5	S	TEX	BNY.
India	Grasim Industries Limited	GSNIF	1:1	S	TEX	CIT.
India	"Grasim Industries Limited "'Gdr'""	GSNTF	1:1	S	TEX	CIT.

COUNTRY	ISSUE	SYMBOL	RATIO	S/U	INDUSTRY	DEPOSITARY
India	Great Eastern Shipping Co. Ltd. 144a	GEGEF	1:5	S	TRN	BNY.
India	Gujarat Ambuja Cements Limited Gdr	GACL	1:1	S	CST	BT.
India	Gujarat Narmada Valley 144A	GNVFYP	1:5	S	CHM	BNY.
India	Gujarat Narmada Valley Reg S Gdr	GNVFRS	1:5	S	CHM	BNY.
India	Himachal Futuristic 144a	HFCLYP	1:4	S	EEI	BNY.
India	Himachal Futuristic Reg S Gdr	HFCLREGS	1:4	S	EEI	BNY.
India	Hindalco Industries Ltd. 144a	HNDCF	1:1	S	MIN	MGT.
India	Hindalco Industries Ltd. Warrant	HINWARR	1:1	S	MIN	MGT.
India	Hindustan Development Corp. Ltd. Gdr	HDCCYGDR	1:1	S	OTH	BT.
India	I.T.C. Limited Gdr	ITCGDR	1:1	S	MUL	CIT.
India	"India Cements Limited 144a, The"	IAMTF	1:1	S	CST	CIT.
India	"India Cements Limited Gdr, The"	ICRPPGDR	1:1	S	CST	CIT.
India	Indian Aluminium Co. Ltd. 144a	IAULY	1:1	S	OTH	BNY.
India	Indian Hotel Co. Ltd.	IDHTF	1:1	S	HOT	CIT.
India	Indian Hotel Company Reg S	INHREGS	1:1	S	HOT	CIT.
India	Indian Petrochemical Corp. Ltd. Reg S	IPETYPGDR	1:3	S	CHM	CIT.
India	Indian Petrochemicals Corp. Ltd. 144a	IPETYP	1:3	S	CHM	CIT.
India	Indian Petrochemicals Corp. Ltd. 144a	IPDRP	1:3	S	CHM	CIT.
India	Indian Petrochemicals Corp. Ltd. Reg S	IPDGP	1:3	S	CHM	CIT.
India	Indian Rayon & Industries Ltd. 144a	INR144A	1:1	S	OTH	CIT.
India	Indo Gulf Fertilizers And Chemical Co	IGF144A	1:1	S	CHM	CIT.

COUNTRY	ISSUE	SYMBOL	RATIO	S/U	INDUSTRY	DEPOSITARY
India	Indo Rama Synthetics (India) Ltd 144A	IRAMYP	1:10	S	TEX	BNY.
India	Indo Rama Synthetics (India) Ltd Reg S	IRAMYPREGS	1:10	S	TEX	BNY.
India	Industrial Credit & Investment Corp	ICI144A	1:5	S	INV	BT.
India	Industrial Credit & Investment Reg S	ICIREGS	1:5	S	INV	BT.
India	Jagatjit Industries Limited Gdr	JAGREGS	1:20	S	FOD	BNY.
India	Jain Irrigation Edr	JNIRF	1:1	S	CHM	BT.
India	Jct Limited 144a	JCCTF	1:10	S	TEX	BNY.
India	Jct Limited Reg S Gdr	JCTLF	1:10	S	TEX	BNY.
India	Jk Corp Limited 144a Gdr	JKCGF	1:1	S	MUL	CIT.
India	"Kesoram Industries Co., Ltd."	KSRPP	1:1	S	CST	CIT.
India	"Kesoram Industries Co., Ltd. Reg S"	KSGPP	1:1	S	CST	CIT.
India	Larsen & Toubro Limited 144a	LTRPP	1:2	S	CST	CIT.
India	Larsen & Toubro Limited Gdr	LTLPP	1:2	S	CST	CIT.
India	Larsen & Toubro Limited Gdr	LTRPPGDR	1:2	S	CST	CIT.
India	Larsen & Toubro Limited Reg S	LTLPPR	1:2	S	CST	CIT.
India	Mahindra & Mahindra Ltd.144a	MANFFP	1:1	S	AUT	BNY.
India	Nepc-Micon Limited 144a	NEPCYP	1:1	S	OTH	BT.
India	Nippon Denro Ispat Ltd GDR	NIPDI	1:1	S	MER	BT.
India	Oriental Hotels Reg S	OHOTGDR	1:1	S	HOT	BT.
India	Ranbaxy Laboratories 144a	RANYPY	1:1	S	DRU	BNY.
India	Ranbaxy Laboratories GDR	RLORF	1:1	S	DRU	BNY.

COUNTRY	ISSUE	SYMBOL	RATIO	S/U	INDUSTRY	DEPOSITARY
India	"Raymond Woollen Mills Ltd. 144a, The"	RWRPP	1:2	S	TEX	CIT.
India	"Raymond Woollen Mills Ltd. Gdr, The"	RWRPPGDR	1:2	S	TEX	CIT.
India	Reliance Industries Limited 144a	RLNGF	1:2	S	CHM	BNY.
India	Reliance Industries Limited Reg S Gdr	RPLREGS	1:15	S	OGS	BNY.
India	Sanghi Polyesters Limited 144a Gdr	SPLYYP	1:5	S	TEX	BNY.
India	Shriram Industrial Enterprises Ltd. G	SIELYP	1:3	S	MUL	BNY.
India	Shriram Industrial Enterprises Ltd. U	SIELUP	1:3	S	MUL	BNY.
India	Siv Industries Limited 144a Gdrs	SIVIYP	1:1	S	TEX	BNY.
India	Siv Industries Limited 144a Units	SIVIUP	1:1	S	TEX	BNY.
India	Siv Industries Limited 144a Warrants	SIVIWP	1:1	S	TEX	BNY.
India	Southern Petrochemical Industries 144A	SXPCF	1:5	S	CHM	BNY.
India	State Bank of India-144A	SBKIYP	1:2	S	BKS	BNY.
India	State Bank of India-Reg S	SBKIYPP	1:2	S	BKS	BNY.
India	Steel Authority of India Limited Gdr	STRPP	1:15	S	STE	CIT.
India	Steel Authority of India Limited Reg S	SKAFF	1:15	S	STE	CIT.
India	Sterlite Industries Gdr	STER	40:1	S	OTH	BT.
India	Tata Electric Companies	TAT144A	1:10	S	EEI	CIT.
India	Tata Engineering and Locomotive Co. Ltd.	TTRPP	1:1	S	AUT	CIT.
India	Tata Engineering and Locomotive Co. Ltd.	TTGPP	1:1	S	AUT	CIT.
India	Tube Investments - 144a.	TUBEYP	1:1	S	STE	BNY.
India	Tube Investments - Reg S Gdr	TIOIF	1:1	S	STE	BNY.

COUNTRY	ISSUE	SYMBOL	RATIO	S/U	INDUSTRY	DEPOSITARY
India	United Phosphorus Limited Gdr	UNPHF	1:1	S	CHM	CIT.
India	Usha Belton Ltd.	USBLF	1:1	S	OTH	BT.
India	Videocon International 144a	VDC144A	1:1	S	CLE	BT.
India	Videocon International Reg S	VDCRGS	1:1	S	CLE	BT.
India	Videsh Sanchar Nigam Ltd (VSNL) 144A	VDSGYP	2:1	S	TEL	BNY.
India	Videsh Sanchar Nigam Ltd (VSNL) Reg S	VDSGYYP	2:1	S	TEL	BNY.
India	Wockhardt Limited	WOCKF	1:1	S	OTH	BT.
Indonesia	"Asia Pulp & Paper Company, Ltd."	PAP	1:4	S	PAP	BNY.
Indonesia	P.T. Indosat	IIT	1:10	S	TEL	BNY.
Indonesia	P.T. Inti Indorayon Utama	PTIDY	1:3	S	PAP	BNY.
Indonesia	P.T. Tambang Timah (Persero) 144a	PTBGF	1:10	S	MIN	CIT.
Indonesia	P.T. Tambang Timah (Persero) Gdr	PTBCF	1:10	S	MIN	CIT.
Indonesia	P.T. Telkom	TLK	1:20	S	TEL	BNY.
Indonesia	P.T. Tri Polyta Indonesia	TPI	1:10	S	CHM	BNY.
Indonesia	Pasifik Satelit Nusantara	PSNRY	1:3	S	TEL	BNY
Indonesia	PT Jakarta Int'l Hotels & Development	PJIHY	1:10	S	HOT	BT.
Indonesia	PT Kawasan Industri Jababeka 144A	PTKWYP	1:10	S	RES	BNY.
Indonesia	PT Kawasan Industri Jababeka Reg S	PTKWYYP	1:10	S	RES	BNY.
Israel	Blue Square–Israel Ltd.	BSI	1:1	S	RET	BNY.
Israel	Elite Industries Limited Nis 1	ELEIY	1:3	S	FOD	BNY.
Israel	Elite Industries Limited Nis 5	ELEDY	1:1	S	FOD	BNY.

COUNTRY	ISSUE	SYMBOL	RATIO	S/U	INDUSTRY	DEPOSITARY
Israel	Formula Systems (1985) Ltd. Reg S	FOMSYYP	1:1	S	CSN	BNY.
Israel	"Israel Land Development Company, Ltd."	ILDCY	1:3	S	RES	BNY.
Israel	Isras Investment Company Ltd. Nis 1	ISIMY1	1:10	S	INV	CIT.
Israel	Isras Investment Company Ltd. Nis 5	ISIMY5	1:10	S	INV	CIT.
Israel	Koor Industries Limited	KOREA	5:1	S	MUL	BNY.
Israel	Kopel Limited	KOPLY	1:2	S	SER	BNY.
Israel	Matav-Cable Systems Media Ltd.	MATVY	1:2	S	TEL	BNY.
Israel	Nice Systems Ltd.	NICEY	1:1	S	TEC	BNY.
Israel	Tadiran Limited	TAD	1:1	S	TEL	BNY.
Israel	Teva Pharmaceutical Industries Ltd.	TEVIY	1:1	S	DRU	BNY.
Kazakhstan	Kazkommertsbank 144A	JSCKRP	1:30	S	BKS	BNY.
Kazakhstan	Kazkommertsbank Reg S	JSCKRPREGS	1:30	S	BKS	BNY.
Korea	"Anam Industrial Co., Ltd."	ANAKYP	1:1	S	EEI	CIT.
Korea	Cho Hung Bank	CHHBYP	1:1	S	BKS	CIT.
Korea	"Goldstar Co, Ltd. Gdr"	GODGDR	2:1	S	CLE	CIT.
Korea	Hana Bank Gdr	HANBYP	1:1	S	BKS	CIT.
Korea	Hankuk Glass Industries Inc.	HAN144A	2:1	S	OTH	CIT.
Korea	Hansol Paper	HAPSF	2:1	S	PAP	MGT.
Korea	"Housing & Commercial Bank, Korea-144A"	HROKYP	1:1	S	BKS	BNY.
Korea	Hyundai Engineering & Construct. 144A	HYUNF	2:1	S	CST	CIT.
Korea	Hyundai Motor Company	HYM144A	2:1	S	AUT	CIT.

COUNTRY	ISSUE	SYMBOL	RATIO	S/U	INDUSTRY	DEPOSITARY
Korea	Hyundai Motor Company	HYMM144A	2:1	S	AUT	CIT.
Korea	Hyundai Motor Company	HYNDYPX	2:1	S	AUT	CIT.
Korea	Kia Motors Corporation 144a	KIAMOT	1:1	S	AUT	CIT.
Korea	Kia Motors Corporation 144a	KIANF	1:1	S	AUT	CIT.
Korea	Kia Motors Corporation Gdr	KNGFYR	1:1	S	AUT	CIT.
Korea	Kookmin Bank Gdr	KKMNYP	1:1	S	BKS	BNY.
Korea	Korea Electric Power Corporation	KEP	2:1	S	UTI	BNY.
Korea	Lg Chemical Ltd. 144a	LGEGF	1:1	S	CHM	CIT.
Korea	Mando Machinery Corp. 144a	MNDOYP	2:1	S	AUT	BNY.
Korea	Pohang Iron & Steel Company Limited	PKX	4:1	S	STE	BNY.
Korea	Samsung Co. Ltd. 144a Gdr	SSGFF	2:1	S	CLE	CIT.
Korea	Samsung Electronics 144a	SAM144A	2:1	S	CLE	CIT.
Korea	"Samsung Electronics Co., Ltd. Gdr"	SEFPP	1:2	S	EEI	CIT.
Korea	Samsung Electronics Convertible Bond	SAMPEZ	2:1	S	EEI	CIT.
Korea	Samsung Electronics Gdr	SAMELEGDR	2:1	S	CLE	CIT.
Korea	Samsung Electronics Non-Voting 144a	SSNEF	2:1	S	CLE	CIT.
Korea	Samsung Electronics Non-Voting Gdr	SELEGDR	2:1	S	CLE	CIT.
Korea	Samsung Electronics Non-Voting Pref 1	SAMPRE144A	2:1	S	CLE	CIT.
Korea	Samsung Engineering & Construction	SAMENG144A	2:1	S	CST	CIT.
Korea	"SK Telecom Co., Ltd."	SKM	90:1	S	TEL	CIT.
Korea	Yukong Limited	YKLLY144A	2:1	S	OGS	CIT.

COUNTRY	ISSUE	SYMBOL	RATIO	S/U	INDUSTRY	DEPOSITARY
Lebanon	Banque Audi Sal Gdr	AUDPP	1:1	S	BKS	BT.
Lebanon	Banque Libanaise Poue Le Commerce 144A	BLPC	1:1	S	BKS	BT.
Lebanon	Soldiere 144A	SLEBYP	1:1	S	CST	BNY.
Lebanon	Soldiere Reg S	SLEBYPP	1:1	S	CST	BNY.
Lithuania	Bankas Hermis Reg S	BKHER	5:1	S	BKS	BNY.
Lithuania	Birzai Milk Joint Stock Company 144A	BMJSC	1:10	S	FOD	BT.
Lithuania	Vilniauc Bankas AB	VILNY	10:1	S	BKS	BT.
Malaysia	Amsteel Corporation Berhad	AMCSY	1:1	S	STE	BNY.
Malaysia	Angkasa Marketing Berhad	AKAMY	1:1	S	MER	BNY.
Malaysia	Bandar Raya Developments Berhad	BRVDY	1:1	U	RES	BNY.CIT.MGT.
Malaysia	Berjaya Corp. Berhad	BJYAY	1:10	S	MUL	CIT.
Malaysia	Boustead Holdings Berhad	BSTHY	1:1	U	MUL	BNY.CIT.MGT.
Malaysia	Genting Berhad	GEBEY	1:1	U	HOT	BNY.BT.CIT.MGT.
Malaysia	Inter-Pacific Industrial Group Berhad	IPIGY	1:10	S	FOD	CIT.
Malaysia	Kesang Corporation Berhad	KSGCY	1:5	S	HOT	BNY.
Malaysia	Kuala Lumpur Kepong Berhad	KLKBY	1:1	U	FOD	BNY.BT.CIT.MGT.
Malaysia	Lion Land Berhad	LONLY	1:1	S	MUL	BNY.
Malaysia	Malayan Credit Limited	MYANY	1:1	U	INV	BNY.CIT.MGT.
Malaysia	Malayan United Industries Berhad	MYLUY	1:1	U	MUL	BNY.BT.CIT.MGT.
Malaysia	MBF Holdings Berhad	MBFHY	1:20	S	MUL	BNY.
Malaysia	Perlis Plantations Berhad	PPBHY	1:1	U	FOD	BNY.MGT.

COUNTRY	ISSUE	SYMBOL	RATIO	S/U	INDUSTRY	DEPOSITARY
Malaysia	Resorts World Berhad	RSWSY	1:5	S	HOT	CIT.
Malaysia	Selangor Properties Berhad	SGPBY	1:1	U	RES	BNY.CIT.MGT.
Malaysia	Sime Darby Berhad	SIDBY	1:1	U	MUL	BNY.BT.CIT.MGT.
Malaysia	Tenaga Nasional Berhad	TNABY	1:4	S	EEI	MGT.
Mexico	"Abaco Grupo Financiero ""C"" Shares"	ABGFY	1:10	S	INV	BNY.
Mexico	Aerovias De Mexico 144a Gdr	AERMY	1:10	S	AIR	CIT.
Mexico	"Alfa, S.A. De C.V."	ALFGDR	1:1	S	MUL	CIT.
Mexico	"Altos Hornos De Mexico, SA"	IAM	1:5	S	STE	MGT.
Mexico	"Apasco, Sa De Cv ""A"""	AASAY	1:5	S	CST	CIT.
Mexico	"Apasco, Sa De Cv ""B"""	AASBY	1:5	S	CST	CIT.
Mexico	Banca Quadrum Units	QDRMY	1:1	S	INV	BNY.
Mexico	"Banpais ""L"" Shares"	BPS	1:6	S	BKS	BNY.
Mexico	"Blockbuster De Mexico ""B"" Shares 144a"	GMEX144A	1:10	S	HOT	BNY.
Mexico	"Bufete Industrial, S.A."	GBI	1:3	S	CST	BNY.
Mexico	"Carso Global Telecom, S.A. De C.V."	CGTVY	1:2	S	TEL	CIT.
Mexico	Cemex S.A. A Shares	CXSSY	1:2	S	CST	MGT.
Mexico	Cemex S.A. De C.V. 144A	CMXOF	1:2	S	CST	MGT.
Mexico	"Cemex, S.A. B Shares"	CMXBY	1:2	S	CST	MGT.
Mexico	"Cifra ""B"" Shares"	CFRAY	1:1	U	MER	BNY.CHS.CIT.MGT.
Mexico	"Cifra ""C"" Shares"	CFRCY	1:1	U	MER	BNY.
Mexico	"Coca-Cola Femsa ""L"" Shares"	KOF	1:10	S	BEV	BNY.

COUNTRY	ISSUE	SYMBOL	RATIO	S/U	INDUSTRY	DEPOSITARY
Mexico	Consorcio Ara Common Shares 144A	CSRAYP	1:10	S	CST	BNY.
Mexico	Consorcio Ara Common Shares Reg S	CSRAYPREGS	1:10	S	CST	BNY.
Mexico	"Consorcio G Grupo Dina ""L""""	DINL	1:4	S	AUT	MGT.
Mexico	Consorcio G Grupo Dina Sa De Cv	DIN	1:4	S	AUT	MGT.
Mexico	"Consorcio Hogar ""B"""" Shares 144A"	HGARYP	1:10	S	CST	BNY.
Mexico	"Consorcio Hogar ""B"""" Shares Reg S"	HGARYPP	1:10	S	CST	BNY.
Mexico	Controladora Commercial Mexicana S.A.	MCM	1:20	S	RET	CIT.
Mexico	"Corporacion Geo, S.A. De C.V."	CVGEY	1:4	S	CST	CIT.
Mexico	"Corporacion Geo, S.A. De C.V. Reg S"	GEOREGS	1:4	S	CST	CIT.
Mexico	Corporacion Industrial San Luis Ser A	SLRPP	1:6	S	MAC	CIT.
Mexico	Corporacion Industrial San Luis Ser A	SLRPPREGS	1:6	S	MAC	CIT.
Mexico	"Desc, S.A. De C.V. Series C"	DES	1:4	S	MUL	CIT.
Mexico	"El Puerto De Liverpool, Sa De Cv Gdr"	ELPLF	1:20	S	RET	CIT.
Mexico	"Empaques Ponderosa ""B"" Shares"	EPQRY	1:25	S	PPP	BNY.
Mexico	"Empresas Ica ""A"""" Cpo"	ICA	1:6	S	CST	BNY.
Mexico	"Empresas La Moderna ""A"""" Cpo"	ELM	1:4	S	FOD	BNY.
Mexico	"Far-Ben, S.A. De C.V."	FRBNY	1:2	S	DRV	CIT.
Mexico	"Femsa, S.A. De C.V."	FEMSA	1:1	S	BEV	CIT.
Mexico	"Femsa, S.A. De C.V. 144a Gdr"	FEM144A	1:1	S	BEV	CIT.
Mexico	G. Accion S.A. De C.V. 144A	GACRP	1:10	S	RES	CIT.
Mexico	G. Accion S.A. De C.V. Reg S	GACRRP	1:10	S	RES	CIT.

COUNTRY	ISSUE	SYMBOL	RATIO	S/U	INDUSTRY	DEPOSITARY
Mexico	"Gruma, S.A. De C.V. 144A"	GRUPYP	1:4	S	FOD	CIT.
Mexico	"Grupo Carso, S.A. De C.V. 144a"	GPOOY	1:2	S	MUL	CIT.
Mexico	Grupo Casa Autrey	ATY	1:4	S	RET	MGT.
Mexico	Grupo Continental S.A.	GPOCY	1:10	S	FOD	BNY.
Mexico	Grupo Elektra Cpo	EKT	1:2	S	MER	BNY.
Mexico	"Grupo Fernandez Editores, S.A. De C.V."	GPOFY	1:25	S	PUB	BNY.
Mexico	"Grupo Financiero Bancomer, ""B"" Shares"	GFNSY	1:20	S	BKS	BNY.
Mexico	"Grupo Financiero Bancomer, 144a ""B"" S"	GFNBY	1:20	S	BKS	BNY.
Mexico	"Grupo Financiero Bital, S.A. De C.V."	GFBLY	1:10	S	INV	BNY.
Mexico	"Grupo Financiero Gbm Atlantico, Sa De"	GRUPY	1:4	S	INV	CIT.
Mexico	"Grupo Financiero Gbm Atlantico, Sa De"	GGDSF	1:4	S	INV	CIT.
Mexico	"Grupo Financiero Invermexico ""C"""	GFXBY	1:10	S	INV	CIT.
Mexico	"Grupo Financiero Prime Int'l, S.A. De"	GRPOTC	1:5	S	INV	CIT.
Mexico	Grupo Financiero Serfin	SFN	1:4	S	BKS	CIT.
Mexico	"Grupo Gigante, S.A. De C.V. 144a Gdr"	GPGTY	1:10	S	MER	CIT.
Mexico	"Grupo Herdez ""B"" Shares"	GUZBY	1:25	S	FOD	BNY.
Mexico	"Grupo IMSA, S.A. De C.V."	IMY	1:9	S	STE	BNY.
Mexico	"Grupo Industrial Durango ""A"" Cpo"	GID	1:2	S	PPP	BNY.
Mexico	Grupo Industrial Maseca S.A. De C.V.	MSK	1:15	S	RET	CIT.
Mexico	"Grupo Industrial Maseca S.A. De C.V. ""A"""	GRIMY	1:10	S	RET	CIT.
Mexico	"Grupo Iusacell Series ""D"" Shares"	CELD	1:10	S	TEL	BNY.

COUNTRY	ISSUE	SYMBOL	RATIO	S/U	INDUSTRY	DEPOSITARY
Mexico	"Grupo Iusacell Series "L"" Shares"	CEL	1:10	S	TEL	BNY.
Mexico	"Grupo Mexicano De Desarrollo "B"" Shares"	GMDB	1:1	S	CST	BNY.
Mexico	"Grupo Mexicano De Desarrollo "L"" Shares"	GMD	1:1	S	CST	BNY.
Mexico	"Grupo Minsa, S.A. De C.V."	GPMNY	1:10	S	FOD	BNY.
Mexico	"Grupo Minsa, S.A. De C.V. 144A"	GPMNYP	1:10	S	FOD	BNY.
Mexico	"Grupo Posadas, S.A. De C.V. "A"" 144A"	GRPALP	1:20	S	HOT	BNY.
Mexico	"Grupo Posadas, S.A. De C.V. "L"" Gdr"	GRPVP	1:20	S	HOT	BNY.
Mexico	"Grupo Pypsa "B"" Shares"	GPPSY	1:2	S	ENG	BNY.
Mexico	"Grupo Radio Centro, S.A. De C.V."	RC	1:9	S	MED	CIT.
Mexico	"Grupo Sidek "B"" Shares"	GPSBY	1:4	S	MUL	BNY.
Mexico	"Grupo Sidek "L"" Shares"	GPSAY	1:4	S	MUL	BNY.
Mexico	"Grupo Simec "B"" Shares"	SIM	1:20	S	STE	BNY.
Mexico	"Grupo Situr "B"" Shares"	GPSRY	1:10	S	HOT	BNY.
Mexico	"Grupo Situr "B"" Shares 144a"	GPSMY	1:10	S	HOT	BNY.
Mexico	"Grupo Synkro "B"" Shares"	GPSYY	1:1	S	RET	BNY.
Mexico	"Grupo Syr, S.A. De C.V."	GSYOTC	1:10	S	RET	CIT.
Mexico	"Grupo Televisa, S.A. Gdr"	TV	1:2	S	MED	CIT.
Mexico	Grupo Tribasa Common Shares	GTR	1:2	S	CST	BNY.
Mexico	"Hylsamex "B"" Shares"	HLETY	1:6	S	STE	BNY.
Mexico	"Hylsamex "B"" Shares	HLEXY	1:6	S	STE	BNY.
Mexico	Iem Sa (Industria Electrica de Mexico)	IEMSY	1:1	U	UTI	BT.CHS.
Mexico	"Industrias Bachoco, S.A. de C.V.	IBA	1:6	S	FOD	BNY.

COUNTRY	ISSUE	SYMBOL	RATIO	S/U	INDUSTRY	DEPOSITARY
Mexico	"Internacional De Ceramica "C"" Shares"	ICDCY	1:1	S	CST	CIT.
Mexico	"Internacional De Ceramica "D"" Shares"	ICM	1:5	S	CST	CIT.
Mexico	"Internacional De Ceramica "B"" Shares"	CEROTC	1:1	S	CST	CIT.
Mexico	Jugos Del Valle Sa De CV	JUVAY	1:5	S	BEV	BT.
Mexico	Kimberly Clark De Mexico	KCDMY	1:5	S	PAP	MGT.
Mexico	Pepsi-Gemex S.A. De C.V.	GEM	1:6	S	BEV	CIT.
Mexico	"Sears Roebuck De Mexico, S.A.Dec.V.14"	SMXBY	1:2	S	RET	MGT.
Mexico	"Sears Roebuck De Mexico, S.A.Dec.V.Gd"	SSSMF	1:2	S	RET	MGT.
Mexico	"Seguros Comercial America, S.A. De C.V."	SCAS	1:1	S	INS	BNY.
Mexico	"Telefonos De Mexico "A"" Shares"	TFONY	1:1	U	TEL	BNY.CIT.MGT.MID.
Mexico	Telefonos De Mexico S.A. De C.V. Ser	TMX	1:20	S	TEL	MGT.
Mexico	"Tolmex, S.A. De C.V. "B"" Shares"	TLMXY	1:10	S	CST	CIT.
Mexico	"Transportacion Maritima Mexicana "A""	TMMA	1:1	S	TRN	CIT.
Mexico	"Transportacion Maritima Mexicana "L""	TMM	1:1	S	TRN	CIT.
Mexico	"Tubos De Acero De Mexico, S.A."	TAM	1:1	S	STE	MGT.
Mexico	"TV Azteca, S.A. De C.V."	TZA	1:4	S	MED	BNY.
Mexico	"Vitro, S.A. De C.V."	VTO	1:1	S	CST	CIT.
Morocco	Banque Marocaine De Commerce Ext 144A	BMDC	3:1	S	BKS	BT.
Morocco	Banque Marocaine De Commerce Ext Reg S	BMDCREGS	3:1	S	BKS	BT.
New Guinea	Bougainville Copper Limited	BOCOY	1:1	U	CST	BNY.BT.CIT.MGT.MID.
New Guinea	Niugini Mining Limited	NGIMY	1:1	S	CST	BNY.

COUNTRY	ISSUE	SYMBOL	RATIO	S/U	INDUSTRY	DEPOSITARY
New Guinea	Oil Search Limited	OISHY	1:10	S	OGS	BNY.
Pakistan	Chakwal Cement 144a	CCRPP	1:25	S	BDM	CIT.
Pakistan	Chakwal Cement Gdr	CCRPPGDR	1:25	S	BDM	CIT.
Pakistan	Hub Power Company Limited 144a	HPCLYP	1:25	S	UTI	BNY.
Pakistan	Hub Power Company Limited Reg S Gdr	HPCLRS	1:25	S	UTI	BNY.
Pakistan	Pakistan Telecommunications	PKTLY144A	1:1	S	TEL	CIT.
Pakistan	Pakistan Telecommunications Gdr	PKTLYGDR	1:1	S	TEL	CIT.
Peru	Banco Weise Limitado	BWP	1:4	S	BKS	MGT.
Peru	Cementos Lima Common Shares	CEMTY	1:1	S	CST	BNY.
Peru	Cementos Lima Common Shares 144a	LIMAYP	1:1	S	CST	BNY.
Peru	"Compania De Minas Buenaventura ""B"""Shares	BVN	1:2	S	MIN	BNY.
Peru	"Corporacion Interbanc ""B"" Shares 144a"	IFNHBYP	1:10	S	INV	BNY.
Peru	"Corporacion Interbanc ""B"" Shares Reg"	IFNHBYS	1:10	S	INV	BNY.
Peru	Ferreyros Common Shares 144A	FRYSYP	1:20	S	MAC	BNY.
Peru	"Ferreyros, S.A."	FERXY	1:20	S	MAC	BNY.
Peru	Luz Del Sur S.A.	LUZZS	1:15	S	UTI	CIT.
Peru	Luz Del Sur S.A. 144A	LUZS	1:15	S	UTI	CIT.
Peru	Peru Real Estate S.A.	PREY	1:25	S	RES	CIT.
Peru	Tele 2000 Common Shares	TLNEY	1:5	S	TEL	BNY.
Peru	Tele 2000 Common Shares 144a	TLNFY	1:5	S	TEL	BNY.
Peru	Telefonica Del Peru S.A.	TDP	1:10	S	TEL	MGT.

COUNTRY	ISSUE	SYMBOL	RATIO	S/U	INDUSTRY	DEPOSITARY
Philippines	Aboitiz Equity Ventures Inc.	ABRPP	1:100	S	MUL	CIT.
Philippines	Aboitiz Equity Ventures Inc. Gdr	ABRPPGDR	1:100	S	MUL	CIT.
Philippines	Ayala Corporation 144a Class B	AYC144A	1:10	S	MUL	MGT.
Philippines	Basic Petroleum & Minerals Inc.	BSPMY	1:2000	S	MIN	BNY.
Philippines	Benpres Holdings Corp.144a	BHCPYP	1:20	S	MUL	BNY.
Philippines	"JG Summit Holdings, Inc. Gdr"	JGSGDR	1:100	S	MUL	CIT.
Philippines	Manila Electric Co (Meralco) Gdr	MAN144A	1:1	S	UTI	CIT.
Philippines	Manila Electric Company (Meralco)	MERAY	1:1	S	EEI	CIT.
Philippines	Petron Corporation	PETCO144A	1:50	S	OGS	CIT.
Philippines	Petron Corporation Gdr	PETCOGDR	1:50	S	OGS	CIT.
Philippines	Philippine First Series F Non-Vote 144A	PHILL	1:1	S	INV	BNY.
Philippines	Philippine First Series F Voting 144A	PHIL	1:1	S	INV	BNY.
Philippines	Philippine Long Distance Telephone	PHILIPPINES	1:1	S	TEL	CIT.
Philippines	Philippine Long Distance Telephone Pr	PHIA	1:1	S	TEL	CIT.
Philippines	"Philodrill Corporation, The"	PHLOY	1:2000	S	MUL	BNY.
Philippines	Rfm Corporation	RFMFY	1:20	S	FOD	BNY.
Philippines	San Miguel Corp.	SMGBY	1:10	S	FOD	MGT.
Philippines	Sm Prime Holdings	SMP144A	1:50	S	RES	MGT.
Philippines	United Paragon Mining Corporation	UNPGY	1:5000	S	MIN	BNY.
Poland	Bank Gdanski 144a	BSKIYP	1:1	S	BKS	BNY.
Poland	Bank Gdanski Reg S	BSKIREGS	1:1	S	BKS	BNY.

COUNTRY	ISSUE	SYMBOL	RATIO	S/U	INDUSTRY	DEPOSITARY
Poland	Bank Handlowy W Warszawie 144A	BKWWYP	1:1	S	BKS	BNY.
Poland	Bank Handlowy W Warszawie Reg S	BKWWYPP	1:1	S	BKS	BNY.
Poland	Bank Inicjatyw Gospodarczych "Big'"" 144A"	BBIGYP	1:15	S	BKS	BNY.
Poland	Bank Inicjatyw Gospodarczych "Big'"" Reg S"	BBIGYPP	1:15	S	BKS	BNY.
Poland	KGHM Polska Miedz S.A.	KGGPP	1:2	S	MIN	CIT.
Poland	KGHM Polska Miedz S.A.	KGPPGDR	1:2	S	MIN	CIT.
Poland	Mostostal Export Corp.	MECOY	1:1	S	CST	BNY.
Poland	"National Invest FDS Reg S '"Nif Progress'"""	NIF4	1:1	S	INV	BNY.
Poland	"National Invest FDS Reg S '"Nif Victoria'"""	NIF5	1:1	S	INV	BNY.
Poland	"National Investment Funds Reg S '"Nif-1'""""	NIF1	1:1	S	INV	BNY.
Poland	"National Investment Funds Reg S '"Nif-2'""""	NIF2	1:1	S	INV	BNY.
Poland	"National Investment Funds Reg S '"Nif-3'""""	NIF3	1:1	S	INV	BNY.
Poland	"Natl Invest Fds Reg S '"Nif-11'""""	NIF11	1:1	S	INV	BNY.
Poland	"Natl Invest Fds Reg S '"'Nif-Fortuna'""""	NIF13	1:1	S	INV	BNY.
Poland	"Natl Invest Fds Reg S '"Nif-Hetman'""""	NIF15	1:1	S	INV	BNY.
Poland	"Natl Invest Fds Reg S '"Nif-K. Wielki'""""	NIF7	1:1	S	INV	BNY.
Poland	"Natl Invest Fds Reg S '"Nif-Octava'""""	NIF8	1:1	S	INV	BNY.
Poland	"Natl Invest Fds Reg S '"Nif-Piast'""""	NIF12	1:1	S	INV	BNY.
Poland	"Natl Invest Fds Reg S '"Nif-Zachodni'""""	NIF14	1:1	S	INV	BNY.
Poland	"Natl Invest Fds Reg S '"Nif-E. Kwiatkowski	NIF9	1:1	S	INV	BNY.
Poland	"Natl Invest Fds Reg S '"Nif-Magna Polonia	NIF6	1:1	S	INV	BNY.

COUNTRY	ISSUE	SYMBOL	RATIO S/U	INDUSTRY	DEPOSITARY
Poland	"Natl Invest Fds Reg S ""Nif-10"""	NIF10	1:1 S	INV	BNY.
Poland	"Republic of Poland ""USC""S Reg S"	RPUSC	1:1 S	MUL	BNY.
Poland	Universal S.A.	UVSFY	1:2 S	MUL	BNY.
Portugal	Banco Comercial Portugues	BPC	1:1 S	BKS	BNY.
Portugal	"Cimpor-Cimentos De Portugal, SA"	CTOSYP	1:2 S	CST	CIT.
Portugal	Electricidade De Portugal	EDP	1:2 S	EEI	CIT.
Portugal	Engil-Sociedad Gestora De Participacoes	ESGPY	1:1 S	CST	CIT.
Portugal	Espirito Santo Financial Holding S.A.	ESF	1:1 S	INV	BNY.
Portugal	Portucel-Industrial 144a	PORTI144A	1:1 S	PAP	CIT.
Portugal	Portucel-Industrial Reg S	PTCIY	1:1 S	PAP	CIT.
Portugal	Portugal Telecom	PT	1:1 S	TEL	BNY.
Portugal	Telecel-Comunicacoes Pessoais 144A	TPORYP	1:1 S	TEL	BNY.
Portugal	Telecel-Comunicacoes Pessoais Reg S	TPORYYP	1:1 S	TEL	BNY.
Russia	Ao Mosenergo 144a	MOSRYP	1:30 S	UTI	BNY.
Russia	Ao Mosenergo Reg S Gdr	AOMOY	1:30 S	UTI	BNY.
Russia	Bank Vozrozhdeniye	BKVZY	1:1 S	BKS	BNY.
Russia	Chernogorneft	CHRHY	1:1 S	OGS	BNY.
Russia	Gazprom 144A	RADGYP	1:10 S	OGS	BNY.
Russia	Gazprom Reg S	RADGYPS	1:10 S	OGS	BNY.
Russia	Gum (A O Torgovy Dom)	GUMRY	1:2 S	MER	BNY.
Russia	Inkombank	IKMBY	1:15 S	BKS	BNY.

COUNTRY	ISSUE	SYMBOL	RATIO	S/U	INDUSTRY	DEPOSITARY
Russia	JSC Irkutskenergo	IKSGY	1:50	S	UTI	BNY.
Russia	JSC Rosneftegazstroy	RFGZY	2:1	S	CST	BNY.
Russia	JSC Surgutneftegaz	JSCSY	1:50	S	OGS	BNY.
Russia	JSC Uralsvyasinform Level I	UVYZY	1:200	S	TEL	BNY.
Russia	Lukoil	LUKOY	1:4	S	OGS	BNY.
Russia	Lukoil 144A	JSCLYP	1:4	S	OGS	BNY.
Russia	Lukoil 144A Global Depositary Receipt	LUKGDR144A	1:4	S	OGS	BNY.
Russia	Lukoil Pref	LUKPY	1:2	S	OGS	BNY.
Russia	Lukoil Reg S Global Depositary Receipt	LUKGDRS	1:4	S	OGS	BNY.
Russia	Menatep Bank	MBRUY	1:10	S	BKS	BNY.
Russia	Menatep Bank-Pref	MBRVY	1:10	S	BKS	BNY.
Russia	Minfin - 5/14/1999 144a	MFINY99	1:1000	S	DEB	BNY.
Russia	Minfin - 5/14/1999 Reg S	MFINRE99	1:1000	S	DEB	BNY.
Russia	Minfin - 5/14/2003 144a	MFINY03	1:1000	S	DEB	BNY.
Russia	Minfin - 5/14/2003 Reg S	MFINRE03	1:1000	S	DEB	BNY.
Russia	Minfin - 5/14/2006 144a	MFINY06	1:1000	S	DEB	BNY.
Russia	Minfin - 5/14/2006 Reg S	MFINRE06	1:1000	S	DEB	BNY.
Russia	Minfin - 5/14/2008 144a	MFINY08	1:1000	S	DEB	BNY.
Russia	Minfin - 5/14/2008 Reg S	MFINRE08	1:1000	S	DEB	BNY.
Russia	Minfin - 5/14/2011 144a	MFINY11	1:1000	S	DEB	BNY.
Russia	Minfin - 5/14/2011 Reg S	MFINRE11	1:1000	S	DEB	BNY.

COUNTRY	ISSUE	SYMBOL	RATIO	S/U	INDUSTRY	DEPOSITARY
Russia	Seversky Tube Works	STBWY	1:10	S	STE	BNY.
Russia	Sun Brewing Limited 144a	SUNBYP	1:1	S	BEV	BNY.
Russia	Tatneft	TTFTY	1:1	S	OGS	BNY.
Russia	Tatneft 144A	ITFTYP	1:1	S	OGS	BNY.
Russia	Tatneft Reg S	ITFTYYP	1:1	S	OGS	BNY.
Russia	Trading House TsUM	TDHSY	1:20	S	HCG	BNY.
Russia	Unified Energy System of Russia Reg S	UESRRYP	1:100	S	EES	BNY.
Russia	Vimpelcom (Open Joint Stock Co)	VIP	4:3	S	TEL	BNY.
Slovakia	Slovnaft As	SLVXF	1:1	S	OGS	BNY.
Slovenia	Btc D.D. 144A	BTCD	10:1	S	CST	BT.
Slovenia	Btc D.D. Reg S	BTCREGS	10:1	S	CST	BT.
Slovenia	SKB Banka D.D. 144A	SKBBYP	1:1	S	BKS	BNY.
Slovenia	SKB Banka D.D. Reg S	SKBBYPP	1:1	S	BKS	BNY.
South Africa	Abercom Group Limited	ABGRY	1:1	U	MAC	CIT.
South Africa	ABSA Bank Limited	ABSA	1:2	S	BKS	BT.
South Africa	Ae And Ci Limited	AECLY	1:1	U	CHM	CIT.
South Africa	AECI Limited 144A	AECIPY	1:3	S	CHM	BNY.
South Africa	AECI Limited Reg S	AECIP	1:3	S	CHM	BNY.
South Africa	Afmin Holdings Limited	AHLOTC	1:1	U	MIN	BNY.BT.
South Africa	"Afrikander Lease Limited, The"	AFKDY	1:1	U	MIN	BNY.BT.CIT.MGT.
South Africa	Anglo American Coal Corporation	ANAMY	1:1	U	COA	BNY.

COUNTRY	ISSUE	SYMBOL	RATIO	S/U	INDUSTRY	DEPOSITARY
South Africa	Anglo American Corporation of SA Ltd.	ANGLY	1:1	U	MIN	BNY.BT.MID.CIT.MGT.
South Africa	"Anglo American Gold Investment Co., L"	AAGIY	10:1	U	MIN	BNY.BT.CIT.MGT.MID.
South Africa	Anglo American Investment Trust Ltd	ANGVY	1:1	U	INV	BNY.CIT.MGT.
South Africa	Anglo American Platinum Corp. Ltd.	RPATY	1:1	U	MIN	BNY.BT.CIT.MID.
South Africa	Anglovaal Holdings Limited	ANHLY	1:1	U	MUL	CIT.
South Africa	"Anglovaal Limited "A""	ANVAY	1:1	U	MUL	CIT.
South Africa	"Anglovaal Limited "N" 144a"	AVAAY	1:1	S	MUL	MGT.
South Africa	"Anglovaal Limited "N" Gdr"	ANAGDR	1:1	S	MUL	MGT.
South Africa	"Anglovaal Limited "Ord""	ANAVY	1:1	U	MUL	BNY.CIT.MGT
South Africa	Avgold Limited	AVGLY	1:10	S	MIN	MGT.
South Africa	Avmin Limited	AVMLY	1:5	S	MIN	MGT.
South Africa	Barlow Limited	BRRAY	1:1	U	MUL	BNY.CIT.MGT.
South Africa	Beatrix Mines	BTRXY	1:1	U	MIN	BNY.BT.CIT.MGT.MID.
South Africa	Bidvest Group Limited	BDVSY	1:2	S	SER	CIT.
South Africa	Blyvooruitzicht Gold Mining Co.Ltd	BLYDY	1:3	S	MIN	BNY.
South Africa	Buffelsfontein Gold Mining Ltd.	BLGMY	1:1	S	MIN	BNY.
South Africa	C.G. Smith Limited	CGSMY	1:1	S	MUL	BNY.
South Africa	Consolidated Murchison Limited	CNMUY	1:1	U	MIN	BNY.CIT.MGT.
South Africa	De Beers Consolidated Mines	DBRSY	1:1	U	MIN	BNY.BT.MID.CIT.MGT.

COUNTRY	ISSUE	SYMBOL	RATIO	S/U	INDUSTRY	DEPOSITARY
South Africa	Deelkraal Gold Mining Company Ltd.	DLKRY	1:1	S	MIN	MGT.
South Africa	Driefontein Consolidated Limited	DRFNY	1:1	S	MIN	MGT.
South Africa	Durban Roodeport Deep Limited	DROOY	1:1	S	MIN	BNY.
South Africa	East Rand Gold And Uranium Company Ltd	EASRY	1:1	U	MIN	BNY.BT.CIT.MGT.MID.
South Africa	East Rand Proprietary Mines Limited	ERNDY	1:1	U	MIN	BNY.CIT.MGT.MID.
South Africa	Egoli Consolidated Mines Limited	ELCMY	1:1	U	MIN	BNY.BT.MGT.
South Africa	Elandsrand Gold Mining Co.	EGMLY	1:1	U	MIN	BNY.BT.CIT.MGT.
South Africa	Energy Africa 144A	ENAFYP	1:5	S	OGS	BNY.
South Africa	Energy Africa Reg S	ENAFY	1:5	S	OGS	BNY.
South Africa	Engen Limited	ENGNY	1:1	S	OGS	BNY.
South Africa	Eskom E167	ESKA	1:10000	S	UTI	MGT.
South Africa	Eskom E168	ESKB	1:10000	S	UTI	MGT.
South Africa	Eskom E169	ESKC	1:10000	S	UTI	MGT.
South Africa	Eskom E170	ESKD	1:10000	S	UTI	MGT.
South Africa	Ettington Investments Limited	ETNVY	1:1	U	MIN	BNY.CIT.MGT.
South Africa	Evander Gold Mines Limited	EGMVY	1:1	U	MIN	BNY.BT.MID.CIT.MGT.
South Africa	Federale Mynbou Beperk	FMBOTC	1:1	U	INV	CIT.
South Africa	"Fedsure Holdings Limited ""Ord"""""	FSURY	1:2	S	INS	BNY.
South Africa	"Fedsure Holdings Limited ""Preference"""""	FSUPY	1:2	S	INS	BNY.
South Africa	Foschini Limited	FHNIY	1:2	S	RET	CIT.
South Africa	Free State Consolidated Gold Mines Ltd	FSCNY	1:1	U	MIN	BNY.BT.MID.CIT.

COUNTRY	ISSUE	SYMBOL	RATIO	S/U	INDUSTRY	DEPOSITARY
South Africa	Free State Development & Invest Corp.	FSDIY	1:1	U	INV	BNY.BT.CIT.MGT.
South Africa	Genbel South Africa Limited	GIVLY	1:1	U	INV	BNY.BT.MID.MGT.
South Africa	Gencor Ltd.	GNCLY	1:1	U	MIN	BNY.BT.MID.CIT.MGT.
South Africa	Gold Fields Of South Africa	GLDFY	1:1	S	MIN	MGT.
South Africa	Gold Fields Property Company Limited	GFPYY	1:1	U	MIN	BNY.BT.CHS.CIT.MGT.MID.
South Africa	Harmony Gold Mining Company	HGMCY	1:1	S	MIN	BNY.
South Africa	Highveld Steel And Vanadium Corp.	HSVLY	1:1	U	STE	BNY.BT.CIT.MGT.MID.
South Africa	Impala Platinum Holdings Limited	IMPAY	1:1	U	MIN	BNY.BT.MID.CIT.MGT.
South Africa	Imperial Holdings Limited	IHSAY	1:1	S	TRN	BNY.
South Africa	Investec Bank Ltd.	IVBOY	1:1	S	BKS	CIT.
South Africa	Iscor Limited	ISCRY	1:10	S	STE	BNY.
South Africa	Jci Limited	JCIOY	1:1	U	MIN	BNY.BT.CIT.MID.
South Africa	JD Group	JDGRY	1:1	S	MER	BNY.
South Africa	Johnnies Industrial Corporation Limit	JICPY	1:1	U	MIN	BNY.CIT.
South Africa	Kloof Gold Mining Company Limited	KLOFY	1:1	S	MIN	MGT.
South Africa	Kolosus Holdings Limited	KOLHY	1:10	S	OTH	CIT.
South Africa	Liberty Life Association Of Africa Ltd	LTYLY	2:1	S	INS	BNY.
South Africa	Malbak Limited	MLBAY	1:1	S	HCG	BNY.
South Africa	Malbak Limited 144a	MLBFF	1:1	S	HCG	BNY.
South Africa	Messina Limited	MESOTC	1:1	U	OTH	CIT.
South Africa	Metro Cash & Carry Ltd.	MECCY	1:4	S	RET	BT.

COUNTRY	ISSUE	SYMBOL	RATIO	S/U	INDUSTRY	DEPOSITARY
South Africa	Metro Cash & Carry	MECREGS	1:4	S	RET	BT.
South Africa	Nampak Limited	NMPKY	1:1	S	PPP	BNY.
South Africa	Nampak Limited Edr	NAMEDR	1:3	S	PPP	BNY.
South Africa	Nedcor	NDCRY	1:2	S	BKS	MGT.
South Africa	Nedcor Ltd 144a	NED144A	1:1	S	BKS	MGT.
South Africa	Nedcor Ltd Reg S	NEDREGS	1:1	S	BKS	MGT.
South Africa	New Wits Limited	NWITY	1:1	U	MIN	BNY.MGT.
South Africa	O'okiep Copper Company Limited	OKP	1:1	U	MIN	OTH.
South Africa	Ocean Diamond Mining Holdings Limited	OCDIY	1:2	S	MIN	BNY.
South Africa	Palabora Mining Company Limited	PBOMY	1:1	U	MIN	BNY.
South Africa	Pepkor Limited	PKRLY	1:2	S	MER	BNY.
South Africa	Pepkor Limited 144a	PEPKYP	1:2	S	MER	BNY.
South Africa	Premier Group Limited	PRRGY	1:5	S	FOD	BNY.
South Africa	Rand Mines Limited	RADMY	10:1	U	MIN	BNY.BT.CIT.MID.
South Africa	Randfontein Estates Gold Mining Co. W	RNDEY	1:1	U	MIN	BNY.BT.MID.CIT.MGT.
South Africa	Randgold & Explorations Co. Ltd 144A	RGEX144A	1:1	S	MIN	BNY.
South Africa	Randgold & Explorations Co. Ltd	RANGY	1:1	S	MIN	BNY.
South Africa	Randgold Resources Ltd 144A	RDGDY	1:1	S	MIN	BNY.
South Africa	Randgold Resources Ltd. Reg S	RDGUF	1:1	S	MIN	BNY.
South Africa	Rembrandt Group Limited	RBDGY	1:1	S	HCG	BNY.
South Africa	Rmp Properties Limited	RMPPY	1:1	U	MIN	BNY.MGT.

COUNTRY	ISSUE	SYMBOL	RATIO	S/U	INDUSTRY	DEPOSITARY
South Africa	Sage Group Limited	SAGEOTC	1:3	S	INS	BT.
South Africa	Samancor Limited	SMNCY	1:1	U	CHM	BNY.CIT.MGT.
South Africa	Sappi Limited	SAPIY	1:1	S	PAP	BNY.
South Africa	Sasol Limited	SASOY	1:1	S	OGS	BNY.
South Africa	Seardel Investment Corp.	SRDLY	1:5	S	TEX	BT.
South Africa	Sentrachem Limited	SNTRY	1:2	S	CHM	BNY.
South Africa	Sentrachem Limited 144a	SNTRY144A	1:4	S	CHM	BNY.
South Africa	Servgro International Limited	SVGRY	1:2	S	SER	BNY.
South Africa	Simmer And Jack Mines Limited	SJACY	1:1	U	MIN	BNY.MGT.
South Africa	"South African Breweries Ltd., The"	SBWRY	1:1	S	BEV	BNY.
South Africa	"South African Breweries 144A	SFABYP	1:1	S	BEV	BNY.
South Africa	South African Breweries Reg S	SFABYPP	1:1	S	BEV	BNY.
South Africa	South African Land & Exploration Co., Ltd"	STHAY	1:1	U	MIN	BNY.BT.CIT.MGT.MID.
South Africa	Southvaal Holdings Limited	STHVY	1:1	U	MIN	BNY.BT.CIT.MGT.MID.
South Africa	St. Helena Gold Mines Limited	SGOLY	1:1	U	MIN	BNY.BT.CIT.MGT.MID.
South Africa	Stilfontein Gold Mining Company	STILY	1:1	U	MIN	BNY.BT.CIT.MGT.MID.
South Africa	Stocks & Stocks Limited	STKKY	1:25	S	CST	BNY.
South Africa	Sub Nigel Gold Mining Co Ltd	SNGOTC	1:1	U	MIN	BNY.
South Africa	Tiger Oats Limited	TIOAY	1:1	S	MUL	BNY.
South Africa	Trans Hex Group Limited	TRHXY	1:1	S	MIN	BNY.
South Africa	Trans-Natal Coal Corporation	TNCCY	1:1	U	MIN	BNY.CIT.

COUNTRY	ISSUE	SYMBOL	RATIO	S/U	INDUSTRY	DEPOSITARY
South Africa	Vaal Reefs Exploration & Mining Compa	VAALY	10:1	U	MIN	BNY.BT.MID.CIT.MGT.
South Africa	West Rand Consolidated Mines. Ltd.	WRCMYC	1:1	U	MIN	BNY.BT.MID.CIT.MGT.
South Africa	Western Areas Gold Mining Co. Ltd.	WARSY	1:1	U	MIN	BNY.BT.MID.CIT.
South Africa	Western Deep Levels Limited	WDEPY	1:1	U	MIN	BNY.BT.MID.CIT.MGT.
South Africa	Witwatersrand Nigel Limited	WWRNY	1:1	U	MIN	BNY.CIT.MGT.
South Africa	Wooltru Limited (Ords)	WLTUY	1:1	S	MER	BNY.
South Africa	"Wooltru Limited Class "N""""	WLTVY	1:1	S	MER	BNY.
Spain	"Antena 3 De Television, S.A. 144A"	ANTDT	1:1	S	PUB	BNY.
Spain	Banco Bilbao Vizcaya	BBV	1:1	S	BKS	BNY.
Spain	"Banco Bilbao Vizcaya (Ser ""A"" Pref)"	BVG+	1:1	S	BKS	BNY.
Spain	"Banco Bilbao Vizcaya (Ser ""B"" Pref)"	BVGB	1:1	S	BKS	BNY.
Spain	"Banco Bilbao Vizcaya (Ser ""C"" Pref)"	BVGC	1:1	S	BKS	BNY.
Spain	"Banco Bilbao Vizcaya (Ser ""D"" Pref) "	BBV144A	1:1	S	BKS	BNY.
Spain	"Banco Bilbao Vizcaya (Ser ""E"" Pref)"	BVGD	1:1	S	BKS	BNY.
Spain	"Banco Central Hispanoamericano, S.A."	BCH	2:1	S	BKS	MGT.
Spain	Banco De Santander	STD	1:1	S	BKS	MGT.
Spain	Banco Espanol De Credito (Banesto)	BNSTY	2:1	S	BKS	BNY.
Spain	Bankinter S. A.	BKISY	4:1	S	BKS	MGT.
Spain	Compania Sevillana De Electricidad S.	COVDY	1:2	S	UTI	BNY.
Spain	Corporacion Bancaria De Espana S.A.	AGR	2:1	S	BKS	MGT.
Spain	Corporacion Mapfre	CRFEY	5:1	S	INS	BNY.

COUNTRY	ISSUE	SYMBOL	RATIO	S/U	INDUSTRY	DEPOSITARY
Spain	"Empresa Nacional De Electricidad, S.A"	ELE	1:1	S	UTI	MGT.
Spain	Repsol S.A.	REP	1:1	S	OGS	BNY.
Spain	Telefonica De Espana Sa	TEF	1:3	S	TEL	CIT.
Sri Lanka	John Keells Holdings Limited	JKHGDR	1:2	S	MUL	CIT.
Sri Lanka	John Keells Holdings Limited 144a	JKH144A	1:2	S	MUL	CIT.
Thailand	Advanced Info Service Plc	AVIFY	1:1	S	TEL	BNY.
Thailand	Asia Fiber Company Limited	ASFBY	1:2	S	TEX	BNY.
Thailand	"Charoen Pokphand Feedmill Co., Ltd."	CPOKY	1:4	S	FOD	BNY.
Thailand	Hana Microelectronics Plc	HANAY	1:2	S	CLE	BNY.
Thailand	Shinawatra Computer & Communications	SHWCY	2:1	S	TEL	BNY.
Thailand	Shinawatra Satellite Public Co. Limiteds	SHTFY	1:4	S	TEL	BNY.
Thailand	Swedish Motors Corporation Public Co. Ltd	SWMTY	1:1	S	AUT	BNY.
Thailand	Telecomasia Corporation Public Co. Ltd	TCMSY	1:10	S	TEL	CIT.
Thailand	Thai Telephone & Telecommunication 14	TTTPYP	1:3	S	TEL	BNY.
Thailand	Thai Telephone & Telecommunication Re	TTTPRS	1:3	S	TEL	BNY.
Thailand	Wattachak Public Company Limited	WAPCL	1:2	S	PUB	BNY.
Turkey	Demirbank	DMRFY	1:500	S	BKS	BNY.
Turkey	Erciyas Bira 144a	ECYAF	1:20	S	BEV	BNY.
Turkey	Erciyas Bira Reg S Gdr	EFEREGS	1:20	S	BEV	BNY.
Turkey	Hace Omer Sabanci Holding S.A.	SARPP	1:250	S	MUL	CIT.
Turkey	Hace Omer Sabanci Holding S.A.	SARPPGDR	1:250	S	MUL	CIT.

COUNTRY	ISSUE	SYMBOL	RATIO	S/U	INDUSTRY	DEPOSITARY
Turkey	Net Holding Inc.	NETHY	1:5	S	HOT	CIT.
Turkey	Raks Electronik Sanayi Ve Ticaret A.S	RKETY	1:20	S	EEI	CIT.
Turkey	Tofas Turk Otomobil Fabrikasi 144a	TOFAYP	1:1	S	AUT	BNY.
Turkey	"Tofas Turk Otomobil Fabrikasi Reg ""S"""""	TOFAYPS	1:1	S	OGS	BNY.
Turkey	Turkiye Garanti Bankasi	TURKY	1:200	S	BKS	BNY.
Turkey	Turkiye Garanti Bankasi 144a	TKGGY	1:200	S	BKS	BNY.
Turkey	Yapi Ve Kredi Banikaisi A.S.-144A	YVKBY	1:1000	S	BKS	BNY.
Turkey	Yapi Ve Kredi Banikaisi A.S.-Reg S	YVKBYREGS	1:1000	S	BKS	BNY.
Uruguay	Banco Comercial S.A. Gdr	BCOMGDR	1:25	S	BKS	BT.
Venezuela	Banco Mercantil & Consorcio	BMIMY	1:10	S	BKS	MGT.
Venezuela	Banco Venezolano De Credito Common	BVZCY	1:1	S	BKS	BNY.
Venezuela	Cantv-National Telefonos De Venezuela	VNT	1:7	S	TEL	CIT.
Venezuela	"Ceramica Carabobo Series ""A"" Shares"	CRCAY	1:1	S	CST	BNY.
Venezuela	"Ceramica Carabobo Series ""B"" Shares"	CRCBY	1:1	S	CST	BNY.
Venezuela	Corimon C.A. S.A.C.A.	CRM	1:250	S	MUL	MGT.
Venezuela	Dominguez Y Cia. Caracas Preferred Share	DCIPY	1:250	S	PPP	BNY.
Venezuela	Dominguez Y Cia. Caracas Common Share	DCIAY	1:25	S	PPP	BNY.
Venezuela	Mantex Common Shares	MTXVY	1:1500	S	CHM	BNY.
Venezuela	"Mavesa ""B"" Shares"	MAV	1:20	S	FOD	BNY.
Venezuela	"Sivensa ""A"" Shares"	SVNZY	1:10	S	STE	BNY.
Venezuela	"Sivensa ""B"" Shares"	SVNYY	1:10	S	STE	BNY.

COUNTRY	ISSUE	SYMBOL	RATIO	S/U	INDUSTRY	DEPOSITARY
Venezuela	"Sivensa ""B""Shares 144A"	SVNXYP	1:160	S	STE	BNY.
Venezuela	"Sudamtex De Venezuela """B"""" Shares"	SDXVY	1:160	S	TEX	BNY.
Venezuela	"Sudamtex De Venezuela C.A. 144A"	SUDXYP	1:160	S	TEX	BNY.
Venezuela	"Sudamtex De Venezuela C.A. Reg S"	SUDXYPREGS	1:10	S	TEX	BNY.
Venezuela	"Venepal, S.A.C.A. 144A"	VNPZY	1:9	S	PAP	BNY.
Venezuela	"Venepal, S.A.C.A. Level I"	VNPSY	1:30	S	PAP	BNY.
Venezuela	"Venprecar """B""" Shares 144A"	VNZZY	1:7	S	STE	BNY.
Venezuela	"Venprecar """B""" Shares Reg S"	VPCGY	1:7	S	STE	BNY.
Zambia	Zambia Consolidated Copper Mines Ltd	ZAMBY	1:1	S	MIN	MGT.
Zambia	Zambia Copper Investments Limited	ZMBAY	1:1	U	MIN	BNY.CIT.MGT.
Zimbabwe	Mhangura Copper Mines Limited	MTDOTC	1:1	U	MIN	BNY.

ABBREVIATIONS

RATIO Number of ADRs: Number of underlying local shares. Example: Brazil Realty has a ratio of 1:100, meaning that one ADR is backed by 100 shares of Brazil Realty on the local Brazilian exchange.

S/U refers to sponsorship. "S" is sponsored; "U" is unsponsored.

SYMBOL	INDUSTRY
AER	Aerospace/Defense Electronics
AIR	Airlines
AUT	Autos, Auto Parts
BKS	Banks
BEV	Beverages
BIO	Biotechnology
CER	Ceramics
CHM	Chemicals
COA	Coal
COM	Computers: Main Frame & Hardware
CSC	Computers: Semiconductors
CSN	Computers: Software & Networking
CSV	Computer Service/Parts
CST	Construction & Building Materials
CLE	Consumer Electronics/Parts
COP	Cosmetics & Personal Care
DEB	All Debt Securities
DRU	Drugs/Healthcare
EEI	Electrical Equipment
EES	Energy Equipment & Services
ENG	Engineering
ENT	Entertainment/Leisure/Toys
FOD	Food Products/Agribusiness
GAM	Gaming
HCG	Household Products & Appliances
HOT	Hotels/Leisure
INS	Insurance
INV	Investment & Financial Services
LUX	Luxury Goods
MAC	Machinery

MAN	Manufacturing
MED	Media/Entertainment
MER	Merchandising
MIN	Mining & Minerals
MUL	Multi-Industry
OFF	Office Equipment/Supplies
OGS	Oil & Natural Gas
PAP	Paper & Forest Products
PHO	Photographic Equipment & Supplies
PLA	Plastic Products
PPP	Packaging/Printing
PUB	Publishing
RES	Restaurants
RRS	Railroads
REL	Real Estate
RET	Retailing
RUB	Rubber Goods & Tires
SHP	Shipbuilding
STE	Steel
SVC	Specialty Services
TEC	Technology/Miscellaneous
TEL	Telecommunications
TEX	Textiles
TOB	Tobacco
TRN	Transportation: Freight & Storage
UTI	Utilities-Gas/Electric
WAS	Waste Management

DEPOSITARY

BNY	Bank of New York
CIT	Citibank
MGT	Morgan Guaranty
CHS	Chase Manhattan
BT	Bankers Trust
MID	Midland

Country Profiles

ARGENTINA

STOCK EXCHANGES. There are 13 stock exchanges in Argentina located in the following cities: Bahia Blanca, Buenos Aires, Cordoba, Entre Rios, La Plata, Mar del Plata, Mendoza, Misiones, Rio Negro, Rosario, San Juan, Santa Fe, Tucuman.

BASE. The largest and most important exchange for foreign investors is the Bolsa de Comercio de Buenos Aires (the Buenos Aires Stock Exchange, BASE). Founded in 1854, the BASE was the first exchange in Latin America.

The BASE accounts for 95 percent of total equity trading. The remaining exchanges have a total of 140 listings, many of which are duplicate listings of issues on the BASE.

TRADING HOURS are from 11:00 A.M. until 6:00 P.M., Monday through Friday (local time). A continuous electronic trading system operates from 10:00 A.M. until 6:00 P.M. Approximately 20 percent of trades on the BASE are contracted by open outcry; the remainder are contracted through the electronic trading system. Both the Rio de Janeiro and São Paulo exchanges provide clearance and custody services.

Argentina's over-the-counter (OTC) market, the Mercado Abierto Electrónico (MAE), was established in 1981. An agreement between the BASE and the MAE, mediated by the Comision Nacional de Valores (CNV), segregates equity and fixed income trading between the two exchanges. Shares trade on the BASE while fixed-income securities trade on the MAE.

STOCK EXCHANGE SUPERVISION. The CNV regulates both the BASE and the MAE. The Mercado de Valores de Buenos Aires regulates and supervises brokers.

TYPES OF SECURITIES TRADED. Securities traded in the Argentine market include common stock and corporate and government bonds. Only a small number of preferred shares exist.

PRINCIPAL MARKET INDEXES Merval (19 blue chips) and Bolsa (all listed stocks) are weighted by traded volume; the Mercap uses the same 19 blue chips as the Merval, but is weighted by market capitalization.

SETTLEMENT takes place on T+3, T+1, or on a spot basis. Approximately 90 percent of equity trades settle on a T+3 basis.

Peso-denominated bonds settle on trade date in same-day funds. USD-denominated bonds usually settle on trade date, with cash settlement on T+1. However, the settlement cycle is open to negotiation between the broker and the customer, and most foreign investor bond trades are now settling on T+3.

THE CAJA DE VALORES S.A. (CDV), the central depository of the Buenos Aires Stock Exchange, is fully computerized.

ANNUAL GENERAL MEETINGS. Proxy cards do not exist in the Argentine market, so shareholders or their legal representatives must attend the Annual General Meeting in person if they wish to vote.

Certified financial statements, annual reports, and other corporate notices are rarely available in English.

TAXATION. Taxes on dividend income capital gains, foreign exchange check payments value-added, stock transfer, stamp duties, and stock dividends have all been abolished. There are no withholding or capital gains taxes in Argentina. There is a 12 percent tax on nonresident investors holding certain debt securities and on time deposits. The tax is withheld at the source and cannot be recovered.

BRAZIL

STOCK EXCHANGES. Brazil has nine stock exchanges, but the Bolsa de Valores in São Paulo (BOVESPA) and the Bolsa de Volares in Rio de Janeiro (BVRJ) account for about 96 percent of all activity. BOVESPA dominates, with around 85 percent and approximately 570 listed companies. The 100 most actively traded represent 98 percent of activity, with a few large firms, such as Telebras, accounting for over 50 percent. The BVRJ lists 569 stocks, but only 8.7 percent are actively traded.

An exchange fee of 0.5 percent per trade is charged automatically. Brokerage commissions are negotiable but generally range from .5 percent to 2 percent. Trading is via open outcry. There are no specialists on the exchange floors or market makers. Both the Rio de Janeiro and São Paulo exchanges provide clearance and custody services.

OTHER EXCHANGES. Belo Horizonte (Bolsa de Valores de Minas Gerais, Espirito Santo e Brasilia); Curitiba (Bolsa de Valores de Parana); Fortaleza (Bolsa de Valores Regional) ; Porto Alegre (Bolsa de Valores de Extremo Sul); Recife (Bolsa de Valores de Pernambuco-Paraiba); Salvador (Bolsa de Valores de Bahia, Sergipe e Alagoas); Santos (Bolsa de Valores de Santos).

There are also two other markets. The Bolsa de Mercadorias y Futuros (BM&F) is the fifth-largest commodities and futures market in the world. The Mercado de Balcao is an OTC market for government securities, corporate bonds, and money market instruments.

Due to extensive cross-listing of securities, it is not possible to accurately measure the market capitalization of securities on each exchange.

TRADING HOURS are from 9:30 A.M. to 1:00 P.M. and from 3:00 P.M. to 4:30 P.M. (local time) on the exchange trading floor via open-outcry auction method. BOVESPA uses CATS, a continuous computer-driven system, for electronic trading of unlisted shares, from 9:00 A.M. to 1:00 P.M. and from 1:00 P.M. to 4:30 P.M. BVRJ also uses the TELEPRAGAO system, and trades from 9:30 A.M. to 5:00 P.M. (local time). All the stock exchanges except BOVESPA are linked through the National Electronic Trading System (SENN), which allows automatic cross-listing of a stock on all eight exchanges.

REGULATORY AGENCIES. The primary regulatory body for the securities market is the Comissao de Valores Mobilarios (CVM). The Conselho Monetario Nacional (CMN or National Monetary Council) makes financial policy including credit regulations, issuance of currency, and monetary guidelines. The Central Bank is responsible for the monetary and credit policies and oversees financial institutions.

TYPES OF SECURITIES TRADED. Common and preferred shares; rights issues; straight, convertible bonds; new money; indexed government bonds; interest-arrears bonds; debentures; money market instruments; CDs; treasury bills; fixed-term bank deposits. Derivatives traded include stock and futures options, gold, currencies, and interest rate futures contracts.

PRINCIPAL MARKET INDEXES. The BOVESPA Stock Index, or IBOVESPA, is the most widely regarded index of overall Brazilian stock market performance. The IBV is based on the BVRJ listings.

The BOVESPA Index represents the present value of a hypothetical stock portfolio organized at the start of 1968. The latest index consists of 54 stocks issued by 49 companies. The IBV is a market-weighted index, with an initial value of 100.00 as of the close of trading in 1983. There are both general and sector IBV indexes.

SETTLEMENT. The settlement process is highly automated. Equities settle at BOVESPA on T+2, and financial settlement takes place on T+3. If a transaction fails to settle on T+2, the financial settlement doesn't occur on T+3.

CLEARING. The BOVESPA depository is CALISPA; BVRJ's is the Camara de Liquidacao e Custodia SA (CLC).

CORPORATE ACTIONS. Corporate actions are announced in newspapers, exchange publications, and electronically. Common stock shareholders have voting rights, but the shareholder, or his or her proxy, must attend the meeting in order to vote. Only major companies issue annual reports in English.

Companies are required to hold Annual General Meetings open to all shareholders, and notification of an AGM must be published at least two weeks in advance. Most local shareholders attend and vote at the meetings.

TAXATION. Nonresident investors are subject to a 15 percent withholding tax on dividends at source. There is no capital gains or value-added tax for nonresident investors. A "fiscalization" tax is payable quarterly directly to the CVM and is based on the portfolio value of the end of the previous year. Brazil maintains double taxation treaties with Argentina, Austria, Belgium, Canada, Czech Republic, Denmark, Ecuador, Finland, France, Germany, Hungary, Italy, Japan, Luxembourg, Norway, Portugal, Spain, and Sweden.

CHILE

STOCK EXCHANGES. Santiago Stock Exchange, the country's principal exchange (*La Bolsa de Comercio de Santiago*); Valparaiso Stock Exchange, Electronic Stock Exchange (*La Bolsa de Valores de Chile*); and an OTC market. The exchanges are not linked and compete for listings.

TRADING HOURS. The Santiago Stock Exchange is open Monday through Friday as follows: electronic trading of equities and fixed income, 9:30 A.M. to 10:30 A.M.; open-outcry equities trading, 10:30 A.M. to 11:30

A.M., 12:00 noon to 1:15 P.M., and 2:30 P.M. to 4:15 P.M., electronic (equities and fixed income). Fixed-income securities are actively traded on the OTC market.

Broker commissions are negotiable, but the minimum rate is higher for nonresidents. The stock exchanges also charge a non-negotiable operations commission on each trade.

STOCK EXCHANGE SUPERVISION. Stock market activity is supervised by the Superintendency of Securities and Insurance (Superintendencia de Valores y Seguros). Foreign investors are regulated by the Foreign Investment Committee and Internal Revenue. The OTC market is regulated by the Superintendencia. Nonlisted OTC companies are not regulated.

TYPES OF SECURITIES TRADED. Common and preferred shares, government securities, mortgage and corporate bonds, repurchase agreements, central bank notes, time deposits, and private equity. Futures contracts and options are also traded on the Santiago Stock Exchange. Fixed income securities can be traded on the stock exchanges and on the OTC market.

MARKET INDEX. The main market index is the General Index of Stock Prices (IGPA). The IGPA uses 1980 as the base year and includes all stocks in the Chilean market. The Selective Index of Stock Prices (IPSA) represents the 40 most important stocks in volume and market presence.

SETTLEMENT. Most equity transactions settle on T+2. Settlement for fixed income transactions varies with type of instrument. Money market instruments settle on trade date (T); long-term instruments (bonds) settle on T+1. All fixed income transactions on the OTC market settle on T. Due to substantial penalties levied by the Stock Exchange, trade settlements rarely fail.

CLEARING. No central depository currently exists in Chile.

CORPORATE ACTIONS. Corporate actions in Chile include rights, subscriptions, and stock splits. Most companies issue annual reports in Spanish only. Corporate actions are typically announced through the stock exchange, and shareholders are advised of meetings via direct mail or newspapers. Most Chilean shareholders attend AGMs and vote. Proxy voting requires attendance of a local administrator or legal representative.

TAXATION. In general, taxes are withheld by the financial institution involved in the transaction. Chile withholds tax on all profits at a flat rate of 10 percent at the time of repatriation, regardless of the source (for example, capital gains, dividends, or interest). Investment funds are taxed at a higher overall rate of 35 percent–42 percent. A Stamp Duty is paid by the debtor on bonds; demand deposit accounts are also subject to Stamp Duty. An 18 percent value-added tax is levied on all service fees, including brokerage and the nonnegotiable operations commission charged by the exchanges.

REGISTRATION AND EXCHANGE FEES. There are no registration fees. A 0.5 percent exchange fee is charged by the broker.

RESTRICTIONS ON FOREIGN INVESTORS. All foreign investors must appoint either a legal representative or, more formally, a local administrator. Foreign investors must obtain approvals from certain agencies, depending on the type of investment. Repatriation of income and capital gains may be restricted for one to five years, depending on which laws apply.

FOREIGN OWNERSHIP CEILINGS. Foreign ownership of television stations, newspaper publishing, and other media companies is restricted. Foreign investment totaling more than 25 percent in any one company is forbidden. There is a 10 percent limit for a single portfolio investing in any single issue except those issued by the government or central bank. The limit is stricter with voting shares, of which a single portfolio cannot hold more than 5 percent; first issues are an exception (a 10 percent limit applies to these shares).

DOUBLE TAXATION TREATIES. Argentina is the only country with such a treaty with Brazil.

COLOMBIA

STOCK EXCHANGE. Colombia has three stock exchanges, located in Bogotá, Medellin, and Cali (De Occidente). The Bogota exchange is the most active, followed by Medellin and the relatively small De Occidente exchange. Shares of actively traded companies are listed on all exchanges, and cross-listing makes market capitalization estimates difficult.

TRADING HOURS. Monday through Friday as follows: Bogota, a single daily equity trading session from 10:00 A.M. to 12:00 noon. Fixed income instruments are traded on the exchange's electronic system in 13 daily sessions from 8:00 A.M. to 4:55 P.M. Medellin trades in two daily sessions, 10:00 A.M. to 12:00 noon and 2:00 P.M. to 2:30 P.M. De Occidente trades from 8:00 A.M. to 12:30 P.M. and 2:00 P.M. to 3:00 P.M.

STOCK EXCHANGE SUPERVISION. The Superintendency of Securities oversees capital markets. A National Planning Department also produces guidelines and general investment policies.

TYPES OF SECURITIES TRADED. Banker's Acceptances, Bonds (fixed and floating rate), corporate, municipal, state, Certificates of Deposit*, Certificados de Cambio*. Commercial Paper, Equities (voting, nonvoting), Eurobonds, Financeria Electrica Nacional (FEN), Government securities*. Mortgaged Transaction Notes, Mutual Funds.*

MARKET INDEX. The main index is the Indice Bolsa de Medellin (IBOMED), which is calculated daily and based on closing prices.

SETTLEMENT. Stocks normally settle on a T+2 basis, but can be as long as T+5. Nonresident investors are recommended to book trades on at least a T+3 basis. Money market and bond market instruments settle on a same-day basis. Certificates of Deposit can be contracted for next-day settlement. Failed trades are almost nonexistent.

CLEARING. The exchanges perform all clearing functions. The Deposito Central de Valores (Deceval) settles fixed income. The Central Bank has its own depository for government issues.

CORPORATE ACTIONS. Information is available through local newspapers, stock market publications, and brokerage firms. Registrars and issuers are required to publish corporate action events in local or national newspapers, but are not obligated to notify shareholders directly. Colombian companies are required to hold Annual General Meetings (AGMs) open to shareholders, but the subjects to be discussed are not disclosed prior to the meeting. A significant number of the listed companies are closely held by family members or small investor groups. As a result, a majority of shareholders vote their shares.

PRICING. Prices are available through the Stock Exchange Bulletin, published by the Bolsa de Bogota.

TAXATION. There is no withholding tax on dividends or capital gains for portfolio (indirect) investors. The issuer pays 30 percent tax on dividends distributed. Interest is taxed at 30 percent, which is withheld by the paying agent. Convertible bonds purchased off the exchanges are subject to a 14 percent withholding tax. All investors must pay 0.5 percent tax on all commissions paid during the year, subject to an annual minimum. This

* Nonresident investors are prohibited from investing in these securities.

minimum is subject to change at the beginning of each year. Colombia's tax authority levies a 14 percent value-added tax on all sales.

REGISTRATION AND EXCHANGE FEES. The issuer pays the costs of registration.

DOUBLE TAXATION TREATIES do not cover profits or any income from nonresident investment in Colombia's capital markets. Therefore, all income is subject to withholding at the full existing rate with no reclamation possible.

RESTRICTIONS ON FOREIGN INVESTORS. Nonresident investors are prohibited from investing in all securities issued by the Central Bank of Colombia and all money market instruments. Legislation requires the registration of capital invested with the Central Bank. Approval is required for investment in certain fields, such as those relating to national security, toxic waste, public service, or communications. Certain bonds are not available to foreign investors, and they may not trade over the counter. No restrictions apply to repatriation of sale proceeds and income, providing they are registered with the Central Bank.

FOREIGN OWNERSHIP CEILINGS. There is a limit of 10 percent of outstanding shares per nonresident investor. Foreign investors holding more than 5 percent of outstanding shares of a company must inform the Superintendency of Securities.

CZECH REPUBLIC

STOCK EXCHANGES. The Prague Stock Exchange (PSE) is the primary stock exchange in the Czech Republic.

TYPES OF SECURITIES TRADED. More than 95 percent of the shares traded are a result of the first round of privatization, and 35 investment funds are currently traded on the PSE. Government bonds are also traded on the PSE. The Prague Options and Futures Exchange (POTB) has been chartered.

MARKET INDEX. The main market index on the PSE is the PX-50. The PX-50 includes the 50 main shares/bonds traded through the PSE. The share/bond base is fixed.

REGULATORY BODIES. The Ministry of Finance supervises stock market activity.

SETTLEMENT. Securities are settled directly through the PSE. The order is executed on "instruction day." Settlement occurs on "instruction day + 3."

CLEARING. The Central Securities Register (SCP) is the central register for dematerialized securities. The Czech National Bank is the Central Register for money market instruments, and Komercni Banka is the central register for physical instruments.

CORPORATE ACTIONS. Most corporate actions are announced through *Hospodarske Noviny*, the daily financial newspaper, and Obchodni Vestnik, the official source of entities registration. FINSAT-PC, a special database, is used to ensure accurate and timely notification of dividends, income payments, and corporate actions. Most shareholders in the Czech Republic attend Annual General Meetings (AGMs). All information relevant to the meeting must be distributed to shareholders 14 days prior to the meeting. If clients want to vote proxies, they must appoint a local or a foreign representative to attend the annual meeting on their behalf.

TAXATION. Withholding tax of 25 percent is applicable on dividends and interest received from equities and fixed-rate securities. There is a 42 percent capital gains tax levied by the Ministry of Finance in the Czech Republic. There are no stamp duties or value-added taxes.

REGISTRATION AND EXCHANGE FEES. The SCP charges Kc 80 (Czech cents) for each transfer of securities, payable by the party who instructed the reregistration.

RESTRICTIONS FOR FOREIGN INVESTORS. Nonresident investment is restricted for certain money market instruments. The first primary issue of government bonds and bank shares require prior approval of the Czech National Bank. Shares of industries of national importance such as defense, salt industry, and telecommunications are prohibited to foreign investment.

FOREIGN OWNERSHIP CEILINGS. There are no ownership or disclosure ceilings for foreign institutional investors. There are no restrictions regarding the repatriation of sale proceeds and income.

DOUBLE TAXATION TREATIES. Austria; Belgium; Brazil; Canada; China; Cyprus; Denmark; Finland; France; FRG; Germany; Greece; India; Italy; Japan; Luxembourg; Netherlands; Nigeria; Norway; Poland; Slovakia; Spain; Sri Lanka; Sweden; Switzerland; Tunisia; United Kingdom; United States; Yugoslavia.

GREECE

STOCK EXCHANGE. The Athens Stock Exchange (ASE) is the sole stock exchange in Greece. It is comprised of two markets; the Main Market and the Parallel Market. Equities and fixed income securities are traded on both markets. The Main Market currently lists 147 large companies with a five-year profitability record. The Parallel Market currently lists six small companies with a three-year profitability record. Trading is automated.

TRADING HOURS. Monday through Friday, 10:45 A.M. to 1:30 P.M. (local time).

STOCK EXCHANGE SUPERVISION. The Ministry of National Economy supervises the operation of the ASE through a Government Commissioner who ensures that rules and regulations are enforced by parties involved in stock exchange transactions. All brokers who are members of the ASE are participants in a common depository fund that provides a form of transaction insurance against failure to fulfill payment obligations.

TYPES OF SECURITIES TRADED. Ordinary shares; preference shares; unit-trust shares; warrants; convertible bonds; corporate bonds; floating-rate bonds; government bonds; bank bonds, certificates of deposit; insurance bonds; repurchase agreements; treasury bills.

MARKET INDEX. There are seven ASE indices as follows: Bank Index (10 banks); Commercial Corporation Index (10 companies); Composite Index (53 shares); Industrial Index (23 companies); Insurance Index (3 insurance companies); Investment Corporation Index (5 companies); Leasing Index (2 companies). The base is the market capitalization as of December 31, 1980 = 100 points.

SETTLEMENT. There is no fixed time frame for settlement. Normally, a T+2/T+3 time frame exists for bearer shares and a T+5/T+7 time frame for registered shares. The settlement cycle for bonds is T+2.

CLEARING. The central depository is the Central Securities Depository (CSD), independent of the stock exchange. The CSD operates under specific legislation as a private company. There are no registration or exchange fees in Greece.

CORPORATE ACTIONS. The primary information source for corporate actions is the ASE Daily Bulletin and various financial newspapers. All corporate actions are open to nonresidents. Corporations are required to notify their registered shareholders directly for actions affecting them, in addition to publishing them in the local newspaper. Voting rights entitle shareholders to vote at AGMs and EGMs. A corporation must call an AGM within six months of the end of its fiscal year and must notify shareholders 20 days prior to the meeting, by publishing a notice in the daily bulletin of the ASE and in at least one financial newspaper. Ten days prior to an AGM, shareholders can obtain financial statements of the company, which should be published at least 20 days prior to the AGM in at least one financial and one daily newspaper. Proxy voting is permitted.

TAXATION. All dividends are taxed at a rate of 35 percent. The tax is withheld at source. Net profits of companies are taxed at 35 percent regardless of securities (bearer, common, not quoted, preferred quoted, and registered), and will be paid by the issuing companies. The respective dividends will be paid to shareholders, net of any tax amount, with no further tax obligation for the shareholder. There is no capital gains or value-added tax in Greece.

RESTRICTIONS FOR FOREIGN INVESTORS. There are no restrictions for foreign investors purchasing securities listed on the ASE. There are no disclosure ceilings in Greece.

DOUBLE TAXATION TREATIES. France; Netherlands; United Kingdom; United States.

HONG KONG

STOCK EXCHANGE. The Stock Exchange of Hong Kong Limited (SEHK) was established in 1986 after the merger of four separate stock exchanges that are no longer in operation (Hong Kong Exchange, Far-East Exchange, Kam NGAN Exchange, and Kowloon Stock Exchange). Trading on the SEHK is carried out on computer terminals in a continuous process in which bid and offer prices are shown and all transactions are recorded.

MARKET STATISTICS. As of December 1992, stock market capitalization was U.S. $194 billion. There are 640 listed stocks, and the average daily turnover is 560.7 million shares.

TRADING HOURS. Monday through Friday, 10:00 A.M.–12:30 P.M. and 2:30 P.M.–3:30 P.M.

STOCK EXCHANGE SUPERVISION. The Stock Exchange of Hong Kong is supervised by the Securities and Futures Commission (SFC).

TYPES OF SECURITIES TRADED. Ordinary; preference; cumulative preference; warrants; preferred ordinary debt securities; loan stock; government bonds; corporate bonds; index-linked bonds; unit trusts; investment trust participation; money market; treasuries; commercial bills; CDs. Derivatives: Futures are traded on the Futures Exchange. Foreign investor participation in the derivatives market is permitted.

MARKET INDEX. The main market index is the Hang Seng Index, computed daily and comprised of 33 blue chip stocks from four different sectors. Other indices are the Hong Kong Index and the All Ordinaries Index.

SETTLEMENT. The settlement period for all SEHK transactions is Trade Date + 2 days (T+2). Buy-ins or sell-outs in the physical market may occur when the buying broker fails to take delivery or the selling broker fails to deliver on settlement date, and either party complains to the stock exchange. Buy-ins are rarely invoked as fails are often negotiated.

CLEARING. CCASS is a continuous computerized book entry clearing and settlement system operated by the Hong Kong Securities Clearing Co., Ltd. (HKSCC).

CORPORATE ACTIONS. The primary sources for corporate action information are the stock exchange and industry securities bulletins as well as local newspapers. Companies are required to hold Annual General Meetings. Investors must be advised of the meeting at least 21 days in advance.

TAXATION. There is no withholding tax on dividends or capital gains. There is a nominal stamp duty on transfer deed, usually paid by the seller, and an *ad valorem* stamp duty payable by both buyer and seller based on the market value of the shares.

RESTRICTIONS FOR FOREIGN INVESTORS. There are currently no restrictions for nonresident investors, but they must submit shares for registration into their nominee or beneficiary name before the books close date in order to protect their entitlements to dividends or corporate actions.

FOREIGN OWNERSHIP CEILINGS. Investors must disclose holdings when they exceed 10 percent of a company's total issued shares.

HUNGARY

STOCK EXCHANGE. The Budapest Stock Exchange (BSE) is the main exchange in Hungary. About 80 percent of the transactions are traded on the OTC market.

STOCK EXCHANGE SUPERVISION. The OTC is not regulated. It has no specific hours of operation, and transactions are not subject to the settlement requirements of the Central Depository. The foreign investor and the counterparty decide when the transaction will settle. The State Securities Supervision regulates the BSE.

There are three categories of traded securities: listed, traded, and OTC. *Listed* securities have very strict disclosure requirements and are at minimum 20 percent publicly held with a minimum book value of Hungarian forint HUF200 million (USD 1.75 million), a minimum of 50 shareholders, and in operation for a minimum of three years. *Traded* securities are 10–20 percent publicly held and must have a minimum nominal value of HUF100 million (USD 877,000), with a minimum of 25 shareholders, and the issuing company must be in business for a minimum of one year. Securities traded on the *OTC* are traded freely with no listing requirements, regulations, or restrictions.

TRADING HOURS are 11:00 A.M. to 12:30 P.M., Monday through Friday (local time).

TYPES OF SECURITIES TRADED. Compensation notes; government bonds; equities (registered shares); investment certificates; options and futures (traded on the fifteenth and on the last business day of the month).

MARKET INDEX. The BSE Index is made up of a basket of the nine most actively traded securities, calculated from a base date of January 2, 1991, and a base value of 1,000.

SETTLEMENT. The trade settlement cycle is T+5 for equities and fixed-income securities. When a broker does not deliver securities by 12:00 P.M. (Hungarian time) on T+3, a buy-in will be initiated by the depositary. The Central Clearing House makes arrangements to settle failed trades and pursues the delinquent party.

CORPORATE ACTIONS. Information about corporate events is provided via notices from registrars, announcements in local newspapers, and state securities publications. Proxies can be voted upon request by clients through an appointed representative who attends the annual or extraordinary general meeting on their behalf. Companies are required to hold AGMs, which are, according to recent practice, well attended.

TAXATION. There is no withholding tax on dividends and interest income for nonresident investors, or capital gains tax on sale proceeds.

REGISTRATION AND EXCHANGE FEES. There are no additional fees charged for registration of securities.

RESTRICTIONS ON FOREIGN INVESTMENT. Foreign investors can buy only registered securities and must pay for the securities in hard currency. Dividend payments may also be converted to hard currency, but this must be reported to the National Bank of Hungary. Citibank will be responsible for reporting the conversion to the National Bank of Hungary.

FOREIGN OWNERSHIP CEILINGS. Nonresidents may own no more than a 10 percent stake in financial institutions.

DISCLOSURE CEILINGS. There are no disclosure ceilings.

DOUBLE TAXATION TREATIES. Austria; Australia; Belgium; Brazil; Cyprus; Denmark; Finland; France; Germany; Great Britain; Greece; India; Ireland; Israel; Italy; Japan; Korea; Luxembourg; Malaysia; Malta; Norway; Poland; Romania; Spain; Sweden; Switzerland; Thailand; United States.

INDIA

STOCK EXCHANGE. India has 25 stock exchanges. The Bombay Stock Exchange (BSE) is the main exchange in the country, with more than 4,500 listings, including equities, bonds, and trusts. Trading is by open outcry. The BSE has a "Circuit Breaker" system that temporarily halts trading for 30 minutes if the BSE-sensitive index fluctuates more than 5 percent from the opening index during the first three hours of the trading session.

The National Stock Exchange, in existence since 1994, has more than 1,000 listings and a trading volume about half that of BSE. The NSE trades equities, debentures, and warrants. The OTC exchange, OTCEI, in Madras, lists small companies that cannot be cross-listed on the BSE. Trading is fully automated, based on the NASDAQ system.

STOCK EXCHANGE SUPERVISION. The Securities and Exchange Board of India (SEBI) is charged with protecting the interests of all securities investors and with regulating the stock market.

TRADING HOURS. Monday through Friday, BSE trading hours are from 12:00 noon to 2:00 P.M. Monday through Friday and Saturday 12:00 noon to 2:30 P.M. for odd lots (local time).

TYPES OF SECURITIES TRADED. "A" stocks, "B" stocks, convertible and nonconvertible debentures, mutual funds, money market instruments (T-bills, deposits, commercial paper).

MARKET INDEX. The BSE Sensitive Index is the main index composed of shares of the 30 leading companies traded on the exchange. Other indexes (the All Industries/All India Index and the RBI Index) are composed of shares of companies in a broad range of industrial sectors. The indexes are calculated on a daily basis.

SETTLEMENT. Almost all of the Indian Stock Exchanges follow an accounting period settlement system, which settles on a T+14 cycle. The less active "B" and "C" shares settle on T+7. The OTCEI is the only exchange that operates on a T+3 settlement cycle. Buy-ins are permitted in the Indian market when a failed trade is reported and the broker fails to deliver within two to four days. The buy-in takes 10 to 12 days.

CLEARING. At present there is no central depository in India. NSE trades are cleared through its own clearing house.

CORPORATE ACTIONS. The primary source of corporate action information is the Bombay Stock Exchange Bulletin, which is published on a daily basis. Event notification is sent via telex, S.W.I.F.T., or fax. A proxy can be voted in person or can be mailed to the company.

TAXATION. The withholding tax on dividends and interest is 20 percent. Those countries that have treaties are subject to a reduced tax rate of 15 percent on income. To be eligible for the reduced rate (in addition to the treaty), clients are required to provide a certificate from the Indian tax authorities acknowledging their eligibility under the double taxation agreement.

Long-term capital gains (holding period of greater than one year) are taxed at a rate of 10 percent. Short-term capital gains are subject to a 30 percent tax. Stamp duty is payable at a rate of 0.5 percent of the market value as of the end of execution date upon registration for all ordinary and preferred shares. A stamp duty on debentures varies according to the rate charged in the state in which the issuing company is registered. There is no VAT tax on foreign institutional investors.

REGISTRATION AND EXCHANGE FEES. A transfer duty of 0.5 percent is applicable for the registration of securities.

RESTRICTIONS ON FOREIGN INVESTMENT. The SEBI requires all foreign institutional investors to file an application and submit other documents to be reviewed and approved prior to investing in the market. When a foreign institutional investor is approved for investment in India he or she is permitted to repatriate and transfer funds without further exchange control clearance.

FOREIGN OWNERSHIP CEILINGS. Foreign institutional investors (including nonresident Indians and overseas corporate entities) are allowed a maximum of 5 percent ownership in any one corporation. The limit imposed for foreign institutional investors collectively is a maximum of 24 percent in any one company.

DISCLOSURE CEILINGS. The Reserve Bank of India (RBI) is required to report to all FII investors when the ceilings are reached. After the ceilings are reached, FII must seek approval from SEBI and RBI.

DOUBLE TAXATION TREATIES. Austria; Belgium; Brazil; Canada; Czech Republic; Denmark; Egypt; Finland; France; Germany; Greece; Holland; Hungary; Indonesia; Italy; Japan; Kenya; Korea; Libya; Mauritius; New Zealand; Norway; Romania; Sierra Leone; Singapore; Slovak Republic; Sweden; Syria; Thailand; United Kingdom; United States (for bond interest only); Yemen; Zambia

INDONESIA

STOCK EXCHANGES. The primary exchange is the Jakarta Stock Exchange (JSE). There are two others, the Parallel Exchange and the Surabaya Exchange. The JSE accounts for most of the activity, but many companies have dual listings on the JSE and the Surabaya Exchange. The Surabaya Exchange is smaller, and is easier to access for companies seeking listings and for regional retail investors who do not live in Jakarta. The Parallel Exchange is for companies not eligible for listing on the JSE. Trading is by open outcry and is automated.

TRADING HOURS. On the JSE, Monday through Thursday, 10:00 A.M. to 12:00 noon and 1:30 P.M. to 3:00 P.M. Friday from 9:30 A.M. to 11:30 A.M., and 2:00 P.M. to 3:00 P.M.

STOCK EXCHANGE SUPERVISION. Badan Pengawas Pasar Modal (BAPEPAM), the Stock Market Supervisory Agency, regulates the JSE, based on directives from the Ministry of Finance.

TYPES OF SECURITIES TRADED. The following are available to nonresidents: commercial bonds, common and preferred equities, government bonds. Fixed-income securities are traded off market. All Indonesian shares start off as local shares; however, when a foreign investor purchases stock, the stock exchange records the shares as "foreign," thereby applying them against the foreign ownership limits. Once this limit has been reached under stock exchange regulations, a foreign investor can purchase stock only from another foreign investor. Foreign investors can buy "local" stock, but have no legal title to it and, therefore, no protection.

MARKET INDEX. The main market index is the Jakarta Composite Index.

SETTLEMENT. The trade settlement cycle for shares is trade date plus four business days (T+4). There is no official trading cycle for fixed-income securities. Settlement date is agreed to by the two counterparties at the time the trade is made. Buy-ins are not common in the Indonesian market. However, there are heavy penalties for failed trades.

CORPORATE ACTIONS. Companies are required to hold Annual General Meetings (AGMs). Information is made available to shareholders 14 days prior to the AGM.

TAXATION. Nonresident withholding tax is applied at the rate of 20 percent and deducted at the source. Residents of countries with double taxation treaties usually pay only 15 percent. Currently, there is no capital gains tax for nonresident investors. However, there is an income tax of 0.1 percent levied on all equity sale transactions. There is a 10 percent value-added tax levied on the brokerage commissions paid on each trade. This tax is payable to the government by the broker executing the transaction. Stamp duty is levied by the government at a rate of IDR1,000 per transaction note. This expense is usually borne by the broker.

REGISTRATION AND EXCHANGE FEES. There is a stock exchange levy of 0.08 percent on the value of all transactions.

FOREIGN OWNERSHIP CEILINGS. There are no industries in Indonesia that are closed to nonresident investors, but all shares currently have a nonresident ownership ceiling of 49 percent. Regulations require disclosure for holdings of 25 percent or greater.

FOREIGN EXCHANGE. There are no restrictions on transferability from local currency.

DOUBLE TAXATION TREATIES. Austria; Australia; Belgium; Bulgaria; Canada; Denmark; Finland; France; Germany; Hungary; India; Italy; Japan; Korea; Malaysia; Netherlands; New Zealand; Norway; Pakistan;

Philippines; Poland; Singapore; Sweden; Switzerland; Thailand; Tunisia; United Kingdom; United States.

ISRAEL

STOCK EXCHANGE. The Tel Aviv Stock Exchange (T.A.S.E.) is the only stock exchange in Israel. A member of the T.A.S.E. who does not belong to the clearing house can clear trades through one of the members. Any investor who wants to buy securities can open an account with one of the T.A.S.E. members.

All trading on the T.A.S.E. takes place Sunday through Thursday. The two trading methods used on the T.A.S.E. are multilateral trading and the auction or *Mishtanim* system.

The multilateral or Computerized Call Market system (CCM) is used for trading shares, convertible securities, and bonds. This method is characterized mainly by the fixing of a price once a day. All transactions on the same day are executed at this price.

The auction or Mishtanim System trades the 100 most active T.A.S.E. issues.

The continuous session trades 40 blue chip stocks of various companies from 10:30 A.M. to 11:30 A.M., Sunday through Thursday (local time). The Variable session trades the same 40 blue-chip securities and begins 20 minutes after the continuous trading session ends. This trading session ends at 3:30 P.M. (local time). The multilateral session trades blue chip stocks plus all other companies (about 210 shares) listed on the T.A.S.E. Trading begins at 12:15 P.M. and ends two to three hours later (local time).

TYPES OF SECURITIES TRADED. Common stock, convertible bonds, corporate bonds, government bonds; options on the MAOF Index; preferred stock; Bank of Israel bonds; warrants.

STOCK EXCHANGE SUPERVISION. The Israeli Securities Authority supervises all T.A.S.E. activity.

MARKET INDEX. The MAOF Index is made up of the 25 leading listed companies in the major sectors.

SETTLEMENT. The trade settlement cycle for equities and fixed income is trade date (T) but the Israeli Discount Bank allows T+2 settlement for foreign institutional investors.

CLEARING. The T.A.S.E. clearing house is represented as the central depositary in Israel.

CORPORATE ACTIONS. Corporate action notices are sent via airmail, fax, S.W.I.F.T., and telex 10–20 days before the actual entitlement is issued. Nonresident investors are permitted to vote proxies by appointing a legal representative. The T.A.S.E. provides its members with information on annual meetings, which is ultimately distributed to the clients.

TAXATION. Dividends and interest are subject to a 25 percent withholding tax with no reclaim. Tax is deducted at source. There is no capital gains tax for foreign investors on the sale of listed securities in Israel. Interest earned on deposits is exempt from taxes. There is no value-added tax or stamp duty in Israel.

REGISTRATION AND EXCHANGE FEES. There are no additional fees charged for registration in Israel.

FOREIGN EXCHANGE RESTRICTIONS. Currency controls require proof of inward remittance for repatriation.

KOREA

STOCK EXCHANGE. The Korea Stock Exchange (KSE) in Seoul is the only stock exchange in Korea. Trading on the KSE is highly automated. Trades are transmitted to the trading floor of the securities company through the use of the stock exchange's computer system, KOSCOM. Trading on the KSE can be done only through a local broker.

TRADING HOURS. Monday through Friday, 9:40 A.M. to 11:40 A.M. and 1:20 P.M. to 3:20 P.M. Saturday from 9:40 A.M. to 11:40 A.M.

STOCK EXCHANGE SUPERVISION. The KSE is controlled directly by the Ministry of Finance (MOF). As agencies of the MOF, the Securities Supervisory Board (SSB) and the Securities and Exchange Commission (SEC) also take part in controlling the exchange.

TYPES OF SECURITIES TRADED. Stocks, bonds, and CDs, but only stocks are open to nonresidents.

MARKET INDEX. The Korea Composite Stock Price Index (KOSPI) is the only official index on the Korea Stock Exchange. It is based on the aggregate market value and has a base date of January 4, 1980, and a base index of 100.

SETTLEMENT. Stocks settle on a T+2 cycle, which is known as a "regular way" transaction. Buy-ins are not common in the Korean market. Funds to cover settlement must be received no later than end of day on T+3. After T+3, the broker must sell the shares at the lowest selling price.

CLEARING. The Korea Securities Depository Corporation (KSDC) operates as both a central depository and a clearing house.

CORPORATE ACTIONS. Corporate actions are reported in the Korean Stock Market (published by the Securities Dealers' Association), *Daily Economic* newspaper, and through direct notification. Companies are required to hold general meetings annually according to Korea's commercial code. Notification of an AGM must be sent to shareholders at least two weeks prior to the meeting.

PRICING. Closing prices are automatically transmitted to BOS through a terminal connected to the Korean Securities Computer Corporation (KOSCOM).

TAXATION. Dividends (stock and cash) and interest are subject to a 25 percent withholding tax. A "Residents Tax" of 7.5 percent of the withholding tax (1.875 percent) is also deducted, making the total amount of tax withheld 26.875 percent. This can be reduced under a double taxation agreement. The current tax treaties allow for reduced withholding, and no reclaims are allowed.

Capital gains from a sale of securities by a nonresident are taxed at 10 percent (or the treaty rate) of the sale proceeds, or 25 percent of the capital gains net of transaction charges, whichever is lower. This amount is deducted by the selling broker. There is also a transaction tax on sales, equal to 0.2 percent on the traded value. A stamp duty of KRW300 is paid when opening a securities account. There are no restrictions regarding the repatriation of sale proceeds and income.

FOREIGN OWNERSHIP CEILINGS. No single nonresident investor may own more than 3 percent of any company's equity. The aggregate foreign ownership limit for Korean companies is 10 percent.

Exceptions exist, such as the higher limit (25 percent) for companies that have issued equities to nonresidents through convertible bonds or the Foreign Capital Inducement Act.

CURRENCY RESTRICTIONS. The currency is not freely convertible. Dealing in Korean won is subject to strict supervision by the Bank of Korea. Currency speculation is not allowed. Transfers of stock to third parties are not permitted.

Double Taxation Treaties. Australia; Austria; Bangladesh; Belgium; Canada; Denmark; Finland; France; Germany; Hungary; India; Indonesia; Japan; Luxembourg; Malaysia; Netherlands; New Zealand; Norway; Pakistan; Philippines; Singapore; Sri Lanka; Sweden; Thailand; Tunisia; Turkey; United Kingdom; United States.

MALAYSIA

Stock Exchanges. There are two stock exchanges: The Kuala Lumpur Stock Exchange (KLSE) and the Bumiputra Stock Exchange (BSE). The KLSE is located in Kuala Lumpur and currently has 59 member firms. The KLSE is automated.

Stock Exchange Supervision. The Kuala Lumpur Stock Exchange (KLSE) is a self-regulatory organization responsible for the surveillance of the marketplace and the enforcement of its listing and disclosure requirements and standards of the listed companies. The Bumiputra Stock Exchange (BSE) is relatively inactive with very few listings.

Trading Hours. Monday through Friday, 9:30 A.M. to 12:30 P.M. and 2:30 P.M. to 5:00 P.M. (local time).

Types of Securities Traded. Stocks, bonds, corporate and government bonds, money market instruments, unit trusts.

Market Indexes. The commonly observed index in Malaysia is the KLSE Composite Index comprised of 85 component stocks. Other indexes are the KLSE Industrial Index and the recently introduced Exchange Main Board All Share Index known as the EMAS Index. These indexes are comprised of equities from various sectors such as consumer products, industrial products, and trading services.

Settlement. Most KLSE purchase transactions are settled on a T+7 basis, and sales transactions are settled on a T+4 basis. However, the buyer and seller can mutually agree on a settlement date other than T+7 for purchase or "off market" transactions. Shares not delivered by the deadline are subject to an exchange-initiated automatic buy-in on T+6. Investors are strongly advised to follow settlement deadlines as buy-ins are strictly enforced by the KLSE.

Clearing. The Central Depository System (CDS) is operated by the Malaysian Central Depository (MCD), which is a subsidiary of the KLSE. The CDS system replaces the existing clearing and settlement system that involves physical movement of shares. Pending full implementation of the CDS, it runs side by side with the existing scrip-based system.

CORPORATE ACTIONS. Consult information circulars, financial newspapers, and the KLSE Daily Diary. Companies are required to hold AGMs. Shareholders must be informed 14 days prior to the meeting unless the Memorandum and Articles of Association of a company stipulate 21 days. Special resolutions require 21 days' notice.

TAXATION. The standard rate of withholding tax in Malaysia is 32 percent on dividends and 20 percent on interest. There is no capital gains tax or withholding tax on dividends in Malaysia. However, dividends are taxed in the form of a 30 percent income tax paid by the distributing corporation.

In general, interest received by nonresidents is subject to Malaysian withholding tax at a rate of 15 percent at source. Interest earned on certain government obligations is exempt from Malaysian withholding tax when received by nonresidents. There is no value-added tax in Malaysia.

REGISTRATION AND EXCHANGE FEES. There is generally a 1 percent exchange fee per transaction and a .05 percent clearing fee paid to Security Clearing Automatic Network Services (SCANS) by both the buyer and the seller. Double taxation treaties do not provide investors with any real benefits from dividend income.

FOREIGN OWNERSHIP CEILINGS. Generally, nonresident investors may hold up to 30 percent of any company. There are exceptions that allow the 30 percent limit to be exceeded, particularly for companies that mainly produce goods for export. The nonresident investor should confirm with the broker the status of the shares prior to entering into a purchase contract for registration purposes.

DISCLOSURE CEILINGS. Currently, disclosures must be made when an investor holds 5 percent of a company's paid-up capital.

DOUBLE TAXATION TREATIES. Albania; Australia; Austria; Bangladesh; Belgium; Canada; Denmark; Finland; France; Germany; Hungary; India; Indonesia; Islamic Republic of Iran; Italy; Japan; Mauritius; Netherlands; New Zealand; Norway; Pakistan; Papua New Guinea; People's Republic of China; Philippines; Poland; Republic of Sudan; Romania; Russia; Saudi Arabia; Singapore; South Korea; Sri Lanka; Sweden; Switzerland; Thailand; United Kingdom; United States; Yugoslavia; Zimbabwe.

MEXICO

STOCK EXCHANGE. Mexico's sole exchange is La Bolsa Mexicana de Valores, S.A. de CV, located in Mexico City. There are two primary markets, the Capital Market and the Money Market. The Capital Market is comprised of long-term investments in equities and bonds. The Money Market is comprised of short- and medium-term investments in government securities, certificates of deposit, bankers acceptances, and commercial paper. There is also a Cobertura market (foreign exchange futures), which is increasingly being used to hedge currency positions.

TRADING HOURS. Monday through Friday, 8:30 A.M. to 3:00 P.M. (local time). During daylight savings time, the trading hours are 7:30 A.M. to 2:00 P.M. (local time).

TYPES OF SECURITIES TRADED. Stocks, bonds, commercial paper, bankers acceptances, convertibles, Nafinsa trust shares. A-Series shares are held by Mexican nationals only. B-, C-, and L-series shares can be held by both nationals and foreign investors. C shares may be nonvoting; L shares may limit voting rights. The Nafinsa trust allows foreign participation in certain shares through CPOs (Certificate of Ordinary Participation). It is limited, however, to ownership rights only.

MARKET INDEX. The Mexican Stock Exchange Equities Index has been published since 1980. Trading volumes are reviewed every two months to determine the index constituents and weightings.

STOCK EXCHANGE SUPERVISION. The Stock Exchange is supervised by the Ministry of Finance (Secretaria de Hacienda y Credito Publico) and the National Securities Commission (Comision Nacional de Valores) or CNV, which is loosely modeled on the U.S. SEC. The Treasury and Public Credit Board, in conjunction with the CNV, determine and establish the policies and standards that guide and supervise the stock market.

SETTLEMENT. Equities settle on a trade date plus 2 days basis (T+2). Bonds generally settle on trade date plus 1 (T+1).

CLEARING. Mexico has a central depository: S.D. Indeval, S.A. De C.V. (Indeval). The long-term objective of Indeval is to dematerialize all securities. Indeval is the sole depository for equities, commercial paper, and bankers' acceptances. Government securities are held at Banco de Mexico, which is the sole depositary for these types of securities.

CORPORATE ACTIONS. Consult daily stock exchange bulletins, local newspapers, the Official Gazette, issuers of corporate action information (special publications devoted to corporate actions), and the weekly newsletter published by Banamex. All companies are required to hold open AGMs. According to Mexican law, all announcements have to be made at least 72 hours before the record date. Most companies announce their meetings several weeks in advance. There is no proxy-card voting in Mexico. Shareholders may be represented at corporate meetings by their designated custodians, who must attend in person.

The CNV requires that listed companies disclose information on performance, policies and projects, as well as the accounting policies, and principles followed in the preparation of all financial information and financial statements.

TAXATION. Taxes are withheld at source by the issuer of each security. There is a 35 percent tax on dividends and a 15 percent tax rate per annum on interest on commerical paper and bankers' acceptances. Mexico does not maintain reciprocal tax treaties with any country.

Government securities are not subject to any withholding taxes. The tax rate on interest for corporate debt paper (such as commercial paper, bankers acceptances, and promissory notes) held for less than one year is 15 percent. No tax is applied to corporate paper held for more than one year. There is no capital gains tax on equities or government securities.

There is a reduced tax rate for foreign investors domiciled in a non-tax-haven country (a tax haven is defined as a country with a corporate tax rate of less than 70 percent of Mexico's). There is no stamp duty or ad valorem tax in Mexico.

DISCLOSURE CEILINGS. There are no disclosure ceilings.

OWNERSHIP CEILINGS. Nonresidents are prohibited from owning more than 49 percent of any Mexican corporation. There are no restrictions on the repatriation of proceeds of sales or income.

PERU

STOCK EXCHANGE. The Bolsa de Valores de Lima [Bolsa, also known as the Lima Stock Exchange—(LSE)] is the largest stock exchange in Peru. There is also an exchange in Arecuipa, and an over-the-counter market that trades primarily corporate bonds and drafts. Unregistered equities trading is permitted but is rare.

TRADING HOURS. Monday through Friday, 11:00 A.M. to 1:30 P.M. (local time).

STOCK EXCHANGE SUPERVISION The Comision Nacional Supervisora de Empresas y Valores, CONASEV (National Commission for the

Supervision of Companies and Securities) supervises the Bolsa. The Comision Nacional de Inversiones y Technologias Extranjeras, CONITE (National Commission for Foreign Investments and Technologies) supervises foreign investments.

TYPES OF SECURITIES TRADED. Bills of exchange, bonds, common shares, drafts, labor shares, promissory notes. The majority of listed shares are labor stocks, which represent workers' participation in the net worth of a company.

Both common and labor shares have the same rights, but only common shares have voting rights and hence generally trade at a premium to labors.

MARKET INDEX. The Stock Exchange General Index (IGB) is the main market index. Its base changes every two years.

SETTLEMENT. Equities settle on T+2 for purchases and T+3 for sales. If a transaction fails to settle, either party may file a claim with the Bolsa within 72 hours. The party filing the claim may then cancel the deal or force a settlement. The Bolsa will buy-in or sell-out the defaulting broker and charge it for any losses. Buy-ins are rare, as brokers may be suspended from trading activities until all outstanding fails are settled.

CLEARING. Peru's central depositary is the Caja de Valores (CAVAL), which. acts as clearinghouse and record keeper for most equities.

CORPORATE ACTIONS. Corporate action announcements are usually published one week before a response is due. Annual General Meetings (AGMs) are required by law and are usually held in March. The Bolsa bulletin usually publishes scheduled meetings and agendas. No regulations exist with regard to the time period between announcement and the AGM, although market average is around 15 days. Shareholders who own a significant number of shares usually attend these meetings.

TAXATION. There is a 10 percent withholding tax on dividends and interest, and no capital gains tax.

REGISTRATION AND EXCHANGE FEES. A tax of 0.05 percent is paid to CONASEV, the regulatory body, and 0.15 percent to the LSE (Lima Stock Exchange).

FOREIGN OWNERSHIP CEILINGS. The Peruvian government makes few distinctions between local and foreign investors, but there is an ownership ceiling that applies to both residents and nonresidents. No investor may purchase more than 15 percent of outstanding shares of a company in the banking, finance, or insurance industries without prior approval of the Superintendencia de Banca y Seguros. Also, majority shareholders, either direct or indirect, of any institution within any of these industries may not hold more than 5 percent of the outstanding shares of any other institution in the same industry.

DISCLOSURE CEILINGS. Custodians are required to submit reports of investment activity and related foreign exchange transactions to the CONITE for statistical purposes.

DOUBLE TAXATION TREATIES. There are no countries that maintain double taxation treaties with Peru.

PHILIPPINES

STOCK EXCHANGE. The Makati and Manila Stock Exchanges recently combined to form the Philippine Stock Exchange (PSE). The Makati Stock Exchange is now the PSE-Ayala, and the Manila Stock Exchange is the PSE-Tektite. The two clearinghouses are linked electronically and now quote one price for all issues. Only equities are listed on the exchanges.

TRADING HOURS. Monday through Friday, from 9:30 A.M. to 12:00 noon (local time). The trading day can be extended to 12:15 P.M. to allow members to complete unexecuted orders received before 9:30 A.M. These orders are executed at the last sale price at 12:00 noon (local time).

STOCK EXCHANGE SUPERVISION Stock exchange activity is regulated by the Board of Investments, the Central Bank of the Philippines, and the Securities and Exchange Commission (SEC). A separate Board of Governors oversees each exchange.

TYPES OF SECURITIES TRADED. Listed securities are generally classified as "A" shares and "B" shares. Class "A" shares are restricted to Filipino investors, and class "B" shares are available to nonresidents as well as Filipino investors and generally trade at a premium. There is currently no trading of futures and options for nonresident investors.

MARKET INDEX. There are three market indexes in the Philippines, the commercial and industrial index, the mining index, and the oil index. Each exchange also maintains a composite index that is based on the changes in price of 25 securities chosen from the commercial, mining, and oil industries.

SETTLEMENT. Shares settle on trade date plus four business days (T+4). Government securities usually settle on a same day (T) basis except for Treasury notes, which settle on trade date plus 2 (T+2). Buy-ins and sell-outs are not permitted, but the defaulting party is expected to compensate the other parties for failed trades should there be any financial loss.

CLEARING. Currently there is no central depository in the Philippines, but there is a project underway to introduce a central depository and clearing system (CDC). Each exchange has an independent corporation acting as a clearinghouse. The PSE-Ayala utilizes Rizal Commercial Banking Corporation, and the PSE-Tektite employs Equitable Banking Corporation. There are plans to consolidate the two clearinghouses in the future.

CORPORATE ACTIONS. Consult the daily stock quotation from the Exchange, the Makati Stock Exchange Monthly Review, the Manila Stock Exchange Monthly Review, newspapers, and notices received from companies. Information relative to corporate actions is generally available as early as one month before payable date. Companies are required to hold AGMs, which are open to all shareholders. The time frame for sending AGM materials to shareholders varies by company.

TAXATION. There is a 35 percent withholding tax on dividends and interest. Taxes are usually withheld by the paying agent. A reduced rate of tax is sometimes available to residents of those countries that maintain a double taxation treaty with the Philippines.

There is no capital gains tax levied on exchange securities transactions. There is a sales tax, however, deducted by the broker, of 1/4 of 1 percent of the selling price on exchange-listed shares levied on the seller on all sale transactions. There is a tax on net capital gains for shares not listed or traded on the stock exchange—10 percent on net capital gains under PHP100,000 (USD3,600); 20 percent on net capital gains over PHP100,000. There is also a Stamp Duty on stock purchases computed as follows: (#of shares) × (par value) × (PHP 1.00). There is no value-added tax.

REGISTRATION AND EXCHANGE FEES. Fees are included in the broker's commission. A registration fee of PHP 49.50 per stock certificate is usually charged by the transfer agent.

FOREIGN OWNERSHIP CEILINGS. Foreign investors may generally own up to 100 percent of most companies' stock. Mining, mass media, and rural banks, however, are restricted by statute to a maximum of 40 percent foreign holding. In addition, certain companies' by laws restrict or prohibit foreign ownership, especially those in the defense and pharmaceutical sectors.

Currently, restricted companies issue A shares and B shares proportionate to the foreign ownership limit. Both have equal shareholder rights and entitlements.

DISCLOSURE CEILINGS. Investors are not required to disclose their holdings upon reaching a threshold, but must register all investments with the Central Bank to secure future repatriation rights.

DOUBLE TAXATION TREATIES. Australia; Austria; Belgium; Canada; Denmark; Finland; France; Germany; Indonesia; Japan; Malaysia; New Zealand; Pakistan; Singapore; Sweden; Thailand; United Kingdom; United States.

POLAND

STOCK EXCHANGE. The Warsaw Stock Exchange (WSE) is the only stock exchange in Poland. The market is divided into five sectors. Off-exchange trading is also allowed, but brokerage firms must be approved by the Securities Commission (SC). Equities and fixed income securities can both be traded off the exchange.

Money Market Instruments, T-Bills, Primary Market. The Primary Market uses the auction system. Foreign investors are allowed to trade on this market.

Money Market Instruments, T-Bills, Secondary Market. The Secondary Market (the OTC market) is not regulated and is dominated by six dealers, one of the dealers being Bank Handlowy. Dealers in the secondary market execute T-bill transactions at net prices based on an agreed upon discounted rate. Other fixed income securities are also traded on the Block and the Common Markets.

The Block Market is a wholesale market for institutional investors, and it deals mostly with Interbank transactions. The smallest lot size traded on this market is 100 units.

The Common Market offers odd and even lots of securities to individual and institutional investors.

The Interbank Bond Market. Trades are executed directly and exclusively between the National Depository of Securities (NDS) participants.

TRADING HOURS. Equities and Common Market Bonds, Monday through Thursday from 11:00 A.M. until 2:00 P.M. (local time). Block Market bonds, Monday through Friday from 11:00 A.M. until 2:00 P.M.

TYPES OF SECURITIES TRADED. Equities, government bonds, government T-bills.

MARKET INDEX. The Warszawski Indeks Fieldowy (WIG-20) is the only index traded on the exchange. The WIG is a market cap index made up of 20 securities with the highest capitalization and volumes of all the securities listed on the WSE.

SETTLEMENT. T+3 for equities and bonds traded on the common market; T+2 in primary and secondary markets; T+1 for bonds traded on the block market. Buy-ins are not permitted in the Polish market.

CLEARING. The NDS is the central depository in Poland.

CORPORATE ACTIONS. Notification of events is sent via fax, S.W.I.F.T., and telex. Polish companies announce annual meetings in public daily publications, describing the agenda of the meetings. Nonresident institutional investors are permitted to vote proxies in Poland. Consult the national daily newspapers and Cedula (a WSE bulletin). Telerate and Reuters are also used.

TAXATION. Dividends are taxed at a rate of 20 percent for nonresident investors. The rate may be less for those countries with double taxation treaties. Investors may file for a tax reclaim if the securities purchased are issued by newly privatized companies on the primary market. In this case, the client is entitled to reclaim the full amount of tax withheld. Financial services fees are VAT exempt.

There is no capital gains tax. Interest earned on T-bills is tax exempt in the Polish market. Transactions executed on the WSE are free of stamp duties, but transactions on the OTC market are exempt only when an SC-authorized Polish broker executes the trade. If no authorized broker is involved, each party is required to pay 2 percent of the transaction amount to the tax authorities. This is applicable only to individual investors.

FOREIGN OWNERSHIP CEILINGS. Foreign investors are permitted to buy all equities traded on the WSE as well as all Treasury bonds. A permit is required for foreign investors to purchase securities in the airports and seaport management and real estate sectors. There are no foreign exchange restrictions for foreign institutional investors. Funds may be repatriated into other currencies with no restrictions.

DISCLOSURE CEILINGS. All investors (foreign and domestic) must announce a takeover bid when the investor acquires more than 5 or 10 percent of a company's issued share capital and this acquisition leads to 33 percent ownership or more. The buyer must also notify the Securities Commission, Anti-Monopoly Office, and the issuing company.

DOUBLE TAXATION TREATIES. Albania; Australia; Austria; Belarus; Belgium; Canada; China; Cyprus; Czech Republic; Denmark; Estonia; Finland; France; Germany; Greece; Hungary; India; Indonesia; Israel; Italy; Japan; Korea; Kuwait; Latvia; Lithuania; Malaysia; Netherlands; Norway; Pakistan; Philippines; Russia; Singapore; Slovak Republic; South Africa; Spain; Sri Lanka; Sweden; Switzerland; Thailand; Tunisia; Turkey; UAE; Ukraine; United Kingdom; United States; Uruguay; Yugoslavia; Zimbabwe.

PORTUGAL

STOCK EXCHANGE. There are two stock exchanges in Portugal. Equities and bonds are traded on the Lisbon Stock Exchange, and futures and options are traded in Porto.

The Lisbon Stock Exchange is divided into four different markets: the Official Market, comprised of shares, bonds, participant bonds, and investment trust units; the Second Market, comprised of shares and bonds of medium-sized companies not listed in the main market; the Market without Quotations, comprised of shares, bonds, warrants, bonus and subscription rights, and investment trust units of small companies without a significant turnover or with economic difficulties; and the Special Market for large transactions of bonds. An OTC Market exists for all purchase and sales transactions of securities not executed on the exchange.

STOCK EXCHANGE SUPERVISION The Comissao do Mercado de Valores Mobiliarios (CMVM) supervises the stock market and is regulated by the Ministry of Finance.

TYPES OF SECURITIES TRADED. Bonds: ordinary, preferred, floating rate, government, zero coupon, medium term treasuries, convertibles; money market instruments; unit trusts; equities; warrants.

On the Porto Exchange, stock index futures, long-term government bonds, and short-term interest rate futures.

MARKET INDEX. The market indices in Portugal are as follows: Lisbon Stock Exchange Index (Bolsa de Valores de Lisboa - B.V.L.), which includes all securities traded on the Lisbon Stock Exchange. Lisbon Stock Exchange 30 Index (B.V.L. 30), the 30 most actively traded companies on the Lisbon Stock Exchange. Continuous Trade System Index (Indice

Nacional do Continuo, I.N.C.), comprised of all stocks traded on the continuous trading system.

SETTLEMENT. The settlement cycle for shares and fixed income instruments is T+4.

CLEARING. Portugal's central depositary, Central de Valores Mobiliarios (CVM), manages the settlement system that is used for both physical and book entry securities.

CORPORATE ACTIONS. Consult the Daily Stock Exchange Bulletin and local press for corporate action information. Annual General Meetings (AGMs) are usually held in February or March. Extraordinary meetings are held throughout the year. When an AGM is announced, the agenda must be published in the Stock Exchange Bulletin 30 days prior to the meeting. The agenda will include a general description of the items on which holders will vote. For voting at AGMs, clients may grant a power of attorney to a representative or an attorney located in Portugal. Local law requires one representative per beneficial owner.

TAXATION. Tax benefits apply and effectively reduce income tax from 25 percent to 12.5 percent for equities listed on the stock exchange. This makes double taxation treaties not applicable as one cannot accumulate both. The rate on unlisted shares is 30 percent, reduced to 25 percent. The tax on interest is 20 percent.

Nonresident investors are fully exempt from capital gains taxes. The withholding tax rates apply to all nonresident investors whose countries have no Double Taxation Agreement with Portugal. There is a Stamp Duty on market trades and Off-Shore trades of 7 percent.

FOREIGN OWNERSHIP CEILINGS. All securities can be traded by foreign investors. Non-Portuguese institutions must obtain authorization from the Portuguese Trade Institute (ICEP) prior to acquiring more than 20 percent of a listed or 30 percent of an unlisted company. Both Portuguese and non-Portuguese investors must report acquisitions exceeding 10, 20, 33.3, and 50 percent of a listed company's total share capital as well as divestment from those levels to the issuing company, the CMVM, and the Stock Exchange.

Some companies have foreign ownership restrictions due to their own bylaws. Registration of such shares in the name of a foreign investor is subject to prior authorization of the issuing company. The only industry sector that has a foreign ownership limit is the gambling and casino business. The limit is 40 percent.

DOUBLE TAXATION TREATIES. Austria; Belgium; Brazil; Denmark; Finland; France; Germany; Italy; Norway; Northern Ireland; Spain; Switzerland; United Kingdom.

SOUTH AFRICA

STOCK EXCHANGE. The Johannesburg Stock Exchange (JSE) is the only stock exchange in South Africa. Dealing is by direct negotiation between traders, as there are no specialists. The bond market is known as the Bond Market Exchange (BME). Most bond trading occurs in the primary market where the bonds are sold directly by issuers to secondary market dealers. Nonresidents can purchase and sell bonds only through the JSE or the BME. The Traded Options Market (TOM) uses the open outcry method. American Put and Call options are available on the All Gold and All Share indexes.

The over-the-counter (OTC) market for options is significantly greater than the TOM, although actual volumes are not measured. The OTC market is used primarily by commercial and trading banks, insurance companies, issuers, and stockbrokers.

TRADING HOURS. Monday through Friday from 9:30 A.M. to 4:00 P.M. for equities and from 7:00 A.M. to 5:00 P.M. for gilt bonds (local time).

STOCK EXCHANGE SUPERVISION The Exchange is supervised by the Financial Services Board, which is a division of the Treasury.

TYPES OF SECURITIES TRADED. Debt: convertible bonds; gilt-edged securities; loans; S. A. Breweries corporate bonds; semi-gilt-edged securities; straight bonds. Equity: convertible preferred; cumulative preferred; deferred; ordinary; participating preferred; preferred Kruggerand gold coins. Money market: bills of exchange; bankers' acceptances; promissory notes; trade bills; land bank bills; land bank debentures; negotiable certificates of deposit; RSA Treasury Bills Unit Trust Certificates; closed-end trusts; open-end trusts.

Options are traded on the JSE while futures, and options on these futures, trade on the South African Futures Exchange (SAFEX).

MARKET INDEX. There are several market indices: JSE All Gold; JSE Fixed Interest; JSE Industrials; JSE Metals and Minerals; JSE Overall. The equity indexes are calculated various times per day and are all based on prices. The fixed-interest index is weighted on the nominal value of outstanding issues.

SETTLEMENT. Settlement takes place on a weekly basis through the computerized clearing system that operates on the JSE. Settlement periods are numbered consecutively from 1 to 52 (1 being the first week in January). The selling brokers stipulate in which settlement period they will deliver scrips. All futures contracts are settled in cash the day after trade date. Although not common, buy-ins do exist in the South African market. If the delivering party fails to deliver the securities in the agreed-upon weekly settlement cycle, the receiving broker can initiate a buy-in on the first day of the next weekly settlement at the delivering party's expense.

CLEARING. The JSE owns and operates the JSE Equity Clearinghouse. UNEXcor clears activities on the BME. A central depository has been developed in South Africa and is still in its very early stages. Futures contracts are cleared through SAFCOM, a clearinghouse owned by SAFEX.

CORPORATE ACTIONS. Consult the JSE daily Gazette and daily newspapers. All publicly traded companies are required to hold Annual General Meetings (AGMs), which are well attended by shareholders. Information relevant to the meetings must be distributed to the registered shareholders no later than 48 hours prior to meetings.

TAXATION. Capital gains and interest income are tax-exempt for nonresidents. A Marketable Securities Tax (MST) exists for all purchases of marketable securities by a stockbroker on behalf of an individual. The tax rate is 1 percent of the gross consideration amount (price × quantity) of the purchase. The tax does not apply to listed debentures and certain marketable securities issued by the government, local authorities and quasi-government institutions.

Securities issued by certain utilities are exempt from stamp duties and MST. Where no MST is chargeable, the stamp duty is 1 percent. There is a VAT at a rate of 14 percent.

FOREIGN OWNERSHIP CEILINGS. Total foreign ownership may not exceed 15 percent of the banking sector and 25 percent of the insurance sector as measured by capital. JSE-traded Kruggerands are not available to foreign investors. Securities owned by nonresidents must be endorsed, and local sale proceeds from these securities cannot be transferred into foreign currency. Nonresident investors may freely transfer dividends and interest earned. The South African Reserve Bank has issued regulations regarding the transfer of accrued interest on interest bearing securities. Nonresidents may purchase call options; however, they are restricted from writing options or buying puts.

DISCLOSURE CEILINGS. A 10 percent disclosure level is required of both local and foreign investors.

DOUBLE TAXATION TREATIES. Germany; Netherlands; Northern Ireland; Switzerland; United Kingdom.

SPAIN

STOCK EXCHANGES. There are four stock exchanges (Bolsas) in Spain. The main exchange is in Madrid, the second largest is in Barcelona, and two smaller exchanges are located in Bilbao and Valencia, all linked through the Computer Assisted Trading Systems (CATS). Fixed-income derivatives are traded at the Mercado de Futuros Financieros, S.A. (MEFF, S.A.). MEFF Renta Variable is the exchange for equity-related derivatives, while the MEFF Renta Fija is the exchange for interest-rate and currency related derivatives.

STOCK EXCHANGE SUPERVISION. The Ministry of Finance and the Comision Nacional Mercado de Valores (CNMV) supervise stock market activity.

TYPES OF SECURITIES TRADED. Securities traded include the following: equities and options; bonds: convertible, mortgage, public debt, and zero coupon; futures, and options contracts on stock market indexes and bonds and short-term interest rates.

MARKET INDEX. The Madrid General Index (IGBM) is the standard stock index for monitoring Spanish stock performance in various sectors. The sectors included in the IGBM are banking, chemicals, communications, construction, food, investments, metals, and oil.

A new index, the IBEX-35, is gaining popularity. The IBEX is composed of the 35 most liquid equity shares on the market. The basket of constituents is rebalanced every six months.

SETTLEMENT. The trade settlement cycle for most equities is T+5.

CLEARING. Spain' s central depository is the Sociedad de Compensación y Liquidación de Valores S.A. (S.C.L.V.), Spain's central depositary. The S.C.L.V. is supervised by the CNMV.

CORPORATE ACTIONS. Consult the Official Gazette and information supplied by the issuing corporation. Spanish companies are required to hold Annual General Meetings (AGMs), which are open to all shareholders. There is no market policy as to when information relevant to the AGM must be distributed to the shareholders. A few companies pay attendance premiums to encourage shareholders to vote.

TAXATION. A 25 percent withholding tax is levied on all dividends and interest income paid to nonresidents. Taxes are withheld at source by the issuer. No capital gains tax is levied on nonresidents whose countries maintain a taxation treaty with Spain. There are no stamp duties or value-added taxes in the Spanish securities market.

REGISTRATION AND EXCHANGE FEES. There are no registration or exchange fees.

FOREIGN OWNERSHIP CEILINGS. The following industries regulate non-resident investments: air transport, construction, defense, finance, information, mining, refineries, sea transport, water, and any company that is the main supplier to a public entity.

DISCLOSURE CEILINGS. All foreign investments must be reported to the CNMV; in addition, the number of shares purchased by nonresidents is subject to the Direccion General de Transacciones Exteriores for the purpose of control and to possibly limit the foreign participation in Spanish companies to 50 percent. The purchase of shares exceeding 5 percent by nonresidents in Spanish banks is subject to approval by the Bank of Spain.

DOUBLE TAXATION TREATIES. Australia; Austria; Belgium; Brazil; Bulgaria; Canada; China; Czech Republic; Denmark; Ecuador; Finland; France; Germany; Hungary; Ireland; Italy; Japan; Korea; Luxembourg; Morocco; Netherlands; Norway; Philippines; Poland; Portugal; Romania; Russia; Sweden; Switzerland; Tunisia; United Kingdom; United States.

SRI LANKA

STOCK EXCHANGE. The Colombo Stock Exchange (CSE) is fully automated. The CSE has primary and secondary markets. On the primary market, investors buy shares directly from the issuing company. On the secondary market, investors buy and sell shares through a broker.

The CSE trades primarily equities securities. Fixed income securities are usually traded off the exchange, directly between issuers and buyers. Local commercial banks trade government bonds, which are mostly three-, six-, and twelve-month T-bills. There is no corporate fixed-income market.

TRADING HOURS. Monday through Friday from 9:00 A.M. to 12:30 P.M.

Types of Securities Traded. Common equities on the CSE.

Market Index. The two main market indexes in Sri Lanka are the All Share Price Index and the Sensitive Price Index. The All Share Price Index is calculated based on the market capitalization of all of the listed companies on the CSE and is adjusted periodically for new listings, delistings, and rights issues. The Sensitive Price Index is calculated based on securities of blue chip companies and identifies general fluctuations in prices of larger capitalization shares.

Settlement. Purchases settle on T+5 and sales settle on T+7, but this two-tiered system will eventually be replaced with a uniform T+5 settlement cycle for all purchase and sale transactions. The percentage of failed trades on the CSE is zero due to implementation of various procedures that serve to prevent trade fails. Selling banks are required to confirm that shares are available prior to executing a trade. On T+4, the broker or custodian bank must confirm the trade. If there is a discrepancy in the transaction information, the trade can be canceled. There is no official or mandatory buy-in procedure. The buyer has the option to repurchase securities if a trade fails for five days. The CSE imposes a daily penalty of 0.25 percent of the market value of the transaction on late deliveries and late payments.

Clearing. The Central Depository System (CDS) facilitates delivery of shares within the settlement system.

Corporate Actions. Most corporate actions are announced through the CSE and are published in the Stock Market Daily report. Most shareholders in Sri Lanka attend Annual General Meetings (AGMs) and vote their shares. Sri Lanka regulations permit nonresident investors to own voting shares and to vote their shares. Shareholders may grant a proxy authority to their custodian bank, if they choose. AGMs take place throughout the year; no regulations define standards for timing and placement of meeting announcements.

Taxation. Tax on dividend income paid to nonresident investors is withheld at a rate of 15 percent at source. Resident investors are exempt from this tax. Nonresident investors are exempt from capital gains tax. Purchases are subject to a 0.5 percent stamp duty on purchases of listed company shares. There is no value added tax in Sri Lanka.

Registration and Exchange Fees. There is no cost for registration. There are no exchange fees in Sri Lanka.

RESTRICTIONS FOR FOREIGN INVESTORS. The following categories of foreign investors are permitted to invest in listed and unlisted securities: country funds and regional/global funds approved by the Ministry of Finance, and individuals residing outside Sri Lanka. Additionally, country funds must maintain minimum investment totals as well as portfolio composition requirements, the terms of which are set by the Ministry of Finance. Local nominee companies are not permitted, although foreign investors may use offshore nominee companies. All nonresident investors are required to open a noninterest-bearing Share Investment External Rupee Account (SIERA) with their local agent. Sales proceeds and income can be repatriated freely with no restrictions or prior approval required. Foreign investment restrictions prohibit nonresidents from investing in fixed-income and money market instruments.

FOREIGN OWNERSHIP CEILINGS. A 40 percent shareholding limit remains in force for investment in companies in banking, finance, residential housing, and mining industries.

DISCLOSURE CEILINGS. There are no disclosure ceilings.

DOUBLE TAXATION TREATIES. Australia; Bangladesh; Belgium; Canada; Czech Republic; Denmark; Finland; France; Germany; India; Italy; Japan; Korea; Malaysia; Netherlands; Norway; Pakistan; Poland; Romania; Singapore; Slovakia; Sweden; Switzerland; Thailand; United Kingdom; Yugoslavia

TAIWAN

STOCK EXCHANGE. The Taiwan Stock Exchange (TSE), located in Taipei, is the only stock exchange in Taiwan. It is fully automated. Most equity trading is effected on the TSE, with the remainder executed on the Over-the-Counter (OTC) exchange. Bonds are primarily traded over the counter.

TRADING HOURS. Monday through Friday, 9:00 A.M. to 12:00 noon and Saturday 9:00 A.M. to 11:00 A.M., local time.

STOCK EXCHANGE SUPERVISION The Taiwan Securities and Exchange Commission (SEC) regulates all stock market activity. The Ministry of Finance supervises the SEC.

TYPES OF SECURITIES TRADED. Corporate bonds; listed beneficiary certificates; listed equity shares.

MARKET INDEX. The main market index in Taiwan is the Taiwan Stock Exchange Index (TAIEX). The index includes most equities listed on the TSE.

SETTLEMENT. The trade settlement cycle for equities is T+1. Fixed-income securities settle on trade date (T), but brokers will allow foreign institutional investors to settle their transactions on T+1. All unlisted securities settle in cash on trade date (T).

Brokers are required to report failed trades to the TSE and settle them either by buy-ins or sell-outs with the TSE. There are strict penalties for failed trades, and frequent offenders will be suspended from trading for a period of up to three years. Due to the preceding, failed trades are rare in the Taiwanese market.

CORPORATE ACTIONS. Listed companies are required to hold an Annual General Meeting (AGM). Shareholders with a minimum of 1,000 shares must be given 30 days' prior notice of an AGM. For special meetings, 15 days' notice must be given.

TAXATION. Dividends and interest paid to foreign investors are subject to a 20 percent tax. Taxes are withheld by the paying agent. There is no capital gains tax or stamp duty, but a value-added tax, called a securities transfer tax of 0.3 percent of the trade value, is charged on equities. Corporate bond sales are taxed at 0.1 percent, but government bonds are exempt.

REGISTRATION AND EXCHANGE FEES. There are no exchange or registration fees.

RESTRICTIONS FOR FOREIGN INVESTORS. Foreign investors are required to obtain approval from the local securities authority, the Securities and Exchange Commission, (SEC), before investing in local securities in Taiwan. All capital inflows and outflows in New Taiwan dollars (NTD) must be registered with the Central Bank of Taiwan. Investment principal may be repatriated after three months. Dividends may be repatriated once per fiscal year. Remittance of currency in and out of Taiwan is strictly controlled.

FOREIGN OWNERSHIP CEILINGS. The ownership ceiling for each foreign investor is 5 percent of any listed company. The ceiling for total foreign holding is 10 percent of any listed company. Foreign investment is prohibited in defense-related industries and certain specified securities in key industries.

DISCLOSURE CEILINGS. The SEC and CBC requires a list of all foreign clients and their holdings.

DOUBLE TAXATION TREATIES. Singapore is the only country that has a double taxation treaty with Taiwan.

THAILAND

STOCK EXCHANGE. Thailand has only one stock exchange, the Stock Exchange of Thailand (SET), located in Bangkok.

Trading is conducted on three separate boards: the Main Board for regular, local trading; the Special Board for large lots, odd lots, special lots, and bonds; and the Alien Board for stocks that are already held in the name of a foreign investor. These stocks may command a premium, but foreign investors are assured stock purchased will be registered, thereby mitigating the risk caused by limits on nonresident ownership of Thai companies.

STOCK EXCHANGE SUPERVISION. The SET is supervised by the Ministry of Finance, the SET's Board of Directors, and the SET Advisory Board. The markets are regulated by the Thai Securities and Exchange Commission (SEC).

TYPES OF SECURITIES TRADED. Common shares, preferred shares, unit trusts, government bonds and debentures; some warrants.

MARKET INDEX. The main market index is the SET Index, which is made up of 494 securities. Other market indexes include the Tisco Index, based on average stock prices, the Book Club Index, a market cap index; and the Capital Market Research Institution index (CMRI), which measures liquidity.

SETTLEMENT. All trades settle on trade date plus three business days (T+3). Buy-ins do not occur in the Thai market. The SET will levy penalties for trades that settle past the standard settlement cycle of T+3.

CLEARING. The Shares Depository Center (SDC) is the central depository of Thailand. The SDC is regulated by the Thai Securities and Exchange Commission (SEC).

CORPORATE ACTIONS. Normally, all corporate actions are open to foreign investors. However, this also depends on the foreign ownership limitation of each company. If the ceiling has not yet been reached, nonresident investors will receive all entitlements due.

Consult the daily SET publication, the SET Daily News, to source corporate action information for all listed companies that use the SET as registrar. For those companies that act as their own registrar, consult corporate action announcements received directly from the companies. All Thai companies are required to hold AGMs. For the majority of companies, information regarding the meeting is distributed approximately seven days prior to the meeting.

TAXATION. The withholding tax on dividends paid to investors is currently 10 percent. The rate of tax withheld on interest payments differs between foreign investors who are considered financial institutions and nonfinancial institutions, 10 percent and 15 percent, respectively. All taxes are withheld at source by the registrar. There is a 15 percent capital gains tax levied on foreign investors. Nonresidents, whose countries have entered into a double- taxation treaty with Thailand are exempt from the capital gains tax. U.S. residents are currently exempt from capital-gains tax through use of the tax treaty between the U.K. and Thailand. Stamp-duty charges exist only when the SET is not the registrar for the shares. There is no stamp duty on government bonds. There is a 7 percent value-added tax in Thailand.

REGISTRATION AND EXCHANGE FEES. There are no exchange fees. However, there is a scrip fee charge for registration.

FOREIGN OWNERSHIP CEILINGS. The foreign ownership limit is 25 percent for banks and financial companies and 49 percent for all other companies. Companies with foreign ownership ceilings are specified by the government and include banks, financial services and brokerage firms, services, hotels, industrial firms, and mining concerns.

DISCLOSURE CEILINGS. Any foreign investor holding more than 5 percent of a company's total amount of issued shares must report that to the SET.

DOUBLE TAXATION TREATIES. Australia; Austria; Belgium; Canada; Denmark; Finland; France; Germany; Hungary; India; Indonesia; Italy; Japan; Korea; Malaysia; Netherlands; Norway; Pakistan; People's Republic of China; Philippines; Poland; Sweden; Singapore; Sri Lanka; UK; Vietnam.

TURKEY

STOCK EXCHANGE. The Istanbul Stock Exchange (ISE) is the only exchange in Turkey. The ISE has been officially recognized by the U.S.

Securities and Exchange Commission (SEC) as a "designated off-shore securities market," thereby putting it on par with only 20 other stock exchanges in the world. Fifty percent of market capitalization and trading activity involves three main sectors: cement/construction, finance, and motor vehicles. The financial sector comprises 26 percent of market capitalization. Banks and licensed brokers also trade on the Repo Market, where government bonds and treasury bills are traded through Reuters. There is also an over-the-counter market.

The ISE also lists foreign securities, which are known as Public Participation Administration Bonds (PPA). These securities are traded in Turkish lira (TRL) and are either foreign currency (BEF, DEM, USD) indexed or foreign currency denominated. With foreign currency indexed bonds, interest and principal are paid in TRL. Foreign currency denominated bonds have interest and principal paid in foreign currency. PPAs mature in four years with semiannual interest payments.

The stock market has been divided into a first market and a second market. The first market accounts for about 85 percent of total market activity. The remaining companies in the stock market are traded in the second market.

Trading Hours. Monday through Friday as follows: The Odd lot and Primary Market, from 9:00 to 9:15 A.M. The Secondary Market, from 10:00 A.M. to 12:00 noon and 2:00 P.M. to 4:00 P.M.

Stock Exchange Supervision. The stock exchange is regulated by its internal Inspection and Control Department, the Undersecretariat of Treasury and Foreign Trade, and the Capital Markets Board (CMB), which is governed by the Minister of State for the Economy.

The CMB has wide regulatory authority and is responsible for issuing directives in the Turkish securities marketplace.

Types of Securities Traded. Ordinary shares, preferred shares, founder's shares, golden shares, fixed income, corporate bonds, government bonds, treasury bills, foreign exchange indexed bonds, revenue sharing certificates, asset-backed securities, bank bills, commercial paper, housing certificates, mutual fund certificates.

Market Index. The main market index is the ISE composite index, made up of the 75 most actively traded companies. There are also both a Financial Index and an Industrial Index.

SETTLEMENT. Stocks settle T+2; government securities settle on T+7 in the primary market, trade date (T) in the secondary market. If a trade does not settle on T+2, an ISE member has one business day to complete the transaction. If, after this time, the broker cannot deliver the securities, the stock exchange committee is authorized to proceed with a buy-in. Nonresidents usually purchase government securities at weekly auctions. Settlement occurs seven days after the auction.

CLEARING. Vakifbank currently acts as the ISE's "Depository, Clearing and Settlement Center." Cash settlement of securities cleared through Vakifbank is handled by another state bank, ISBANK.

CORPORATE ACTIONS. The Stock Exchange Bulletin is the primary source of corporate action information. Reuters and local newspapers are also utilized. Nonresidents are allowed to vote at an AGM or EGM. These meetings are announced in the Stock Exchange Bulletin and local newspapers. AGM and EGM agendas are announced two to four weeks prior to the meeting date. Resolutions are reported through the ISE media news and daily newspapers.

TAXATION. Nonresident investors are not subject to withholding tax on Turkish dividends, but there is a 10.5 percent withholding tax on interest from corporate bonds withheld at source. Foreign portfolio managers operating on an institutional basis are considered exempt from capital gains tax so long as they fulfill certain requirements.

REGISTRATION AND EXCHANGE FEES. There are no registration or exchange fees in Turkey

FOREIGN OWNERSHIP CEILINGS. There are no restrictions or limitations on foreign ownership. However, government approval is required for foreign control of a traded company. There is no restriction on the inflow and outflow of foreign currency, but all transfers in excess of 2.06 billion Turkish lira must be reported to the Central Bank of Turkey to comply with EC policy on money laundering.

DISCLOSURE CEILINGS. Any individual or entity owning 10 percent or more of a company's equity is required to report those holdings to the Treasury.

DOUBLE TAXATION TREATIES. Australia; Belgium; Cyprus; France; Germany; Italy; Jordan; Korea; Netherlands; Norway; Finland; Northern Ireland; Pakistan; Romania; Saudi Arabia; Sweden; Tunisia; United Kingdom.

URUGUAY

STOCK EXCHANGES. There are two stock exchanges in Uruguay, the Montevideo Stock Exchange (MSE) and the electronic exchange, La Bolsa Electronica de Valores (BEVSA). There are primary, secondary, and as over-the-counter market. Trading occurs by open outcry on the MSE.

The Uruguayan equity market is extremely thin at present, but it is expected to grow considerably as the privatization program of state-owned enterprises progresses and as a result of the potential cross-listings through the federation of Ibero American stock exchanges. A substantial market exists in Uruguay for the trading of Argentine and Brazilian fixed income securities.

TRADING HOURS. Monday through Friday from 2:00 P.M. to 3:00 P.M. local time.

STOCK EXCHANGE SUPERVISION. The stock exchange and its participants are supervised and regulated by the Camara Nacional De Comercio.

TYPES OF SECURITIES TRADED. Equity securities; treasury bills (denominated in pesos, U.S. dollars and deutschemarks); treasury bonds (denominated in U.S. dollars); OHR short-term certificates (issued by BHU State Mortgage Bank); CPI short-term certificates (issued by BHU State Mortgage Bank). Trading is primarily centered around mortgage certificates (OHR and CPI) and Treasury securities.

MARKET INDEX There is no formally calculated stock market index.

SETTLEMENT. Government securities (bills and bonds) purchased in the primary auction market settle on the trade date. Equity securities (must be executed through a local broker); money market instruments; government securities (bills and bonds) traded in the secondary market; and OTC securities all settle T+1. There is no standard market practice with regard to failing trades and buy-in procedures.

CLEARING. There is no central securities depository in Uruguay. All securities are held in custody in physical form by banks, brokers, and individual investors.

CORPORATE ACTIONS. Consult the following sources to monitor corporate actions: Stock Exchange Report; local newspapers; trade journals; local brokers; and the corporation itself. Shareholders may be represented by a proxy providing the proxy is not a board member, syndicate, or employee of the corporation that will be affected by the vote. A proxy may be granted without any formalities if it is for a specific meeting; otherwise, a notarized and legalized letter of appointment is necessary. All companies are required to publish an annual balance sheet and to communicate to all investors any and all changes in the Board of Directors or Auditing Committee.

There is no law requiring companies to hold annual general meetings (AGMs). However, the law does require that a company's balance sheet be approved by a general meeting within 180 days of the date the company closes its books. Companies usually provide shareholders with AGM information prior to the meeting.

TAXATION. A 30 percent withholding tax on dividends from industrial and commercial companies applies only if the investor's country of residence also taxes dividends from industrial and commercial companies and if there is a fiscal credit for taxes paid in Uruguay. Interest paid to nonresidents is not subject to withholding tax. Nominal shares issued by Uruguayan companies are subject to a net-worth tax of 2 percent per annum (for legal entities) or a progressive scale of up to 3 percent per annum in the case of individual shareholders. The net worth of companies issuing nominative shares is considered capital owned by the shareholders in proportion to their participation. Items exempt from VAT are sales of real estate, precious metals, shares and negotiable instruments, and medical and dental services. Custody services are subject to a 22 percent VAT.

FOREIGN OWNERSHIP CEILINGS. There are no foreign exchange controls or restrictions on capital movements. However, nonresidents may not invest in the broadcasting industry. The Uruguayan market does not require the appointment of a local administrator or a legal representative.

DOUBLE TAXATION TREATIES. Uruguay maintains a tax treaty with Germany.

VENEZUELA

STOCK EXCHANGES. The Caracas Stock Exchange (CSE) and the Maracaibo Stock Exchange are the only two exchanges in Venezuela with the CSE accounting for more than 90 percent of market volume. All equities are traded on a system modeled after that used by the Vancouver Stock Exchange, the Systema Automatica Transaction Bursatiles (SATB). Fixed-income trading is by open outcry.

TRADING HOURS. Monday through Friday, from 10:30 A.M. to 12:30 P.M.

STOCK EXCHANGE SUPERVISION. Market activity is supervised by the National Securities Commission (Comision Nacional de Valores or

CNV). The Superintendency of Foreign Investment (SIEX) is responsible for regulating foreign investment.

TYPES OF SECURITIES TRADED. Virtually all investment in Venezuela is in equities and treasury bills, though some treasury notes D-P-N (government term), and corporate bonds are traded. At present, there is no futures and options market in Venezuela.

MARKET INDEX. The Caracas Stock Exchange Index is comprised of 17 companies. The index is reviewed periodically to ensure the composition adequately reflects trading volume. The index was established at a base of 100 in 1971 and is measured by closing sale prices of the composite stocks adjusted for dividends, splits, reverse splits, and rights.

SETTLEMENT. Settlement of both equities and bonds is by mutual arrangement (T+1 to T+120) but usually occurs on T+3; Treasury bills settle on T+2. Buy-ins are rare in the Venezuelan market.

CLEARING. Clearing is performed by the Caracas Stock Exchange's Systema Automatica Liquidacion Bursatiles (SALB), which receives its information from the SATB (equity trading system). There is no central depositary at present.

CORPORATE ACTIONS. Delayed notices on corporate actions as well as last-minute changes in dates are common. Companies are required to hold annual general meetings, and shareholders generally attend. Consult the Caracas Stock Exchange Bulletin for daily announcements of corporate actions.

TAXATION. Nonresidents are exempt from withholding tax on dividends, and there is presently no withholding tax on interest income. There is a capital gains tax, paid annually. There are no stamp duties or VAT.

REGISTRATION AND EXCHANGE FEES. There are no exchange or registration fees in Venezuela.

FOREIGN OWNERSHIP CEILINGS. Nonresidents are prohibited from owning shares in certain industries such as oil and gas and communications (except telecommunications). Foreign ownership of Venezuelan banks and financial institutions must be approved by the Superintendency of Banks.

DISCLOSURE CEILINGS. All nonresident investment must still be reported to the Superintendency of Foreign Investment (SIEX). Reporting of such activity is the responsibility of the registrar.

The subject matter contained herein has been derived from several sources believed to be reliable and accurate at the time of publication. The author does not accept any liability for losses either direct or consequential caused by the use of this information. The author is neither making any investment recommendation nor providing any professional or advisory services relating to the activities described herein.

Sources: The Bank of New York, local stock exchanges.

Emerging Market Web Sites

The Internet is a rich source of valuable information on emerging markets, and I have compiled a list of my favorite sites. Keep in mind that sites have a way of going "dead," that is, the provider no longer maintains them. Web addresses can change frequently, but are current as of this writing. Individual country sites are best found using search engines such as Yahoo, which offer up a page of world stock markets as well as country and regional links.

EMERGING MARKETS GATEWAY
(www.emergingmarkets.com)

This is the emerging market Web site of yours truly. I maintain current links to the best emerging market Web pages, and useful information on emerging market investing. I have gathered what I believe is some of the most useful information on emerging markets available anywhere on the Web. Much of the information is free to the public, but there are also special features for owners of this book.

AFRICAN STOCK EXCHANGE GUIDE
(http://africa.com/pages/jse/page1.htm)

One of the few sites to offer an overview of the companies listed on the stock exchanges in Africa. Includes a search engine by company or sector. Updated very infrequently.

ASIA, INC. ONLINE
(www.asia-inc.com/index.html)

The site of *Asia, Inc.*, a regional business magazine, features valuable and insightful articles of interest to Asian emerging market investors. You'll

347

also find Asian stock market closings and some commentary, a reference library, *Who's Who in Asia,* and an Asian Internet directory. Attractive and useful. There is also something called the Prudential Perspective Index provided by Prudential Asia, which offers economic analysis of Asian economies.

BANK OF NEW YORK
(www.bankofny.com/adr/index.htm)

The Bank of New York's ADR Web site is the most comprehensive source of ADR information currently available. Not surprising, since the Bank of New York is the leading sponsor of ADRs. The site includes a complete directory listing all the ADRs, downloadable in Microsoft Excel format by region, industry, or alphabetically. The site also contains year-end and quarterly market reviews, as well as more than 300 individual company profiles, available for downloading in Adobe Acrobat format. There are also hypertext links to foreign company home pages, the SEC, all the major U.S. stock exchanges, and more than 40 international stock exchanges. An excellent site for emerging market watchers.

BARRA
(www.barra.com)

A highly regarded firm that serves professional money managers. Offers very limited material for the general public, but what it does offer is worth a look. For example, the BARRA Emerging Markets Volatility Index compares emerging market volatility for the latest 13-week period. The index calculations are based upon the International Finance Corporation (IFC) investable total return indexes (in U.S. $). No historical figures posted (just current rank, previous week, four and twelve weeks prior), so you must check regularly if you want to follow a trend. The BARRA site also includes a financial links page, which includes many interesting sites and research publications not found elsewhere.

BATTERYMARCH FINANCIAL MANAGEMENT, INC.
(www.batterymarch.com/index.html)

This firm has been an innovator in global equity investing, including emerging markets, for more than 25 years. The site features selected articles on global investing and a virtual research sites that include some valuable and unusual links to emerging market company and country reports.

BLOOMBERG PERSONAL:
WORLD EQUITY INDEXES
(www.bloomberg.com/markets/wei.html)

This page on the much-praised Bloomberg Web site monitors world stock market performance. Tables with levels of 20 major indexes from North/Latin America, Europe/Africa, and Asia/Pacific are on the front page, and there are dozens more on the inside pages. Choose Asia/Pacific's inner pages, for example, and Turkish, Malaysian, Japanese, Israeli, and New Zealand indexes are some you will come across. Some inexes are presented up to the minute, while others are on 20-minute delay. When you get to this page, click on the region of choice. This will take you to the inside page, which offers many more indexes than are displayed on the front page.

BRADYNET
(www.bradynet.com)

While this site is primarily devoted to Brady Bonds and other emerging market debt issues, it is one of the best overall emerging market sites, with excellent research reports on selected emerging markets, provided by partners such as Bankers Trust, DLJ, The Weston Group, and Socimer Capital Markets. Prices and ratings are available, and a premium service offers even more. An enhanced service for market professionals and serious investors, BradyNet Pro, provides Brady Bond pricing information combined with portfolio analysis software. BradyNet Pro also provides a comprehensive database of other emerging markets' fixed-income instruments as well as the tools to analyze them and integrate them to your portfolio. Some of this information can also be received via e-mail.

BUSINESS MONITOR - ECONOMIC ANALYSIS INDEX
(www.businessmonitor.co.uk)

This is an excellent site intended for professionals and businesspeople involved in international trade and investment, but it offers much useful data for emerging market investors. The site provides global coverage of legislation and regulations, corporate finance, offshore finance, market analysis, economic analysis, risk management, and worldwide business news. Use the search engine to find the country of choice or search "emerging markets" for many interesting articles. Go to (www.business-monitor.co.uk/bbp_index/economic_analysis/emerging_markets.html)

for an index of useful and current economic analyses of emerging markets.

BUTTONWOOD INTERNATIONAL GROUP
(www.buttonwood.com)

Buttonwood International provides a high-quality management consulting service to the global securities industry with some emphasis on emerging markets. One page, "Emerging Markets on the Net," features issues and trends and timely and useful articles. Limited free access to survey results and summaries from its Global Custody Yearbook; unlimited access is fee-based. It also provides excellent information on the leading global custodians.

CAMPBELL R. HARVEY
(www.duke.edu/~charvey)

The home page of Professor Campbell Harvey, who has published some very interesting data on emerging market investing, some of which is cited in this book. Papers, charts, and lectures available on-line. The Country Risk page at (www. Duke.edu/~charvey/Country risk/couindex.htm) is particularly interesting. Much of the data is a few years old, but it is still useful.

CAPITAL DATA
(www.capitaldata.com)

An excellent site for reports on international bond, equity, and syndicated loan issues, including daily updates and limited historical data in Microsoft Excel format. There is also a link page to the bond rating services such as Moody's and S&P.

CDA/WIESENBERGER
(www.cda.com/wiesenberger)

An excellent source of mutual fund Internet links from a leading data provider. CDA also offers an excellent product, FundEdge for Closed-Ends, which gives you instant access to data on the complete universe of closed-end funds and over 65 indexes. FundEdge allows you to screen the database to find funds that meet your specific investment and risk statistics. FundEdge also graphs the premium/discount, distributions, market price, NAV, and volume on a specified fund.

CHICAGO MERCANTILE EXCHANGE
EMERGING MARKETS PRODUCTS
(www.cme.com/market/emerging/index.html)

The CME offers several interest rate, currency, and index contracts based upon the emerging markets of the world, providing tools for managing the risk associated with emerging market financial flows, investments, and foreign exchange transactions. The home page provides a search engine, and if you enter "emerging markets," the site will offer even more information and tips on trading emerging market derivatives.

CLOSED-END FUNDS AND QUOTES
(www.site-by-site.com/usa/cef/cef.htm)

This site offers closing prices and news on many, but not all, closed-end funds. Simple to navigate.

CLOSED-END FUNDS CHARTS
(www.icefi.com/info/chart.htm)

This subscription-based service offers five types of daily and weekly charts specially tailored for closed-end funds. Some excellent information on closed ends is available free of charge, including an on-line tutorial on closed-end investing, an on-line forum, quarterly performance figures, a database of closed-end fund information, and market sentiment indicators.

DATASTREAM INTERNATIONAL:
COMPLIMENTARY DATA
(www.datastream.com)

Datastream International is a U.S.-based information services company offering a simple and clean, free interface for retrieving quotes for over 32,000 world equities. The quote includes p/e, EPS, dividend yield, and currency denomination. Datastream provides other complimentary data including exchange rates, economic indicators (GDP, current account) updated monthly, and Datastream Global Market Indices charts updated daily for many countries.

ECONOMEISTER HOME PAGE
(www.economeister.com/index.htm)

A collection of reports on the world's major economies, monetary policy, currencies, bonds, derivatives. Much of the information is the same as the data used by traders, but it isn't provided in real time. Emerging market coverage is limited to the largest markets. The site is a freebie designed to induce you to order the real-time fee-based services of Market News. Like Bloomberg, this company is generating lots of goodwill among Internet investors with useful offerings free of charge.

ECONOMIST USA
(www.economist.com)

Solid research, excellent insights on emerging markets, in both weekly news and special sections. Some emerging market indexes each week. To start receiving *Business This Week,* send an e-mail with the message "join economist-business" to newscaster@postbox.uk.

EMERGING MARKETS COMPANION
(www.emgmkts.com)

A convenient window into the emerging economies of Asia, Latin America, Africa, and Eastern Europe, with content contributed by premier-market participants and news organizations, and access to economic and political events, market activity, and investment strategies. The site also maintains a bulletin board where it posts e-mails to the site. This site currently offers free news, pricing data, and research on emerging market securities, although at this writing there is little that isn't available elsewhere. ADR prices and stock indexes for the previous five trading days are also available. The country profiles are from the CIA World Factbook, which appears on the Web in dozens of locations masquerading as proprietary material. It's thorough but dated, and isn't intended for investors. There are also primers on emerging markets and Brady Bonds. The premium service offers real-time broker/dealer price feeds and other features, including news feeds, research, and economic indicators.

EUROMONEY
(www.euromoney.com)

Don't let the name fool you. The Euromoney site offers some of the best emerging market coverage available on the Net. The articles are informative and current, and there are also special sections devoted to various countries. The site is well designed and a pleasure to browse. Best of all, it's free.

FINANCIAL DATA FINDER
(www.cob.ohio-state.edu/dept/fin/osudata.htm)

Hosted by Ohio State University, this is the best and most comprehensive set of links to Web sites that provide financial and economic data. You'll have to do some surfing to find emerging markets data, because it isn't always apparent from the descriptions. Still, this is one to check out early and often.

FINANCIAL INFORMATION LINK LIBRARY (FILL)
(www.mbnet.mb.ca:80/~russell)

An extensive but far from complete list of links, organized by country. A grab bag of banks, central banks, brokerage firms, and information services, the site is worth browsing. Just remember that the list isn't all-inclusive. Includes some emerging market links. The list has some useful sites but has no established patterns. Some countries have stock exchange links, others just brokerages or consulting firms.

FINANCIAL TIMES
(www.ft.com)

This "FT" covered emerging markets before they were fashionable. It is by far the best business daily for emerging market investors. The site has some search capabilities on-line. Track latest and closing prices for shares, managed funds, and currencies.

FINWEB FINANCIAL ECONOMICS
(www.finweb.com)

FINWeb is a financial economics Web site managed by James R. Garven, Ph.D. The primary objective of FINWeb is to list Internet resources providing substantive information concerning economics- and finance-related topics including journals, working papers, research tools, and databases; includes a search engine for the site.

GLOBAL FINANCIAL DATA
(www.globalfindata.com)

This unique, entertaining, and informative site offers historical stock market, currency, inflation, interest rate, and commodity data. The difference is that some data go back hundreds of years. You can view global stock market performance since 1800. The site is maintained by economist Bryan Taylor who will sell you entire datasets on CD-ROM.

GLOBAL INVESTOR
(www.global-investor.com)

This comprehensive site offers global financial data and analysis, including a news service that tracks Internet-related financial news and a good list of links to other sites dealing with global finance. It includes an ADR directory with a "portfolio" feature that allows you to track news and prices of particular ADR issues. The Global Investor Directory ranks the relative performance of 12 key stock markets as well as several bond indexes and a few commodities such as gold. Users can recalculate for any time period since January 1995 in 18 currencies.

IFC EMERGING MARKETS DATABASE (EMDB)
(www.ifc.org/emdb/emdbhome.htm)

Home page of IFC Indexes. The site includes IFC index definitions, weekly and daily market feeds of emerging market IFC indexes. Also browse the home page at www.ifc.org for more information on emerging markets. There is also a good links page at (www.ifc.org/EMDB/LINKS.htm).

INTERNATIONAL FINANCE BUSINESS GUIDE
(http://web.idirect.com/~tiger/money.htm)

This page offers links divided into three groups. The "World & US Stocks" group offers financial information, quotes, and investment tools. The "Stocks by Country" links take you to some of the emerging market stock exchanges, and the "Foreign Investment" links offer some insights into the investment climates of some emerging markets. The Foreign Investment group offers "investment" guides for various countries, with an emphasis on direct investment.

INTERNATIONAL MONETARY FUND
(www.imf.org)

The home page of the IMF offers news releases and other resources of interest to emerging market investors. Go to their publications page, where you can find excerpts of their World Economic Outlook survey, free for the downloading. The data is very valuable and comes to you undiluted by the news media or business press.

INTERNET SECURITIES, INC. (ISI)
EMERGING MARKETS SERVICE
(www.securities.com)

ISI Emerging Markets provides hard-to-get information about emerging market economies including financial, economic, and political news and information, and transmits that data through the Internet. Full-text news articles, financial statements, industry analyses, equity quotes, macroeconomic statistics, and market-specific information, which are derived directly from local information providers, appear in both English and the local language. Fee-based.

INVESTMENT RESEARCH VIA THE INTERNET
(www.ibbotson.com/Research/iafp96.htm)

This page is located on the Web site of Ibbotson and Associates, a well-known consulting firm. It contains an excellent collection of investment research links. The site also includes a library of selected articles by Ibbotson employees on investing and portfolio management.

J. P. MORGAN EMERGING MARKET
BOND INDICES (EMBI)
(www.jpmorgan.com/MarketDataInd/EMBI/embi.html)

The site for J. P. Morgan's Emerging Market Bond Indices. A good if basic site for emerging market debt watchers.

MEXICO OFFICIAL ECONOMIC INFORMATION
(www.shcp.gob.mx/english)

An excellent site for Mexico watchers, indicative of the government's change in attitude after the peso crisis. Hosted by the Mexican Finance Secretariat, this site includes information on public finance, economic programs, and financial activities in Mexico. This represents a great step forward for the emerging market sector, where governments are often vague and ambiguous about their financial policies. It is designed to increase confidence in the Mexican economy and is a must for anyone owning Mexican stocks.

MORGAN STANLEY GLOBAL ECONOMIC FORUM

(www.ms.com/GEFdata/digests/latest.html)

Daily commentary on global economies from Morgan's team of analysts. Currently not searchable, but you can access the commentary of the day and past dates by clicking on a calendar. Morgan Stanley offers excellent emerging market data, including all its MSCI indexes and valuable insights in its Global Economic Forum. The forum has archives, but they aren't searchable; you click the date it appeared on the linked calendar, and it's anyone's guess what you will find.

MORGAN STANLEY MSCI GLOBAL INDICES

(http://www.ms.com/mscidata/index.html)

MSCI, the world leader in global equity indexes, provides daily performance reporting on over 3,000 indexes, including 49 countries, 17 regions, and 38 industries. MSCI data is free as of this writing, but Morgan has indicated that they may restrict access.

NEW YORK FEDERAL RESERVE DAILY FOREIGN EXCHANGE RATES

(www.ny.frb.org/pihome/mktrates/forex10.html)

Daily 10 A.M. midpoint foreign exchange rates from the New York interbank market, certified by the New York Federal Reserve Bank for customs purposes.

NEW YORK TIMES ON THE WEB

(www.nytimes.com)

The *New York Times's* electronic edition allows you to create a personalized search page that allows you to retrieve articles on your country or region of choice on a daily basis. Free with registration as of this writing.

ONLINE INTELLIGENCE PROJECT
(www.cig.org/intelweb/index.html)

The Online Intelligence Project is oriented to individuals and professionals with an interest in international news, commerce, and references. It uses an intelligence service model to array Internet resources into departments and regional desks. Well-organized source of news and analysis.

PACIFIC EXCHANGE RATE SERVICE
(http://pacific.commerce.ubc.ca/xr)

This service provides access to current and historic daily exchange rates through an on-line database retrieval and plotting system. Also provided is a list of all the currencies of the world and the countries' exchange rate arrangements. Some historical rates back to 1971. Easy to use.

POLITICAL AND ECONOMIC RISK CONSULTANCY (PERC)
(www.asiarisk.com/perc.html)

This firm specializes in strategic business information and analysis for companies doing business in the countries in East and Southeast Asia. PERC produces risk reports on the individual countries of Asia on a quarterly basis. Features free executive summaries of country risk reports and economic indicators for China, Hong Kong, Indonesia, Malaysia, Philippines, Singapore, South Korea, Taiwan, and Thailand. There is a charge for the complete reports.

PRIVATIZATION MONITOR
(www.trace-sc.com/private.htm)

Includes a useful list of privatization links, which includes countries all over the world from Estonia to Uganda, and selected World Bank articles. Note that some are out-of-date, "dead," or empty.

PRIVATIZATION NEWS
(www.privatization.net)

A clearinghouse for news and information about privatization activities around the world. A paid subscription service.

PRS ONLINE
(www.prs.group.com)

A fee-based site provides current country-specific information such as international investment restrictions; regimes and probabilities; investment restrictions; equity restrictions; operations restrictions; taxation discrimination; repatriation restrictions; exchange controls; five-year forecasts; political and economic turmoil; investment restrictions; trade restrictions; domestic economic problems; international economic problems.

REFERENCE STATISTICS EVERY WRITER SHOULD KNOW
(www.nilesonline.com)

A great site for those seeking clear explanations of statistical terms, apparently provided as a public service.

RESOURCES FOR ECONOMISTS ON THE INTERNET
(wwww.econwpa.wustl.edu/EconFAQ/EconFAQ.html)

A sprawling list of just about every Web site that touches on economics or finance.

SEI INVESTMENT REVIEW
(www.seic.com/investmentreview)

SEI is a research and fund management firm. This site provides SEI's monthly report on the economy, markets, asset allocation, and indexes. It can be especially helpful for recent past return data. Quarterly investment reviews are downloadable in Adobe Acrobat format.

STANDARD AND POOR'S GLOBAL RATINGS BOOK
(www.ratings.standardpoor.com/funds)

Standard & Poor's Managed Funds Ratings group rates money market funds, bond funds, local government investment pools, and unit-investment trusts. S&P monitors and rates for credit and market risk over 550 funds with over $270 billion under management.

STRATEGIC FORECASTING
(www.stratfor.com)

Strategic Forecasting describes itself as a "private intelligence center" that looks for geopolitical trends around the world. This interesting site offers free commentaries on global regions, frequently updated, plus "Red

Alerts" on urgent developments, and longer-term (one-year and ten-year) geopolitical forecasts.

VENTURE CAPITAL WORLD ON THE WEB
(www.vcword.com)

This site is an attempt to match entrepreneurs and venture capitalists on-line. It is interesting to emerging market direct investors, because some of the funding requests come from emerging market entrepreneurs as far away as Latvia.

WALL STREET JOURNAL INTERACTIVE EDITION
(www.wsj.com)

An excellent source of general business news; emerging market coverage grows stronger every year. This site provides an updated version of the *Wall Street Journal.* It includes all stories in the U.S., Asian, and European editions. In addition, it provides a Personal Journal, which allows one to customize news reports. Quotes are still very limited. "Briefing Book" section provides some ADR coverage. Search engine covers only prior 14 days. The site also includes access to the on-line edition of *Barron's,* which offers excellent emerging market insights. Fee-based.

WORLD BANK
(www.worldbank.org)

This is a big, somewhat disorderly site in keeping with a bureaucracy, but well worth the mouse clicks. Some of the data are very technical, but invaluable. Many are free, the rest are reasonably priced. The World Bank is a valuable source of data on emerging markets. This page is a gateway to its many divisions, including the IFC, creator of the IFC indexes. A fair amount of useful information is available free of charge, and the publications are quite reasonable.

WORLD EQUITY BENCHMARK SHARES
(www.websontheweb.com/)

A site devoted to passive index management using the WEBS Index Series. There's a WEBS for each of 17 different countries. Each WEBS Index Series seeks to track the performance of a specific MSCI Index. WEBS are listed on the American Stock Exchange and trade like any other listed stock. Emerging market WEBS include Mexico and Malaysia, with more to come. The site includes prospectuses, prices, and index constituents.

WORLD TRADE ORGANIZATION
(www.unicc.org/wto/)

The World Trade Organization is the international body that governs matters of world trade. Trade agreements influence emerging market economies and many of their largest companies. This site features valuable information on important trade topics such as goods and services, intellectual property, environment, and dispute settlement. Documents and downloads are also included online, plus a terrific selected trade research links page.

Nasdaq Emerging Market Listings

Country	Symbol	Company Name	Market Value ($000s)	Date Listed	SIC/ Industry Code
Argentina	BGALY	Banco de Galicia y Buenos Aires S.A.	440,816	6/11/93	6029
	CRESY	Crésud S.A.C.I.F. y A.	38,500	3/19/97	19
Belize	BHIKF	B.H.I. Corporation	128,571	5/13/95	671
Brazil	MPARY	Multicanal Participacoes, S.A.	153,013	11/1/96	4841
Chile	CCUUY	Comania Cervecerias Unidas S.A.	166,701	9/24/92	2082
Finland	INMRY	Instrumentarium Corporation	3,735	8/18/83	384
Greece	ASIPY	Anangel-American Shipholdings Limited	64,019	3/2/89	4412
Hong Kong	BNSOF	Bonso Electronics International, Inc.	5,122	6/27/89	382
	BNSWF	Bonso Electronics International, Inc.	825	12/16/94	382
	RADAF	Radica Games Limited	98,230	5/13/94	5092
	CPLNY	Concordia Paper Holdings, Ltd.	4,964	12/2/94	6719
	OLSAY	OLS Asia Holdings, Limited	12,650	12/18/95	1542
	OLSWF	OLS Asia Holdings, Limited	2,565	12/18/95	1542
	HIHOF	Highway Holdings Limited	12,159	12/11/96	3469
	HIHWF	Highway Holdings Limited	459	12/11/96	3469
	TRFDF	Tramford International, Ltd.	47,355	12/13/96	3431
	TRFWF	Tramford International, Ltd.	250	12/13/96	3431
	ZNDTY	Zindart Limited	13,650	3/4/97	3944
	CLWTF	Euro Tech Holdings Company Limited	15,375	3/14/97	5090
	CLWWF	Euro Tech Holdings Company Limited	3,251	3/14/97	5090
	DCPCF	Dransfield China Paper Corporation	44,713	5/21/97	2676
Indonesia	PSNRY	P.T. Pasifik Satelit Nusantara	70,263	6/11/96	4899
Israel	ELRNF	Elron Electronic Industries Ltd.	263,731	3/19/82	3669
	ELRWF	Elron Electronic Industries Ltd.	3,534	11/30/94	3669

Country	Symbol	Company Name	Market Value ($000s)	Date Listed	SIC/ Industry Code
Israel	LASRF	Laser Industries Limited	122,202	7/30/96	3841
	SCIXF	Scitex Corporation Ltd.	384,210	5/16/80	357
	TEVIY	Teva Pharmaceutical Industries Ltd.	2,679,060	2/17/82	2834
	TAROF	Taro Pharmaceutical Industries Ltd.	54,196	9/14/82	2834
	ECILF	ECI Telecom Ltd.	1,732,271	1/25/83	362
	ELBTF	Elbit Ltd.	62,821	9/13/83	3573
	ORBKF	Orbotech Ltd.	349,274	2/9/88	737
	IISLF	I.I.S. Intelligent Information Systems Ltd.	23,402	11/8/84	357
	RADIF	Rada Electronic Industries Ltd.	13,301	6/24/85	382
	OSHSF	Oshap Technologies Ltd.	49,398	11/26/85	7373
	TATTF	TAT Technologies Ltd.	10,367	9/30/91	357
	IDANF	Idan Software Industries-I.S.I. Ltd.	14,829	10/31/88	737
	HCTLF	Healthcare Technologies Ltd.	6,092	2/16/89	283
	ILDCY	Israel Land Development Company Ltd. (The)	5,156	12/4/90	651
	BVRTF	B.V.R. Technologies Limited	36,450	8/6/91	369
	MGICF	Magic Software Enterprises Ltd.	26,406	8/28/91	737
	ROBOF	Eshed Robotec (1982) Ltd.	9,171	10/7/91	356
	TLDCF	Teledata Communications Ltd.	305,000	4/16/92	3661
	EDUSF	EduSoft Ltd.	25,581	7/14/92	7372
	DDDDF	New Dimension Software Ltd.	107,954	10/6/92	7372
	LNOPF	LanOptics Ltd.	38,142	11/19/92	7373
	SISGF	ISG International Software Group Ltd.	61,296	12/17/92	7372
	TCNOF	Tecnomatix Technologies Ltd.	240,004	2/26/93	7372
	FLSHF	M-Systems Flash Disk Pioneers Ltd.	34,304	3/4/93	3845
	MAGSF	Magal Security Systems Ltd.	23,531	3/23/93	3669
	GILTF	Gilat Satellite Networks Ltd.	316,071	3/26/93	4899
	TVGUF	T.V.G. Technologies Ltd.	1,800	8/9/93	3577
	TVGTF	T.V.G. Technologies Ltd.	7,287	8/13/93	3577
	TVGWF	T.V.G. Technologies Ltd.	116	8/13/93	3577
	TVGZF	T.V.G. Technologies Ltd.	78	8/13/93	3577
	TVGLF	T.V.G. Technologies Ltd.	39	8/13/93	3577
	ALDNF	Aladdin Knowledge Systems Limited	105,748	10/12/93	7372
	MDSLF	Medis El Ltd.	41,250	12/21/93	3826
	SILCF	Silicom Ltd.	21,500	2/18/94	3577
	SILZF	Silicom Ltd.	250	2/18/94	3577
	TSEMF	Tower Semiconductor Ltd.	169,000	10/26/94	3674
	ARLCF	Arel Communications & Software Ltd.	7,425	12/2/94	7373
	ARLWF	Arel Communications & Software Ltd.	41	12/2/94	7373
	ACNTF	Accent Software International	23,958	7/21/95	7372

Country	Symbol	Company Name	Market Value ($000s)	Date Listed	SIC/ Industry Code
Israel	ACNUF	Accent Software International	3,488	11/22/96	7372
	RELEF	Ariely Advertising, Limited	8,481	9/20/95	7311
	NURTF	Nur Advanced Technologies, Ltd.	8,170	10/6/95	3555
	SVECF	ScanVec Company (1990), Ltd.	11,000	10/19/95	7372
	HOMEF	Home Centers, (DIY), Limited	25,960	12/21/95	5311
	ESCMF	ESC Medical Systems, Limited	421,200	1/25/96	5047
	NICEY	NICE-Systems Limited	131,547	1/25/96	3571
	VOCLF	VocalTec, Limited	58,765	2/7/96	7373
	ARZNF	Arzan International (1991), Limited	4,569	3/13/96	2099
	ARZWF	Arzan International (1991), Limited	313	3/13/96	2099
	LOGLF	Logal Educational Software & Systems, Ltd.	15,675	3/20/96	7372
	CIMTF	Cimatron, Limited	10,638	3/21/96	7373
	TTELF	Tadiran Telecommunications, Limited	453,125	3/29/96	3661
	BOSCF	B.O.S. Better Online Solutions	34,500	5/15/96	7373
	BOSWF	B.O.S. Better Online Solutions	1,050	5/15/96	7373
	WIZTF	Wiztec Solutions, Limited	42,050	4/18/96	7371
	MATVY	Matav-Cable Systems Media Ltd.	47,933	6/13/96	4841
	CHKPF	Check Point Software Technologies, Ltd.	915,600	6/28/96	7372
	EVSNF	Elbit Vision Systems, Limited	99,671	7/3/96	3823
	ORCTF	Orckit Communications, Limited	190,823	9/27/96	3661
	MEMCF	Memco Software Limited	268,357	10/16/96	7373
	ZAGIF	ZAG Industries Ltd.	125,847	11/1/96	3089
	TISAF	Top Image Systems, Ltd.	16,560	11/22/96	7372
	TISWF	Top Image Systems, Ltd.	600	11/22/96	7372
	EMITF	Elbit Medical Imaging Ltd.	134,999	11/27/96	3845
	ESLTF	Elbit Systems, Ltd.	211,187	11/27/96	3812
	TTILF	TTI Team Telecom International Ltd.	42,538	12/4/96	7372
	ELTKF	Eltek Ltd.	12,883	1/22/97	3672
	GDCOF	Genesis Development and Construction, Ltd.	6,000	1/30/97	1521
	GDCUF	Genesis Development and Construction, Ltd.	10,000	1/30/97	1521
	GDCWF	Genesis Development and Construction, Ltd.	3,375	1/30/97	1521
	GDCZF	Genesis Development and Construction, Ltd.	1,500	1/30/97	1521
	CRYSF	Crystal Systems Solutions, Ltd.	237,500	1/31/97	7371
	WILCF	G. Willi-Food International, Ltd.	20,250	5/20/97	5149
	WILWF	G. Willi-Food International, Ltd.	488	5/20/97	5149
	MTSLF	MER Telemanagement Solutions Ltd.	44,787	5/21/97	5065
Mexico	TFONY	Telefonos de Mexico, S.A. de C.V.	224,611	1/17/80	4813
	QDRMY	Banca Quadrum S.A.	17,244	7/29/93	5112
	ELAMF	Elamex S.A. de C.V.	60,125	3/20/96	3672
New Guinea	LIHRY	Lihir Gold, Limited	152,831	10/9/95	1041

Country	Symbol	Company Name	Market Value ($000s)	Date Listed	SIC/ Industry Code
South Africa	AAGIY	Anglo American Gold Investment Company, Limited	46,271	12/1/70	1041
	ANGLY	Anglo American Corporation of South Africa Limited	256,191	12/1/70	1499
	BLYDY	Blyvooruitzicht Gold Mining Co.	14,845	12/1/70	1041
	DBRSY	De Beers Consolidated Mines	775,535	12/1/70	1499
	DRFNY	Driefontein Consolidated, Ltd.	173,009	6/16/76	1041
	GLDFY	Gold Fields of South Africa Limited	54,582	12/25/70	1049
	KLOFY	Kloof Gold Mining Co., Ltd.	136,850	1/1/78	1041
	SGOLY	St. Helena Gold Mines Limited	11,976	12/1/70	1041
	VAALY	Vaal Reefs Exploration and Mining Company Limited	153,210	1/1/78	1041
	WDEPY	Western Deep Levels Ltd.	147,687	12/1/70	1049
	HSVLY	Highveld Steel and Vanadium Corporation Limited	1,806	10/26/81	3339
	SASOY	Sasol Ltd.	25,309	4/23/82	1321
	FSCNY	Free State Consolidated Gold Mining Company Ltd.	175,247	2/19/86	1041
	GVPMY	Grootvlei Proprietary Mines	5,503	10/2/96	1041
	HGMCY	Harmony Gold Mining Co., Ltd.	32,176	10/2/96	1041
	BLGMY	Buffelsfontein Gold Mines, Ltd.	15,984	10/2/96	1041
	DROOY	Durban Roodepoort Deep, Ltd.	10,474	10/2/96	1041
	RANGY	Randgold & Exploration Company, Limited	251,281	3/10/97	1041
Taiwan	MXICY	Macronix International Co. Ltd.	101,842	5/9/96	3674
	ASTSF	ASE Test, Limited	616,272	6/6/96	3674
United Arab Emirates	IRPPF	International Petroleum Corporation	186,309	7/17/92	1382

These listings are current as of June 30, 1997. Over two-thirds are Israeli companies and 10% are South African. Many emerging market companies are listed as ADRs on the NYSE and AMEX, as well as Nasdaq (see Appendix A for ADRs).

Index